S EXTON
Selected Criticism

SEXTON
Selected Criticism

EDITED BY
Diana Hume George

UNIVERSITY OF ILLINOIS PRESS
Urbana and Chicago

© 1988 by the Board of Trustees of the University of Illinois
Manufactured in the United States of America
C 5 4 3 2 1

This book is printed on acid-free paper.

Library of Congress Cataloging-in-Publication Data

Sexton : selected criticism / edited by Diana Hume George.
    p.   cm.
  ISBN 0-252-01552-5 (alk. paper)
  1. Sexton, Anne—Criticism and interpretation.   I. George, Diana
Hume, 1948–
PS3537.E915Z87   1988
811'.54—dc 19   87-36540
                                                       CIP

Contents

Acknowledgments   vii

Introduction   ix

Anne Sexton Chronology   xxiii

Two Types of Seduction

Anne Sexton and the Seduction of the Audience
ALICIA OSTRIKER   3

Seduction in Anne Sexton's Unpublished Play *Mercy Street*
DIANE WOOD MIDDLEBROOK   19

Sexton through Freud and Psychoanalytic Theory

Anne Sexton: Somehow to Endure
J. D. McCLATCHY   29

Beyond the Pleasure Principle: The Death Baby
DIANA HUME GEORGE   73

Jungian Feminist Readings

The Double Image and the Division of Parts: A Study of
Mother-Daughter Relationships in the Poetry of Anne Sexton
MARGARET HONTON   99

Goddess Manifestations as Stages in Feminine Metaphysics
in the Poetry and Life of Anne Sexton
STEPHANIE DEMETRAKOPOULOS   117

Anne Sexton's "Radical Discontent with the Awful Order
of Things"
ESTELLA LAUTER   145

The Awful Rowing Toward God

The Hungry Beast Rowing Toward God: Anne Sexton's
Later Religious Poetry
KATHLEEN L. NICHOLS   165

Mysticism and Suicide: Anne Sexton's Last Poetry
    WILLIAM H. SHURR   171

On the Poetic Biography

How It Was: Maxine Kumin on Anne Sexton
    MAXINE KUMIN   197

Anne Sexton at the Radcliffe Institute
    DIANE WOOD MIDDLEBROOK   211

Influences and Connections

"Daddy": Sylvia Plath's Debt to Anne Sexton
    HEATHER CAM   223

45 Mercy Street and Other Vacant Houses
    LINDA WAGNER-MARTIN   227

Personal and Public: Controlling the Material

That Story: Anne Sexton and Her Transformations
    ALICIA OSTRIKER   251

The Witch's Life: Confession and Control in the Early Poetry
of Anne Sexton
    JEANNE KAMMER NEFF   274

The Troubled Life of the Artist
    STEVEN E. COLBURN   283

What Poetry Can and Cannot Do

Seeking the Exit or the Home: Poetry and Salvation in
the Career of Anne Sexton
    SUZANNE JUHASZ   303

Not That It Was Beautiful
    KIM KRYNOCK   312

Notes on the Contributors   317
Index   321

Acknowledgments

This book was completed with assistance provided by a grant from Penn State University at Erie, The Behrend College. My thanks to Provost John Lilley at Behrend and to Charles Hosler at University Park.

Ann Lowry Weir, Aaron Appelstein, and Harriet Stockanes of the University of Illinois Press have my gratitude once again. Aaron Appelstein is the finest, most meticulous copy editor an author could hope to have, a mean detailman with the nerves of a bibliographical midwife. He expects more of himself than he does of his authors and editors.

Linda Wagner-Martin first urged me to proceed with this project despite my own reservations, and I appreciate her encouragement. Diane Wood Middlebrook and Alicia Suskin Ostriker were similarly supportive. Steven E. Colburn and I also found ways to cooperate with and encourage each other, despite the fact that we were editing potentially competitive volumes.

I thank Norma Hartner, as I repeatedly and happily must, for invaluable assistance. My family has been supportive in undocumentable ways: Mac Nelson, my son Bernie George, my daughter Kris Luce, and Mary Ellen Sullivan have all contributed to this project. And I appreciate my granddaughter, Ayron Luce, for supplying comic relief.

My thanks to all of the contributors to this volume, whose words are the body of the book. All of them know my estimation of their works.

Diana Hume George

Introduction

The essays assembled in this collection present the best previously published criticism on Anne Sexton, together with new evaluations that demonstrate the range and diversity of recent perspectives on her achievement. While conducting research for Contemporary Authors Bibliographical Series and for *Oedipus Anne: The Poetry of Anne Sexton*, I became increasingly aware of the exceptionally high quality of critical attention that Sexton has attracted and retained. The majority of essays reprinted here were first published in the late 1970s and the early 1980s, in diverse and occasionally obscure sources not always easily available to a reading public interested in Sexton's writing.

The endurance of that public interest is clear and has been enlivened by a number of factors. *The Complete Poems*, published by Houghton Mifflin in 1981, complemented but did not completely replace Sexton's individual volumes, which have only recently begun to go out of print. Response to *The Complete Poems* indicates that Sexton's readership has increased in the years following her death in 1974. In 1988 Houghton Mifflin published Sexton's *Selected Poems*, a collection designed to represent the poet at the height of her powers throughout her writing career. Diane Wood Middlebrook's forthcoming biography is certain of a wide readership. Sexton's life appeared to be—but was not—fully explained or understood as a result of the highly personal nature of her poetry. Middlebrook's preliminary research, published in essays in *Parnassus*, the *Denver Quarterly*, and the *New England Quarterly*, clarifies that the story of Sexton's life remained largely untold at her death.

Sexton now appears as a represented poet in most standard anthologies of the moderns, as well as in specialist collections on women poets. Critics writing (or rewriting) histories of modern poetry are beginning to place her near the center of enormous mid-century changes in American poetry, changes not confined to the "confessional" context. I am thinking especially of Alicia Ostriker's *Stealing the Lan-*

guage: The Emergence of Women's Poetry in America. Many of the critics now making large claims for Sexton's poetry are feminists who find in Sexton's work a set of resonant and sometimes enabling myths, as well as a critique of those that disabled Sexton herself.

If Sexton is an enduringly popular poet in the 1980s, she is also a highly controversial one who has been criticized for various failings and excesses, some imagined, some real, all certainly overblown. These three factors—popularity, controversy, and quality—are conflicting and complementary, and all three are among the most persuasive reasons to assemble essays that address such issues both implicitly and explicitly. The controversy regarding her quality and the appropriateness of her subject matter and style will not be settled here, but it will be aired in such a way as to dismiss the extremes of her detractors, create a forum for those who find her achievement significant, and keep alive the productive tension surrounding her work.

Several of the contributions in this collection first appeared in books; a few come from previous anthologies of criticism on poetry; most were published in scholarly journals. Readers interested in extensively annotated bibliographical citations on Sexton should consult *American Poets* (ed. Ronald Baughman, Contemporary Authors Bibliographical Series, vol. 2 [Detroit: Gale Research Co., 1986]), where my entry on Sexton includes everything of substance published on her work through 1985. Steven E. Colburn's *Anne Sexton: Telling the Tale* (Ann Arbor: University of Michigan Press, 1988) includes an updated, comprehensive bibliography.

The critical approaches in the present volume include diverse perspectives. Several articles concentrate on one period or one volume, or a series of poems, or one individual selection; a few present overviews of her canon. All of Sexton's major themes and subjects are represented through these discussions: religious quest, transformation and dismantling of myth, the meanings of gender, inheritance and legacy, the search for fathers, mother-daughter relationships, sexual anxiety and love, madness and suicide, issues of female identity. The critics share an always acute and close attention to the language of poetry, but their interpretations are not always similar, nor do I necessarily indicate agreement with their conclusions by representing them here. The writers' specialized perspectives include feminism, psychoanalytic and myth criticism, theology, poetic style and technique, and biography. While almost all of the essays are feminist, lively differences inform even the fundamental agreements this approach implies.

The recent or previously unpublished essays in this collection offer original and provocative ways to read Anne Sexton. Heather Cam of Macquarie University in Australia is the author of " 'Daddy': Sylvia Plath's Debt to Anne Sexton," an important piece of scholarly sleuthing that will be of interest to Plath and Sexton readers alike. Although it is technically a reprint because it recently appeared as a note in *American Literature*, for most readers it will still bring surprising news. Cam supports a startling thesis about Sexton's impact on one of the most celebrated works of modern poetry. Her demonstration that Plath's "Daddy" was influenced by an early, uncollected poem of Sexton's (unreprinted since its original publication in the *Antioch Review* in 1959 but included in the new *Selected Poems*) is detailed, complete, and convincing.

Steven E. Colburn's "The Troubled Life of the Artist" examines a group of personal poems in which Sexton discusses the special gifts of the poet and the obstacles she or he is presented with in our culture. He argues that in a number of poems composed throughout her career, Anne Sexton explored the nature of the poet's work deliberately and in detail; ironically, many readers have dismissed these same poems as "merely" confessional, ignoring both Sexton's elaborate storytelling devices and her penetrating exploration of creative process.

Like many readers of Sexton criticism, I have known for several years about the unpublished work of Stephanie Demetrakopoulos on Sexton's mother-daughter poetry. A series of mishaps prevented the publication of this important essay until now. Space constraints still prevent printing the entire text of Demetrakopoulos's "Goddess Manifestations as Stages in Feminine Metaphysics in the Poetry and Life of Anne Sexton," but the substance of her argument is included here. Demetrakopoulos sees her essay on transformations of the Demeter-Kore archetypes in Sexton's poetry as a continuation of Sexton's task of "naming the significance of the feminine self, a bringing to collective consciousness both strong, positive feminine values and some especially powerful feminine sources of despair."

Kim Krynock's "Not That It Was Beautiful" is a short piece that will illuminate how Sexton may be read and received by contemporary students in the college classrooms where her work is taught. Krynock is one of my students at Penn State at Erie, The Behrend College.

While few students of poetry could be expected to approach Sexton with Krynock's degree of readerly sophistication, she is representative of student response in that the relationship between Sexton's life and her death—between her poetry and her suicide—remains a central issue often impossible to sidestep for teacher and student alike. This is how one student reader confronted the problem.

While Diane Wood Middlebrook has shared some of her biographical research with audiences through several recent journal articles, her "Anne Sexton at the Radcliffe Institute" is the first published excerpt from the manuscript of the forthcoming biography. Readers of this collection are thus given access to the results of archival research not previously available. Some source material is now accessible to scholars at the Harry Ransom Humanities Research Center at the University of Texas, Austin, but much of it is still restricted. Middlebrook's account of an important moment in Sexton's early career and her informed interpretation of events in Sexton's professional and personal life are thus invaluable.

Middlebrook's "Seduction in Anne Sexton's Unpublished Play *Mercy Street*" also appears in print here for the first time. Because the play remains unpublished, readers will be interested in the segments of dialogue reproduced here, especially as they illuminate Middlebrook's thesis that the play explores two "axes of desire" in its representation of seduction. Father-daughter and mother-daughter incest are included in Middlebrook's conjectures, which are both biographical and psychoanalytic.

Alicia Ostriker's "Anne Sexton and the Seduction of the Audience" provides a new and elegantly suggestive perspective on the dynamics of Sexton's relationship to her readers. Ostriker explodes the confessional issue by reading it anew and then transcending it. Her examination of the dynamics between Sexton's speaker and the many forms of "you" the poems address—i.e., the reader—clarifies our discomfort and reveals the ways in which Sexton's voice is one of many in a chorus of modern and contemporary female poets. Insistence on intimacy redefines and eroticizes the relationship between speaker and reader. Ostriker's reading through Marvell's "To His Coy Mistress" provides an orthodox analogy to the heterodox strategies of female poetic seduction.

Among the previously published essays, my own "Beyond the Pleasure Principle: The Death Baby" presents Sexton's sequence of poems from *The Death Notebooks* as a poetic analogue to Freud's "death instinct." I try to demonstrate that in "The Death Baby" the wish for and the fear of death—representing a psychic orientation to all primary oppositions—are functionally identical. The death baby image is seen as the humanized, internalized metaphor for the repetition compulsion.

Margaret Honton's "The Double Image and the Division of Parts," like Demetrakopoulos's essay, deals with Sexton's poetry about mother-daughter relationships. Honton describes the struggle against the devouring mother myth embodied in Sexton's work on this subject. In the poet's double image of that myth, the speaker must accept both blame from her predecessor and guilt concerning her inheritor.

Suzanne Juhasz's "Seeking the Exit or the Home" is a sober meditation on what poetry can and cannot do. She discusses Sexton's special "rat" as an alien aspect of self that simultaneously obstructs salvation and yet is the source of creativity. Poetry gave Sexton something to do with the rat's knowledge, but the rat of death cannot be killed without also murdering the vision that gives life to the poetry. Juhasz hopes that Sexton's poetry can have meanings and functions for its readers quite different from those for its writer.

In "The Witch's Life: Confession and Control in the Early Poetry of Anne Sexton," Jeanne Kammer Neff counters the claim that Sexton writes "raw" instead of "cooked" verse. Kammer Neff demonstrates that the writer imposes "the boundary and counterpoint of intense control" on her chaotic experience. Sexton's use of language in the early work is consummately controlled, in Kammer Neff's view, by directness, economy, and technical skill.

Maxine Kumin has written a number of valuable reminiscences on her long poetic collaboration and personal friendship with Anne Sexton. Among these, her "How It Was: Maxine Kumin on Anne Sexton" is the most detailed and critically useful. The story of the development of their friendship is recapitulated here, with detailed enumeration of their working habits. Most important is that Kumin presents her own valuable and special perspective on Sexton's originality and achievement.

In "Anne Sexton's 'Radical Discontent with the Awful Order of Things,' " Estella Lauter contends that between 1970 and 1974 Sexton created an extraordinary body of poetry based on images that have "profound psychological and religious significance for our age." Sexton's quest for a relationship with traditional Christianity "broke open under the pressure of her imaginative scrutiny." The archetypal figures Lauter identifies in the later poetry are best understood as an act of Jungian "soul-making," although Sexton was finally not able to name her own new and female deities. Lauter places Sexton's discontent with a patriarchal God and her alternative deities in the contexts of archetypal psychology and feminist theology. Readers might be interested to know that Estella Lauter and Stephanie Demetrakopoulos originally intended the extended versions of their essays here to form the core of a feminist and Jungian study of Sexton's poetry.

The first critic to make serious exegetical use of the psychoanalytic framework of Sexton's poetry was J. D. McClatchy in his "Anne Sexton: Somehow to Endure." Employing Freud, Ernst Kris, and Theodor Reik's theories on psychic exorcism and absolution, McClatchy examines the confessional context and identifies "endurance" as Sexton's consistent concern. McClatchy does not reduce poetry to symptom but rather uses theory as an illuminating subtext. Confessional poets, among whom McClatchy counts Sexton the most daring, functioned as witnesses to the inner lives of many people.

Kathleen Nichols shares Estella Lauter's Jungian perspective in her examination of the compensatory function of religious myth in Sexton's later work. She emphasizes Sexton's need to find in death the idealized male and female archetypes of the unified self. In Nichols's reading Sexton's sea journey toward God is a regressive quest for primal sources, or mythic parents, especially the lost father.

Alicia Ostriker's "That Story" focuses on the problematic relationship of Sexton to her critics. She suspects that the "sneer" toward Sexton derives from fear of being "stung into imaginative sympathy." Ostriker's major discussion is of *Transformations* and *The Book of Folly*'s "Jesus Papers," in which Ostriker finds a brilliant fusion of the public and the personal. She maintains that the later poetry tackles increasingly ambitious themes, with correspondingly significant cultural implications.

William Shurr's perspective in "Mysticism and Suicide: Anne Sexton's Last Poetry," is entirely different from the fundamental assumptions of the feminist critics here, who tend to find the later work personally distressing and poetically undistinguished. Shurr calls *The Awful Rowing Toward God* "the book of a mature poet whose dedication to art was single-minded and supreme." In place of the feminist concentration on patriarchal elements in Sexton's religious quest, or on negatively maternal meanings, Shurr reads Sexton's final, fluid medium as a Sea of Life and a source of creative vitality, an embodiment of Logos mysticism. Hers is the traditional journey of the ascetic soul toward encounter with the divine. For Shurr the suicide of "St. Anne" is grounded in "magnanimity" and is an authentic act of spiritual completion.

Linda Wagner-Martin extends the comparison with Emily Dickinson suggested by other critics, in "45 Mercy Street and Other Vacant Houses." Like Dickinson, Sexton addressed the need for identity as a writer and for a male authority figure to support the writing process. Their work shares exuberance, anger, guilt, frustration, and an uneasy measure of self-acceptance. Dickinson, Sexton, and Plath are joined by their mutual alienation from the traditional sphere of femininity because of their identities as poets, and from the traditional territory of poetry because of gender.

Many organizations of this richly interrelated collection of essays suggested themselves. The one I chose is simply explained. I begin with two new essays by Ostriker and Middlebrook, grouped as "Two Types of Seduction." Ostriker's essay brings up many questions regarding how to read Sexton; the reader will find answers to some of them in the articles that follow. Ostriker deals with the seduction of the reader by the poet and the text. Middlebrook concentrates on one possible archetype or paradigm for such seduction, the incest scenario in which interpenetration of personal and poetic (or dramatic) is concretely and disturbingly realized.

The second section, titled "Sexton through Freud and Psychoanalytic Theory," groups my own essay with J. D. McClatchy's "Anne Sexton: Somehow to Endure." The psychoanalytic conjectures explicit in Middlebrook are explored through a theoretical examination of the entire canon by McClatchy and one sequence of poems by George. The Freudian discussion is complemented by the "Jungian Feminist Readings" that follow, in which mother-daughter configurations in Sexton's poetry receive interpretation by Honton and Demetrakopoulos, and the feminine mythmaking activity is explored by Lauter. Because Lauter and Demetrakopoulos originally conceived of their essays as complementary, my presentation of them here tries to retain their original integrity.

Estella Lauter's reading of "The Jesus Papers" brings up the questions of the nature and the success or failure of the religious quest in Sexton, and in the section titled "The Awful Rowing Toward God," Kathleen Nichols's and William Shurr's contrasting readings of the late religious poetry offer keenly differing perspectives on the situation. Because Shurr's interpretation regards the last act of the life as a kind of final poem for the poet, the section "On the Poetic Biography" follows his essay. Here Diane Middlebrook gives us the details of Sexton's time at the Radcliffe Institute, a period that intersects the longer span of time Maxine Kumin deals with in "How It Was." Kumin describes the shape of a long poetic and personal friendship and the course of the poets' influence on each other and on American poetry.

"Influences and Connections" takes a deeper look at two specific connections of the kind Kumin establishes above. Heather Cam discusses Sexton's influence on another poet, Sylvia Plath, and Linda Wagner-Martin connects Sexton to the mainstream of American literature through Emily Dickinson. Although many of Sexton's poetic influences are male, the two examined here are specifically and significantly female.

In "Personal and Public: Controlling the Material," three essays expand upon the exploration of the poetic biography. Ostriker's "That Story" might have been placed near Lauter, since it, too, deals in part with "The Jesus Papers"; but Ostriker's emphasis is on the fusion of public and personal as a form of poetic achievement, so I group her with Jeanne Kammer Neff, whose essay concentrates on formal control, and Steven E. Colburn, whose subject is narrative control.

In the final section, "What Poetry Can and Cannot Do," Suzanne Juhasz explores the issue through concerns about female identity that have been raised in one form or another by almost every essay in this assemblage. Her conclusions, like Kim Krynock's, are "not beautiful," but they are clear-eyed, critically significant, and perhaps also personally valuable.

An Overview of Sexton's Canon

Anne Sexton would have been sixty years old in November 1988. When she died in 1974, her reputation as an important member of a misnamed and misapprehended movement in modern American poetry was secured. She had become almost entirely identified with the controversial "confessional school," and she was generally regarded as among that mode's most accomplished practitioners. In company with such poets as Robert Lowell, Sylvia Plath, and W. D. Snodgrass, she had risen to fame well beyond the boundaries of New England. She received the Pulitzer Prize and numerous other awards, including nomination for the National Book Award, and fellowships from the American Academy of Arts and Letters, the Ford Foundation, and the Guggenheim Foundation. She taught at Radcliffe and Harvard, lectured at Bread Loaf, held the Crashaw Chair at Colgate University, and was a full professor at Boston University by 1972. She was much in demand on the poetry reading circuit, where her flamboyant, dramatic performances were celebrated and criticized.

Yet the confessional label had become a trap that prevented readers and critics from interpreting the range of her achievement. Poetic typecasting did not prevent Sexton from writing poems that reached beyond the personal boundaries that ostensibly formed the confessional territory; it merely kept readers from noticing that she had done so. Robert Lowell escaped confinement because of his established reputation and his stature as a major modern poet before the publication of *Life Studies,* the single volume usually cited to mark the beginning of the confessional movement. Sylvia Plath's early death and the strategic release of her late poetry over a period of years combined to make her a cult poet, but one whose niche in the academy was well carved and well deserved. W. D. Snodgrass has long since moved far away from the style and subject that first brought him renown. Only Sexton seemed identified with and limited by the confines of the moment that had given her poetic birth.

The academic feminist movement has been central to a reconsideration of this misdirected judgment. At first feminism's appropriation of Sexton was superficial and constituted another form of limitation. Anthologies of poetry by women kept her work visible, but the selections were predictable and limited to a few poems that celebrated feminist subjects or reflected feminist concerns. "Little Girl, My String Bean, My Lovely Woman" and "In Celebration of My Uterus" are examples of good work by Sexton kept before a large public. Recent feminist approaches, such as the ones represented in this collection of essays, have cracked open the critical bell jar to clarify the range of her themes, the territory of her poetics, and the radical nature of her vision.

Sexton's early poetry dealt with her recovery from a mental break-down, the deaths of her parents, her relationship to her daughters, and her suicidal impulses. *To Bedlam and Part Way Back* documented the breakdown and constituted a poetic declaration of independence. The second part of *Bedlam* begins with "For John, Who Begs Me Not to Enquire Further," which asserted her determination to pursue the dangerous poetic path that her mentor had urged her to abandon. The second volume, *All My Pretty Ones*, continued to deal with themes established in *Bedlam*, but its major concern was the loss of the beloved others that gave the speaker her fragile sense of identity.

In the early work the confessional label is useful, if limiting. If Lowell and Snodgrass are the fathers of confessional poetry, it is legitimate to claim for Sexton the role of mother. She served her apprenticeship as a daughter figure to both male poets, but they could not validate, on behalf of the reading public, the excruciatingly female statements she was making on behalf of herself and other women. She repeatedly acknowledged her debts to both Lowell and Snodgrass, specifying that the latter's "Heart's Needle" had given her "permission" to write about loss, neurosis, even madness.

That permission could not extend to writing about such experiences from a female point of view, and early criticism of her work clarifies the strength of the special resistance of the critical and poetic establishments to such revelations. We are accustomed to thinking that Sylvia Plath was the first of the female moderns to break these taboos, but, in fact, Sexton was writing in the personal mode well before Plath, and she probably served as an enabling model for some of Plath's more celebrated work.

Her third book, *Live or Die*, which won the Pulitzer Prize, was concerned with a progress from sickness toward health; she was, after all, only "part way back" from Bedlam. While the poetically successful shape of the collection constituted a fiction—Sexton experienced remission in her emotional difficulties but obviously not "cure"—it was a powerful one that spoke to many readers. *Love Poems*, thematically tight and popular, was organized around the project of building a "love's body" through the mediation and transforming power of the beloved.

Critics have located a shift in theme, subject, and style in Sexton's fifth volume, *Transformations*. This collection of modernized fairy tales uses the Grimm brothers' versions of culturally resonant myths to suggest that their meanings are both different from and darker than the public that consumed them had imagined. The volume's title is an elaborate pun; each of the tales turns on a magical transformation, and Sexton transformed each one further in two respects: she updated their contexts and language to point out their applications to and parallels with modern life, and she exposed the dark psychic core of each tale in ways that inverted or even reversed their normative meanings.

In Sexton's hands a genre that appears radically to reverse the normal social order in which the poor become rich, the ugly become beautiful, and the powerless gain power is exposed as deeply conservative in values and reflective of massive anxieties about gender. This was the first, but not the last, time that Anne Sexton engaged in a radical critique of cultural values. In this case Sexton anticipated (and in some respects bettered) cultural analysts such as Bruno Bettelheim.

While *Transformations* marks a shift in style and approach, it is important to recognize that Sexton is still dealing with the subjects that have concerned her from the start: personal transformations from housewife to poet, from sanity to madness, from love to loss, and from life to death were always her subjects. Sexual anxiety, relationships between parents and children, the ambiguity of role reversals were her firmly established territory. Yet the distinction customarily made between the early work and *Transformations* is useful. Henceforth, Sexton would increasingly become what critics have variously called surreal, mythic, visionary, or prophetic.

The Book of Folly contains many poems on Sexton's customary themes, but she also becomes more poetically ambitious in the series of poems on which some of her greatness rests. In "The Death of the Fathers" sequence, she anatomizes the love affair between father and daughter, which deals with seduction, betrayal, and deaths both symbolic and actual. The "Angels of the Love Affair" invokes a religious rhetoric not new to her work, one she employs in more radical form to critique Christianity's central drama in "The Jesus Papers." Her earlier identifications with Christ as the ragged brother and fellow sufferer are not abandoned, but here she begins a sustained consideration of the distance between the female sufferer and the male deity, as he is embodied in the infant and adult figure of Christ. As in *Transformations*, she performs an elegant, impudent misprision of the parental text, exposing its misogyny and the nature of its sacrificial ges-

ture. The quester here is the doubter, but the quest is genuine, such
that it is appropriate to call Sexton one of our most important religious
poets, as well as an accomplished deconstructor of patriarchal religion.

The Death Notebooks continues the mythic reach, returning first
to personal, early material. In "The Death Baby" Sexton re-creates and
transforms the psychoanalytic consideration of the "death instinct"
and the "repetition compulsion." The subtle but pervasive subtext
penetrated by the poem is Freud's Beyond the Pleasure Principle. Her
earlier suicide poetry was explanatory, self-justifying, and engaged primarily in a poetic form of translation from the language of the suicide;
"The Death Baby" embodies theory in mythopoesis. While she was
never psychoanalyzed, years of psychotherapy and of reading allowed
her to traverse the boundaries between one system of metaphor (psychoanalytic theory) and another (poetry). Here the pitched battle between Eros and Thanatos is enacted at the personal level but is clearly
meant to be read as a cultural drama. While gender is not the poem's
only or primary concern, the scenario in "The Death Baby" is reso-
nantly feminine.

"The Furies" sequence is not specifically religious or spiritual,
but its rhetoric and stance belong to the visionary tradition. The speaker
voices the prophecies given to one who sees with spiritually naked
eyes the passionate contraries of joy and despair. "O Ye Tongues" is
Sexton's rendering of both Psalms and Genesis, in which she invents
herself as the god who gives form to poetic voice.

The final phase of Sexton's work is inaugurated by the last volume
that she prepared for publication, The Awful Rowing Toward God.
While many poems in Rowing remain impudent and joyous, or suf-
fused with the longing of the quest, it is generally (though not universally) agreed that here the imagery is less powerful, less imaginative,
and less successful than in her earlier work. Sexton wrote these poems
at white heat over a period of less than three weeks, and it shows. In
thematic and tonal terms the project is less ambitious. The voice is
increasingly desperate, ready to settle for less than the demands she
made upon the deities or the cosmos in previous volumes. The collection ends with a capitulation to the imaginatively small God of an
orthodox religious hope. In feminist terms the female voice of rebirth
and transformation turns into the conservative voice of feminine sup-
plication.

It is important not to equate the quality of the poems with their adherence to the voice of power and doubt, need and strength, challenge and acceptance established in the middle period; that voice vibrated in the gap between everlasting certainty and everlasting doubt and traveled swiftly and compellingly between the intricate contraries it found or formed. If the need for certainty softened the strong voice, that is not necessarily equivalent to a loss of poetic power—or it need not be. But in this case the loss of voice and the loss of poetic resonance seem to be simultaneous. It is of course possible that a feminist viewpoint permits its politics to interfere with or to define its poetics. A longer perspective may be necessary to settle the issue. The posthumously published work, consisting of *45 Mercy Street* and *Words for Dr. Y.*, was not prepared by Sexton for publication. It therefore lacks her editorial hand and her selection process. While little has been written about the very late work, individual poems in the posthumous volumes show Anne Sexton still writing some fine poems that deserve to survive.

Anne Sexton Chronology

Compiled with information supplied by Diane Wood Middlebrook

1928	Born Anne Gray Harvey on November 9 in Newton, Massachusetts.
1934–47	Educated in Wellesley public schools; graduated from Rogers Hall, Lowell, Massachusetts.
1947	Attended the Garland School, a Boston finishing school for women.
1948	August 16: eloped with Alfred Muller Sexton II ("Kayo").
1949–52	Lived in Boston area, with brief residence in Cochituate, Baltimore, and San Francisco.
1953	July 21: Linda Gray Sexton born.
1954	July 15: Anna Ladd Dingley ("Nana") died at age eighty-six.
1955	August 5: Joyce Ladd Sexton born.
1956	July 13–August 3: hospitalized for treatment of anxiety; children sent to grandmothers.
1957	January: enrolled in John Holmes's poetry workshop at Boston Center for Adult Education. Met Maxine Kumin.
1958	Scholarship to Antioch Writers' Conference to work with W. D. Snodgrass. Began attending Robert Lowell's writing seminar at Boston University. Met George Starbuck.
1959	January: Sylvia Plath joined Lowell's seminar. March 10: Mary Gray Staples died of cancer. May 19: Houghton Mifflin accepted *To Bedlam and Part Way Back* for publication. June 3: Ralph Churchill Harvey died of cerebral hemorrhage. August: received Robert Frost Fellowship to attend Bread Loaf Writers' Conference.
1960	April: *To Bedlam and Part Way Back* published; nominated for National Book Award. June–July: courses in modern literature with Irving Howe and Philip Rahv at Brandeis University.
1961	Began writing play. Appointed to Radcliffe Institute for Independent Study.
1962	October: *All My Pretty Ones* published; nominated for National Book Award. November: Levinson Prize from *Poetry*.
1963	May 22: awarded traveling fellowship by American Academy of Arts and Letters. August 22–October 27: tour of Europe with neighbor Sands Robart.

1964   *Selected Poems* published in England. September–March 1965:
        Ford Foundation grant for residence with the Charles Playhouse,
        Boston.
1965   Elected a Fellow of the Royal Society of Literature, London. Re-
        ceived the first literary magazine travel award from the Interna-
        tional Congress of Cultural Freedom.
1966   August: hunting safari in Kenya with Kayo Sexton.
1967   May: awarded Pulitzer Prize for *Live or Die*. Shelley Award from
        the Poetry Society of America.
1968   July: formed rock group "Anne Sexton and Her Kind." Taught
        poetry at McLean's Hospital in Belmont, Massachusetts.
1969   April: Guggenheim Fellowship for work on play *Mercy Street;*
        produced at American Place Theater, New York City, October 8–
        November 21. Began teaching at Boston University and conduct-
        ing workshops for Oberlin College Independent Study students.
1970   June: honorary doctor of letters, Tufts University, Medford, Mas-
        sachusetts.
1972   Promoted to full professor at Boston University. May–June: Cra-
        shaw Chair in Literature at Colgate University. Honorary doctor
        of letters, Fairfield University, Fairfield, Connecticut.
1973   May 5: *Transformations* in opera version by Conrad Susa pre-
        miered by the Minneapolis Opera Company. August: lectured at
        Bread Loaf Writers' Conference.
1974   October 4: died of carbon monoxide poisoning in the garage of
        her home.

Editor's Note

In its original form in *The Death Notebooks* (abbreviated *DN*), the "O Ye
Tongues" sequence consists of nine numbered "psalms." *The Complete Poems*
(abbreviated *CP*) includes an addition to the sequence, designated as "Second
Psalm," that changes all subsequent title numbers. This addition produces a
discrepancy in critics' references to the poems by title and number, depending
on whether the critic cites *The Death Notebooks* or *The Complete Poems*.
All references to the sequence in this collection retain the reference used by
the essay's author, with parenthetical clarification of the poem's title in the
other source.

TWO TYPES OF SEDUCTION

Anne Sexton and the Seduction of the Audience

I

In the most famous seduction poem in English, Andrew Marvell reminds his coy mistress that "The grave's a fine and private place / But none, I think, do there embrace."[1] The final turn of his syllogism then begins:

> Now, therefore, while the youthful hue
> Sits on thy skin like morning dew,
> And while thy willing soul transpires
> At every pore with instant fires—

We are all familiar with the strategy: "thy willing soul transpires / At every pore with instant fires"—you're blushing, baby, I know you really want it, don't be shy. Earlier in the poem Marvell has engaged in some clever bullying, mocking the conventions of courtship and of courtly love poetry he pretends to respect. At its close he anticipates a lovemaking that will transgress social and literary rules in its combination of indelicate violence and startling intimacy. "Like amorous birds of prey," the lovers must "Rather at once our Time devour / Than languish in his slow-chapt power." It is either eat or be eaten, in the world of the flesh. This metaphor is followed by one yet more insistently carnal, and at the same time more genuinely loving, than the rhetoric of flattery the poet has rejected:

> Let us roll all our strength, and all
> Our sweetness up into one ball,
> And tear our pleasures with rough strife
> Thorough the iron gates of life.
> Thus, if we cannot make our sun
> Stand still, yet we will make him run.

If we take Marvell's poem as an epitome of seduction, the activity of seduction is quite a subtle matter. It differs on the one hand from the act of rape, where x subdues y by force, and on the other from the proposal, where x promises y an exchange of goods and services: come live with me and be my love, and I'll give you this and that. In both rape and the proposal, x and y remain distinct beings with separate sets of wishes. In the seduction this separation is less certain, less absolute. As Marvell suggests, seduction depends on x convincing y that she already secretly desires the same amorous play that x desires, and that she has the potential to amalgamate with y into a single being, a "we" that will replace "I" and "you" as it does at the poem's close. Note that Marvell does not make the gender distinction we would expect, my strength and your sweetness, but invokes "all our strength, and all / Our sweetness," implying that both man and woman possess both strength and sweetness.

"To His Coy Mistress" is also a poem about poetry, and not only about a poetics of the contra-conventional, composed under pressure of lust and of mortality; it is a poem about the poet-reader relation. For if all works of literature construct their proper audience, a work that addresses a "you" within itself does so doubly. In the transaction taking place between "To His Coy Mistress" and each of its readers, the reader as well as the mistress plays the part of "you," and the poet is seducing the reader by suggesting that the reader's resistance disguises a deeper desire to be seduced. The poet promises that, when certain foolish literary formalities are dropped, the reader can become— excitingly, violently, strongly and sweetly, transcending gender distinction and the distinction between self and other—one with the poet.

Anne Sexton's poem "For John, Who Begs Me Not to Enquire Further," composed as the apologia for what we might call an erotic poetics at the very outset of Sexton's career, resembles "To His Coy Mistress" in a number of ways. First, the title constitutes a witty piece of bullying mockery, as we learn from Diane Middlebrook's reconstruction of Sexton's early apprentice relationship with John Holmes.[2] Holmes, Sexton's teacher, fellow poet, and supposed friend, wrote her an admonitory letter after seeing the manuscript that was to become *To Bedlam and Part Way Back*, advising her not to publish the poems she had written about her mental breakdowns and hospital experiences:

> I am uneasy . . . that what looks like a brilliant beginning might turn
> out to be so self-centered and so narrowed a diary that it would be clinical
> only. Something about asserting the hospital and psychiatric experiences
> seems to me very selfish—all a forcing others to listen to you, and nothing

given the listeners, nothing that teaches them or helps them. . . . It bothers me that you use poetry this way. It's all a release for you but what is it for anybody else except a spectacle of someone experiencing release?

Holmes accuses Sexton, in other words, of attempted emotional rape. His assumption is that her experiences are not only painful but intrinsically worthless, and that others cannot identify with her or them.

Sexton's reply begins by accepting the premise of difference between "I" and "you" but, like Marvell, gives that difference a twist of the tail. She has quoted as her epigraph to *Bedlam* a letter from Goethe to Schopenhauer: "[The true philosopher] must be like Sophocles's Oedipus, who, seeking enlightenment concerning his terrible fate, pursues his indefatigable enquiry, even when he divines that appalling horror awaits him in the answer. But most of us carry in our heart the Jocasta who begs Oedipus for God's sake not to inquire further." The title "For John, Who Begs Me Not to Enquire Further," then, accomplishes a neat role reversal. Anne Sexton assumes the mantle of the tragic hero-philosopher (male, of course, and celebrated by a long line of high-cultural males), while John Holmes is relegated to the position of timid female. As Marvell mocks the coy mistress, Sexton mocks the resistant mentor.

Second, as Marvell seems to agree that conventional courtship would be desirable if we had world and time enough, Sexton seems to agree that her poetry is "not beautiful." She uses Holmes's own language, calling her mind a "narrow diary" and herself "selfish." She appears to accept his values: "I tapped my own head; / it was glass, an inverted bowl. / It is a small thing / to rage in your own bowl." We may take these concessions to the adversary as sincere or insincere; they are probably in some sense both; either way, they establish a kind of authority of empathy. The poet knows what the adversary thinks and likes, and this gives the poet a bit of moral edge, or at any rate wedge.

A third and crucial similarity is that Sexton tells Holmes he is not really different from her: "At first it was private. / Then it was more than myself; / it was you, or your house / or your kitchen." As Diane Middlebrook has observed, "Sexton insists to Holmes that his rejection of her poetry is in part a defense against the power of her art, which tells not a private but a collective truth, and, to his horror, includes and reveals him." For Holmes's first wife was a suicide, and he himself was a recovered alcoholic. The poet then continues:

> And if you turn away
> because there is no lesson here
> I will hold my awkward bowl,
> with all its cracked stars shining
> like a complicated lie,
> and fasten a new skin around it
> as if I were dressing an orange
> or a strange sun.

As Marvell reminds his coy mistress of human mortality, so Sexton in this beautiful passage offers her resisting reader the truth of human vulnerability. The awkward bowl of her creativity, mysteriously precious, will be wounded by his disdain. Still, she will continue to care for it, continue to write, even if her truths are taken to be a lie. There is fear of rejection and contempt here, but also a pursuit of the point that rejection of one another derives precisely from the dread of contemplating our shared, frightening lives, and that denial can only exacerbate suffering:

> This is something I would never find
> in a lovelier place, my dear,
> although your fear is anyone's fear,
> like an invisible veil between us all . . .
> and sometimes in private,
> my kitchen, your kitchen,
> my face, your face.

The tone is at once pleading and condescending, with its masterstroke rhyming of "dear" and "fear." The idea of the personal as transpersonal expands, as she urges Holmes to recognize that his fear of accepting a shared human condition is itself a shared fear; that it is perhaps responsible for making that human condition as sad as it is; and that resistance is a kind of spiritual virginity. The "invisible veil" returns us to the image of Holmes as woman, as Jocasta, while it suggests that all of us may be in the position of protecting ourselves like fearful women. But as Jocasta already intuitively knows the secret she hopes to deny, so Holmes is not really an emotional virgin. He has suffered like Sexton, even if he wishes to deny it, and she has already penetrated his veil by naming his disapproval "fear." They are, as the undifferentiated parallelism of kitchens and faces urges, alike.

As a poem of seduction and an apologia for a poetics of seduction, "For John" addresses—indeed creates by addressing—a reader who is at once in the poem and outside it, who is both John and "anyone," and who both resists the poet's claim and secretly wants to accept it. "I" and "you" are different and also the same, is the claim, and the attempt is to seduce the reader into empathizing both with Holmes's position and with Sexton's, into finding both the Oedipus and the Jocasta within the self, and, ultimately, into recognizing that our normal sense of self as rigidly bounded ego committed to protecting its boundaries is a fiction that damages more than it sustains us. As a critique of conventional aesthetics, "For John" does not so much dismiss conservative expectations that poetry must be impersonally "beautiful" as it introduces the liberal possibility that poetry may legitimately be personal and intimate and that a poet's introspection may yield a "certain sense of order . . . worth learning" to others as well as herself. Note, however, that while Sexton offers the notion that such poetry is cognitively significant, something one can "know," a "lesson," the poem's most original and provocative metaphoric sequence is generated by the expectation of rejection. If the cracked stars of the poet's glass head shine "like a complicated lie," which is to say that poetry is a truth that seems to be a lie, the poet will veil it with new skin "as if . . . dressing an orange / or a strange sun," which is to say that she will write irrationally, surreally, healingly, ornamentally, childishly, playfully, protectively. One dresses wounds, one dresses dolls. These are metaphors that will recur in Sexton's poems, and they are metaphors for the activity of metaphor making. Thus the critic-reader's assumed antagonism becomes incorporated into the act of the poem, becomes transformed to poetic energy.

II

To penetrate the invisible veil between us all was Anne Sexton's literary calling, much as the justification of God's ways to men was Milton's, the articulation of the true voice of feeling was Keats's, or the recovery of the tale of the tribe was Pound's. The poetic program Sexton announced in her first volume of poems continued to be hers throughout her career. She had committed herself to an erotic view of art and life and remained committed to it. Having grown up in a family and society that resisted reading her and each other, among "people who seldom touched— / though touch is all" ("Rowing," CP, 417),[3] she places the issue of human intimacy at the center of her writing,

both thematically and as the source of poetic language itself. In a letter
to a psychiatrist friend, Sexton wrote:

> It is hard to define. When I was first sick I was thrilled . . . to get into
> the Nut House. At first, of course, I was just scared and crying and very
> quiet (who me!) but then I found this girl (very crazy of course) (like
> me I guess) who talked language. What a relief! I mean, well . . . someone!
> And then later, a while later, and quite a while, I found out that [Dr.]
> Martin talked language. . . . By the way, Kayo [Sexton's husband] has
> never understood one word of language. (*Letters*, 244)

When she began taking classes in poetry and meeting poets, Sexton discovered another group who spoke "language." "I found I belonged to the poets, that I was *real* there." As Diane Middlebrook
remarks, what Sexton means by "language" is something compressed,
elliptical, metaphoric. "Schizophrenics use language this way, and so
do poets: 'figurative language' is the term Sexton might have used here,
except she meant to indicate that the crucible of formation was urgent
need."[4] Clearly, too, "language" in Sexton's account is what people
speak when they are free of the censor's invisible veil of ordinary
intercourse; "language" is intimacy, authenticity, love in a loveless
world; it is what the inner self uses to communicate with other inner
selves. What a relief! But inevitably temporary, inevitably to be sought
and resought. Longing always "for something to touch / that touches
back" ("The Touch," *CP*, 173), a kiss is for her "Zing! A resurrection!"
("The Kiss," *CP*, 174); a lover caressing a breast is "the key to everything" ("The Breast," *CP*, 175); at the consummation of any lovemaking, "Logos appears milking a star"; and, with a variation on the
figure of the hymeneal veil of separation, the man and woman "with
their double hunger / have tried to reach through / the curtain of God"
("When Man Enters Woman," *CP*, 428), much as Sexton has tried to
pierce the veil of the anxious male authority. All her books contain
recurrent images of undressing, nudity, skin, the parts and parcels of
the body. Her work repeatedly implies that self is constituted by other(s)
or that self and other overlap: "Mother, father I'm made of" is for her
one key constellation; another is what she confesses to her daughter,
"I made you to find me" ("The Double Image," *CP*, 42). She remembers becoming "a we . . . a kind company" in infancy, inventing her
imaginary supportive twin Christopher (based on Christopher Smart,
another madman who spoke "language") for the times "when the big

balloons did not bend over us" ("O Ye Tongues: Fourth Psalm," *CP*, 402—ED. "Third Psalm" in *DN*). Lovers "gnaw at the barrier because we are two" and swim "up and up / the river, the identical river called Mine" ("Eighteen Days without You," *CP*, 214). Friends "reach into my veins" ("The Witch's Life," *CP*, 423). In *The Awful Rowing Toward God*, Sexton advises us to take off our lives like trousers, shoes, underwear, take off our flesh, "In other words / take off the wall / that separates you from God" ("The Wall," *CP*, 446).

That opening the self to intimacy means leaving oneself open to pain and guilt continues to be a deep assumption in Sexton's late work as in her early. The same poem that advises stripping ourselves for God also describes us as earthworms underground, who, were Christ to come in the form of a plow, "would be blinded by the sudden light / and writhe in our distress. / As I write these lines," she adds, "I too writhe." To surrender a lover is to annihilate the self: "As for me, I am a watercolor. / I wash off" ("For My Lover, Returning to His Wife," *CP*, 190). In the posthumously published "Food," the dependency on love is described as profoundly infantile, a need that continuously reproduces the infant's need for the breast—"I want mother's milk, / that good sour soup"—a need that can never be satisfied; rejection takes the form of impersonal discourses antithetical to the "language" of intimacy:

> I am hungry and you give me
> a dictionary to decipher.
> I am a baby all wrapped up in its red howl
> and you pour salt into my mouth.
> . . . .
> Tell me! Tell me! Why is it?
> I need food
> and you walk away reading the paper.
>
> (*CP*, 489)

From the beginning Sexton saw readers and audiences as potential intimates, and consequently potential sources of pain, much as she sees the other beings who populate her poems. Indeed the condition of her poetry is the presence of an audience, whom she needs to need her; Sexton's vocation as a poet was determined to an extraordinary degree by an assumption of and dependence on readerly empathy. "My doctor encouraged me to write more. 'Don't kill yourself,' he said. 'Your poems might mean something to someone else someday,' " she says of her first poems (*No Evil Star*, 85). Recalling the course she took with Robert Lowell, she describes letting her poems "come up, as for a butcher, as for a lover" (*No Evil Star*, 6). Describing the agonies she endured as a performer reading her poetry to thrill-seeking audiences in the essay "The Freak Show," she also makes clear how significant performance was to her: "Don't kid yourself. You write for an audience. I think of myself as writing for . . . that one perfect reader who understands and loves" (*No Evil Star*, 33). She touchingly relates occasions when audience members shouted encouragement, declares that readings traumatize her for a month, and quotes in full an adulatory letter from a fan. Her letters, too, are full of references to her "fans," references at once self-dramatizing, self-congratulatory, and self-pitying.

We may easily find Sexton's addiction to love, her insistence on need, infantile and repellent. She clearly finds it repellent herself, thereby somewhat outflanking us. What must mitigate our judgment is the recognition that we, too, are such addicts, were truth told. Imagine the veil lifted, "language" spoken. Hence the centrality of a strategy of seduction.

The single most crucial device whereby Sexton pursues a seductive poetics is her use of "you," a pronoun she employs, I would not be surprised to learn, more than any other poet in English. Over and over the poems address a "you" who may be mother, father, daughter, husband, lover, friend, psychoanalyst, or God, and who is always also the reader. More powerfully than any other poet in English (only D. H. Lawrence comes close) she renders the complexity of intimate relationships—the way they involve the desire to merge with the other and the desire to resist merger; the way the other can be seen both as antagonist and as lover-beloved; the way joy, sympathy, affection, admiration, resentment, fear, anger, and guilt may (must?) coexist at any moment in a relationship of sufficient nearness and dearness. When we include the inevitable actuality of the readerly "you" within the dynamic of these poems, their potential meaning increases several fold, for the reader may at any moment be identifying/resisting identification with both the "I" and the "you" of the poet's text. Further, those Sexton poems that deal most self-referentially with language gestures of various kinds are often, precisely, addresses to "you" that, in effect, invite "you" to reconsider the meaning of language, of poetry.

For example, the early elegy "The Division of Parts" oscillates, as do all Sexton's mother poems, between entanglement and disentanglement of their two identities and between motherly and daughterly dominance. The mother is half-identified as a martyred Christ whose daughter is "one third thief" of her inheritance; "division" signifies both the dividing of the dead from the living and the apportionment of the dead among the living—whether or not they want her "parts." The poet describes her discomfort with the mother's burdensome legacy of money, coat, jewels, and furs, the mother's Christ, and the mother *as* Christ. Simultaneously this is a text about textuality, "your will" (a legal, moral, and religious text, especially if we hear the echo of "thy will be done") versus the poet's work: "I . . . poke at this dry page like a rough / goat" (*CP*, 44). Visited in a dream by her dead mother, "I cursed you, *Dame / keep out of my slumber. / My good Dame, you are dead*" (*CP*, 45). At the poem's climax, however, she wants both to "curse / you with my rhyming words" and to "bring you flapping back, old love . . . god-in-her-moon . . . my Lady of my first words" (*CP*, 45–46). The poet speaks, as we all do, a mother tongue; to recognize this is to recognize that the mother-daughter bond is the source of the poetic language whereby the poet both exorcises the mother, rupturing the connection, and guarantees her perpetual presence.

Like her mother poems, Sexton's daughter poems revolve around issues of identification and separation as well as the inevitable superseding of mother by daughter. Just as "I did not know / that my life, in the end, / would run over my mother's like a truck," so to the growing daughter, "I'm there, an old tree in the background." In "Mother and Daughter" (*CP*, 305–7), a poem celebrating the advent of her daughter's puberty:

> Linda, you are leaving
> your old body now.
>
>   . . . .
>
> You've picked my pocket clean
> and you've racked up all my
> poker chips and left me empty.

I have presided over more than one classroom of women arguing over whether this is a poem of love or hate, pleasure or jealousy, satisfaction or dread. I have tried to suggest that it is all these things.

It is also a poem about language, juxtaposing an aging mother's discourse of words with a ripening daughter's discourse of proud bodily gesture. "Question you about this" is the poem's refrain:

> Question you about this
> and you hold up pearls.
>
> . . . .
>
> Question you about this—
> you with your big clock going,
> its hands wider than jackstraws—
> and you'll sew up a continent.
>
> . . . .
>
> Question you about this
> and you will see my death
> drooling at these gray lips
> while you, my burglar, will eat
> fruit and pass the time of day.

The daughter's response is frightening, gratifying, tragic, and comic. It is both a failure of response, as the daughter cannot or will not answer the mother in words, and precisely the response the mother desires, as it indicates that the daughter has successfully entered her own life; therefore the mother's mothering has succeeded. One must perhaps be a mother to recognize in these lines the maternal wry pride in the daughter's free vitality; that the daughter is a new Eve whose casual fruit eating is being endorsed as safe to herself if fatal to her mother, and that the mother would not have it otherwise, should be apparent to any reader.

Another ambiguous alternative to the "language" of intimate communication in Sexton is laughter, specifically the laughter of the fathers. The first poem of "The Death of the Fathers," called "Oysters" (*CP*, 322–23), again has puberty as its subject:

> Oysters we ate,
> sweet blue babies,
> twelve eyes looked up at me,
> running with lemon and Tabasco.
> I was afraid to eat this father-food
> and Father laughed
> and drank down his martini,
> clear as tears.

She eats the oysters, successfully completing an initiation that she also calls a death, as she joins her father's laughter: "Then I laughed and then we laughed . . . for I was fifteen / and eating oysters / and the child was defeated. / The woman won." But won what, we are made to wonder. The child has been seduced, or is it raped, into womanhood, in a scene that seems to balance intimidation and enticement. One becomes a woman by eating "father-food," which suggests both the father's genitals and the unborn children she may now bear, but which also suggests that she will now be *like* her father, able to do frightening adult things. To enter womanhood, sexuality, is to enter a condition in which sophistication and humiliation, power and grief ("his martini, / clear as tears"), will be inextricably combined. The powerful and sinister paternal laughter of this poem resembles that of "Death, with his ho-ho baritone." It reappears in "Santa," "Grandfather, Your Wound," and, above all, "The Rowing Endeth," where the Father-God's laughter rolls out of his mouth and into the speaker's after the notorious crooked game of poker; the scene of daughterly compliance with paternal force is at once physical and spiritual. In the tremendously glamorous shadow of the Father, one must die to be saved; one ceases to speak in words. Whether or not the paternal laughter can be said to constitute a superior "language" of intimacy remains a question. Sexton's propitiatory tone at the close of "The Rowing Endeth" suggests that it is and is not. For her, however, it is unquestionably seductive.

III

At this point let me indicate two issues that I believe the foregoing discussion of Sexton opens up. The first is the relation of Sexton's work to issues of gender, the second to the issue of the boundary between life and art.

Readers of feminist theory will of course recognize the context in which this discussion of Sexton's poetics belongs. Students of female psychology such as Jean Miller, Nancy Chodorow, and Carol Gilligan define female personality in terms of its fluid ego boundaries, its permanent tendency to oscillate between mother and father as erotic objects, its often self-destructive capacity for empathy, and its relatedness. Literary critics, including Sandra Gilbert and Susan Gubar, Nancy Miller, Judith Kegan Gardiner, Mary Jacobus, Rachel DuPlessis, and others concerned with avant-garde writing, propose that the woman writer's culturally marginal status gives her what DuPlessis calls a "both/and vision" opposed to the "either/or" of the dominant culture. Iragaray tells us that the female sex is never "one" but is always fluid, multiple, plural:

> "She" is indefinitely other in herself. This is doubtless why she is said to be whimsical, incomprehensible, agitated, capricious. . . . It is useless, then, to trap women in the exact definition of what they mean, to make them repeat (themselves) so that it will be clear; they are already elsewhere in that discursive machinery where you expected to surprise them. . . . Their desire is often interpreted, and feared, as a sort of insatiable hunger, a voracity that will swallow you whole. Whereas it really involves a different economy more than anything else, one that upsets the linearity of a project, undermines the goal-object of a desire, diffuses the polarization toward a single pleasure, disconcerts fidelity to a single discourse.[5]

Female "difference," according to feminist thought in our time, is female fluidity, diffusion, affiliation, multiplicity. To write in ways that violate our normal notions of a unitary self and of simply definable self-other relationships, then, is to write like a woman. Readers of contemporary women's poetry will also recognize that others besides Sexton attempt to engage the reader in participatory acts that will rupture both literary rules and the rule that we must not try to penetrate "the invisible veil between us all." As I have elsewhere argued, writers as various as Sylvia Plath, Diane Wakoski, Adrienne Rich, Ntozake Shange, June Jordan, Audre Lorde, and Judy Grahn—to name a few—employ strategies designed to put the reader in a problematic position, to make it impossible for us to read "objectively" whether or not we identify with the author or approve of the strategies.[6] Forced to relinquish the role of reader-looking-at-artifact, forced to respond personally to the poetic fiction of a direct address expressing need, hope, pain, joy, anger, and despair, calling on our love and sympathy, or attacking us for our indifference and neglect, we may be delighted, we may be repelled. Either way, we have been, to some undetermined degree, seduced. Insofar as "love" is woman's topic and the need to transform a phallocentric literature is the woman writer's larger project, the seductiveness of women's writing is almost an inevitable consequence.

Yet does it make sense, finally, to look at literature in this rigidly gendered fashion? I began this essay by noticing the way Andrew Marvell invokes, at the climax of his poem, not man's strength and woman's sweetness but all *our* strength, all *our* sweetness. I should add that this gesture moves me deeply; I am very grateful for it. I went on to suggest that Anne Sexton at the outset of her career perceived that self and other may, if they penetrate the invisible veil of fear between them, discover likeness as well as difference. Now I must wonder what I am liable to find when I penetrate the veil of other poets I love, men as well as women.

Diana Hume George in her powerful study of Anne Sexton's poetry argues both that Sexton's work constitutes the "psychic biography of a gender" and that it tells not merely a gendered but a human story, "not the story only of personal pathology but of a people, a culture, perhaps all cultures, all individuals."[7] This is contradictory only if we are unwilling to suppose that a generic "she" may represent humanity, may probe the universal human condition, in precisely the way the generic "he" has always done. What if we were to *expect* the woman writer to compose in "the first-person universal?" Would we not then *expect* the male writer to write like a woman?

The woman reader, the woman critic should, I think, be especially alert to the possibility that "female" literary techniques, values, and forms may exemplify human universals. For are not writers marginal just as women are marginal? May not the search of women writers for continuity and community exemplify the larger, though veiled, quest implicit in all literature? Thus it is proper to hypothesize that if we reexamine the long tradition of poetry by men with the light offered us by a poet like Sexton, we may well find more "female" eroticism, more fluidity, more dissolving of self-other boundaries than we presently suppose. Certainly with the help of Sexton and other writers like her, we may learn to recognize that the quality of relationship between poet and reader is in fact never neutral. A poem is in fact never simply an artifact, is always a transaction, a personal transaction. We do not have a critical vocabulary to describe the many types of response poets may demand of their readers or the many kinds of responses readers may bring their poets. But by asking ourselves what happens to us when we read—when we read Shakespeare, Swift, Shelley, as well as Sexton—we might begin to develop one.

A second issue raised by Sexton's seductiveness concerns the moral resonance of her art and its relation to the real lives of women. There is a sense in which all art affirms what it represents, a sense in which all viewers consent to what is viewed—a sense in which the category of the good is dissolved into the true, the beautiful—whenever we apprehend a thing as art. Tragedy does not oppose the hamartia of its hero; rather it celebrates it. We deeply consent, watching *King Lear*, to Lear's death, to the fact of evil and suffering in the world. Tragedy by no means wishes suffering away from us but on the contrary ennobles it, sweetens it, makes us feel it is good, and thus disarms us of the will to change. To take an example closer to Sexton, when we read *Anna Karenina* or *The Mill on the Floss*, we consent to the death of a passionate woman—or do we? If we are feminists, must we not object that the passionate woman's death, so dear to nineteenth-century fiction, reflects nothing but the dread of woman's autonomous sensuality and is both an effect and a cause of woman's oppression?

A few years ago in a session of the Modern Language Association devoted to "Anne Sexton: The Daughter's Seduction," several members of the audience were distressed at my neutral-to-positive use of the term *seduction*. We had heard a paper by Diane Wood Middlebrook on Sexton's play *Mercy Street* and one by Diana Hume George on the theme of incest in Sexton's poetry and in her life. It is clear enough at the present moment that the term *seduction* is often a euphemism in public discourse (beginning with Freud) for incest; that the trauma suffered by incest victims is deepened by social denial that incest exists; and that incest victims live—in our culture—with shame, self-hatred, inexpressible anger, much as do rape victims. We had, then, in our audience, women who were or who knew incest victims and who were appalled at the absence of protest in my, in our, discussion of seduction. That absence of protest, it must be said, is a defining characteristic of Sexton's. Both in *Mercy Street*, where the daughter's adolescent body is the locus of the father's and the great-aunt's selfish desires, and in the lyrics that hint at incestuous desire and exploitation by Anne Sexton's father and grandfather, Sexton withholds the anger we may wish her to feel, just as she withholds it when she writes of or to her mother, daughter, lover, God. The story Sexton tells about love says, in part, that normative femaleness means falling in love with the father, being seduced by him, being complicit in that seduction, and proceeding to resurrect his deified image in other men. This is a plain enough pattern in Sexton. But it is complicated by the poet's awareness of male failure. The father in all his incarnations is, as Diana Hume George points out, "a god not sufficiently omnipotent, a man not sufficiently humane, a male principle not sufficiently able to accommodate feminine powers and desires. But this ultimate failure is never judged harshly. . . . In the world of Sexton's poetry, the men born into their myths are often as helpless and hapless as the women born into theirs."[8] If love, in Sexton, is inextricable from pain, it is also inextricable from compassion. To love is to experience an other as a self in a way that undermines anger, protest, and judgment. When Sexton claims to write "with mercy for the greedy," she means by "the greedy" not merely herself but everyone. And it is to this vision that her art is designed to seduce us.

How is the feminist reader, or any reader who is committed to changing his or her own life and the life of society, to respond to an art seemingly so complicit with female victimization? I believe there is no plain and simple answer to this question, but I would like to suggest a set of possible responses. First, it may well be that some readers will find the values of Sexton's erotic poetics thoroughly repellent; they will view her neediness and greediness, her insistent vulnerability and excessive generosity with horror; they will not find these qualities in themselves, and they will not be seduced by her into doing so. Other readers may recognize the Sexton in themselves and want to expel or alter her. Yet others may believe that Sexton's "weird abundance" of erotic openness is or might be normative and benign and that it is only society that needs transforming. It is a conviction of one branch of feminism, at least, that if everyone spoke the "language" of intimacy we would be, as it were, out of the woods. Interestingly, I do not think Sexton encourages simple imitation. There was never a Sexton cult comparable to the Plath cult. This is because she does not herself glamorize madness, suicide, or pain. She represents; she does not endorse, just as she does not condemn. However we respond to her poetry and life, it will be useful to remember that she, too, looked "for uncomplicated hymns / but love has none" ("A Little Uncomplicated Hymn," *CP*, 152).

NOTES

1. Andrew Marvell, "To His Coy Mistress," in *Selected Poetry and Prose*, ed. Dennis Davison (London: George D. Havrap and Co., 1952), 83–84.

2. See Diane Wood Middlebrook, " 'I Tapped My Own Head': The Apprenticeship of Anne Sexton," in *Coming to Light: American Women Poets in the Twentieth Century*, ed. Diane Wood Middlebrook and Marilyn Yalom (Ann Arbor: University of Michigan Press, 1985), 195–203, to which the following discussion is indebted.

3. Quotations from Anne Sexton's works and writings are cited in the text using the following abbreviations:

CP:	*The Complete Poems*, ed. Linda Gray Sexton (Boston: Houghton Mifflin Co., 1981)
Letters:	*Anne Sexton: A Self-Portrait in Letters*, ed. Linda Gray Sexton and Lois Ames (Boston: Houghton Mifflin Co., 1977)
No Evil Star:	*No Evil Star: Selected Essays, Interviews and Prose*, ed. Steven E. Colburn (Ann Arbor: University of Michigan Press, 1985)

4. Middlebrook, "Apprenticeship of Anne Sexton," 198.

5. Luce Irigaray, "This Sex Which Is Not One," in *This Sex Which Is Not One*, trans. Catherine Porter (Ithaca: Cornell University Press, 1985), 28–32.

6. Alicia Ostriker, *Stealing the Language: The Emergence of Women's Poetry in America* (Boston: Beacon Press, 1986), 205–9.

7. Diana Hume George, *Oedipus Anne: The Poetry of Anne Sexton* (Urbana: University of Illinois Press, 1987), 24, 181.

8. Ibid., 25.

DIANE WOOD MIDDLEBROOK

Seduction in Anne Sexton's Unpublished Play *Mercy Street*

In the fall of 1969 a one-act play by poet Anne Sexton ran for six weeks off-Broadway in New York at the American Place Theater. Titled *Mercy Street*,[1] the play starred an Anne Sexton look-alike named Marian Seldes in the role of Daisy, a suicidal woman, thirty years old. The setting is an Episcopal High Mass, where Daisy has come to take communion; the priest elevates the host, and the play takes place in the space of a heartbeat as Daisy's imagination flashes back over episodes in the past from which she seeks redemption through the sacrament of Holy Communion. The priest becomes Daisy's psychiatrist, Dr. Alex; the altar becomes a consulting room, Daisy a hysteric; the stage fills and empties with ghosts from Daisy's past: her mother, Judith, her father, Arthur (a salesman, nicknamed "Ace"), and her great-aunt Amelia ("Amy").

The play's main action takes place in the doctor's consulting room. Daisy revisits in memory—sometimes in hallucination—significant episodes related to her illness and despair: a trip to Europe, based on her great-aunt Amelia's itinerary fifty years before; her father's seduction of her, witnessed by Amelia; Amelia's subsequent madness; Daisy's twenty-seventh birthday, which she spends on furlough from the mental hospital. In the penultimate scene Daisy, hallucinating the presence of great-aunt Amelia, feels herself caught between Amelia and Dr. Alex for the possession of her body, her sanity. But the doctor sees her retreating further and further into fantasy. Discovering that Daisy has inflicted herself with wounds on her palms, claiming these are stigmata, Dr. Alex decides to send her back to the hospital. For all his compassion he has failed to interpret the signs inscribed on her body. But the end of the play returns to the Mass: to Daisy's hunger for release from her body's afflictions. "Grant us rest eternal," intones the priest-psychiatrist, who turns to Daisy saying: "Daisy, the body of Christ. / Daisy, the blood of Christ."

Sexton characterizes Daisy as a particular kind of hysteric: an incest survivor whose defense lies in splitting off parts of her body from consciousness. Setting the play in an Episcopal High Mass, Sexton brings together the social context of Daisy's illness—upper-middle-class New England family life—with the promise of redemption of the body symbolized in the mystery of the Eucharist, wherein bread and wine are transubstantiated into the presence of Christ, infusing with spirit the flesh of the partaker. The curtain falls before Daisy has taken the eucharist onto her tongue: we do not know whether she chooses the sacrament or suicide.

Daisy's body is thus the site of dramatic conflict in *Mercy Street;* "Take me out of my body," she prays to Christ, "and give me back my soul." Throughout the play Daisy has the dissociated relation to her body characteristic of the hysteric. But the play offers an account of this condition from the inside, as the audience reexperiences with Daisy significant occasions on which her body has been appropriated by others for interpretation and manipulation. The most significant of these is Daisy's memory of a night of family quarreling that culminated in a seduction by her father.

The scene takes place in three bedrooms that remain simultaneously visible to the audience: Amelia's, stage left; Daisy's, stage center; Judith's, stage right. Amelia goes to Daisy's mother's bedroom to confront her with a financial crisis. Amelia reveals that Ace is broke and that she's been supporting him—but she's spent her capital, used up all her stocks, and Ace has sold the family's summer home in Maine. Judith denies that Ace is a weak man and dismisses Amelia as crazy. Amelia leaves angrily, returning to her room.

Daisy, aware of trouble, comes into Judith's room, concerned about Amelia's strangeness. Judith comforts her as if she were a little child but worries aloud about Daisy's habit of cuddling with Amelia: "It makes me shiver the way Aunt Amy keeps touching you and stroking you. . . . Women don't touch women that way."

Daisy goes off to her own room; Ace comes in drunk, and Judith asks him about the money and property—Aunt Amelia's charges. Learning the worst, Judith locks Ace out of their bedroom.

Ace goes into Daisy's room, looking for company. Daisy greets him tenderly, and together they sing the song she's named for: "Daisy, Daisy, tell me your answer true / I'm half crazy. . . ." Gradually the scene grows erotically charged: Ace forces whiskey on Daisy, praises her "little peachy breasts," begins rubbing her back. As Ace gathers his daughter into a sexual embrace, Amelia enters the room, and Ace exits to her shocked cries.

The mood of this scene is surprisingly tender and subtly comic. Oblivious to the double entendres, Daisy is a generic naive, while Ace's drunken clumsiness delays the register of horror, until an adult witness intrudes and labels the action "filthy and disgusting."

While the drama of seduction is being enacted in Daisy's bedroom, the scene contains another figure, stage left: great-aunt Amelia, shut away in her own room, pacing and twisting her hands in an obsessive private ritual, chanting and raving, cracking a small riding whip. In the earlier part of this act, Amelia has played a get-tough role with Daisy's mother: it is Amelia who wears the pants in this family. ("You're hard, like a man—a two-fisted man," Daisy's mother complains.) But this scene reveals another side of her: the sex-obsessed spinster whose masculine character traits cover hysterical disgust for her body. Amelia's "garbage bible" is a psalmlike litany that she has evolved as a mode of acting out her thwarted Oedipal desires. Modeled by Anne Sexton on the mad lyrics of Christopher Smart and the Bible's Song of Songs, Amelia's self-abusive chant weaves like a chorus through the lines exchanged between the seductive father and his prey: an operatic trio that blends only in the ears of the audience.

> ACE: Here, we'll make a woman of you yet. (*Holds bottle to her lips.*) Take some. No. Three swallows.
> DAISY: I don't like it.
> ACE: A few more swallows. You will. It's good for you, prewar scotch, like medicine. Here, have another swig.
> AMELIA: Once I was a shedder of blood and the great eagle took me in his claws and came into my mouth and ate thereof. He traded me for figs and oil and wine. He drank of me and caused me shame.
> DAISY: It burns like fire.
> ACE: Now, you're really grown up, had your first drink with your old man, got the—menstruated last month.
> DAISY: How did you know?
> ACE: Your mother said.
> DAISY: Do you know if it only happens once a year?
> AMELIA: The days of the month are sacred, and I will wash them.
> ACE: No, once a month if you're lucky.
> DAISY: Lucky?
> ACE: Just a joke of your mother's.

AMELIA: I am fighting with my groaning all night. All night I am swimming in oil and it clouds my eyes.

ACE: Lie back now and I'll give you a back rub the way Aunt Amy does. You have breasts, too, don't you. Nice little peachy breasts. Does it feel good?

AMELIA: I am clean. I am sweeter than honeycomb and the bees buzz over my mouth.

ACE: Oh, Daisy, I'm so lonely. I need someone to love me.

AMELIA: I will stroke my skin with cream and let the virgins admire me. I will build my womb like the ribs of a dory and when my little girl comes to me I will let her lie betwixt my breasts.

ACE: (*Holding tight.*) Daisy, lie close to me.

DAISY: Yes, Daddy, yes.

(*Amelia opens door of bedroom to see Ace and Daisy side by side.*)

AMELIA: Were you calling, Daisy? I thought I heard a voice—Ace!

ACE: (*Gets off bed quickly.*) Amelia, I—

AMELIA: Disgusting!

(*Ace starts to cry.*)

DAISY: Why do you cry, Daddy?

AMELIA: Filthy . . . both of you!

DAISY: Only fire water, Aunt Amy—only—

AMELIA: And drinking, too . . . oh, the filth of it, the horrible filth of it!

ACE: Go to sleep, little flower girl.

AMELIA: And a seed shall serve him and it shall be accounted to the Lord for a generation.

(*Ace exits, stumbling out.*)

DAISY: (*Dazed.*) I want my teddy bear.

AMELIA: (*Hurling the teddy bear at the bed.*) Take your filthy teddy bear!

DAISY: Oh, teddy, what happened to you?

Two axes of desire cross in this scene, crucifying the pubescent female child. One is the axis of daughter-father eroticism that Freud descried as the basis of normal *adult* female sexual identity, the other a surprising treatment of pre-Oedipal female desire underlying adult heterosexuality.

Daisy's erotic feeling for her father surfaces throughout this scene. As it opens, Daisy is singing to herself a little song, "Hey Daddy! . . . You wanna get the best for me, de-ah, de-ah, de-ah." Later, when Ace enters the room, Daisy, pretending to be chilly, dives under the covers in coy retreat; and the scene culminates in her assent to her father's embrace: "Yes, Daddy, yes." In ensuing scenes Daisy's heterosexual

desire emerges as full-blown transference toward Dr. Alex, who alternately bullies and seduces her into accepting the reality principle: to
give up her hallucinations and accept her destiny as a grown-up woman,
mother, and wife. Sexton's play is non-Freudian, however, in that it
acknowledges the *father's* desire, with surprising empathy. Ace, un-
manned by his aunt, by his wife, and by his bottle, yearns first toward
the moon (an infantile memory of mother, red-faced, up there, out
there, "eyes bulging like an old prostitute"), then toward his own
erection. It is his erection that he desires in this scene:

> ACE: When you drink all day no one wants you, if you do get a woman
> to bed, it doesn't work—you lose your erection.
> DAISY: What's an erection?
> AMELIA: The man will wait with his enemies at my city gate. And with
> his quiver empty.
> ACE: Nothing—just something men get when they get to be men.
> DAISY: Do girls get it too?
> ACE: Nope. Doesn't work that way.

Aunt Amelia calls Ace "filthy and disgusting"; but we remember
that the scene has another witness: grown-up Daisy, suicidal and despairing at the play's opening, in whose memory the episode is re-
played. In *her* eyes, it would seem, her father's behavior appears not
threatening but decisively self-absorbed; it is not herself but his own
potency that he seeks in her arms. Daisy's memory unmasks the ideal
of paternal love as specular—casting into doubt the possibility that any
masculine figure with authority over her life may be trusted to love
her for herself, and not as a screen for the projection of his compelling
power. Drawing the theme of father-daughter incest into the larger
arena of Daisy's spiritual questioning, Sexton's play anticipates by several years current debates in both feminist psychoanalysis and feminist
theology.

Of even greater interest is Sexton's non-Freudian extension of
the incest theme to include the relation between Daisy and Amelia,
which Amelia acts out as *both* pre-Oedipal and phallic. Sexton situates
Amelia in a "phallic" social position by making her both rich and
unmarried (that is, economically autonomous); and it is Amelia's control of the family's capital that exposes Ace's impotence. Significantly,
in the incest scene Ace offers to take Amelia's place: "I'll give you a
back rub, the way Aunt Amy does." This practice has troubled Daisy's
mother: "Women don't touch women that way." Sexton seems to

imply that the pre-Oedipal bond of daughter with mother, mother with daughter is the basis of the spinster's attachment to the little girl, an attachment that must now be abandoned. But Amelia's garbage-bible also reveals heterosexual deformations in her own father-fixated desire: "He drank of me and caused me shame. . . ." Amelia's desire profoundly confuses Daisy's body and her own; and her litany substitutes herself for Daisy, as the virgin body men covet: "I am sweeter than honeycomb and the bees buzz over my mouth." As the scene goes on she is seen to participate in the script of incest, playing both roles—seducer and seduced; and it is she who disrupts the script, usurping the father's place even as she calls him to account for his crime. Thus Amelia's desire may be described as daughter-daughter incest; her garbage-bible litany yearns toward Daisy's body because of its privileged position in patriarchy as the object of male desire. Young Daisy doesn't register the abusiveness; but the mother does, and so does the play, for it is Amelia's desire for the daughter that catalyzes adult Daisy's madness; she has become Amelia's "double," bent on self-destruction.

It is possible that a personal crisis stimulated the design of *Mercy Street:* Anne Sexton's own fear of reproducing the damage an erotic mother does to a pubescent daughter by engaging in an infantile erotic relation to her. "Transference" is the feared love: love that does not recognize the autonomy—let us say the soul—of its object, the young girl. The theme of incest asserts a strong gravitational pull in the play, partly because it seems so personally referential. But Sexton's play is not about incest as a social phenomenon; it is about a specifically female quest for spiritual redemption. The play's action takes place as an instant of consciousness in which adult Daisy witnesses the interlocking memories that underlie her despair. Watching the play's action, the audience is situated with Daisy, as in a dream, where the dreamer's subjectivity provides the empathy and affect attributed to each of the characters. Daisy and the audience are trapped in the script of a woman's place in the dynamic of heterosexual desire. Daisy's struggle to redeem her flesh from the male gaze *and* from the boundlessness of the female bond is "explained" by the incest episode and the voice-over commentary of Amelia's self-castigation.

Taken together these situations express the spiritual horror of the daughter's position in patriarchy. Daisy is *twice* a daughter in the play, and twice the object of desire: object of incestuous father love and object again of incestuous female love. Father-daughter incest has been well theorized in feminist scholarship; less well understood is the phenomenon of the acting-out woman who appropriates the daughter's body to gratify unconscious sexual desires frustrated in her adult life as a stunted sexual being—in the play, a virginal spinster fixated on her punitive, puritanical father. Aunt Amelia's affection for Daisy is revealed as perverse not when she touches her—Daisy needs to be held and loved—but when she symbolizes the daughter's body in florid, masochistic images.

Daisy's plight, then, can be theorized psychoanalytically. However, classical psychoanalysis offers no "cure" for the patriarchal system that places women's bodies at the disposal of male fantasy. Sexton's play is an act of resistance to patriarchy and does, tentatively, propose a cure: in the crucified body of Christ, to which Daisy turns with the hope of redemption. In *Mercy Street*, Sexton's "Christ" stands for the transcendence of social relations through the soul's intuition of love's possibilities: the possibility of separating conditions of dominance from the social dyad where love occurs. Christ calls upon Daisy to surrender her body—her social identity. Helpless as any infant, Christ on the cross signifies, in this play, the surrender of male dominance. He is rendered both passive and available to any vulgar stare, like a woman. But he is not in the woman's position because his sacrifice was—though predestined—freely chosen. His influence causes Daisy to un-daughter herself in relation to her therapist, by bringing him a state of mind that resists psychiatric interpretations.

Not that Sexton's Christ has no body: crucified, he is all body, body without masculine prerogatives, thus freed for redefinition in relation to woman. In Daisy's visionary hallucinations, Christ comes to her kitchen: his face appears to her at the bottom of a frying pan. He calls her away from woman's place, into what is perceived by others as madness, by Daisy as terrifying possibility. He *calls* her but does not *teach* her, does not try to assimilate her into a system of belief.

Thus the central action of *Mercy Street* can be expressed as a conflict between normalcy and salvation, between masculine culture (the Oedipal configuration) and the redemptive possibilities latent in desire. The end of the play is completely ambiguous; we do not know whether Daisy takes sleeping pills or a eucharist, death or rebirth. The actors and director who worked on the production of *Mercy Street*, gripped by the luxuriously suggestive "middle" of the play, lamented this lack of closure or point.[2] Daisy neither recovers nor dies; she exits the scene with her conflicts intact, violating the first principle of dramaturgy. In life Sexton could not locate a resolving insight either: "I keep looking for Mercy Street, and there isn't any!" she raged to her therapist during the period of the play's composition;[3] perhaps that is why Sexton turned away from the play after its production and refused to publish it. But Daisy is not Anne Sexton. She is a condition of gendered insight, a female subjectivity in a dialogue with itself; and it is in this capacity that "Daisy" reappears in the lyric voice of Sexton's later religious poetry. Increasingly, Sexton returned to the questions posed in *Mercy Street* about the impossibility of loving a God who is a Father, the need for a redeemer who has broken out of the prison house of gender and provides a model of love entirely different from father-daughter love. The play's setting, which nests the consulting room into the Episcopal Mass so that the audience necessarily loses a base in "reality," conveys that Daisy's construction of *everything*, including the incest episode, may be "all in her head." But like all of Sexton's most original and most misunderstood late work, *Mercy Street* is an act of resistance to the patriarchy in us all. The play names the enemy and refuses to envision either the choice of "mental health"—succumbing to the female role—or despair. In what sense is Daisy's the body of Christ? The site of the question is the female body poised on the brink of womanhood, and that is what *Mercy Street* is about.

NOTES

1. Unpublished manuscript deposited in the Anne Sexton Archive, Harry Ransom Humanities Research Center, University of Texas, Austin; permission to quote courtesy of Linda Gray Sexton and the Harry Ransom Humanities Research Center.

2. Interviews in 1983 with Charles Maryan, director, and Marian Seldes and Virginia Downing, actors in the American Place production.

3. Unpublished therapy journal, under restriction in the Anne Sexton Archive; quoted by permission of Linda Gray Sexton.

SEXTON THROUGH FREUD AND PSYCHOANALYTIC THEORY

Anne Sexton: Somehow to Endure

Even the covers of an Anne Sexton book are contradictory. The poet posed demurely on their jackets: a sun-streaked porch, white wicker, the beads and pleated skirt, the casual cigarette. Their tame titles—literary or allusive: *To Bedlam and Part Way Back, All My Pretty Ones, Love Poems, Transformations, The Book of Folly.* And yet beyond, inside, are extraordinary revelations of pain and loss, an intensely private record of a life hungering for madness and stalked by great loves, the getting and spending of privileged moments and suffered years. The terrible urgency of the poems, in fact, seems to invite another sort of contradiction, the kind we feel only with strong poets: disappointments. Occasionally there are poems that frankly misfire for being awkward or repetitious, stilted or prosaic. One critic has caught it:

> So her work veers between good and terrible almost indiscriminately. It is not a question of her writing bad poems from time to time, like everybody else; she also prints them cheek by jowl with her purest work. The reason, I suppose, is that the bad poems are bad in much the same way as her good ones are good: in their head-on intimacy and their persistence in exploring whatever is most painful to the author.[1]

The influences on her poetry—ranging from Rilke, Lawrence, Rimbaud, and Smart to Jarrell, Roethke, Lowell, Plath, and C. K. Williams—were easily acquired, obviously displayed, and often quickly discarded, while a few deeper influences—like that of Neruda—were absorbed and recast. She described herself as "a primitive" yet was a master of intricate formal techniques. Her voice steadily evolved and varied and, at times, sought to escape speaking of the self, but her strongest poems consistently return to her narrow thematic range and the open voice of familiar feelings. *Do I contradict myself? Very well then I contradict myself.* For the source of her first fame continued

Reprinted from *Anne Sexton: The Artist and Her Critics*, ed. J. D. McClatchy (Bloomington: Indiana University Press, 1978), 244–90.

as the focus of her work: she was the most persistent and daring of the confessionalists. Her peers have their covers: Lowell's allusiveness, Snodgrass's lyricism, Berryman's dazzle, Plath's expressionism. More than the others, Sexton resisted the temptations to dodge or distort, and the continuity and strength of her achievement remain the primary witness to the ability of confessional art to render a life into poems with all the intimacy and complexity of feeling and response with which that life has been endured.

Endurance was always her concern. Why must we? How can we? Why we must, how we do: "to endure, / somehow to endure." It is a theme that reenacts not only the sustained source of her poetry but its original impulse as well. At the age of twenty-eight, while recovering from a psychotic breakdown and suicide attempt, she began writing poems on the advice of her psychiatrist: "In the beginning, the doctor said, 'Write down your feelings because someday they might mean something to somebody. No matter how despairing you are, there are other people going through this who can't express it, and if they should read it they would feel less alone.' And so he gave me my little reason to go on; it shifted around, but that was always a driving, driving force."[2] The essentially practical motive here, and the fact of her coming to write so late and unlearned, accounts for her ironic fortune in pursuing a poetry not only then unfashionable but also difficult to achieve without a kind of clumsy innocence: "I couldn't do anything else," she said.

The spur to more serious concentration—the conscious conversion of a means for survival into a necessary art—was her reading of five poems by W. D. Snodgrass from his "Heart's Needle" sequence, published by Hall, Pack and Simpson in their important 1957 anthology, *New Poets of England and America.* The impact of Snodgrass's poems came as an affirmation of Sexton's own effort to write personally. Not the influence of his achievement but the encouragement of his example mattered, and she left to study with him at the 1958 Antioch Writers' Conference, where she showed him her poem "Unknown Girl in the Maternity Ward," written in direct response to "Heart's Needle" and dealing, too, with the loss of a child. Snodgrass sensed that her poem was a disguise and advised her simply, "Tell the real story." The result, written over many months and in obvious imitation of the strategies of "Heart's Needle," became one of her best-known poems, "The Double Image." Snodgrass also told her to study with Robert Lowell, which she returned to Boston to do in the fall of 1958. She later evaluated Lowell's influence: "He helped me to distrust the easy musical phrase and to look for the frankness of ordinary speech. If you have enough natural energy he can show you how to chain it in. He didn't teach me what to put in a poem, but what to leave out."[3] At the same time, she was studying at the Boston Adult Center with John Holmes, who discouraged her confessional impulse and tried to impose a more traditional subject matter on her. "I couldn't do anything else. I tried, but I couldn't do it. I mean, I did a couple. There's a stupid poem called 'Venus and the Ark,' which should never have been in that first book, that is the sort of thing that was approved of. That's one of the attempts; I do it, and then think, 'No!' "[4] There are a few other false starts among the poems she had gathered by 1959, but *To Bedlam and Part Way Back* (1960) has fewer hollows and sags than betray most beginners because it is the product not only of several years of determined effort but of the longer years that, to paraphrase Shelley, had learned in suffering what they teach in song.

It may be appropriate first to consider the general problem of the confessional aesthetic that Sexton's poetry helped establish. Even if it were possible, any description of the psychogenesis and psychopathology of confessionalism could only be reductive. More general psychoanalytical theories of poetry are either so broad as to be impractical for this special use of poetry or so vague and unmanageable as to be of no use at all. Freud's sense of poetry as compensatory gratification is not really applicable for confessional poetry, and more recent theories—for instance, art as "restitution" or symbolic re-creation of what the artist's aggressive fantasies have already destroyed—still cannot account for a poetry that largely avoids the symbolic approach and instead seeks naked revelation. In fact, surprisingly little has been written with any authority on the subject of confessionalism, which has become, under the rubric of "sincerity," an impulse behind many of the significant social movements and styles since 1960.

One of the few studies available is Theodor Reik's *The Compulsion to Confess*, a work that, while hardly exhaustive, at least opens up a few theoretical approaches toward an understanding of the "compulsion" and its results. Broadly, Reik defines a confession as "a statement about impulses or drives which are felt or recognized as forbidden," and their expression involves both the repressed tendency and the repressing forces. If this secular interpretation seems to exclude the usual religious (and even legal) sense of the term as narrowed to facts and intentions, they can easily be added to Reik's definition without any loss to the force of his point. The confessional situation—most obvious in analytical sessions—resides in "the transformation of a primitive urge for expression into the compulsion to confess," occasioned by social and psychic restraints and "the reactive reinforcement which the intensity of the drive experiences through repression," so that "confession is a repetition of action or of certain behavior substituted by displacement and with different emotional material, as words must substitute for action." This weakened repetition allows its own gratifications, indulging as it does both guilt and the need for punishment, even while the "reproduction through narration" achieves "the retroactive annulment of repression." That is to say, confession is at once the process of exorcism and the plea for absolution. And the result, in Reik's view, is that "the disintegrating of the personality is at least temporarily halted by the confession. The communication between the ego and that part of the ego from which it was estranged is restored."[5]

Although Freud recognized the "flexibility of repression" in artists, allowing them greater access to the unconscious and what Ernst Kris calls "functional regression" in service to the ego and its art, Reik's discussion is more directly apt for the poetry by Sexton under discussion in this essay. At the same time, it must be admitted that however much such sequences as "The Death of the Fathers" (in *The Book of Folly*) or "The Divorce Papers" (in *45 Mercy Street*) may have served Sexton as punishments for sins confessed, such an explanation, if it doubles as evaluation, cannot be finally satisfactory. It is their importance as art rather than as mere self-expression that matters. Even with that caution, Reik's explanation can be used to describe the impulses behind the expression that a confessional art then transforms. The repression through which such poems as Sexton's "The Double Image" or Sylvia Plath's "Daddy" explode is a part of their compulsive force. In fact, the great poems of madness and loss in Sexton's early books had their deeply personal source in what she once described as "a terrible need to kill myself."[6]

To some extent, then, the poetry is therapeutic; or as D. H. Lawrence said, "One sheds one's sicknesses in books—repeats and presents again one's emotions, to be master of them." Erik Erikson underscores this aspect of the situation by reminding that "the individual's mastery over his neurosis begins where he is put in a position to accept the historical necessity which made him what he is."[7] Acceptance becomes survival. Anne Sexton: "Writing, and especially having written, is evidence of survival—the books accumulate ego-strength."[8] And so confessional poets are driven back to their losses, to that alienation—from self and others, from sanity and love—which is the thematic center of their vision and work. The betrayals in childhood, the family romance, the divorces and madnesses, the suicide attempts, the self-defeat and longing—the poets pursue them in their most intimate and painful detail. The pressure of public events, of the world outside the skin, is rarely felt, except perhaps in Robert Lowell's work. But the lives these poets have survived in their poems become emblems of larger forces. In answer to a question about putting "more of the political and cultural life of the country into [his] verse," W. D. Snodgrass once remarked on the way in which confessional poems are subjective correlatives:

> A psychoanalyst a couple of years ago said, someplace or other, that family trouble, troubles in your love life, have caused people a hundred times more real agony than all the wars, famines, oppressions and the other stuff that gets in the history books. If those were your only troubles, boy would you be lucky. No, it's the fact that you keep devouring the person you love, that you keep throwing people away and sitting there saying "Where'd everybody go?" And you can't help it. And you just keep doing it. These are agonies much more important, and it seems to me that they are the agonies out of which we create our other agonies: that's one of the things I try to say in my poems, that it is out of the pattern of the life you know, with the people you love, that you create these larger patterns. It seems to me that Freud would have seen it that way entirely, and I must say that I do, but I don't think I get that from him, I hope I don't.[9]

Whether or not Snodgrass got that from Freud, there is much else that confessional poetry owes to the human science Freud inaugurated. All the contemporary poets central to confessionalism have undergone extensive psychotherapy, and while it would be foolish to account for their poetry by this experience, it would be careless to ignore its influence, especially given the strong similarities between the process of therapy they have needed as individuals and the poetic process by which they have then sought to express the lives they have come to explore or understand. Psychotherapy and psychoanalysis, abstractly outlined, involve a process during which the patient recounts his or her most intimate experiences, both conscious and unconscious, memories and fantasies. Though these "spots of time" overlap and perhaps even contradict each other, their deeper continuities assume the crucial patterns by which a life was led and sense is made. Both the experiences still painfully central and the unaccountable gaps are endlessly recircled, and those recountings—themselves depending on the same sense of experience-in-time—not only reveal the neuroses that have obscured the real experience and self but also work toward what Freud once called a *Nacherziehung*, an after-education. We learn what we are by relearning what we have become. But what is important to note now is the essentially narrative structure of the process, of one's experiences recounted in this time as remembered in their own past time. And narrative is likewise the most distinctive structural device in confessional poetry. The importance and integrity of chronology affect both the way in which individual poems are composed and the way they are collected into sequences and volumes, and these arrangements, in turn, are of thematic importance as facts or memories, shifting desires or needs, or anxieties or gratifications change the landscape of personality. Sexton's poem "The Double Image," for instance, is a closely written and carefully sectioned account of her hospitalization and her necessary separation from her mother's shame and her daughter's innocence. The poem opens with the specificity of the achieved present—"I am thirty this November. . . . We stand watching the yellow leaves go queer"—and then drifts back through three years of madness and bitter history, to Bedlam and part way back, its larger thematic concerns held in precise details—dates, objects, places, names— among which are studded still smaller stories that memory associates with the main narrative. The destructions that survival implies in the poem are given their haunting force and authenticity by the history that the narrative leads readers through so that they themselves experience the dramatic life of events and feelings.

In the same way, the poems of the confessionalists—Sexton especially—have a kind of chronicle effect on readers, as one keeps track volume by volume. This pervasive need to follow the contours of time, as if they sanctioned the truth they contain, is most clearly exemplified by *Live or Die*, where the poems are arranged in no particular narrative chronology but rather according to the compositional chronology, with the date carefully added to each poem like a clinching last line—from "January 25, 1962" to "February the last, 1966." Such a dependence on the details of time and place becomes a rhetorical method of definition and discovery and points finally to the essentially epistemological concern of confessional poetry: since all that can meaningfully be known is my individual self, how is that self to be known and communicated except through the honest precision of its cumulative experience?

The rhetorical importance of confessional subject matter—especially insofar as it involves a characteristically Freudian epistemology—leads, in turn, to another consideration. In his most important gloss on the mediation of art, Freud wrote: "The essential *ars poetica* lies in the technique of overcoming the feeling of repulsion in us which is undoubtedly connected with the barriers that rise between each single ego and the others."[10] Or between the single ego and its history, he might have added. And among the barriers the self constructs are the familiar defense mechanisms: repression, displacement, suppression, screen memories, condensation, projection, and so on. Such psychological techniques, in turn, have their rhetorical analogues, not surprisingly those most favored by modernist poets and their New Critics: paradox, ambiguity, ellipsis, allusion, wit, and the other "tensions" that correspond to the neurotic symptoms by which the self is obscured. And in order to write with greater directness and honesty about their own experiences, Sexton and the other confessional poets have tended to avoid the poetic strategies of modernism—to derepress poetry, so to speak—and have sought to achieve their effects by other means. Sexton's turn toward open forms, as though in trust, is an example. In general, it can be said of Sexton's poems, as of other confessional poems, that the patterns they assume and by which they manage their meanings are those which more closely follow the actual experiences they are re-creating—forms that can include and reflect direct, personal experience; a human rather than a disembodied voice; the dramatic presentation of the flux of time and personality; and the drive toward sincerity. By this last concept is meant not an ethical imperative but the willed and willing openness of the poet to her experience and to the character of the language by which her discoveries are revealed and shared. Not that the structures of sincerity abandon every measure of artifice. While she may have associated the imagination strongly with memory, Sexton realized as well that the self's past experiences are neither provisional nor final, that even as they shape the art that describes them, so, too, they are modified by that very art. The flux of experience, rather than its absolute truth, determines which concerns or wounds are returned to in poem after poem, either because they have not yet been understood or because the understanding of them has changed. And Sexton is sharply aware, in her work, of the difference between factual truth and poetic truth—of the need to "edit" out, while trying not to distort, redundant or inessential "facts" in the service of cleaner, sharper poems. In a crucial sense, confessional art is a means of *realizing* the poet.

As the poet realizes himself, inevitably he catches up the way we live now: especially the personal life, since our marriages are more difficult than our wars, our private nightmares more terrifying than our public horrors. In addition, then, to our sense of the confessional poet as a survivor, he or she functions as a kind of witness. What may have begun as a strictly private need is transformed, once it is published, into a more inclusive focus—and here one recalls Whitman's "attempt, from first to last, to put a *Person*, a human being (myself, in the latter half of the Nineteenth Century, in America) freely, fully, and truly on record." The more naked and directly emotional nature of confessional poems heightens the integrity and force of their witness to the inner lives of both poets and readers; or, as Sexton has remarked, "poems of the inner life can reach the inner lives of readers in a way that anti-war poems can never stop a war." The final privatism of poetry itself, in other words, affords the confessional poet a certain confidence in using the details of intimate experience in ways that earlier would have been considered either arrogant or obscure. And the ends to which those details are put are not merely self-indulgent or self-therapeutic—or, in Robert Lowell's phrase, "a brave heart drowned on monologue." Of her own work, Anne Sexton once reminisced: "I began to think that if one life somehow made into art, were recorded—not all of it, but like the testimony on an old tombstone— wouldn't that be worth something? Just one life—a poor middle-class life, nothing extraordinary (except maybe madness, but that's so common nowadays)—that seems worth putting down. It's the thing I have to do, the thing I want to do—I'm not sure why." And she went on to describe a reader's response to this "testimony": "I think, I hope, a reader's response is: 'My God, this has happened. And in some real sense it has happened to me too.' This has been my reaction to other poems, and my readers have responded to my poems in just this way."[11]

Perhaps the most telling evidence of this sort of response are the countless letters that anonymous readers sent to Sexton explaining how her poetry revealed their own troubled lives to them and often making impossible demands on the poet, so strong was the readers' sense of the real, suffering person in the poetry. It is no wonder that, with bitter wit, Sexton once described herself in a poem as "mother of the insane." But at a deeper level there is some dark part in any one of us which her work illuminated, often distressingly. Like Wordsworth, who wished to allow his audience "new compositions of feeling," Sexton's response to her own experience becomes a model for a reader's response to his or her own. The poems function as instruments of discovery for the reader as well as for the poet, and the process of discovery—ongoing through poems and collections, as through life—is as important as the products, the poems that the poet has drawn directly out of her experience, often as isolated stays against confusion. The immediacy of impact and response and the mutual intimacy between poet and reader correspond with an observation by Ernst Kris on aesthetic distance: "When psychic distance is maximal, the response is philistine or intellectualistic. At best, the experience is one of passive receptivity rather than active participation of the self. . . . [But] when distance is minimal the reaction to works of art is pragmatic rather than aesthetic."[12] To emphasize the "pragmatic" response of the readers to this poetry—even though the term describes the response of most poets to their experience, however the subsequent poem may inform it—may be viewed as an effort to minimize the "art" of the poems. I hope my subsequent remarks will describe that art sufficiently, or at least with more attention to real questions than most critics have so far paid Sexton.

Despite the authority and abundance in *To Bedlam and Part Way Back*, Sexton was careful, perhaps compelled, to include an apologia, a poem called "For John, Who Begs Me Not to Enquire Further"—addressed to her discouraging teacher John Holmes, and so finally to the critic in herself. The poem's title echoes the book's epigraph, from a letter of Schopenhauer to Goethe concerning the courage necessary for a philosopher: "He must be like Sophocles's Oedipus, who, seeking enlightenment concerning his terrible fate, pursues his indefatigable enquiry, even when he divines that appalling horror awaits him in the answer. But most of us carry in our heart the Jocasta who begs Oedipus for God's sake not to inquire further. . . ." The sympathy she can afford for Holmes—"although your fear is anyone's fear, / like an invisible veil between us all"—recalls Freud's sense of the repulsion with the self and others that art overcomes. Her cautious justification is modeled on her psychiatrist's plea: "that the worst of anyone / can be, finally, / an accident of hope." And the standard she sets herself is simply making sense:

> Not that it was beautiful,
> but that, in the end, there was
> a certain sense of order there;
> something worth learning
> in that narrow diary of my mind,
> in the commonplaces of the asylum
> where the cracked mirror
> or my own selfish death
> outstared me.

Part of that order is substantive and thematic, the urge to recover and understand the past: "I have this great need somehow to keep that time of my life, that feeling. I want to imprison it in a poem, to keep it. It's almost in a way like keeping a scrapbook to make life mean something as it goes by, to rescue it from chaos—to make 'now' last."[13] But if the ability to extend the past and present into each other further depends upon the orders of art, that art cannot succeed without a prior commitment to honesty—or, to use Sexton's peculiar term, as a confessional poet she must start with a wise passivity, with being "still." That word occurs in her poem about the tradition, "Portrait of an Old Woman on the College Tavern Wall," where the poets sit "singing and lying / around their round table / and around me still." Why do these poets lie? the poem goes on to question, and leaves them with mortal irony "singing / around their round table / until they are still." Whether death or silence, this "stillness" is the view of experience, both prior to and beyond language, from which her ordering proceeds. The difficulty, as she knows in another poem, "Said the Poet to the Analyst," is that "My business is words":

> I must always forget how one word is able to pick
> out another, to manner another, until I have got

> something I might have said . . .
> but did not.

The business of the analyst—again, an internal figure, a sort of artistic conscience—is "watching my words," guarding against the Jocasta who would settle for "something I might have said" instead of what must be revealed.

Sexton's business with words—the ordering of statement and instinct—is the adjustment of their demands to her experience: in her figure, to make a tree out of used furniture. Though her attitudes toward form evolved, from the beginning there was an uneasy ambivalence: the poet insisting on control, the person pleading, "Take out rules and leave the instant," as she said in one interview. Her solution was to use the metaphor of deceit, but to reverse it into a very personally inflected version of form:

> I think all form is a trick to get at the truth. Sometimes in my hardest poems, the ones that are difficult to write, I might make an impossible scheme, a syllabic count that is so involved, that it then allows me to be truthful. It works as a kind of super-ego. It says, "You may now face it, because it will be impossible ever to get out." . . . But you see how I say this not to deceive you, but to deceive me. I deceive myself, saying to myself you can't do it, and then if I can get it, then I have deceived myself, then I can change it and do what I want. I can even change and rearrange it so no one can see my trick. It won't change what's real. It's there on paper.[14]

Though her early work occasionally forces itself with inversions and stolid high style, her concern for the precisions of voice and pace reveal her care in indulging a lyric impulse only to heighten the dramatic. What Richard Howard has said of her use of rhyme is indicative of her larger sense of form: "Invariably it is Sexton's practice to use rhyme to bind the poem, irregularly invoked, abandoned when inconvenient, psychologically convincing."[15] The truth-getting tricks, in other words, serve as a method of conviction for both poet and reader. For the poet form functions to articulate the details and thrust of her actual experience, while for readers it guides their dramatic involvement in the re-creation: both convictions converging on authenticity, on realization. And so the voice is kept conversational, understated by plain-speech slang or homely detail—its imagery drawn from the same sources it counterpoints, its force centered in the pressure of events it contours, the states of mind it maps. This is clearly the case with the poems of madness in the first section of *To Bedlam and Part Way Back*. Compared with Sexton's powerful control in this group, a similar but more celebrated poem, Lowell's "Waking in the Blue," seems faded with retrospective observation rather than immediate involvement. True to the several experiences, cut across time, that they describe, the poems vary the means they take to explore the common meaning. They range from expressionistic projections:

> It was the strangled cold of November;
> even the stars were strapped in the sky
> and that moon too bright
> forking through the bars to stick me
> with a singing in the head.
>   ("Music Swims Back to Me")

to the menacing, flat accent of life-in-death:

> and this is always my bell responding
> to my hand that responds to the lady
> who points at me, E flat;
> and although we are no better for it,
> they tell you to go. And you do.
>   ("Ringing the Bells")

Together they devise, in Michel Foucault's phrase, "the formulas of exclusion."

M. L. Rosenthal has seen in these poems "the self reduced to almost infantile regression,"[16] but more often the voice is that of an older child, which implies a consciousness that can experience the arbitrariness of authority and the sufferings of loss without understanding either chance or cause. The inferno of insanity opens, appropriately, with the poet lost in the dark wood of her "night mind":

> And opening my eyes, I am afraid of course
> to look—this inward look that society scorns—
> Still, I search in these woods and find nothing worse
> than myself, caught between the grapes and the thorns.
>   ("Kind Sir: These Woods")

The disorientation necessitates the search: here, the descent into her own underworld, as later she will ascend part way back. Likewise, the figure of the child—so important in part 2, where it subsumes both

the poet and her daughter—introduces the themes of growth and discovery, of the growth into self by discovering its extremes, as in the
poem addressed to her psychiatrist:

> And we are magic talking to itself,
> noisy and alone. I am queen of all my sins
> forgotten. Am I still lost?
> Once I was beautiful. Now I am myself,
> counting this row and that row of moccasins
> waiting on the silent shelf.
> ("You, Doctor Martin")

The "private institution on a hill," like Hamlet's nutshell, is finally
the self in which she is confined:

> They lock me in this chair at eight a.m.
> and there are no signs to tell the way,
> just the radio beating to itself
> and the song that remembers
> more than I. Oh, la la la,
> this music swims back to me.
> The night I came I danced a circle
> and was not afraid.
> Mister?
> ("Music Swims Back to Me")

The struggle to find "which way is home" involves the dissociation
and resumption of different personalities ("Her Kind," "The Expatriates," "What's That"), the limits of paranoia and mania ("Noon
Walk on the Asylum Lawn," "Lullaby"), and the dilemma of memory
that drives pain toward exorcism ("You, Doctor Martin," "Music Swims
Back to Me," "The Bells," "Said the Poet to the Analyst").

Though, as she says, there is finally "no word for time," the need
to restore it is the essential aspect of the ordering process:

> Today is made of yesterday, each time I steal
> toward rites I do not know, waiting for the lost
> ingredient, as if salt or money or even lust
> would keep us calm and prove us whole at last.
> ("The Lost Ingredient")

What has been lost, along with sanity, is the meaning of those who
made her, and this first book introduces us to the cast she will reas-
semble and rehearse in all her subsequent work, even through "Talking

to Sheep" and "Divorce, Thy Name Is Woman" in *45 Mercy Street*: the hapless boozy father, the helpless cancer-swollen bitch of a mother, the daughters as both victims and purifiers, the shadowy presence of her husband, the analyst as dark daddy and muse, the clutching company of doomed poets—and most touchingly, the great-aunt whom she calls Nana. Sexton's obsession with her Nana—the "Nana-hex" she calls it later—results from both sympathy and guilt. "She was, during the years she lived with us, my best friend, my teacher, my confidante and my comforter. I never thought of her as being young. She was an extension of myself and was my world."[17] For this very reason, when her great-aunt, after a sudden deafness, had a nervous breakdown from which she never recovered, the poet could find her both an emblem of her own suffering and a source of guilt for fear she had somehow caused it. Nana is brought on tenderly in the lyrical elegy "Elizabeth Gone," but in the next poem, "Some Foreign Letters," her life is used as the focus of the poet's own anxieties as she sits reading the letters her great-aunt had sent to her family as a young woman on her Victorian grand tour. The poem proceeds by verse and refrain—Nana's letters of her youth, the poet's images of the same woman different—to point up the disjunction between memories: Nana's diaried ones, which have trapped her youth in an irretrievable past, and the poet's own memories of Nana trapped in age and lost to death:

> Tonight your letters reduce
> history to a guess. The Count had a wife.
> You were the old maid aunt who lived with us.
> Tonight I read how the winter howled around
> the towers of Schloss Schwöbber, how the tedious
> language grew in your jaw, how you loved the sound
> of the music of the rats tapping on the stone
> floors. When you were mine you wore an earphone.

The "guilty love" with which the poem ends is the poet's own ambivalent response to her inability to have rescued her Nana—even as she realizes she will not be able to save herself—from the facts that are fate, a life that cannot be unlived or chosen. The last stanza's pathos derives from its prediction of what has already occurred, the proof that guilt is suffered again and again:

> Tonight I will learn to love you twice;
> learn your first days, your mid-Victorian face.

> Tonight I will speak up and interrupt
> your letters, warning you that wars are coming,
> that the Count will die, that you will accept
> your America back to live like a prim thing
> on the farm in Maine. I tell you, you will come
> here, to the suburbs of Boston, to see the blue-nose
> world go drunk each night, to see the handsome
> children jitterbug, to feel your left ear close
> one Friday at Symphony. And I tell you,
> you will tip your boot feet out of that hall,
> rocking from its sour sound, out onto
> the crowded street, letting your spectacles fall
> and your hair net tangle as you stop passers-by
> to mumble your guilty love while your ears die.

The poet speaks her warning here not as a suspicious Jocasta but as a knowing Tiresias, helpless before time, that most visible scar of mortality. And the family to which she resigns Nana is, of course, her own as well, and the self-recovery that the volume's arrangement of poems plots necessarily moves to recover her parents, as so much of her later work too will do.

The book's second section is the part way back, in the sense of both return and history. The painful realizations of adjustment, the lessons of loss and recovery weight the book's two anchor poems—"The Double Image" and "The Division of Parts." They are long poems, explorations lengthened to accommodate their discoveries and unresolved dilemmas, and extended by subtle modulations of voice and structure to dramatize their privacies. "The Double Image," the book's strongest and most ambitious poem, is actually a sequence of seven poems tracing the terms of Sexton's dispossession—similar to Snodgrass's "Heart's Needle," which was its model. The other poem, which clearly echoes Snodgrass's voice as well, is an independent summary of her losses and makes the subsequent poems seem to have insisted themselves on her later. If that was the case, there is reason for it, since the jagged lines of the first poem reflect the uncertain hesitancy in naming the guilt that had caused her self-hatred and her suicide attempts and breakdown. It is addressed, in retrospect, to the daughter whose infant illness released the long-held guilt:

> a fever rattled
> in your throat and I moved like a pantomime

above your head. Ugly angels spoke to me. The blame,
I heard them say, was mine. They tattled
like green witches in my head, letting doom
leak like a broken faucet;
as if doom had flooded my belly and filled your bassinet,
an old debt I must assume.

She tries to solve her life with death—"I let the witches take away
my guilty soul"—but is forced back from the "time I did not love /
myself" to face the new life she has made in her child and the old life
she had made for herself. She assumes the old debts in the following
narrative of her recovery. If the first poem turned on her commitment
and the loss of her daughter, the second turns on her release and the
loss of her mother, to whom she returns as "an angry guest," "an
outgrown child." The poet had grown "well enough to tolerate / myself," but her mother cannot forgive the suicide attempt and so cannot
accept her daughter: she "had my portrait / done instead," a line that
refrains the tedium and repressed menace that punches out each stanza.
The tension of presence begins to sort the past; the church is another
Bedlam, her parents her keepers:

There was a church where I grew up
with its white cupboards where they locked us up,
row by row, like puritans or shipmates
singing together. My father passed the plate.
Too late to be forgiven now, the witches said.
I wasn't exactly forgiven. They had my portrait
done instead.

The third poem opens up the deaths in and of relationships.
Sexton's distance from her own daughter gains its double reference:
"as if it were normal / to be a mother and be gone." As the poet gathers
her strength, her mother sickens, and madness, love-loss, and death
are drawn into a single figure that points again at guilt. Her mother's
cancer—"as if my dying had eaten inside of her"—accuses Sexton with
questions that "still I couldn't answer." The fourth poem is centered
as an interlude of partial return and acceptance: Sexton back from
Bedlam, her mother from the hospital, her daughter from the exile of
innocence. The fact of survival converts its sterility into patience; the
blank, facing portraits mirror the reversal of concern:

> During the sea blizzards
> she had her
> own portrait painted.
> A cave of a mirror
> placed on the south wall;
> matching smile, matching contour.
> And you resembled me; unacquainted
> with my face, you wore it. But you were mine
> after all.

The fifth poem begins to draw the women together into a chorus, their roles merging into a new knowledge:

> And I had to learn
> why I would rather
> die than love, how your innocence
> would hurt and how I gather
> guilt like a young intern
> his symptoms, his certain evidence
>
> . . . .
>
> We drove past the hatchery,
> the hut that sells bait,
> past Pigeon Cove, past the Yacht Club, past Squall's
> Hill, to the house that waits
> still, on the top of the sea,
> and two portraits hang on opposite walls.

The sixth is a self-study, the poet finding herself in the distanced image of her mother, as in the next poem she discovers how selfish are the maternal motives of love. But in this poem it is the process of life that learns from *la nature morte:*

> And this was the cave of the mirror,
> that double woman who stares
> at herself, as if she were petrified
> in time—two ladies sitting in umber chairs.
> You kissed your grandmother
> and she cried.

The final poem, again addressed to the poet's daughter, summarizes her learning:

> You learn my name,
> wobbling up the sidewalk, calling and crying.

> You call me *mother* and I remember my mother again,
> somewhere in greater Boston, dying.

But the last stanza unwinds into a tentative resumption of guilt—its last line speaking, with an odd irony, the voice of Jocasta: "And this was my worst guilt; you could not cure / nor soothe it. I made you to find me."

In "The Division of Parts" Sexton carries the account past her mother's death, which has left her, on Good Friday, with "gifts I did not choose." The last hospital days are retold, and the numbness with which they stun her implies the larger truth of the poem:

> But you turned old,
> all your fifty-eight years sliding
> like masks from your skull;
> and at the end
> I packed your nightgowns in suitcases,
> paid the nurses, came riding
> home as if I'd been told
> I could pretend
> people live in places.

But people live not in space or places but in time and in others, and their demands puzzle the poet's guilt: "Time, that rearranger / of estates, equips / me with your garments, but not with grief." Her inheritance steals on her "like a debt," and she cannot expiate her loss: "I planned to suffer / and I cannot." Unlike "Jesus, *my stranger*," who assumed "old debts" and knew how and why to suffer, Sexton is emptied of belief by need:

> Fool! I fumble my lost childhood
> for a mother and lounge in sad stuff
> with love to catch and catch as catch can.

> And Christ still waits. I have tried
> to exorcise the memory of each event
> and remain still, a mixed child,
> heavy with cloths of you.
> Sweet witch, you are my worried guide.

And she realizes the motive of her subsequent books: "For all the way I've come / I'll have to go again." Only ever part way back, she tries her art against her mind—"I would still curse / you with my rhyming words / and bring you flapping back, old love"—but her litany of incantatory adjectives cannot lose loss, and if she cannot love it, she has learned to live it.

The religious note introduced at the end of *To Bedlam and Part Way Back*, evoked by the death that aligns it with other needs and losses, is even more apparent in her next book, *All My Pretty Ones* (1962). Two of its best-known poems—"For God while Sleeping" and "In the Deep Museum"—are really part of a much larger group that threads through all her collections, on through "The Jesus Papers" in *The Book of Folly* and into "Jesus Walking" in *The Death Notebooks* and the major poems in *The Awful Rowing Toward God*, whose title best describes the project. Though she herself referred to these poems as "mystical," they are more obviously religious since their concerns are always the human intricacies of need and belief, and their context is Sexton's need for belief and her inability to believe as that dilemma interacts with her relationships to herself and others, the dead and dying. This explains, too, why her religious poetry centers almost exclusively on the person of Jesus, the central figure of belief who himself despaired at the end, who brought love and found none, who gave life and was nailed to a tree. But her relationship to Jesus, as it develops through the books, is an ambivalent one. On the one hand, he serves as a sympathetic emblem of her own experience: "That ragged Christ, that sufferer, performed the greatest act of confession, and I mean with his body. And I try to do that with words."[18] This is the force of the poems in *All My Pretty Ones*. To touch a crucifix—"I touch its tender hips, its dark jawed face, / its solid neck, its brown sleep"—is to remind herself of poetry's work for salvation:

> My friend, my friend, I was born
> doing reference work in sin, and born
> confessing it. This is what poems are:
> with mercy
> for the greedy,
> they are the tongue's wrangle,
> the world's pottage, the rat's star.
>   ("With Mercy for the Greedy")

The Christ who is "somebody's fault," like the poet, is "hooked to your own weight, / jolting toward death under your nameplate" ("For God while Sleeping"). But at the same time, Sexton is fascinated by another Jesus: "Perhaps it's because he can forgive sins."[19] Like her psychiatrist, Jesus is a man who can take on her guilt, a man who suffers with her and for her. This is the Jesus of "In the Deep Museum," where gnawing rats are the "hairy angels who take / my gift," as he blesses "this other death": "Far below The Cross, I correct its flaws." Her purest statement of this sense of Christ comes in *The Death Notebooks*, in "Jesus Walking": "To pray, Jesus knew, / is to be a man carrying a man." It is the simplicity of such strength that takes the measure of weaker men in her life, especially her father, whose death brings him into the poetry of *All My Pretty Ones*.

This second book is less an extension than a completion of her first, just as its epigraph—from Kafka—describes the motive and effect of the courage invoked earlier: "the books we need are the kind that act upon us like a misfortune, that make us suffer like the death of someone we love more than ourselves, that make us feel as though we were on the verge of suicide, or lost in a forest remote from all human habitation—a book should serve as the ax for the frozen sea within us." But Sexton's own evaluation is misleadingly neat: "Well, in the first book, I was giving the experience of madness; in the second book, the causes of madness."[20] That account of "causes" is not sustained, and most of this book—whose poems are more expert but less urgent than before—catches the reader up with the poet's life. That is to say, its confessions converge toward the present, and the chronicle begins to include more immediate and intimate events. Previously worked aspects of and approaches to her experience are here retried: "The Operation" clearly derives from "The Double Image," "The House" expands "Some Foreign Letters." The greater assurance of her verse likewise allows Sexton to experiment successfully with open forms and new voices. Besides the religious poems already mentioned, *All My Pretty Ones* includes several distinctive love poems, real and invented, of which "Flight" and "Letter Written on a Ferry while Crossing Long Island Sound" are most incisive, the latter poem recalling Whitman's "Crossing Brooklyn Ferry," whose "dumb, beautiful ministers" are redressed as nuns who float up in a fantasy of redemption.

But Sexton's burden remains her inward argument: "I cannot promise very much. / I give you the images I know." The effort in these early books remains to get back at herself. The dead haunt like "bad dreams," and the heart loves only "the decay we're made of." The poem addressed to her "Old Dwarf Heart," in lines that echo Roethke and fold back in their rhymes like a trap, sets the stakes for *All My Pretty Ones*:

> Good God, the things she knows!
> And worse, the sores she holds
> in her hands, gathered in like a nest
> from an abandoned field. At her best
> she is all red muscle, humming in and out, cajoled
> by time. Where I go, she goes.
>
> Oh now I lay me down to love,
> how awkwardly her arms undo,
> how patiently I untangle her wrists
> like knots. Old ornament, old naked fist,
> even if I put on seventy coats I could not cover you . . .
> mother, father, I'm made of.

The book opens on "The Truth the Dead Know," which is their absolute isolation, against which the poet fights to save both herself and her dead parents. Her father's death, three months after her mother's, intervened not only between the different concerns of these first two books but also between the completed realization of her inheritance: in the fine print of their wills, the poet fears to find her father's alcoholism and her mother's cancer, which would at the same time prove her their daughter and destroy her. The sins of the father are revisited in the title poem, which blends memories and objects like snapshots out of order to invoke the man's loss and, again, her guilt:

> This year, solvent but sick, you meant
> to marry that pretty widow in a one-month rush.
> But before you had that second chance, I cried
> on your fat shoulder. Three days later you died.

The fear that she has somehow killed her father is the familiar origin of guilt for which she seeks both the retribution of punishment and the reconciliation of a forced forgiveness:

> I hold a five-year diary that my mother kept
> for three years, telling all she does not say
> of your alcoholic tendency. You overslept,
> she writes. My God, father, each Christmas Day
> with your blood, will I drink down your glass
> of wine? The diary of your hurly-burly years
> goes to my shelf to wait for my age to pass.
> Only in this hoarded span will love persevere.
> Whether you are pretty or not, I outlive you,
> bend down my strange face to yours and forgive you.

The volume's most striking poem, "The Operation," returns to her mother's death, which the poet must now have cut out of herself: "the historic thief / is loose in my house / and must be set upon." Unconscious under the surgeries of survival, her experience is another madness:

> Next, I am hung up like a saddle and they begin.
> Pale as an angel I float out over my own skin.
>
> I soar in hostile air
> over the pure women in labor,
> over the crowning heads of babies being born.
> I plunge down the backstair
> calling *mother* at the dying door,
> to rush back to my own skin, tied where it was torn.
> Its nerves pull like wires
> snapping from the leg to the rib.
> Strangers, their faces rolling like hoops, require
> my arm. I am lifted into my aluminum crib.

Reborn from death, as in "The Double Image" she was from insanity, her scarred, scared response to life is inadequate to its new demands, and the poem ends understated, with a child's diction, a deflecting image:

> Time now to pack this humpty-dumpty
> back the frightened way she came
> and run along, Anne, and run along now,
> my stomach laced up like a football
> for the game.

Much more is faced in "The House," which loosens its regard and drifts back over her childhood, dream-distorted and so clarified. Reruns of "the same bad dream . . . The same dreadful set, / the same family of orange and pink faces" are set spinning to portray the atmosphere in which death was first preferred. These three album photographs, each a collage of hurt and menace—in ways that oddly prefigure *Transformations*—are sufficient example of the poem's force:

> Father,
> an exact likeness,
> his face bloated and pink
> with black market scotch,
> sits out his monthly bender

in his custom-made pajamas
and shouts, his tongue as quick as galloping horses,
shouts into the long distance telephone call.
His mouth is as wide as his kiss.

Mother,
with just the right gesture,
kicks her shoes off,
but is made all wrong,
impossibly frumpy as she sits there
in her alabaster dressing room
sorting her diamonds like a bank teller
to see if they add up.

The maid
as thin as a popsicle stick,
holds dinner as usual,
rubs her angry knuckles over the porcelain sink
and grumbles at the gun-shy bird dog.
She knows something is going on.
She pricks a baked potato.

The poet then walks into her own dream, "up another flight into the penthouse, / to slam the door on all the years / she'll have to live through . . ." until she wakes in italics: "*Father, father, I wish I were dead.*" She wakes as well into the self she has become, caught between neurosis and nostalgia: "At thirty-five / she'll dream she's dead / or else she'll dream she's back." In the death that poses desire as dream nothing has changed, and it merges in her awareness with history— again, facts are fate, the infernal machine: "All day long the machine waits: rooms, / stairs, carpets, furniture, people— / those people who stand at the open windows like objects / waiting to topple." What the past has lost cannot be salvaged in the future, and her poem "The Fortress," a meditation over her sleeping daughter Linda, submits to a life other than hers:

Darling, life is not in my hands;
life with its terrible changes
will take you, bombs or glands,
your own child at
your breast, your own house on your own land.
Outside the bittersweet turns orange.
Before she died, my mother and I picked those fat

> branches, finding orange nipples
> on the gray wire stands.
> We weeded the forest, curing trees like cripples.

Time draws on change, and the love she leaves her child seems as fragile as innocence. That, too, is part of the weary acceptance of this book.

The oneiric organization of "The House" looks forward to the important changes that her next and decisive book, *Live or Die* (1966), announces. With its longer poems in open forms that more subtly accommodate a greater range of experience, and with a voice pitched higher to intensify that experience, *Live or Die* represents not a departure from her earlier strengths but the breakthrough into her distinctive style. Perhaps the most immediate aspect of that style is more extravagant use of imagery:

> I sat all day
> stuffing my heart into a shoe box,
> avoiding the precious window
> as if it were an ugly eye
> through which birds coughed,
> chained to the heaving trees;
> avoiding the wallpaper of the room
> where tongues bloomed over and over,
> bursting from lips like sea flowers. . . .
> ("Those Times . . .")

This is the sort of imagery that will be even more exploited in later books where *like* becomes the most frequently encountered word. It is a technique that risks arbitrary excesses and embarrassing crudities, that at its best can seem but a slangy American equivalent of Apollinaire's surrealism: *Les nuages coulaient comme un flux menstruel.* But it is crucial to remember, with Gaston Bachelard, that "we live images synthetically in their initial complexity, often giving them our unreasoned allegiance."[21] And Sexton's use of images is primarily psychotropic—used less for literary effect than as a means to pry deeper into her psychic history, to float her findings and model her experience. As she said: "The poetry is often more advanced, in terms of my unconscious, than I am. Poetry, after all, milks the unconscious."[22] And so she came increasingly to identify the imagination less with her memory than with her unconscious: "Images are the heart of poetry. And this is not tricks. Images come from the unconscious. Imagination and the unconscious are one and the same."[23] Sexton's commitment to honest realization is thus only carried to a deeper level. And if Rimbaud was right to demand of such associative poetry a *"dérègle-ment de tous les sens,"* it can be seen as Sexton's necessary road of excess through her experiences of madness and the disorientation of her past, so that her metaphors are a method not to display similarities but to discover identities.

Although *Live or Die* shows, for this reason, the influence of her readings in Roethke and Neruda, a more important factor was the new analyst she began seeing while at work on this book. He was more interested in dreams than her earlier doctors had been, and Sexton found herself dealing more directly with her unconscious: "You taught me / to believe in dreams; / thus I was the dredger" ("Flee on Your Donkey"). Several poems in *Live or Die* are direct dream-songs—"Three Green Windows," "Imitations of Drowning," "Consorting with Angels," "In the Beach House," and "To Lose the Earth." The latent content in these poems—such as the primal scene of "the royal strapping" in "In the Beach House"—is expressive but abandoned to its own independence, unlike more conscious fantasies such as "Menstruation at Forty," in which themes of death and incest are projected onto the imagined birth of a son. The insistence of the unconscious also draws up the poems of her childhood—"Love Songs," "Protestant Easter," and especially "Those Times . . .," one of the book's triumphs. Robert Boyers has described *Live or Die* as "a poetry of victimization, in which she is at once victim and tormentor,"[24] and "Those Times . . ." torments the poet with her earliest memories of victimization: "being the unwanted, the mistake / that Mother used to keep Father / from his divorce." Her suffering was as silent as her envy of a doll's perfection: "I did not question the bedtime ritual / where, on the cold bathroom tiles, / I was spread out daily / and examined for flaws." But her felt exclusion was assumed and rehearsed in a closet's dark escape, where she sat with her hurts and dreams, as later she would sit in madness and poetry:

> I did not know that my life, in the end,
> would run over my mother's like a truck
> and all that would remain
> from the year I was six

was a small hole in my heart, a deaf spot,
so that I might hear
the unsaid more clearly.

The other crucial influence on *Live or Die* is the play she wrote
at the time—first titled *Tell Me Your Answer True* and eventually
produced in 1969 as *Mercy Street*—sections of which were carried
over as poems into *Live or Die* and lend the book its character of
psychodrama. Sexton's description of herself during a poetry reading
could apply to her presence in this book as well: "I am an actress in
my own autobiographical play."[25] The vitality, even the violence, of
the book's drama of adaptation recall Emily Dickinson's sly lines: "Men
die—externally— / It is a truth—of Blood— / But we—are dying in
Drama— / And Drama—is never dead." To match the expansive forms
and intense imagery of these poems, the voice that speaks them grows
more various in its effects, matching a strident aggression or hovering
tenderness with the mood and matter evoked. Above all, there is energy, whether of mania or nostalgia. And it is more expressly vocative
here, as her cast is introduced separately and her relationship to each
is reworked: her father ("And One for My Dame"), mother ("Christmas Eve"), daughters ("Little Girl, My String Bean, My Lovely Woman,"
"A Little Uncomplicated Hymn," "Pain for a Daughter"), husband
("And One for My Dame," "Man and Wife," "Your Face on the Dog's
Neck"), and Nana ("Crossing the Atlantic," "Walking in Paris"). There
is a very conscious sense about these poems of the times since her first
book that she has spent with her living and her dead. "A Little Uncomplicated Hymn," for instance, alludes directly to "The Double
Image" to catch at a perspective for the interval; the new poem, according to Sexton, was the "attempt to master that experience in light
of the new experience of her life and how it might have affected her
and how it affects me still; she wasn't just an emblem for me any
longer. Every book, every poem, is an attempt to master things that
aren't ever quite mastered."[26] And so one watches her recircling her
experiences to define and refine her understanding of them. Her parents
are written of more sharply, and her regret is less for what she has
lost than for what she never had. Her great-aunt's account of her youth
in Europe, which structures "Some Foreign Letters," was the motive
for Sexton's attempt to retrace in person Nana's journey—"I'd peel
your life back to its start"—both to solve the riddle of other people—
"I come back to your youth, my Nana, / as if I might clean off / the

mad woman you became, / withered and constipated, / howling into your own earphone"—and so to solve her own origins—"You are my history (that stealer of children) / and I have entered you." But the attempt is impossible; she cannot walk off her history, the past cannot be toured, only endured: where I am is hell.

The hell in her head is the subject of "Flee on Your Donkey," whose title and other details are taken from Rimbaud's "Fêtes de la faim." Begun in a mental hospital and worked over four years, the poem draws the past into the present to realign the poet's perspective on both:

> Recently I noticed in "Flee on Your Donkey" that I had used some of the same facts in *To Bedlam and Part Way Back*, but I hadn't realized them in their total ugliness. I'd hidden from them. This time was really raw and really ugly and it was all involved with my own madness. It was all like a great involuted web, and I presented it the way it really was.[27]

The madness that in "The Double Image" had been an escape from guilt has become a "hunger": "Six years of shuttling in and out of this place! / O my hunger! My hunger!" The hospital scene this time resembles a sort of religious retreat—"Because there was no other place / to flee to, / I came back to the scene of the disordered senses"—and the poet inventories her time, fingers the black beads of loss. Like Rimbaud, she has been "a stranger, / damned and in trance" during the years huddled in her analyst's office. This ambivalent love song to her doctor is the pleas to her father, and the self he helps her deliver describes a birth. (Another poem, "Cripples and Other Stories," makes explicit the connection implied here.)

> O my hunger! My hunger!
> I was the one
> who opened the warm eyelid
> like a surgeon
> and brought forth young girls
> to grunt like fish.
>
> I told you,
> I said—
> but I was lying—
> that the knife was for my mother . . .
> and then I delivered her.

Similarly, "For the Year of the Insane" invokes "Mary, fragile mother," the name of both the Virgin and Sexton's own mother. And again, her prayer for rebirth fantasizes a return: "A beginner, I feel your mouth touch mine." But more striking still is the repetition of the image of the eye as vagina in the call for delivery into light:

> O Mary, open your eyelids.
> I am in the domain of silence,
> the kingdom of the crazy and the sleeper.
> There is blood here
> and I have eaten it.
> O mother of the womb,
> did I come for blood alone?
> O little mother,
> I am in my own mind.
> I am locked in the wrong house.

This demand for release into life, as the title *Live or Die* balances her options, is the counterweight to the measure of death in the book, scaled from suicide attempts ("Wanting to Die," "The Addict") to the deaths of past figures who were part of her—John Holmes ("Somewhere in Africa") and Sylvia Plath ("Sylvia's Death"). "Flee on Your Donkey" struggles with the ambiguous impatience, introducing it first as weariness with "allowing myself the wasted life": "I have come back / but disorder is not what it was. / I have lost the trick of it! / The innocence of it!" Her desire for communion—"In this place everyone talks to his own mouth"—reverses her earlier escape inward: "Anne, Anne, / flee on your donkey, / flee this sad hotel." And by the time she can write the simple title "Live" over the book's last poem, the "mutilation" that previous poems had struck off is renounced. The evidence of survival is enough: "Even so, / I kept right on going on, / a sort of human statement" that says finally: "I am not what I expected." If her guilt has not been solved, it has at least been soothed by her acceptance of it and by her "dearest three"—her husband and daughters. And if the resolution of "Live" sounds unconvinced, unconvincing, it is because of Sexton's dependence on others, lulling the self into a passive tense.

The survival achieved, the rebirth delivered, is then praised in *Love Poems* (1969), in many ways her weakest collection since most of it is sustained by language alone. Its self-celebration tends either to avoid or to invent the experience behind it or revolves on minimal events: a hip fracture, a summer safari. Secure in her use of free verse, Sexton crafts these poems with equivalents: litanies of images that are more often additional than accumulative. As before, the book's epigraph—this time from Yeats—defines its intention, and here the concern is with roles: "One should say before sleeping, 'I have lived many lives. I have been a slave and a prince. Many a beloved has sat upon my knees and I have sat upon the knees of many a beloved. Everything that has been shall be again.' " And so she explores her womanhood ("The Breast," "In Celebration of My Uterus") and her roles as woman, wife, and lover. Not surprisingly, she is best when describing how lovers swim "the identical river called Mine": "we are a pair of scissors / who come together to cut, without towels saying His. Hers" ("December 10th"). The poem to her husband, "Loving the Killer," speaks of the selfishness carved out by the past:

> Though the house is full of
> candy bars the wasted ghost
> of my parents is poking
> the keyhole, rubbing the bedpost.
> Also the ghost of your father,
> who was killed outright.
> Tonight we will argue and shout,
> "My loss is greater than yours!
> My pain is more valuable!"

The masks she wears in *Love Poems* don't hide Sexton's confessional impulse; they avoid it. Her motive may well have been to search out new voices. Certainly this is the case with her next work, *Transformations* (1971). She began these versions of Grimms' tales on the advice of her daughter after an extended dry spell in her work, and, when, five poems later, she had written "Snow White and the Seven Dwarfs," she felt she should continue the experiment into a book that would release a more playful aspect of her personality neglected in her earlier books.[28] The result—considering its cloyingly "cute" Kurt Vonnegut introduction, its illustrations, and commercial success—seems at most a divertissement and surely a conscious effort to avoid her confessional voice. Like *Love Poems*, it seems content to present women in their roles, from princess to witch, with the poet merely presiding as "Dame Sexton," as the introductory poem, "The Gold Key," explains:

> The speaker in this case
> is a middle-aged witch, me—
> tangled on my two great arms,
> my face in a book
> and my mouth wide,
> ready to tell you a story or two.

And the poem goes on to offer a key to her technique here:

> It opens this book of odd tales
> which transform the Brothers Grimm.
> Transform?
> As if an enlarged paper clip
> could be a piece of sculpture.
> (And it could.)

That is to say, her "transformations" exaggerate and so distort the originals. And indeed the tales are blown up like pop art posters by means of an irreverently zippy style, slangy allusions, and a strongly Freudian slant to her stories. But what draws *Transformations* more centrally into this discussion is Sexton's inability to keep her characteristic concerns from seeping into what would otherwise seem her most distanced work.

The book's Ovidian title points to Sexton's first fascination with Grimm—one that Randall Jarrell spoke of in his poem "The Märchen":

> Had you not learned—have we not learned, from tales
> Neither of beasts nor kingdoms nor their Lord,
> But of our own hearts, the realm of death—
> Neither to rule nor die? to change, to change!

The power of fairy tales has always resided in their "changed" dream-landscapes, and Freud discussed them as "screen memories," survivals of persistent human conflicts and desires, narratives whose characters and situations are symbolic of the unconscious dramas in any individual's psyche.[29] With this in mind, the psychoanalytical uses of the word *transformations* bear on Sexton's work. It can refer both to the variations of the same thematic material represented in a patient's dreams of experience and to the process by which unconscious material is brought to consciousness. So, too, Sexton's poems are variations on themes familiar from her earlier work—at one point she says, "My guilts are what / we catalogue"—transformed into fantasies or dreams discovered in the Grimm tales, which are anyone's first "literature" and become bound up with the child's psyche. The introductions that precede each story—replacing the analogous moral pointing in the fairy tale—usually isolate her more private concern in each, and the tales that elaborate them include subjects ranging from adultery ("The Little Peasant") to despair ("Rumpelstiltskin") to deception ("Red Riding Hood") to parents' devouring their children ("Hansel and Gretel"). Other poems are even more explicit in that their subjects allude directly to earlier poems: "The Operation" is recalled in "The Maiden without Hands" with its lines "If they have cut out your uterus / I will give you a laurel wreath / to put in its place." "Rapunzel" fantasizes on her "Nana-hex," and "The Frog Prince" is a daring exploration of her father-feelings: "Frog is my father's genitals. . . . He says: Kiss me. Kiss me. / And the ground soils itself." But a majority of these poems link their dreams with those of madness and with Sexton's strong poem on its asylum. "The White Snake," "Iron Hans," "One-Eye, Two-Eyes, Three-Eyes," "The Wonderful Musician," "The Twelve Dancing Princesses," and "Briar Rose (Sleeping Beauty)"—each is set at an outpost of psychosis, the often bizarre details creating a narrative of insanity from the inside. "Briar Rose (Sleeping Beauty)," the final and most intense poem in the book, was actually written while Sexton was hospitalized and loosens its disguise into an identity. Once awake, Briar Rose cannot bear to sleep again, to imprison herself in the dreams that are Sexton's:

> There was a theft.
> That much I am told.
> I was abandoned.
> That much I know.
> I was forced backward.
> I was forced forward.
> I was passed hand to hand
> like a bowl of fruit.
> Each night I am nailed into place
> and I forget who I am.
> Daddy?
> That's another kind of prison.
> It's not the prince at all,
> but my father

> drunkenly bent over my bed,
> circling the abyss like a shark,
> my father thick upon me
> like some sleeping jellyfish.
>
> What voyage this, little girl?
> This coming out of prison?
> God help—
> this life after death?

The fabular impulse behind *Transformations* is resumed in *The Book of Folly* (1972), both in the three short stories included among the poems and in "The Jesus Papers" sequence, which is a taunting, Black Mass transformation of the salvation story. The entire book, in fact, has a summary quality to it. The forged stylization of *Love Poems* returns in "Angels of the Love Affair," six sonnets on love's seasons. The angel in each is the "gull that grows out of my back in the dreams I prefer," and those dreams are hushed, flamboyant, touching memories of certain sheets, bits of dried blood, lemony woodwork, a peace march—all the abstracted details of moments that are warm only in her darknesses. But what is more important is her return to the fully confessional mode: "I struck out memory with an X / but it came back. / I tied down time with a rope / but it came back" ("Killing the Spring"). At the simplest level the detritus of time has clustered new collisions or crises: the death of her sister—"her slim neck / snapped like a piece of celery" in a car crash—or the national disasters ("The Firebombers," "The Assassin"). Generally, the subjects she recircles are familiar, but her angle of attack is new: more self-conscious, often more strident and defiant, more searching. Like the later Lowell, Sexton's self-consciousness results from the ironies of exposure, the logistics of fame. These permit her both a guilty longing:

> I would like a simple life
> yet all night I am laying
> poems away in a long box.
>
> It is my immortality box,
> my lay-away plan,
> my coffin.
>   ("The Ambition Bird")

and an empty pride:

> Now Sweeney phones from London, W. 2,
> saying *Martyr, my religion is love, is you.*
> Be seated, my Sweeney, my invisible fan.
> Surely the words will continue, for that's
> what's left that's true.
>
> ("Sweeney")[30]

Both her art and her audience, her fans and family exist beyond their ability to help her, as a poem to her now-grown daughter Linda laments:

> Question you about this
> and you will sew me a shroud
> and hold up Monday's broiler
> and thumb out the chicken gut.
> Question you about this
> and you will see my death
> drooling at these gray lips
> while you, my burglar, will eat
> fruit and pass the time of day.
>
> ("Mother and Daughter")

It is this sense of what still remains to be lost that occasions the tonal shift. In contrast with "You, Doctor Martin" or "Cripples and Other Stories," a new poem to her psychiatrist, "The Doctor of the Heart," is scornfully reductive, resentful of the soothing instead of solving, challenging the doctor with her history and her art:

> But take away my mother's carcinoma
> for I have only one cup of fetus tears.
>
> Take away my father's cerebral hemorrhage
> for I have only a jigger of blood in my hand.
>
> Take away my sister's broken neck
> for I have only my schoolroom ruler for a cure.
>
> Is there such a device for my heart?
> I have only a gimmick called magic fingers.

Whether the mind is too strong or not strong enough to adjust to the violent changes that death forces on us no longer seems to matter to the poem's manic finale:

> I am at the ship's prow.
> I am no longer the suicide
>
> with her raft and paddle.

Herr Doktor! I'll no longer die

to spite you, you wallowing
seasick grounded man.

This defiance of death demands, first of all, that the tyranny of her
own impulse toward suicide be fully evoked: she must "lie down /
with them and lift my madness / off like a wig," since "Death is here.
There is no / other settlement" ("Oh"). And for this reason she returns,
in "The Other," to what has always terrified her poetry: the alien self
she cannot escape, who insanely possesses her and can keep her from
the self that makes poems and love and children:

When the child is soothed and resting on the breast
it is my other who swallows Lysol.
When someone kisses someone or flushes the toilet
it is my other who sits in a ball and cries.
My other beats a tin drum in my heart.
My other hangs up laundry as I try to sleep.
My other cries and cries and cries
when I put on a cocktail dress.
It cries when I prick a potato.
It cries when I kiss someone hello.
It cries and cries and cries
until I put on a painted mask
and leer at Jesus in His passion.

As in *Live or Die*, these are the dreams that confront endurance. Re-
formulated, death and madness, which had once seemed her only innocence, come to the silence she is writing against:

The silence is death.
It comes each day with its shock
to sit on my shoulder, a white bird,
and peck at the black eyes
and the vibrating muscle
of my mouth.
                                        ("The Silence")

The Book of Folly's remembrance of things past is likewise more
direct when it turns to her family. "Anna Who Was Mad"—Anna, the
anagram for the Nana whose namesake Sexton is—alternates interrog-
ative and imperative lines to force the guilt of cause and effect: "Am
I some sort of infection? / Did I make you go insane?" This paralyzing

guilt, itself a form of self-hatred, is "all a matter of history" in "The Hex," a poem that links her relationship with the same great-aunt to that with "The Other": "Every time I get happy / the Nana-hex comes through." This strong poem on how "The dead take aim" to leave her "still the criminal" is an angry pacing off of the past's cage:

> Sitting on the stairs at thirteen,
> hands fixed over my ears,
> the Hitler-mouth psychiatrist climbing
> past me like an undertaker,
> and the old woman's shriek of fear:
> You did it. You are the evil.
> It was the day meant for me.
> Thirteen for your whole life,
> just the masks keep changing.

But this is a prelude to the book's centering six-poem sequence, "The Death of the Fathers"—surely one of Sexton's triumphs, daring in its explorations and revelations, its verse superbly controlled as the voice of each poem is modulated to its experience, now shifting to the declaratives of a child, now heightening to involved regrets and prayers. While watching Sexton trace memories of her father mixed with sexual fantasies, one must recall Freud's sense of the origin of childhood memories:

> Quite unlike conscious memories from the time of maturity, they are not fixed at the moment of being experienced and afterwards repeated, but are only elicited at a later age when childhood is already past; in the process they are altered and falsified, and are put into the service of later trends, so that generally speaking they cannot be sharply distinguished from phantasies.[31]

Similarly, since fantasies become memories, it becomes impossible and useless beyond a certain point to distinguish between "events" that happened and fears or desires imagined so strongly that they might as well have happened. And further, Freud writes that the "screen memories" made of childhood traumas "relate to impressions of a sexual and aggressive nature, and no doubt also to early injuries to the ego (narcissistic mortifications). In this connection it should be remarked that such young children make no sharp distinction between sexual and aggressive acts, as they do later."[32]

Sexton's sequence divides naturally into two parts of three poems each, the first set in childhood to evoke her father, and the second set in the present to focus his double death and the "later trends" that have occasioned the fantasies in the first. The opening poem, "Oysters," is her initiation, at once a fantasy of self-begetting and a memory of desire that, once conscious, defeats innocence. She is Daddy's girl having lunch with her father at a restaurant, and fearfully eats her oysters—"this father-food," his semen: "It was a soft medicine / that came from the sea into my mouth, / moist and plump. / I swallowed." Then they laugh through this "death of childhood"—"the child was defeated. / The woman won." The second poem, "How We Danced," continues the fantasy in an Oedipal round:

> The champagne breathed like a skin diver
> and the glasses were crystal and the bride
> and groom gripped each other in sleep
> like nineteen-thirty marathon dancers.
> Mother was a belle and danced with twenty men.
> You danced with me never saying a word.
> Instead the serpent spoke as you held me close.
> The serpent, that mocker, woke up and pressed against me
> like a great god and we bent together
> like two lonely swans.

And the third poem, "The Boat," though it reverts to an earlier time, is a kind of coital coda to her subconscious victory. This time Leda's swan is her godlike captain, out in the same sea from which the oysters came, "out past Cuckold's Light," where "the three of us" ride through a storm that her father masters, but at its height there is the moment that both resolves her fantasies and predicts their destruction, in a memory of violence both sexual and aggressive:

> Now the waves are higher;
> they are round buildings.
> We start to go through them
> and the boat shudders.
> Father is going faster.
> I am wet.
> I am tumbling on my seat
> like a loose kumquat.
> Suddenly
> a wave that we go under.

> Under. Under. Under.
> We are daring the sea.
> We have parted it.
> We are scissors.
> Here in the green room
> the dead are very close.

The second part narrates the death of the fathers. In "Santa" the child's mythic sense of her father is killed: "Father, / the Santa Claus suit / you bought from Wolff Fording Theatrical Supplies, / back before I was born, / is dead." After describing how her father dressed up her childhood—when "Mother would kiss you / for she was that tall"—she comes to liquor's reality principle: "The year I ceased to believe in you / is the year you were drunk." And by the time her father, in turn, dressed up for her own children, the emptiness of having replaced her mother is apparent: "We were conspirators, / secret actors, / and I kissed you / because I was tall enough. / But that is over." "Friends" details another death, as her father is distanced by doubt. The stranger in her childhood could have been any of the men who would come to steal her from her father, but this family friend is more ominous:

> He was as bald as a hump.
> His ears stuck out like teacups
> and his tongue, my God, his tongue,
> like a red worm and when he kissed
> it crawled right in.
>
> Oh Father, Father,
> who was that stranger
> who knew Mother too well?

The question this poem ends on—"Oh God, / he was a stranger, / was he not?"—is answered brutally in the last poem, "Begat," a kind of family romance in reverse:

> Today someone else lurks in the wings
> with your dear lines in his mouth
> and your crown on his head.
> Oh Father, Father-sorrow,
> where has time brought us?
>
> Today someone called.
> "Merry Christmas," said the stranger.
> "I am your real father."

That was a knife.
That was a grave.

The father she had called hers dies again—the stranger takes "the *you* out of the *me*"—and the poems end with a pathetic elegy on the distance she has come since childhood and the first poem of this sequence, since the understood desire. The end rises to a last regret with the simple details of intimacy's allowances and sadnesses, and the memory of her father dressed as Santa turns as raw as the blood they no longer share, the "two lonely swans" who danced in fantasy are now fired by betrayal and loss:

> Those times I smelled the Vitalis on his pajamas.
> Those times I mussed his curly black hair
> and touched his ten tar-fingers
> and swallowed down his whiskey breath.
> Red. Red. Father, you are blood red.
> Father,
> we are two birds on fire.

The blend of memory and fantasy in "The Death of the Fathers," each sharpening and supporting the effect of the other, is the culmination of Sexton's confessional style. Her next book, *The Death Notebooks* (1974), develops this technique still further but without any consistency. The reason for this is that the book collects poems she had written over many years without intending to publish them, and as meditations on her own death they tend to fantasize forward rather than remember back. But with their frequent sense of having been written from beyond death, there is a retrospective character to them that continually catches up long memories and fragments of experience. And the exercise itself—especially its eventual publication, which seems reluctant but inevitable, even in its duplication of the smaller deaths she had detailed before—adds a note of shabby self-consciousness to "this last peep show" ("Making a Living," "For Mr. Death Who Stands with His Door Open," "Faustus and I," "Clothes"). But the book's powerful confrontation with death—and even its cover schemes in black and blue—tries to work its way toward the accommodations of understanding: "For death comes to friends, to parents, to sisters. Death comes with its bagful of pain yet they do not curse the key they were given to hold" ("Ninth Psalm"—ED. "Tenth Psalm" in *CP*). So Sexton sees herself "knitting her own hair into a baby shawl" because "There is a death baby / for each of us. / We own him" ("Baby"), carried for a lifetime, delivered slowly, and rocked into darkness. And as she sits "in the dark room putting bones into place" ("Seventh Psalm"—ED. "Eighth Psalm" in *CP*), she edges "the abyss, / the God spot" ("The Fury of Sundays")—a dilemma first raised in "The Division of Parts" back in *To Bedlam and Part Way Back* and left as ambiguous here in several religious poems. That personal paradox reflects the difficulty with the book itself, whose "summing-up" remains too immediate and unresolved.

The title of the book implies excerpts of unfinished spontaneity, and there are two long experiments that, by their very nature, could have been continued or concluded at the poet's will. "The Furies" was written while the poet was recuperating in bed from an illness and began associating at the typewriter on suggestive topics. Their antecedent is "Angels of the Love Affair" (or even the variant form in the uneven sequence titled "Bestiary U.S.A.," later included in *45 Mercy Street*), and their energy is their own rather than the poet's. And a sequence of psalms called "O Ye Tongues" attempts to adapt the patterns of Smart's *Jubilato Agno* and to identify Smart with both herself and the *other*, combined into "the mad poet":

> For I am an orphan with two death masks on the mantel and came from the grave of my mama's belly into the commerce of Boston.
>
> For there were only two windows on the city and the buildings ate me.
>
> For I was swaddled in grease wool from my father's company and could not move or ask the time.
>
> For Anne and Christopher were born in my head as I howled at the grave of the roses, the ninety-four rose crèches of my bedroom.
>
> ("Third Psalm"—ED. "Fourth Psalm" in *CP*)

Her success is variable, but when the excess is simplified the result is the genuine pathos of Smart's own verse: "For in my nature I quested for beauty, but God, God, hath sent me to sea for pearls."

But the most significant and successful poem in *The Death Notebooks* is "Hurry Up Please It's Time," a sort of long, hallucinatory diary entry: "Today is November 14th, 1972. / I live in Weston, Mass., Middlesex County, / U.S.A., and it rains steadily / in the pond like white puppy eyes." The style is pure pastiche, mixing dialect and dialogue, nursery rhymes and New Testament, references ranging from Goethe to Thurber, attitudes veering between arrogance and abasement. At times she is "Anne," at times "Ms. Dog"—becoming her own mock God. She can sneer at herself ("Middle class lady, / you make me smile") or shiver at what "my heart, that witness" remembers. The recaptured spots of time—say, a quiet summer interlude with her husband and friends—are run into projected blotches spread toward the death to come. And though its expansive free form dilutes all but its cumulative force, the poem is an advance on the way "The Death of the Fathers" had whispered its confessions.

Sexton's two posthumously published collections—*The Awful Rowing Toward God* (1975) and *45 Mercy Street* (1976)—are largely disappointing and anticlimactic, except when isolated poems in either book echo earlier successes. The last volume is particularly flat—because, one presumes, the poet did not revise the poems or arrange the selection. Its dominating section is a painful sequence called "The Divorce Papers," an entirely unresolved series of reactions to "the dead city of my marriage" and to the ways in which divorce exhumes it. The ambivalence that informs these seventeen poems—alternating relief and regret, guilt, despair, and exhilaration—is less enriching than enervating. One reason for that is the very immediacy of the work, which is not grounded in an adequate perspective on the history of her marriage, the evolution of her feelings, or the complication of two lives lived together. It is as if the poet—and her poetry—simply resigned themselves to necessary conditions. And that aspect of autopsy is also apparent elsewhere in *45 Mercy Street*, for instance in the title poem, the book's best. Here we are given glimpses of a dream vision whose burden is the inability to recover what has been lost in and to the past, whose own character shifts from history to hallucination. This can result in bursts of self-disgust or helpless bewilderment, which are combined in the poem's final lines and testify to the blind end these last poems embody:

> Next I pull the dream off
> and slam into the cement wall
> of the clumsy calendar
> I live in,
> my life,

and its hauled up
notebooks.

The stronger and more fluent book is *The Awful Rowing Toward God*, which consolidates her experiments in *The Book of Folly* and *The Death Notebooks*. Like the latter, it is thematically organized into a series of variations on a religious doubt that swerves between exorcism and exultation. What she calls "my ignorance of God" is figured as a cancerous crab "clutching fast to my heart" ("The Poet of Ignorance"), while on the other hand there is an ecstatic, almost murderous release of desire:

> I am on the amphetamine of the soul.
> I am, each day,
> typing out the God
> my typewriter believes in.
> Very quick. Very intense,
> like a wolf at a live heart.
>
> ("Frenzy")

Within such a dialectic, "You have a thousand prayers / but God has one," and she repeats her poems as if hoping they accumulate into *his* prayer. But though this may be a God a typewriter can believe in, it seems questionable that Sexton does. At the very least, he is an abstracted presence—perhaps merely an obvious displacement of the father with whom she is attempting to effect a reconciliation. This may be one reason why the religious experience she records in this book is transposed into an almost mythic mode—one that, for instance, projects a version of her asylum life into a vision of an afterlife. As if to underscore this mode, both her voice and her line have the poise and concision of proverbs. There is little interest in elaborate exposition or explanation; instead there is a dialogue with herself, private and associative. The surrealistic and domestic imagery employed have considerable authority, and the book's long—and usually successful—poem "Is It True?" is a continuation of the diaristic "Hurry Up Please It's Time," though the later poem has a quiet control that strengthens the free form's urgent sprawl. Though still intensely personal, the book's privatism is of the peculiar variety that renders it accessible, undoubtedly because its subject is one in which the individual personality is less prominent than the character of the quest itself. At its best moments Sexton's voice swells to assume that character, her rhetoric pur-

ified to austere grandeur. The conclusion of "The Big Heart," a poem
addressed to her intimate companions, is one such moment:

> They hear how
> the artery of my soul has been severed
> and soul is spurting out upon them,
> bleeding on them,
> messing up their clothes,
> dirtying their shoes.
> And God is filling me,
> though there are times of doubt
> as hollow as the Grand Canyon,
> still God is filling me.
> He is giving me the thoughts of dogs,
> the spider in its intricate web,
> the sun
> in all its amazement,
> and a slain ram
> that is the glory,
> the mystery of great cost,
> and my heart,
> which is very big,
> I promise it is very large,
> a monster of sorts,
> takes it all in—
> all in comes the fury of love.

That very fury of love, occasionally so moving in the posthumous
books, does tend to distort or diffuse their force. Still, they remain as
flawed evidence of Sexton's steady boldness, her readiness to risk new
experiments in verse to record renewed perceptions of her experience
in life, in the manner Emerson claimed that art is the effort to indem-
nify ourselves for the wrongs of our condition. There is, as one critic
has said of her, "something awesome, even sublime in a woman who
is not afraid to sound crude or shrill so long as she is honest, who in
her best work sounds neither shrill nor crude precisely because she is
honest."[33] Her courage in coming true not only made Sexton one of
the most distinctive voices in this generation's literature, and a figure
of permanent importance to the development of American poetry, but
has revealed in its art and its honesty a life in which we can discover
our own.

NOTES

1. A. Alvarez, *Beyond All This Fiddle* (New York: Random House, 1969), 14–15. It is important to add that Sexton herself conceded the point: "There is some very bad writing in some of my best poems, and yet those flaws seem to me to make them even better. They are with all their flaws, a little more human, you might say" (Patricia Marx, "Interview with Anne Sexton," *Hudson Review* 18 [Winter 1965–66]: 569).

2. Anne Sexton (hereafter AS) to J. D. McClatchy (hereafter JDMcC), recorded conversation, Sept. 23, 1973.

3. "Classroom at Boston University," *Harvard Advocate* 145, special suppl. (Nov. 1961): 14.

4. AS to JDMcC, recorded conversation, July 3, 1973.

5. Theodor Reik, *The Compulsion to Confess* [1925] (New York: Farrar, Straus and Cudahy, 1959), 195–99, 206–7, 347.

6. AS to JDMcC, recorded conversation, Sept. 23, 1973.

7. Erik H. Erikson, *Identity: Youth and Crisis* (New York: Norton, 1968), 74.

8. AS to JDMcC, recorded conversation, Sept. 23, 1973.

9. "W. D. Snodgrass: An Interview," *Salmagundi* 22–23 (Spring-Summer 1973): 150.

10. "Creative Writers and Day-Dreaming" (1907), in *The Standard Edition of the Complete Psychological Works of Sigmund Freud*, ed. James Strachey (London: Hogarth Press; Institute of Psycho-Analysis, 1953–), 153.

11. AS to JDMcC, recorded conversations, July 3 and Sept. 23, 1973. This sense of witness is shared by poets with very different approaches. For instance, in the preface to a collection of her work, Denise Levertov writes of her hope that the book will be seen "as having some value not as mere 'confessional' autobiography, but as a document of some historical value, a record of one person's inner/outer experience in America during the '60s and the beginning of the '70s, an experience which is shared by so many and transcends the peculiar details of each life, though it can only be expressed in and through such details" (*To Stay Alive* [New York: New Directions, 1971], ix).

12. Ernst Kris, *Psychoanalytic Explorations in Art* (New York: International Universities Press, 1952), 256.

13. Marx, "Interview," 563.

14. Ibid., 568.

15. Richard Howard, *Alone with America* (New York: Atheneum, 1971), 445.

16. M. L. Rosenthal, *The New Poets: American and British Poetry since World War II* (New York: Oxford University Press, 1967), 134.

17. *Poet's Choice*, ed. Paul Engle and Joseph Langland (New York: Dial Press, 1962), 227.

18. Barbara Kevles, "The Art of Poetry XV: Anne Sexton," *Paris Review* [13,] no. 52 (Summer 1971): 187.

19. Beatrice Berg, " 'Oh, I Was Very Sick,' " *New York Times*, Nov. 19, 1969, D7.

20. Kevles, "Art of Poetry," 171–72.

21. Gaston Bachelard, *L'Eau et les rêves* (Paris: J. Corti, 1942), 10. See also Kris, *Psychoanalytic Explorations in Art*, 258.

22. Kevles, "Art of Poetry," 162.

23. William Packard, "Craft Interview with Anne Sexton," *New York Quarterly* 3 (Summer 1970): 11.

24. Robert Boyers, "*Live or Die:* The Achievement of Anne Sexton," *Salmagundi* 2, no. 1 (Spring 1967): 64.

25. Kevles, "Art of Poetry," 189.

26. AS to JDMcC, recorded conversation, Sept. 23, 1973.

27. Kevles, "Art of Poetry," 180.

28. AS to JDMcC, recorded conversation, Sept. 23, 1973.

29. Sigmund Freud, "The Occurrence in Dreams of Material from Fairy Tales" (1913), in *The Standard Edition* 12:279–87. See also Freud and D. E. Oppenheim, "Dreams in Folklore" (1911), in *The Standard Edition* 12:175–203; Emanuel K. Schwartz, "A Psychoanalytic Study of the Fairy Tale," *American Journal of Psychotherapy* 10 (Oct. 1956): 740–62; Ernest Jones, "Psychoanalysis and Folklore," in *Essays in Applied Psycho-analysis* (London: Hogarth Press, 1951), 2:1–21. For a more general discussion of the unconscious motives and strategies of fairy tales, see Bruno Bettelheim, *The Uses of Enchantment: The Meaning and Importance of Fairy Tales* (New York: Knopf, 1976), which singles out Sexton's *Transformations* for its powerful insights.

30. For an interesting example of the continuity between her life, poetry, and fiction, see the reappearance of Sweeney (an Australian businessman and fan) in "A Small Journal," *Ms.* 2, no. 5 (Nov. 1973): 60–63, 107. This journal in the form of a confessional story is reprinted with the title the poet herself preferred, "All God's Children Need Radios," in *The Poet's Story*, ed. Howard Moss (New York: Macmillan, 1973), 214–22.

31. Sigmund Freud, "Leonardo da Vinci and a Memory of His Childhood" (1910), in *The Standard Edition* 11:83.

32. Sigmund Freud, "Moses and Monotheism: Three Essays" (1934–38), in *The Standard Edition* 23:74.

33. Boyers, "*Live or Die*," 71.

DIANA HUME GEORGE

Beyond the Pleasure Principle:
The Death Baby

Let us suppose, then, that all the organic instincts are conservative, are acquired historically and tend towards the restoration of an earlier state of things. . . . Every modification which is thus imposed upon the course of the organism's life is accepted by the conservative organic instincts and stored up for further repetition. Those instincts are therefore bound to give a deceptive appearance of being forces tending towards change and progress, whilst in fact they are merely seeking to reach an ancient goal by paths alike old and new. Moreover it is possible to specify this final goal of all organic striving[,] . . . it must be an *old* state of things, an initial state from which the living entity has at one time or other departed and to which it is striving to return by the circuitous paths along which its development leads. If we are to take it as a truth that knows no exception that everything living dies for *internal* reasons—becomes inorganic once again—then we shall be compelled to say that *"the aim of all life is death"* and, looking backwards, that *"inanimate things existed before living ones."*

. . . Seen in this light, the theoretical importance of the instincts of self-preservation, of self-assertion and of mastery greatly diminishes. They are component instincts whose function it is to assure that the organism shall follow its own path to death, and to ward off any possible ways of returning to inorganic existence other than those which are immanent in the organism itself. . . . What we are left with is the fact that the organism wishes to die only in its own fashion.

—Sigmund Freud, *Beyond the Pleasure Principle*

The soul, is I think, a human being who speaks with the pressure of death at his head. . . . The self in trouble . . . not just the self without love (as us) but the self as it will always be (with gun at its head finally). . . . To live and know it is only for a moment . . . that is to know "the soul" . . . and it increases closeness and despair and happiness.

—Anne Sexton, *Anne Sexton: A Self-Portrait in Letters*

What does it mean to be a *self-conscious* animal? The idea is ludicrous, if it is not monstrous. . . . This is the terror: to have emerged from nothing, to have a name, consciousness of self, deep inner feelings, an excruciating inner yearning for life and self-expression—and with all this yet to die.

—Ernest Becker, *The Denial of Death*

Reprinted from Diana Hume George, *Oedipus Anne: The Poetry of Anne Sexton* (Urbana: University of Illinois Press, 1987), 164–85.

Becker and Freud

Freud published *Beyond the Pleasure Principle* in 1920, and ever since its publication, Freudians have been trying to beat anti-Freudians to the draw in the effort to unwrite it. Even classical analysts tend to consider it erratic and easily dismissible, almost an aberration in the career of an otherwise authoritative theorist. Indeed, its appeals to biology seem quaint and easy to patronize. That Freud wrote this book during his intellectual maturity and that he never refuted it, but rather made its premises the basis of all subsequent theory, seem not to matter. It is as though most readers agree that *Beyond the Pleasure Principle* represents a momentary lapse of concentration and intellectual vitality.

The thesis that so upsets even aficionados is relatively simple: in *Beyond the Pleasure Principle* Freud proposed the existence of a "death instinct," a biologically rooted urge in organic life to reachieve the inorganic state. Among the factors that led him to this hypothesis is the "repetition compulsion" he had noted in the course of analytic treatment and of world events, what he later called a "piece of unconquerable nature" or a "force which is defending itself by every possible means against recovery."[1]

No one likes the idea that the enemy has outposts in our heads. The proposition that there is in all of us an urge toward death competitive with the urge toward life seems outrageous, even ridiculous. If Freud had proposed that this was true of only severely neurotic or psychotic individuals, no one would have argued the point. But he posited that "we must suppose [the death instincts] to be associated from the very first with life instincts" in all living beings, and that is simply beyond the pale, to say nothing of the pleasure principle.[2] In the dramatic battle he staged between Eros and Thanatos in the germ plasm of all living creatures, Freud still gave the impression of championing Eros, but he implied that if "the aim of all life is death," Thanatos will always, eventually, win out. Between birth and death Freud envisioned the organism vibrating anxiously: "[The sexual instincts] are the true life instincts. They operate against the purpose of the other instincts, which leads, by reason of their function, to death; and this fact indicates that there is an opposition between them and the other instincts. . . . It is as though the life of the organism moved with a vacillating rhythm."[3]

His conclusions in *Beyond the Pleasure Principle* led to significant shifts in the rest of psychoanalytic theory. For example, he was forced now to consider that there *might* be such a thing as primary masochism, whereas before he had regarded masochism as sadism or aggressiveness turned inward upon the subject. But the fear of death, as opposed to the wish for it, remained for Freud at this time a special case of displaced sexual anxiety associated primarily with the castration complex.

The dismissal of a tract as hypothetical as *Beyond the Pleasure Principle* is inevitable in a culture that represses and avoids death as ours does. In his *The Denial of Death*, Ernest Becker proposes that the fear and dread of death is the primary repression in almost all cultures, and in this he means to contradict Freud: *"Consciousness of death* is the primary repression, not sexuality. . . . *This* is what is creaturely about man, *this* is the repression on which culture is built, a repression unique to the self-conscious animal."[4]

A psychoanalytic theorist himself, Becker agrees with Otto Rank that Freud was unable to establish "man's continuity and his difference from the lower animals on the basis of his *protest* against death rather than on his built-in instinctive urge toward it."[5] In this judgment he concurs with both popular and scholarly opinion. As Gregory Zilboorg remarks ironically in his introduction to an edition of *Beyond the Pleasure Principle*, the consensus has it that "the book in question is therefore more or less superannuated and deserves but a respectful historical glance before we put it back on the shelf to gather more dust."[6] Becker's own judgment is as damning and dismissive as any qualified opinion could be: "Freud's tortuous formulations on the death instinct can now securely be relegated to the dust bin of history."[7]

Becker refers to "Freud's unfortunate habit of forming polarities in his thought" but fails to see similarly structured polarities in his own thought. Becker may be right that *Beyond the Pleasure Principle* patched up the instinct libido theory into another comfortable duality, but it is just as true that Becker's own theses about death fear are based on polarities and dualities, in this case the unquestioning acceptance of mind/body dichotomies on which our culture may be based, but which are not necessarily productive or "true" on that account. Becker is eloquent in his defense of dualism *as truth:*

> This is the paradox: he (man) is out of nature and hopelessly in it; he
> is dual, up in the stars and yet housed in a heart-pumping, breath-gasping

body that once belonged to a fish and still carries the gill-marks to prove it. His body is a material fleshy casing that is alien to him in many ways—the strangest and most repugnant way being that it aches and bleeds and will decay and die. Man is literally split in two: he has an awareness of his own splendid uniqueness in that he sticks out of nature with a towering majesty, and yet he goes back into the ground a few feet in order blindly and dumbly to rot and disappear forever.[8]

If Becker's repugnance toward the body sounds overly disgusted, he is only reflecting a paradox to which we are all heirs. The most significant thing about Becker's fine book, it seems to me, is that it was regarded as new, radical, and bold when it was published in 1973. He speaks here, after all, of a dualism so commonly held that it is nearly definitive of Judeo-Christian culture's body politic and personal. But I do not quote him here just to argue with him—he is now dead and cannot argue back, at any rate—for I believe he is right, irrefutably so, in his contention that the repression of the knowledge and fear of death is primary to humankind in a sophisticated culture, that we are faced with what seems an impossible paradox: constant fear of death in the biological functioning of our self-preservative instincts, as well as obliviousness to this fear in our conscious life. So awful is the thought of our mortality, contends Becker, that "those who speculate that a full apprehension of man's condition would drive him insane are right, quite literally right." The essence of normality, in the face of this terrible and definitive fact of our lives, is the "refusal of reality." Some people have more trouble with their lies than others, and these people we call neurotic or, depending on the severity of symptoms, psychotic.[9]

As a counter to the Freudian contention that the fear of death is not primary and is not repressed, but is rather only a displacement for the fear of castration, Becker's reminder is necessary. It has always seemed to me ingenuous of Freud to dismiss the fear of death primarily because he believed that the unconscious has no knowledge of its own death. That he altered this position to permit himself to think that we do have unconscious knowledge of our own deaths but that the knowledge can take the form only of an instinct *toward* it or wish *for* it seems to me lopsided, and Becker joins those who point out this lapse of attention to possibilities. There is indeed *no theoretically necessary reason* why Freud should have restricted our relationship to our own mortality in such an intellectually and imaginatively cramped fashion.

He need not have insisted that sexuality is the only primary repression, nor that the wish for death is not accompanied by the greatest fear of it.

But I have a similar objection to Becker. Refuting Freud's contention that all primary repressions are sexual in nature, Becker counterasserts that all primary repression has to do with death rather than sexuality. Just as Freud shuts his door on the possibility of a primary death fear, Becker slams his own on the possibility of a primary death wish, as though the primacy of fear could not be mutually compatible with the primacy of wish—or tendency or urge or instinct. These are ironically rigid pronouncements, given that psychoanalytic thought is built upon the accommodation of paradoxes that seem, on the face of it, mutually exclusive. The reconciling of opposites through overdetermination, projection, reaction formation, and other psychic mechanisms is perhaps the greatest contribution of psychoanalytic thought. But at bedrock (which Freud located by definition in biology), the tendency toward either/or structures seems to defeat even the groundbreakers—or especially the groundbreakers.

It is my assumption that wish and fear, symbolic of our psychic orientation to all primary oppositions, are elaborately intertwined in unconscious mental life. In Anne Sexton's death poetry, wish and fear are often functionally identical. This does not mean that it is useless to distinguish the separable components of wish and fear, to identify one human urge juxtaposed with its opposite, when that is poetically possible; any analysis of tonal complexities must at least attempt to do this. But Sexton's poetry on death absolutely defies the desire finally to sunder wish and fear. Perhaps that is why this poetry is so disconcerting, so uncomfortable to assimilate. It speaks to our deepest identifications and defenses and rouses our need to protest against the blurring of boundaries, the obliteration of distinctions among objects and feelings people need to think of separately. It embodies the anomalies that call up our need for purity and our flight from danger.

The Dumb Traveler

"The Death Baby" (*The Death Notebooks*) is among the most psychoanalytic of Sexton's poems. By this I do not mean that it merely confesses to a neurosis that may be analyzed psychoanalytically or that the critic can dissect as case history. Rather, I mean that in "The Death

Baby" Sexton presents in poetry a persuasive case for a controversial
piece of Freudian theory, providing a poetic analogue for the hypothesis Freud outlined in *Beyond the Pleasure Principle.* I have no reason
to suppose that she set out to achieve this or that she conceived of
"The Death Baby" as supportive of any psychological theory. Finding
such correspondences is the critic's job, not the poet's. But while Sexton
was not a psychoanalytic theorist by any measure, she was preemi-
nently a psychoanalytic poet, and in "The Death Baby" she clearly
wishes to convey not only a truth she has lived but something close
to a thesis about the workings of unconscious mental life. She proceeds
toward her thesis inductively, and my exploration follows that method.

"The Death Baby" is a sequence of six poems interconnected by
dreams, dolls, and death. In the first poem, "Dreams," the speaker
imagines herself a frozen blue ice baby, "my mouth stiffened into a
dumb howl." She has been told this is only a childhood dream, but
she knows better than to dismiss it on that account: "I remember that
hardening." Without ever refuting that it was indeed a dream, she
asserts the authenticity of the experience and the memory. Sexton's
use of the dream-state here and throughout the canon insists upon
this authenticity of dreams, in exactly the way analytic theory insists
upon it. For Sexton the mind dreaming is "she of the origin, / she of
the primal crack," and the bed is an "operating table," where dreams
"slice me into pieces" ("January 24th," *Words for Dr. Y;* and "The
Lost Lie," *45 Mercy Street).* In "Dreams" an unspecified "they" attempt to dismiss the memory by calling it dream, but the speaker
knows that the images in dreams are emblems of psychic reality. The
first stanza leaves the reader contemplating a double image: the adult
speaker superimposed on a howling baby frozen into ice.

The second stanza calls into question whose dream we are dealing
with:

> My sister at six
> dreamt nightly of my death:
> "The baby turned to ice.
> Someone put her in the refrigerator
> and she turned as hard as a Popsicle."

This was not the speaker's dream after all, as the first stanza had let
the reader assume. Rereading, I am struck by how easy it would have
been to reverse the first two stanzas to avoid confusion about the

identity of the dreamer. But the ambiguity is purposeful. Sexton wants us to be confused about identities here, and she will deepen that confusion by creating identifications not only between the speaker and her sister but also between the speaker and her mother. Finally, such ambiguity serves to establish that the poem will concern itself with the wish to kill as well as to die, with the hostility and aggression toward others that may be part of our species' urge toward death.

The third stanza is among the most grotesquely powerful in Sexton's canon. The speaker places herself in the refrigerator in her incarnation as ice baby. She remembers "how I was put on a platter and laid / between the mayonnaise and the bacon." As is so characteristic of Sexton's manipulation of the grotesque, the image is softened, or twisted, by the humorous specificity of mayo and bacon. What might otherwise be merely maudlin and shocking is rendered almost funny, yet still terrifying. Readers would soon wilt under the burden of the images that follow—"The tomatoes vomited up their stomachs"—if such wince-making metaphors were not accompanied by others that bring a degree of levity to an unimaginably horrible scenario in which a baby, its mouth stiffened into a dumb howl, is placed on a platter in a refrigerator along with other leftover edibles. Sexton saves the situation, and our sensibilities, with "the pimentos kissed like cupids." This stanza ends with the ice baby moving on its platter, "like a lobster, / slower and slower," suffocated by the "tiny" air.

Next we are taken into the black core of another dream, this one also the sister's dream, but belonging to the speaker as her own lived reality:

> I was at the dogs' party.
> I was their bone.
> I had been laid out in their kennel
> like a fresh turkey.

Just as she "remembers" the hardening in the refrigerator, she remembers "that quartering" by Boston bull terriers, "ten angry bulls / jumping like enormous roaches" over her body. First the dogs lap her "very clean." Then they begin with their teeth, "those nails," to dismember her.

> I was coming apart.
> They loved me until
> I was gone.

In each of these two segments, the speaker has been transformed by the wish of another, her sister, into an object stripped of humanity, a kind of stillborn baby; and in each she is further objectified and transformed into food, first for people, finally for dogs. By the end of the first poem in the sequence, then, the speaker has been born and has died in infancy. Sexton does not explain or labor the Oedipal scenario so clearly enacted by the sister, who, at age six, sees the new-comer as intruder and competitor for the affections of the parents and wishes her dead. She concentrates instead on the degree of internalization the speaker experienced when she was old enough to be told about the dream, and still experiences as an adult. Having learned about the ice baby of her sister's dream, she identifies with that image; or perhaps the ice-baby image corresponds uncannily to the sense she has always had of herself. Someone else's dream has always been true for her, has always been the lived nightmare of her own reality.

Significantly, the adult agents of her transformation are entirely absent in this segment of the poem. No mother or father comes to rescue this helpless infant trapped in the hideous half-light we know not only from dreams but also from fairy tales. This may be Sexton's own private image for the menace of obliteration, but the author of *Transformations* already knew that her own private pantheon of demons belonged to everyone, was derived from the storehouse of cultural nightmare she milked from her own unconscious depths. Sexton's ice baby on a platter draws from the same source of horror in domestic disguise as do fairy tales. The fear of children transformed into food for giants or monsters or wolves or consuming mothers is familiar from *Hansel and Gretel, Little Red Riding Hood, Jack and the Beanstalk;* the kitchen is the right room in which to stage a scenario about fears of consumption, just as it was in the early poem "For John, Who Begs Me Not to Enquire Further" (*To Bedlam and Part Way Back*). In this case the child is helplessly sunk in motor incapacity, without language, reduced to a frozen howl.

Becker says of young children: "In their tortured interiors radiate complex symbols of many inadmissible realities—terror of the world, the horror of one's own wishes, the fear of vengeance by the parents, the disappearance of things, one's lack of control over anything, really." If "to grow up at all is to conceal the mass of internal scar tissue that throbs in our dreams," then Sexton is here engaged in opening the wounds, driving back to the beginning the lack of control epitomized by infancy, exposing the "tortured interior."[10] And although the agent of her transformation to frozen food is not named—"Someone put her in the refrigerator"—the absent parents are surely among the suspects. Who puts food in the refrigerator? Usually the mother or, in the case of Sexton's own household, the maid, the mother's kitchen surrogate. Even if the parents did not put her in the fridge—and on a platter— they did not save her. There is no help here; the infant's world is all unmanageable violence.[11]

The "quartering" of the baby's body by the dogs constitutes sexual violation as well as murder. "They loved me until / I was gone." The desire to consume, experienced by every infant, is closely related to the fear of being consumed, and both are connected to the mode of sexuality characteristic of the oral stage of psychic development. Infantile sexuality is polymorphous, experienced as far as we can tell throughout the body and not necessarily focused on or restricted to the genitals. (Some of the best anecdotal evidence for the dispersed, polymorphous nature of infantile sexuality comes from adult memories of earliest sexual fantasies. One woman I know describes her earliest sexual fantasy like this: "I am riding on the seat in a train, watching the lights go by. I am naked, possibly about to be diapered. My entire body is vibrating with the train. I don't even know why I call this a 'sexual' fantasy, but it is.") Creating an unimaginably horrible sense of a baby's rape and murder by ravenous dogs, Sexton's poem alludes to unconscious connections between death and sexuality even in infancy and relates such connections to the aggression of orality, of consuming and being consumed.

Before language, prior to the sense of control that develops as a child grows, the possibility of nightmare victimization, of consumption, and of violation and finally obliteration is a fundamental human fear. And the infant—this infant, any infant—can respond only with a "dumb howl." Sexton renders a universal human condition—the helplessness of infancy, the fear of obliteration that lives on in nightmares—through the particularities of her speaker's dream life. These are only dreams, only someone else's dreams, not even the speaker's, and yet the poem makes me see that baby on a platter in the refrigerator, see her torn in pieces and eaten by dogs, so clearly that I wonder, indeed, whose dream this is.

The second poem in "The Death Baby" sequence is "The Dydee Doll," who, the speaker says, died twice:

Once when I snapped
her head off
and let it float in the toilet
and once under the sun lamp
trying to get warm
she melted.

The matter-of-fact and unapologetic tone emphasizes the shadowy presence of the child whose baby doll this was. (The doll represents an infant rather than a child—a "Dy-dee" is a doll that can be diapered.) The placement of "The Dy-dee Doll," following the "Dreams" sequence, brings the nightmare aura of the earlier poems into the reenacted remembrance of childhood reality. Sexton plays here on the familiar pattern of the doll as surrogate self—children often punish and mistreat dolls in exact reenactments of their own punishments and real or imagined mistreatments by parents. A beloved doll can be literally torn apart in the service of vengeance against the paternal powers in whose presence the child herself is helpless.

The degree of malicious motivation differs in the two deaths of the doll. In the first we are told that the speaker "snapped / her head off"; the incident is reported without emotional content. We see a child purposely and determinedly snapping off a doll's head and then casting it in the toilet, enacting a murder that is only vicious play, for the head floats and can apparently be replaced. The second, final death seems less purposeful; the doll was "trying to get warm." But anyone who remembers such play, with pets as well as with dolls, knows how thin is the line between cruelty and carelessness, between innocence and malicious self-deception. Here we cannot judge for certain, but we can suspect. After the flat, toneless relating of facts, the speaker ends with:

She was a gloom,
her face embracing
her little bent arms.
She died in all her rubber wisdom.

I read a certain amount of irony in the last line. Rubber wisdom? That is no wisdom at all—or no more wisdom than can be attributed to a frozen baby with a dumb howl on its face. But genuine sympathy and regret are present in the description of the dying doll, whose face embraces her arms, melting into rubber soup just as the refrigerated baby froze into ice. In the dreams and the play of children, these first two poems assert, is enacted the business of horror, mutilation, objectification, and bodily obliteration we know perfectly well resides there but like to pretend does not. Just as people know that children are not innocent of sexuality, we know that they are not innocent of murderous thoughts. We somehow relegate these experienced and remembered kinds of knowledge, which we observe again as parents, to a safe place, thinking that the real business of death gets done in hospitals or on battlefields. We repress what we know of the horror of infancy and childhood, the fear of dying, the wish to kill, the fear of being consumed, the wish to consume.

A later poem provides support for connections between the dydee doll and the abandoned ice baby of the first segment. In "The Falling Dolls" (45 Mercy Street), Sexton dreams that "Dolls, / by the thousands, / are falling out of the sky." She wonders who will catch them and imagines the carnage of doll bodies smashing to earth. Some of them will fall on highways, "so that they may be run over like muskrats," and some will land in national parks, where centuries later "they'll be found petrified like stone babies." The speaker tries to catch as many as she can, knowing that they are "the babies I practice upon." The dolls "need cribs and blankets and pajamas / with real feet in them." She wants to know "Why is there no mother?" and "Was there a father?"—the same questions I asked as a reader of "Dreams." The final stanza serves as a bridge between "Dreams" and "The Dy-dee Doll":

> Or have the planets cut holes in their nets
> and let our childhood out,
> or are we the dolls themselves,
> born but never fed?

Thus far Sexton has restricted the sequence to examination of the *fear of dying* and the *wish to kill*, all placed in the psychoanalytic and poetic context of infancy and early childhood and anatomized through the agency of dreaming. Now she builds outward from that chronology, moving toward another dimension of psychic reality. The third poem, "Seven Times," is a ritual reiteration of the speaker's many deaths:

> I died seven times
> in seven ways

> letting death give me a sign,
> letting death place his mark on my forehead,
> *crossed over, crossed over.*

The experienced Sexton reader is likely to interpret the seven deaths as suicide attempts, half- or wholehearted. But this poem stands on its own without such personal context, and since she does not say that the seven deaths are self-inflicted, I am inclined to honor that ambiguity, or that refusal of clarity. Rather than being an active participant in her own deaths, the speaker assumes a passive role here, so that she might be referring to grave illnesses or psychic deaths. She "lets" death give her a sign and place his mark on her, a mark that says she is *"crossed over."* But these are not final deaths, although they may be real in some sense. They are, instead, deaths of the kind described in the first two poems: dream deaths, play deaths, deaths that can be taken back. If the mark on her forehead says she is *"crossed over,"* it is only temporary, like the dream-state, like the snapped-off doll's head. But the deaths are no less serious for being temporary or partial; rather, the fact that the speaker comes to life again with death's mark still on her forehead means that she wears the mark continuously through life. One wakes from a dream but goes to sleep again, to dream again:

> And death took root in that sleep.
> In that sleep I held an ice baby
> and I rocked it
> and was rocked by it.
> Oh Madonna, hold me.
> I am a small handful.

Now the speaker holds her own ice baby, the stillborn aspect of herself from her sister's dream of many years before. As a child she mothered her doll, whom she also murdered. The central images of both "Dreams" and "The Dy-dee Doll" are conflated in this rocking scene, which takes place in sleep. In a peculiar twist on the ordinary relationship of mother and infant, she not only rocks this alien yet intimate death baby; she is also "rocked by it." Instantly, she transforms it into a Madonna, whom she begs to hold her. If we are to make sense of this unintelligible switch, that sense must be psychoanalytic.

In dreams people and objects transform into their opposites, or merely into other objects or people, through the agencies of projection, displacement, and condensation. Freud originally proposed that all dreams are fulfillments of disguised wishes and that upon analysis such disguised wishes will always reveal their sexual, infantile sources. But in *Beyond the Pleasure Principle* he proposed significant exceptions to this rule. "It is impossible to classify as wish-fulfillments the dreams . . . which occur in traumatic neuroses, or the dreams during psychoanalyses which bring to memory the psychical traumas of childhood. They arise, rather, in obedience to the compulsion to repeat. . . ."[12]

This "repetition compulsion" is the foundation of Freud's theory on the death instinct. In popular usage it has come to signify any repetitive behaviors that are "neurotic," that keep people from progressing or changing in ways they consciously believe they want to. Freud eventually came to think of such repetitive behavior as inevitable or inescapable. The compulsion to repeat is ascribed by Freud to the unconscious repressed and is thus a manifestation of the power of repressed material to influence the conscious behaviors of normal as well as ill people. Freud found that in analysis patients repeat "unwanted situations and painful emotions" and "revive them with the greatest ingenuity." Eventually, he came to see this force as so powerful that it defended itself against cure at any cost. People in treatment returned to the same traumatic events of their pasts again and again, "under pressure of a compulsion."[13] The clearest way to characterize the tendency Freud is speaking of is to quote his comments on the repetition compulsion in the lives of normal people:

> Thus we have come across people all of whose human relationships have the same outcome, such as the benefactor who is abandoned in anger after a time by each of his proteges . . . and who thus seems doomed to taste all the bitterness of ingratitude; or the man whose friendships all end in betrayal by his friend; . . . or, again, the lover each of whose love affairs with a woman passes through the same phase and reaches the same conclusion.[14]

Most important for my purposes here, Freud relates the repetition compulsion to the kind of dream discussed above and to the impulse that leads children to play. In the first two poems of "The Death Baby" sequence, Sexton has explored exactly these activities, traumatic dreaming and playing. In the first sequence the speaker returns, apparently under force of a compulsion, to a traumatic dream of childhood, which she has erected into a memory she must resuscitate even though it does not bring her pleasure. The dream in question is the sister's, and it is clear how for the sister it would have been a wish-fulfillment dream: it gets rid of the new baby in the house. As the speaker's own dream, vicarious but real, it cannot be said to fulfill any pleasurable wish, as we conceive of pleasure. But the need to repeat overrides what Freud called the dominance of the pleasure principle in instinctual life.

The example of child's play that Sexton produces in the second poem is similarly unpleasurable as a memory, but it must be repeated. Such examples, says Freud, "give the appearance of some 'daemonic' force at work," as do all manifestations of the repetition compulsion when they seem to act against the best interests of the agent.[15] There may indeed be something pleasurable for the child who acts out murderous wishes against her doll, and perhaps the adult remembering the incident is able to recapture the sense of power she felt as a child. But the memory is clearly more unpleasant than pleasant, more traumatic than healing. Speaking of children's play, Freud writes, "Children repeat unpleasurable experiences for the additional reason that they can master a powerful impression far more thoroughly by being active than they could by merely experiencing it passively."[16] The speaker's enactment of the doll's death serves this purpose of attempting to master a traumatic experience, that experience being the dream-state of helplessness in "Dreams." But it is not only for purposes of mastery that the speaker returns and returns to unpleasant childhood memories. The compulsion to repeat embodies urges literally *beyond* the pleasure principle.

The thesis that Freud eventually builds on the foundation of the repetition compulsion is the urge toward death in all organic life, the need to return to the quiescence of the inorganic state. By the third poem in the sequence, Sexton is already synthesizing the same psychic mechanisms that Freud delineated in *Beyond the Pleasure Principle*, by placing herself in the sleep of death with the ice baby in her lap, rocking.

But baby as Madonna? In this dream- and sleep state near to death, the speaker makes identifications out of near opposites. The logic of the poem is circular and cyclical: mother turns into baby in her relationship to daughter. "Madonna," meaning originally "my lady," had the more specific meanings to Sexton of the Virgin Mary *and* her own mother, whose name was Mary. Sexton played with this accident of nomenclature throughout her career. From her many poems about Mary the mother of Christ, it is also clear that Sexton saw Mary as wise but thoroughly victimized and institutionally infantilized, especially in her relationship to her own infant son, who, although he grows up and away from her, is always an infant himself because his human development is sexually arrested. Sexton was also deeply and painfully aware of the exchange of places between mother and daughter when a mother grows into old age and disease. That the ice baby of death has turned into a Madonna is an appropriate juxtaposition of the themes of the first two sections; and the subject of the fourth poem, "Madonna," is the role reversal of mother and daughter:

> My mother died
> unrocked, unrocked.

Beside a hospital deathbed, the speaker relives her mother's death from cancer. She watches her mother "thrust herself against the metal bars," with "vomit steaming from her mouth." The speaker remembers herself

> wanting to place my head in her lap
> or even take her in my arms somehow
> and fondle her twisted gray hair.

Throughout the poem, Sexton intertwines images of mothering and being mothered, nurturing and being nurtured, repeatedly changing places with her mother. In the example above she wants to place her head in her mother's lap, i.e., to be mothered by her; and she wants to "take her in my arms," to mother her mother in her pain.

Playing on the pregnancy that brought her own life forth from her mother's body, the speaker finds "Her belly . . . big with another child, / cancer's baby, big as a football." There is nothing she can do to help, so she must watch her mother diminish into death before her eyes:

> With every hump and crack
> there was less Madonna
> until that strange labor took her.

The "strange labor" is the reversal of ordinary birthing, the birth into death. "Cancer's baby" is a parody sibling of those other infants, the ice baby and the doll. "Cancer's baby" replaces the baby the speaker once was and answers to the speaker's conviction that she, too, was born of death-in-life.

Fifth in the sequence, "Max" refers to Sexton's closest friend, poet Maxine Kumin. "Max and I" are "two immoderate sisters, / two immoderate writers, / two burdeners," whose understanding of each other's relationship to death ended in a "pact":

> To beat death down with a stick.
> To take over.
> To build our death like carpenters.

This poem reverses the trend of passivity toward her own death that has been characteristic of the speaker in earlier poems in the sequence. As the ice-dream baby she was completely passive and helpless and overwhelmed; in "Seven Times" she has let death give her a sign, allowed him to place a mark on her forehead; at her mother's deathbed she has been the passive and helpless observer. Only in "The Dy-dee Doll" segment has she been active in relation to death, and that was only a play death. In "Max" she takes over, protesting the power-lessness of her position. If death is her lot, as it is everyone's, she will not wait for it quietly but will defeat it, "beat [it] down with a stick." But to beat it down might mean to refute it, to fight against it; to clarify, she says she and Max will "build" their deaths like "carpenters" (see "Wanting to Die," *Live or Die*). They will struggle against it until they are ready; but then they will take death into their own hands instead of being taken *by* it. (This position bears remarkable similarities to the arguments of euthanasia proponents, who advocate just such active participation in one's own death.) Their agreement is that when they know "the moment" has come,

> we'll talk turkey,
> we'll shoot words straight from the hip,
> we'll play it as it lays.
> Yes,
> when death comes with its hood
> we won't be polite.

The stance of "Max" is courageous and unblinking. Sexton here insists on resisting death before embracing it, creating an adversary as well as a seductive relationship to one's own death.

"Baby," the finale of "The Death Baby" sequence, synthesizes the first five poems and goes far beyond them—and far beyond the separate implications of pain and pleasure principles. "Baby" is addressed directly to death, resurrected from the first poem as a "cherub." Now the infant is more luminous than frozen, more mythic than ordinarily mortal:

> Your milky wings are as still as plastic.
> Hair as soft as music.
> Hair the color of a harp.
> And eyes made of glass,
> as brittle as crystal.

Whereas the ice baby was helplessly fixed into a silent howl of pain, the death baby is an embodiment of power, a delicate and dangerous force field. The speaker rocks the death baby in her arms, staring at its eyes, which are wise with primal knowledge: "Glass eye, ice eye, / primordial eye, / lava eye, / pin eye, / break eye, / how you stare back!" Like the Homunculus in Goethe's *Faust*, this baby contains the essence and recapitulation of all that is peculiarly human, but the knowledge in its eyes gazes out from the face of a cherub. Its knowledge is not only universal—it knows what it is to be human and mortal—but particular; the death baby knows the speaker's own life history. "You know all about me."

> You have worn my underwear.
> You have read my newspaper.
> You have seen my father whip me.
> You have seen me stroke my father's whip.

These intimacies cannot be known by anyone except the self, and this is the point: the death baby *is* the speaker, what Estella Lauter calls "the still-born aspect of the self."[17] It is thus the aspect of the self that is subject to the repetition compulsion, to urges toward primary masochism, to the fusion of Eros and Thanatos, sexuality and death. The cameo appearance of the father comes as a surprise in this feminine poem of mothers, sisters, daughters, babies, and female friends. His function is to bring the patriarchal order into the self-enclosed circle of women, infants, and death; it might be said that his earlier surrogates were the angry dogs who "quartered" the ice baby. Once again the speaker reenacts or reevokes an experience that cannot have been pleasurable, in the ordinary sense, but that *is* pleasurable in the perversely erotic sense experienced by the masochistic daughter in relation to the patriarchal father. The death baby knows all about this kind of pleasure, for the baby is the literal, infantilized embodiment of the urge to experience pain, shame, and finally death.

The speaker rocks the death baby as they "plunge back and forth / comforting each other." Together they are a stone "pietà," the Madonna and child of the earlier poems. In this rocking all else is obliterated. The world outside may be the scene of larger events, even "Pakistan is swallowed in a mouthful," but here in the room of rocking, there is only the self and the self's own death baby, "my stone child / with still eyes like marbles."

Now the poet swerves without warning or apology into a didactic mode. The story of "The Death Baby" has a moral, reminiscent of the morals in *Transformations*, but entirely without the wry tone Sexton saved for fairy tales. This is the meaning she cannot allow us to miss— and that, without the admonitory tone, we might easily wish to avoid:

> There is a death baby
> for each of us.
> We own him.
> His smell is our smell.

Were she speaking here to other suicidal people, our agreement would be easy and immediate. But she is speaking to "each of us." The grotesquely intimate death baby belongs not just to Sexton or her kind but to everyone. She insists that this is not the story only of personal pathology but of a people, a culture, perhaps all cultures, all individuals. The death baby is the clearest possible humanized metaphor for the processes Freud delineated in *Beyond the Pleasure Principle*. Sexton is "supposing," with Freud, that organic instincts are "conservative," that they "tend towards the restoration of an earlier state of things." We mistake matters if we think all of our "instinctual" urges are directed toward prolonging life indefinitely. "Those instincts are . . . bound," Freud writes, "to give a deceptive appearance of being forces tending toward change and progress, whilst in fact they are merely seeking to reach an ancient goal by paths alike old and new."[18]

The stillborn aspect of each life, its glass and ice eye calcified into a stare that peers into the soul of the living self, remains in Sexton's mythopoeic terms a baby we rock, are rocked by, throughout life and into death. This corresponds exactly to Freud's "final goal of all organic striving": "If we are to take it as a truth that knows no exception that everything living dies for *internal* reasons—becomes inorganic once again—then we shall be compelled to say that *the aim of all life is death.*'"[19] One may, of course, quarrel with the validity of that "truth." Freud carefully specifies that the conclusion he is compelled toward is conditional upon the hypothesis that everything dies for internal reasons. With the exception of death by accident from outer agencies, I find Freud's statement one way of stating the facts: if we live to be old enough, we do die for internal reasons. And the extremities of old age are closely united to the extremities of infancy, making the death baby an appropriate image for the ironic circularity of the life cycle.

The "ancient goal" of inorganic quiescence, the "*old* state of things," is emphasized in Sexton's poem in the "primordial" gaze of the death baby's eyes. In the sense that the "primordial" is first in order of appearance in the growth or development of an organism, it is fundamental, present at and participating in the very process of ordering, of coming into being: the death baby is born with and within the "life" baby. Or, as Freud expresses the same principle, "We must suppose [the death instincts] to be associated from the very first with life instincts."[20]

Although the death baby's visage is compelling and even seductive, Sexton does not embrace it without anxiety, nor does she suggest that any of us rock our death babies without being aware of what we thus nurture:

> Beware. Beware.
> There is a tenderness.
> There is a love
> for this dumb traveler
> waiting in his pink covers.

The warning is clear: watch out for your death baby, in whatever guise he comes to you. She tells us that we need beware not only his presence but also our affection for this death-in-life principle. The death baby appears harmless, clothed in the colors of innocence and purity, and therein lies the danger that we will mistake it, not be sufficiently on guard against the seductive tenderness we feel. And we cannot expect the baby to tell us who he is: he is "dumb," without language, before language, even if wise *beyond* language.

The ending of "The Death Baby" sequence imagines the moment when it will be time, when the speaker will know the necessity of finally and completely embracing her own death:

> Someday,
> heavy with cancer or disaster
> I will look up at Max
> and say: It is time.
> Hand me the death baby
> and there will be
> that final rocking.

If she seems to be succumbing here to the seductiveness of the death baby, there are significant qualifications upon that relinquishing of life, and for the substance of them we must return to "Max," and to Freud.

Even after he formulated his death-instinct hypothesis, Freud felt that urges toward self-preservation, assertion, and mastery were still very important; he had merely qualified what had been an exclusive emphasis on their power and significance. To go *beyond* the pleasure principle, where Eros reigns, is not to abandon the pleasure principle but merely to temper it to accord with clinical experience and observation on the behavior patterns of real people. If he could no longer suppose the sexual or life instincts to be all-powerful, he still found a place for them even within the death instinct, for they "assure that the organism shall follow its own path to death" and "ward off any possible ways of returning to inorganic existence other than those which are immanent in the organism itself."[21] Readers of Freud have found this a depressing hypothesis; but given that death is inevitable for all living creatures, the idea that "the organism wishes to die only in its own fashion" accords at least the semblance of internal choice. Note that it is not the death instinct itself that governs this choice, in Freud's scheme, but rather the life-preserving urges, engaged in negotiating a compromise between their own single-minded direction and the equally single-minded direction of the death urge. Seen in this light, the choice of the moment of death is a decision, albeit usually an unconscious one, on the part of a living being.

But the "final rocking" that Sexton speaks of involves an element of conscious choice on the speaker's part, in delicately negotiated compromise between Eros and Thanatos. Cancer or disaster may not be her conscious choices, may be the result of a struggle between internal, unconscious motivations, some directed toward living and some toward dying. But Sexton speaks here of her own *conscious* and *rational* decision to take control over both. The decision-making process was described in "Max," where the speaker and Max made the "pact" to "take over" their deaths. When Max had a broken back, the two women "built" her sleep nightly over the phone. Max had not chosen her broken back in any conscious way; but given her pain, undeniable and irrefutable, the building of sleep to ease that pain and to lead toward recovery was the life-affirming choice. Similarly, the "building" of death will take place in the clear-eyed recognition of the facts—this time cancer or disaster—and will affirm the power of the individual to choose her moment, when there is nothing else she can hope to gain by staying alive. In the face of cancer the speaker will not passively await the helpless, "unrocked" death that befell her mother while she watched; she will elect to take the death baby, humanized symbol of her own necessary and always-waiting death, into her arms for that "final rocking." It is better, this poem suggests, to rock your own death baby in your arms than to die, as her mother did, "unrocked, unrocked." For to rock your own death baby, *when it is time*—"I will look up at Max / and say: It is time"—is also to *be rocked by it*, to accept it, to receive comfort, to let go.

I am aware that many readers, many people who cared about Anne Sexton, will feel the irony inherent in my reading of "The Death Baby." The source of the irony is the manner and timing of Anne Sexton's death, which we are not accustomed to see as a rational, courageous embrace of death at the "right" time, in the "right" way. This poem articulates a thesis about death that is uncomfortable even for people used to seeing the world psychoanalytically, even, as I have said, for Freudians. Yet the poem concludes with a movement, a decision, that militates against the dark, almost demonic direction of the rest of the poem, at least as I read it. The choice to die, in the face of "cancer" or its substitutes, is one that many people now agree or at least sympathize with; and I have suggested that the position Sexton takes here is similar to the positions advocated by euthanasia activists. But we do not extend the same agreement and sympathy to what Sexton here designates as "disaster."

Anne Sexton took the death baby in her arms for that final rocking at a time most people would consider premature. According to her lights, disaster was upon her, if not cancer. It is difficult to see how that could have been so; in 1974 she was a renowned poet living almost anyone's version of the good life. That she was fresh from a divorce seems insufficient cause for such drastic action, and the divorce is the only public indication we have of the straits she was in. Her death was immeasurably painful for her family and friends, premature by any ordinary measure. She responded to the call of her own death baby or her green girls or her Mr. Death before we would have wanted her to. "The Death Baby" can be read as a sad commentary on her own pathology, and to the extent that it is just that, we will distance ourselves from its implications, fail to see what she was in fact saying about everyone.

We cannot judge the depth of Sexton's despair, the manner of "disaster" she was encountering at the time of her death. For her the moment of her death was by definition the right time to rock the death baby—even if, knowing Max might not agree, she could not ask Maxine Kumin to hand it to her. It is certain that Sexton knew her own death baby far better than I know mine, far more intimately than most people know theirs.[22] This is a matter of poetic and personal insight, a mark of her special knowledge, as well as a clinical fact that can be translated into aberration. The timing and manner of the poet's death does not compromise the special knowledge conveyed in "The Death Baby." If the suicidal poet can show us the commonality of our "normal" neurosis and her psychosis, those of us who sometimes respond with cramped and alienated sympathies will have learned something needful about ourselves. Perhaps we will consider our tenderness for our own dumb travelers.

NOTES

1. Sigmund Freud, "Analysis Terminable and Interminable," trans. Joan Riviere, in *The Standard Edition of the Complete Psychological Works of Sigmund Freud,* ed. James Strachey (London: Hogarth Press; Institute of Psycho-Analysis, 1953–), 23:242.

2. Sigmund Freud, *Beyond the Pleasure Principle,* trans. James Strachey, in *The Standard Edition of the Complete Psychological Works of Sigmund Freud,* 18:57.

3. Ibid., 40–41.

4. Ernest Becker, *The Denial of Death* (New York: Free Press, 1973), 96.

5. Ibid., 98–99.

6. Gregory Zilboorg, introduction to Freud, *Beyond the Pleasure Principle,* trans. James Strachey (New York: Bantam Books, 1972), 1.

7. Becker, *Denial of Death,* 99.

8. Ibid., 26.

9. Ibid., 27, 178.

10. Ibid., 19, 29.

11. The resonance of the fear of consumption may well be inevitable in a carnivorous culture. For many years I was frequently visited near sleep by a scene from a Porky Pig cartoon I saw as a young child. Porky fell asleep while fishing in a boat. In his dream he was the "fish" and the fish were his predators. The father fish caught Porky on the hook and took him home to the mother fish, who bustled about the kitchen in a parody of middle-class human cookery, cleaning Porky and preparing to bake him. I remember distinctly that the mother fish, clad in apron and dress, placed Porky on a platter, lovingly plumping him about into aesthetically appetizing position. As she was about to put him in the oven, Porky woke up in his boat and rowed to shore double-speed. It must have been thirty years ago that I saw this cartoon, but I remember it vividly—and the moment I remember best is the placement on a platter, which produced in me feelings of horror and, although I could not have named it at the time, of sexuality. A hideously erotic component was attendant upon the presentation of live Porky for food, a component completely lacking in, say, Sylvester's near-gobble of Tweetie. I wonder how many children were both mesmerized and repulsed by that cartoon, especially at a time when the cartoon genre had taken on some of the functions of the fairy tale.

12. Freud, *Beyond the Pleasure Principle*, 32.

13. Ibid., 21.

14. Ibid., 22.

15. Ibid., 35.

16. Ibid.

17. The only critic who has noted the mythic qualities of Sexton's "The Death Baby" is Estella Lauter, who calls the death baby an image "stunning in the context of Western iconography where death is often figured as an adult skeleton posing as lover or monk." "Sexton's image is an externalization of an ever-present, all-seeing eye within all human lives—an entity that is at once the most private aspect of one's life (one's smell), and the most universal aspect (primordial eye). It is an aspect of self and world within the person that never grows and can elicit tenderness in moments of despair, presented here as maternal self-sacrifice." ("Anne Sexton's 'Radical Discontent with the Awful Order of Things,' " *Spring: An Annual of Archetypal Psychology and Jungian Thought* [1979]: 77–92, and *infra*, 145–61.) To Lauter's assessment, with which I agree, I would add that Sexton envisioned and re-visioned death in many mythic guises throughout her poetic career, and that the death baby is only the most original and successful of these reimaginings. She also sees death as God, as an elegant lover and then a beer-bellied Lothario, as her father and mother, and as a series of "green girls," seductive young women superficially similar to the sirens of mythology. But whereas in all the other guises of death

she is calling upon a minor historical tradition for the portrayal of death, the death baby is her own creation and corresponds to no other poetic or artistic rendering of which I am aware.

18. Freud, *Beyond the Pleasure Principle,* 38.

19. Ibid.

20. Ibid., 57.

21. Ibid., 39.

22. One reader of this essay, Kim Krynock, writes to me about her way of understanding death as a man and the relationship between wish and fear that Anne Sexton's suicide and death poetry embodies. Both Sexton's poetry and my arguments in these chapters "meet with great resistance in me," writes Ms. Krynock. But "one of the most impressive things about Sexton, and probably the most difficult to ignore, is her ability to give me common ground, a place to meet her. . . . I do identify with her, I do feel for her. The past two weeks, I've been sleeping alone in an apartment for the first time in my life. I've been staying up late, sleeping with the radio on, or a light, frightened and conscious of the person who is not behind the door, the demons in my bed. I've noticed that it gets past fear to a wish that my intruder-man would get it over with, break through the damn window, already. It has to do with a special dual fear that comes from being very female and very mortal—any finality seems better than this vulnerable not knowing. I think of Sexton feeling like this all of the time, or most of the time—that, ultimately, is how I understand her." Krynock's "Not That It Was Beautiful" (*infra*, 310–13) is her response to my request that she expand upon these perceptions.

JUNGIAN FEMINIST
READINGS

MARGARET HONTON

The Double Image and the Division of Parts: A Study of Mother-Daughter Relationships in the Poetry of Anne Sexton

Anne Sexton and Her Personae

A major premise in this essay is that in a fashion similar to the way one perceives Antigone through Sophocles, Anna Karenina through Tolstoy, or Annabelle Lee through Poe, one perceives Anne Sexton through the Anne Sexton speaking at the moment. Here I choose to discuss her writing in terms of poet and personae, not in terms of Anne Sexton and her autobiography. This approach allows universal meanings to emerge from highly personal writing and allows "confessional" poetry several meanings: acknowledgment, avowal, public profession of belief and values, as well as admission of guilt.

In "Talking to Sheep" (*45 Mercy Street*),[1] a poem dealing with public confession over the centuries, Sexton says that her life "has appeared unclothed in court, / detail by detail, / death-bone witness by death-bone witness." The poet admits that, though "shamed at the verdict," she has gone on confessing. "It was a compulsion," she says, "but I denied it, called it fiction / and then the populace screamed *Me too, Me too* / and I swallowed it like my fate." Yet, in summing for her defense, she makes this observation:

> or if it is not my life I depict
> then someone's close enough to wear my nose—
> My nose, my patrician nose
> sniffing at me or following theirs down the street.

Reprinted from the *Journal of Women's Studies in Literature* 1, no. 1 (Winter 1979): 33–50.

Whether the reader is one of the populace screaming "*Me too, Me too,*" or someone close enough to Sexton to wear her nose, or someone at a much greater remove, will influence the reader's interpretation of her poetry. For me Anne Sexton's writing evidences a terrible struggle against the devouring mother myth, and the struggle is important, regardless of the final outcome.

The Poet's Relationships with Her Mother

The first words on the subject of mother-daughter relationships that Anne Sexton spells out are *blame, debt,* and *guilt* in a poem called "The Double Image" in *To Bedlam and Part Way Back.* In this poem the speaker blames herself for the illness of her infant daughter, "as if doom had flooded my belly and filled your bassinet, / an old debt I must assume," and very soon takes on another load of guilt when her mother claims Anne "gave her cancer." To the extent that Sexton's mother is shown to be unforgiving, as are the witches in the speaker's mind who say, "Too late to be forgiven now," so is the speaker consciously unforgiving of herself, barely tolerating herself before and after suicide attempts. Even as the daughter in the poet accuses her mother of having preferred a mirror image or an oil portrait to the life-size original that is Anne, the mother in the poet admits that she herself made a genetic reproduction, an image in the form of Joyce, and accuses herself of this "worst guilt . . . I made you to find me."

In Sexton's double image of the devouring mother myth, the speaker accepts blame from her predecessor as well as guilt concerning her successor. Moreover, she equates *blame* with *guilt* in some sort of inverse functioning, never quite stated, but throughout this poem implied: As my mother's sufferings were caused by me, so I am the cause of my daughter's sufferings. With this distorted perception, she encounters the double terror of likenesses and unlikenesses, of reflections and foreshadowings, of apparent answers to *how* and *why* mother and daughter are so much alike, without asking the proper antecedent question *if* the mother's and daughter's "smiles held in place" are really, or even symbolically, matching smiles.

In "The Double Image" the chief metaphor of portraits/mirrors is sustained throughout. Even a single word related to the subject can set up puns and take on progressively greater significance, carrying the burden well. An example is the portrait painter's "matching me to keep me well," his later rendering the mother's portrait, too, with "matching smile, matching contour," and his artistically catching "us at the turning; / we smiled in our canvas home / before we chose our foreknown separate ways." A phrase, "the cave of the mirror," first appearing when the portraits are hung to face each other, is later augmented to a definition in which mother and daughter cannot be distinguished, one from the other.

> And this was the cave of the mirror,
> that double woman who stares
> at herself as if she were petrified
> in time—two ladies sitting in umber chairs.

The poet, staring back, remembers the petrified time of "holding my smile in place, till it grew formal." Yet, even while viewing the artfulness of her mother's and her own smile "held in place," she has the vision of some separateness. While calling her mother "my mocking mirror . . . my first image," she is able to say, "my overthrown / love," and to assert that "The artist caught us at the turning; / we smiled in our canvas home / before we chose our foreknown separate ways."

Just how difficult of achievement separation will be for the speaker is suggested in a refrain of "The Double Image" that ties together early and recent experiences of mother, artist, father, and witches—for whom the convalescent "had my portrait done instead" of pleasing or placating them. Emotionally tied in a bundle by the poet, the persons are not readily released.

The reader faces a similar dilemma, needing for the purpose of discussion to untie and separate relationships in Sexton's overall mother-daughter theme. This article will proceed on the assumption that one can discuss first the speaker's relationships with her mother, next her relationships with her daughters, and then whatever personal integration may be evidenced in the poetry—even though these relationships occur in writing like simultaneous equations, the solution to one of the variables expressed in terms of the others.

Appropriately, the next poem to be considered is "The Division of Parts" (Bedlam). Addressed by the poet to her mother, Mary Gray, it is couched in terms of the Good Friday sacrifice. The conflict again hinges on indebtedness. Sexton, reading her mother's will, feels her inheritance settling like a debt, a debt she would not willingly incur.

Referring to herself as "one third / of your daughters counting my bounty," she proceeds to draw parallels between her mother's death and that of Christ. Self-accusation follows immediately: "I have cast my lot / and am one third thief / of you." Though she argues with herself that she grieved with her mother daily for the final three months of her illness, the fact remains that she has "never said goodbye."

Sexton, "bundled out with gifts I did not choose" when her mother's "things: / obstacles" were sorted out, wants to shake off her sense of indebtedness. Calling herself a fool for fumbling "my lost childhood / for a mother" and for lounging "in sad stuff," she combats memories of her mother and her mother's version of Christ without much success:

> Since then I have pretended ease,
> loved with the trickeries of need, but not enough
> to shed my daughterhood
> or sweeten him as a man.

Sexton will not appropriate the "clutter of worship / that you taught me, Mary Gray." What the poet chooses for herself is to maintain her own version of religion and her own vision of Christ, even though haunted by her mother's ghost calling her to convert to the "grotesque metaphor" of sacrifice. Sexton discovers that cursing her good Dame does not exorcise memories. Neither does reciting a litany of loving supplications unless it ends in a statement of separateness. A passage of sixteen lines includes all three attempts:

> Now it is Friday's noon
> and I would still curse
> you with my rhyming words
> and bring you flapping back, old love,
> old circus knitting, god-in-her-moon,
> all fairest in my lang syne verse,
> the gauzy bride among the children,
> that fancy among the absurd
> and awkward, that horn for hounds
> that skipper homeward, that museum
> keeper of stiff starfish, that blaze
> within the pilgrim woman,
> a clown mender, a dove's
> cheek among the stones,

> my Lady of my first words,
> this is the division of ways.

Though emotional conflicts persist in this relationship—cursing and loving are still possible choices—the speaker is able to verbalize some sense of independence, saying to her good Dame, to the Lady of her first words, "this is the division of ways."

In "The Division of Parts" Sexton chooses not to be emotionally beguiled by the "brave ghost" of her mother, that "sweet witch" and "worried guide" to paradise. The poet makes an intellectual commitment, however, to a "love as reasonable / as Latin, as solid as earthenware: / an equilibrium / I never knew." Precise lines like these speak well for Sexton's early writing. The reader profits by not dismissing them when, as in this instance, the choice lines are surrounded by less propitious ones:

> Sweet witch, you are my worried guide.
> Such dangerous angels walk through Lent.
> Their walls creak *Anne! Convert! Convert!*
> My desk moves. Its cave murmurs Boo
> and I am taken and beguiled.
>
> Or wrong. For all the way I've come
> I'll have to go again. Instead, I must convert
> to love as reasonable
> as Latin, as solid as earthenware:
> an equilibrium
> I never knew. And Lent will keep its hurt
> for someone else. Christ knows enough
> staunch guys have hitched on him in trouble,
> thinking his sticks were badges to wear.

In this passage are examples of what I find weakest in Sexton's early poetry. Reading this, I am distracted enough by inadequate referents to question: Do angels' walls creak? Frequent shifts in vantage point (from you/witch/guide/angel to walls, desk, I, Lent, Christ, some other guys) weaken the passage, as do shifts occurring with changeable and sometimes pretentious vocabulary (from sweet witch, worried guide, and dangerous angels to a cave that murmurs boo and a Christ who knows enough staunch guys).

The poet's pledge to do what she "must" is easier spoken than fulfilled. Other poems show her continued striving for the equilibrium that she never knew in daughterhood. "After the sweet promise" comes a new shock that the poet sketches in "The Operation" (*All My Pretty Ones*).

> After the sweet promise,
> the summer's mild retreat
> from mother's cancer, the winter months of her death,
> I . . .
>
>   . . . .
>
> hear the almost mighty doctor over me equate
> my ills with hers
> and decide to operate.

The doctor's equation gets internalized by the poet as, "I, too, have cancer; I, too, will bear the lie of all who have loved, 'No reason to be afraid'; I, too, will die of the affliction." Yet this poem, for all its subjectivity, succeeds as dramatic monologue. In the immediacy of this situation, "No reason to be afraid" conjures every possible reason, and Sexton's particulars evoke in the reader memories or fears of similar experiences. Now the involved reader becomes a participant, plunging when the speaker being anesthetized plunges down the backstair "calling *mother* at the dying door"; reviving when she comes out thick with shock calling "mother to help myself"; and sharing the wonder when she finds herself alive "recalling mother, the sound of her / good morning, the odor of orange and jam."

In "The Operation" can be noticed a mellowing in the speaker's tone when she refers to her mother as "Always my most gentle house before that embryo / of evil [cancer] spread in her shelter and she grew frail." In this poem Sexton voices no recriminations against her mother or herself. Subsequently, the poet develops the ability to remember or to reconstruct loving moments with her mother, recording for instance, in "Three Green Windows" (*Live or Die*) that "She will tell me a story and keep me asleep / against her plump and fruity skin." Even a scene of psychic violence narrated in "Christmas Eve" (*Live or Die*)—when the speaker admits: "I thought of your body / as one thinks of murder"—is ameliorated by other memories and ends with another kind of confession that indicates a growing understanding of her mother:

> Then I said Mary—
> Mary, Mary, forgive me
> and then I touched a present for the child,
> the last I bred before your death;

> and then I touched my breast
> and then I touched the floor
> and then my breast again as if,
> somehow, it were one of yours.

This yielding of Anne Sexton is not to her mother's demands or to whatever is symbolized by her mother's portrait presiding over the family reunion but to her own inner being "that does not lie."

The poet shows some growth in personal relationship between her salutation, "Mother, / strange goddess face," and her valediction, "Mother, dear dead human," in her poem "Dreaming the Breasts" (*The Book of Folly*). In this poem Sexton fills in some ellipses concerning her daughterhood by regressing in imagination to the oral stage, and she does the same thing more successfully in "Food" (*45 Mercy Street*). The first of these paired poems begins with self-accusation: "Mother . . . I ate you up. / All my need took / you down like a meal." Then the central drama follows:

> In the end they cut off your breasts
> and milk poured from them
> into the surgeon's hand
> and he embraced them.
> I took them from him
> and planted them.

But the drama is upstaged by the final strophe's awkward bid for attention. Let me make myself clear: I take no exception to the images of "breasts hanging like two bats / and then darting at me," of breasts beating "like the sea in me now," or of breasts like "great bells." What I object to is a final strophe that cancels the inner consistency of dreamstage effects, a statement not paradoxical but contradictory:

> I have put a padlock
> on you, Mother, dear dead human,
> so that your great bells
> those dear white ponies,
> can go galloping, galloping,
> wherever you are.

The second poem on the subject of ungratified oral needs, "Food," is more successful than the first because it operates simultaneously at two levels, expressing hunger in terms of adult needs as well as infantile demands. The speaker, whether infant or adult, not only lists her wants but also catalogues a description of them: "mother's milk, / that good sour soup," breasts with "nipples like shy strawberries," a mouth that kisses, and arms that rock. In this second poem the self-accusation of the first is replaced by anger outwardly directed, in a voice neither squalling nor whimpering:

> I am hungry and you give me
> a dictionary to decipher.
> I am a baby all wrapped up in its red howl
> and you pour salt into my mouth.
> Your nipples are stitched up like sutures
> and although I suck
> I suck air
> and even the big fat sugar moves away.
> Tell me! Tell me! Why is it?
> I need food
> and you walk away reading the paper.

Here the speaker makes a declaration of human rights rather than an apology for helplessness.

Sexton the poet regresses in imagination to the anal stage in "The Hoarder" (*The Book of Folly*). Going through layers and layers of memories, digging and digging into the subconscious, she gets back to diaper days

> and the dirt thereof and my
> mother hating me for it and me
> loving me for it but the hate
> won didn't it yes the distaste
> won the disgust won and because
> of this I am a hoarder of words
> I hold them in though they are
> dung oh God I am a digger
> I am not an idler
> am I?

Reading this unpunctuated poem with even the slightest pause at the end of each short line suggests a halting question. The poem's epigraph from Ecclesiasticus, "An idler is like a lump of dung; whoever picks it up shakes it off his hand," enlarges the plea voiced in the last few lines—that the daughter not be considered an idler, a lump of dung, a person to be shaken off. It appears that, even after a dozen years of digging and writing, Sexton has not achieved the equilibrium in daughterhood that she desires.

If Sexton is a "hoarder of words," yet another explanation can be found in her writing on mother-daughter relationships, in "Dancing the Jig," one of the short stories at the end of *The Book of Folly*. Sexton illustrates with such emotional intensity her mother's "talking, talking" that one paragraph after another qualifies as a prose poem. Here are some of the lines describing a dinner table scene:

> I am beginning to watch Mother and watch her words coming out. I am trying to answer but I must be very careful with this meat in my mouth. Now I am talking. I am trying to change the subject; trying to keep control. . . .
>
>   . . . . Mother is talking. I am starting to talk myself. The words are running out of my mouth and she is catching them and hurling them back at me. My eyes are beginning to smart, the candlelight hurts. It is starting now—I can feel it begin and I can't help myself. I am trying to chew the meat and the words get mixed up together. . . . Mother is talking. I am talking. My arms move like a shuttle. My lips move on words and meat. I can't control anything. (Pp. 69–70)

If one technique can be ascribed to Sexton's work, it is this: *trying to change the subject in order to keep control*, not to gain control of others as much as to keep control of the unruly self. Many artists make it their life work visually to change the subject—shaping through exaggeration and distortion, eliminating distracting lines, coloring with a new palette, achieving new textures with new materials or the stretching of old ones beyond their previous dimensions. Sexton, the artist-poet, tries verbally to change the subject—to change the speaker of the poem and the spoken word—in order to control the socially unacceptable jabbering, crying, or "dancing the jig" that jolt her from her unconscious.

In one of her late poems, "The Death Baby" (*The Death Notebooks*), the poet makes the imaginative leap from "recalling" her infancy to "remembering" the nightly death dreams her sister had when she, Anne, was born. "Remembering" when someone put her in the refrigerator and she turned "as hard as a Popsicle," here is Sexton at her imaginative best:

> I remember the stink of the liverwurst.
> How I was put on a platter and laid

between the mayonnaise and the bacon.
The rhythm of the refrigerator
had been disturbed.
The milk bottle hissed like a snake.
The tomatoes vomited up their stomachs.
The caviar turned to lava.
The pimentos kissed like cupids.
I moved like a lobster,
slower and slower.
The air was tiny.
The air would not do.

The rhythm of family life has been disturbed by the display of a new baby, and only the death of the baby will be retribution for its birth.

The second of her sister's repeated dreams—imagistically very different but symbolically very close—is that of a death bone laid out for a dogs' party, lapped, chewed, and finally devoured. In both instances the principal figure accepts the laying out and the violence done to her while she is still alive. In "The Death Baby" Sexton's principal motif of the sky blue ice baby with tears like glass beads is carried through successive images of glass to ice, crystal to rock, and rocking to death. Single words, inconspicuous in themselves, help build to the climax: rock, weeks, hook, crack, stick, take, back, talk, think, break. The poet progresses from imagining her death in infancy, to recalling her mother's death, to speculating about her own death in adulthood. Again the daughter feels guilty for not having held in her arms her dying mother whose "rocking horse was pain." Even though Sexton eventually finds "Death [lying] in my arms like a cherub," the poem in its entirety indicates that the poet never completely resolves the conflicts regarding her own daughterhood.

The Poet's Relationships with Her Daughters

Verses can be quoted from almost any of Sexton's books to support the charge that she perpetuates the stereotype "like mother, like daughter." Certainly she struggles with the idea. An early poem called "Housewife" (All My Pretty Ones) concludes epigrammatically: "A woman is her mother. / That's the main thing." A dozen years later, in "Hurry Up Please It's Time" (The Death Notebooks), her inference is about the same, though stated conversely: "The trouble with being a woman, Skeezix, / is being a little girl in the first place. / Not all the books in the world will change that."

Yet Sexton's lyrics over the years want to deny any such categorical statements. Even in "The Double Image," that early poem so full of guilt and self-accusations, the poet makes a distinction between her behavior and that of her daughter. She says, "I lived like an angry guest [in my mother's house]," and later gives a contrasting description of her daughter's arrival and loving welcome.

> You came like an awkward guest
> that first time, all wrapped and moist
> and strange at my heavy breast.
> I needed you. I didn't want a boy,
> only a girl, a small milky mouse
> of a girl, already loved, already loud in the house
> of herself. We named you Joy.

Even while the poet confesses in "The Double Image" details of the time "I did not love myself," she has hope for the baby daughter who "wears her face" and counsels, "Today, my small child, Joyce, / love your self's self where it lives." In another lyric, "The Fortress" (*All My Pretty Ones*), a similar distinction is made. The woman taking a nap with her little Linda is not a Mary Gray reproving her daughter, nor is Linda another Anne feeling chastised and guilty. The poet, promising her daughter little, gives her the best of her world—the images she knows, a laugh, a touch, and love.

Another example of Anne Sexton's growing maturity in relation to her daughters can be found in her rendition of the "Ninth Psalm" (*The Death Notebooks*—ED. "Tenth Psalm" in *CP*). Here are four verses that can stand alone, or together, and contribute to an understanding of the poet's progress:

> For as the baby springs out like a starfish into her million light
> years Anne sees that she must climb her own mountain.
>
> . . . .
>
> For as her child grows Anne grows and there is salt and canta-
> loupe and molasses for all.
>
> . . . .
>
> For I am placing fist over fist on rock and plunging into the
> altitude of words. The silence of words.
>
> . . . .

For that daughter must build her own city and fill it with her
own oranges, her own words.

The increasing surety of maternal love and familial love expressed
in poems dedicated to her daughters helps account for Anne Sexton's
gradual yielding to herself—the self she previously could not love.
Simultaneously, the poet shows a greater trust in her rhythmic lines
and her images, allowing them to carry emotions without invoking or
imposing the ordering principle of rhyme. Two important dedicatory
poems are the much anthologized "Little Girl, My String Bean, My
Lovely Woman" (*Live or Die*) for Linda and the worthy "A Little
Uncomplicated Hymn" (*Live or Die*) for Joyce.

The reader introduced to Anne Sexton by "Little Girl, My String
Bean, My Lovely Woman" would not guess at the anger and guilt
feelings the poet deals with elsewhere. Speaking in this poem of womanhood, Sexton does say, "I remember that I heard nothing myself,"
but this contributes to making other remarks more poignant, especially
those about *forming* her daughter ("there would have been such ripening within: / your embryo, / the seed taking on its own") and *informing* her Linda in life. Here the poet reassures herself that she has
prepared her daughter for the physical and emotional changes of young
adulthood *before* the young men come to Linda at her high noon:
"But before they enter / I will have said, *Your bones are lovely,* / and
before their strange hands / there was always this hand that formed."

"Little Girl, My String Bean, My Lovely Woman," after the introductory flat statement, "My daughter, at eleven / (almost twelve),
is like a garden," continues with a hundred lines of exclamation. It
carries a sense of jubilation even in, especially in, the mother's words
of advice, "Oh, darling, let your body in, / let it tie you in, / in comfort." Linda's sexual budding reminds her mother of "mushroom-
s / and garlic buds all engorged"; the orchard next door, where the
berries are done and the apples are beginning to swell; an acre of yellow
beans, "too many to eat." Yes, Linda is like a garden, and her mother
is a tree standing by, observant and approving. "I'm here, that somebody else, / an old tree in the background."

Sexton's companion piece to her second daughter, Joyce, is "A
Little Uncomplicated Hymn." In this, the poet regrets that there is for
Joy, even for her asking, no "hymn without guilt"—other than her
name. There *was* such a song, the poet says, and she rehearses lines
for Joy's knee bones, her ribs, her "twenty grubby fingers," and for
the rage of her 104° fever. There *was* a song for her flight from a tree

and for the humpty-dumpty girl's fall, but now the poet has only words, "words that dog my heels, / words for sale you might say." Yet the words soar like a love song, in a self-fulfilling prophecy.

> You will jump to it someday
> as you will jump out of the pitch of this house.
> It will be a holiday, a parade, a fiesta!
> Then you'll fly.
> You'll really fly.
> After that you'll quite simply, quite calmly
> make your own stones, your own floor plan,
> your own sound.

Sexton's attempt at hymning, even though "complicated" by regrets, is here not bogged down by the breast-beating and remorse evident in some of her early writing.

This poem for Joyce follows immediately the one for Linda in Sexton's chronologically arranged book *Live or Die*. Both poems contain a symbol of strength and stability—a good stone. In the piece for Linda the final figure is this:

> Darling,
> stand still at your door,
> sure of yourself, a white stone, a good stone—
> as exceptional as laughter
> you will strike fire,
> that new thing!

In the hymn for Joy—less exclamatory, wanting to be uncomplicated—there is assurance for the poet's younger daughter: "you'll quite simply, quite calmly / make your own stones, your own floor plan, / your own sound."

Another poem of initiation comes six years later, this addressed to the eighteen-year-old Linda. Entitled "Mother and Daughter" (*The Book of Folly*), it carries Sexton's fear concerning the inevitable separation, "the river between us . . . [my] shroud . . . death / drooling at these gray lips," a fear that the incantation "Question you about this" does not remove. The triumphant notes of the earlier pieces for her daughters are missing. Only a pedal point continues: explicitly, "Linda, you are leaving / your old body now," and implicitly, "Linda, you are leaving me."

In "Mother and Daughter" the speaker, after comparing Linda's recent growth to the metamorphosis of a butterfly, laments that "I am motherwarm and used, / just as your childhood is used." Yet she realizes that her questions are equally as inappropriate to her daughter's thinking as Linda's answers in body language ("calisthenics, / that womanly semaphore") are to hers. In the middle part Sexton declaims, without even expecting a response:

> Question you about this
> and you'll not know the answer—
> the muzzle at the mouth,
> the hopeful tent of oxygen,
> the tubes, the pathways,
> the war and the war's vomit.

The war is not a military foray but a continuous battle for life, against death. "The muzzle at the mouth" may represent violence from without or suicidal urgings from within; whichever, Linda seems to be too young to care, too unconcerned to suppose it has anything to do with her present activities. In the rhetoric of a propagandist, the mother urges her to "Keep on, keep on, keep on" with the battle, to engage in the thick of it, even to the point of "carrying, my Linda, blood to / the bloodletter." The implication here is that the daughter does not understand the range or intensity of warfare in her mother's life, so she cannot appreciate the victories that have accrued "booty" and "spoils." But, even if Linda is not interested in heroics now, she may sometime in the future remember her mother's urgings.

In the third and final part of "Mother and Daughter," the poet admits that she is fearful of the very steps she had previously encouraged in her daughter. The concept that her "daughter must build her own city and fill it with her own oranges, her own words," now takes shape as, "you will see my death / drooling at these gray lips / while you, my burglar, will eat / fruit and pass the time of day."

Fears that were voiced by the poet long years before take on more substance during Anne Sexton's middle years. By the time she is in her forties and Linda is eighteen, there seems to be biological reason for including in her "Mother & Co." not only the assets of booty and spoils but also the deficits of "ailments." In the posthumously published *45 Mercy Street* are two poems relating to this possibility. In "The Child Bearers" the poet speaks of a daughter "pushed into gnawing a stilbestrol cancer / I passed on like hemophilia." Two pages later is "The Risk," a poem whose structure—it may be all subject or all predicate complement—emphasizes the circularity in life that the poet finds distressing. This circularity seems to corroborate for the poet her early fears of "passing on doom" to her daughters. Here is the catalogue of "The Risk" in its entirety:

> When a daughter tries suicide
> and the chimney falls down like a drunk
> and the dog chews her tail off
> and the kitchen blows up its shiny kettle
> and the vacuum cleaner swallows its bag
> and the toilet washes itself in tears
> and the bathroom scales weigh in the ghost
> of the grandmother and the windows,
> those sky pieces, ride out like boats
> and the grass rolls down the driveway
> and the mother lies down on her marriage bed
> and eats up her heart like two eggs.

In "The Risk" the speaker exaggerates ordinary functions (the toilet's flushing) and everyday mishaps (the vacuum cleaner's not working, the kitchen kettle's exploding), showing how out of proportion they get to be, how monumental, when one is under duress. The little things are listed in the same manner as the traumatic event that heads her list, "When a daughter tries suicide." This time the whole house is disturbed, as the refrigerator's rhythm was disturbed when the "death baby" was laid in it. Everything and everyone is active—even the grandmother's ghost is weighed in the balance—except for the mother, laid out on her marriage bed, eating her heart away. Functioning in one's daily life is a risk, Sexton indicates, but so is lying down; either way, heartaches are inevitable. The poet's risk taking should not be overlooked, especially when the poetry seems most subjective.

The Poet's Growing Concern with Integration in Personae

The study of mother-daughter relationships in the poetry of Anne Sexton indicates a partial resolution of conflicts with her mother and considerable success in establishing a joyous relationship with her daughters. Furthermore, the poet in the process of writing, at any rate

in the poems that record her discoveries, achieves a new self-awareness
that encourages a lighthearted self-acceptance. Often quoted from Sexton's Pulitzer prize-winning volume, *Live or Die*, are the lines, "I say
Live, Live because of the sun, / the dream, the excitable gift" ("Live").
What is "the excitable gift"? Neither her private writing nor her public
reading, neither her publishing nor the popular acclaim of her books.
"The excitable gift" is that she—Anne—is lovable. Moreover, she is
loved by "a husband straight as a redwood" and "two daughters, two
sea urchins, / picking roses off my hackles." The family "trust my
incalculable city, / my corruptible bed" and—almost as important to
the poet—understand her moods and adapt to them.

> If I'm on fire they dance around it
> and cook marshmallows.
> And if I'm ice
> they simply skate on me
> in little ballet costumes.
>   . . . .
> Even crazy, I'm as nice
> as a chocolate bar.

Largely through the love of her husband and daughters, Anne Sexton
learns to love herself.

I realize that for some readers there is a difficulty if much of
Sexton's writing is interpreted as affirming life when her final unwritten
act was to deny life; or if Sexton's writing is credited with working
through negative feelings of her own daughterhood and conveying
positive attitudes to her daughters when ultimately, though nonver-
bally, she denied them her very presence. What I say here in response
is simply that mother-daughter relationships were not the sole cause
of Anne Sexton's suffering, and suicide was not the sole result of her
suffering. What I understand as the definitive statement concerning
Sexton's career, and what justifies my distinguishing between the poet
and her personae, can be found in an interview in which Anne Sexton
says, "To really get at the truth of something is the poem, not the
poet. . . . The poem counts for more than your life."[2] Therefore, readers interested in the complexities and stresses of Anne Sexton's life
should consult the body of her work even when they refer to biographical material and recently published letters.[3]

Sexton's poems repeatedly rejoice in "the sun, the dream, the
excitable gift." Even in the sometimes morbid "Hurry Up Please It's

Time," the yellow sun figures as a "honeysuckle mama [pouring] your blonde on me!" The poet's self-image is that of a "fortunate lady" who is "clothed in gold air," and the woman emerging is glad.

> I've come a long way to peel off my clothes
> and lay me down in the grass.
> Once only my palms showed.
> Once I hung around in my woolly tank suit,
> drying my hair in those little meatball curls.
> Now I am clothed in gold air with
> one dozen halos glistening on my skin.
> I am a fortunate lady.
> I've gotten out of my pouch
> and my teeth are glad
> and my heart, that witness,
> beats well at the thought.
>
> Oh body, be glad.
> You are good goods.

Another poem in which Anne Sexton shows loving acceptance of herself as woman and mother is "In Celebration of My Uterus" (*Love Poems*). Although the beginning seems to allow female sexuality and responsiveness only to the physiologically complete, uncut person, the poem goes beyond that. Sexton develops it into a love poem to womanhood. Even before embarking on a travelogue that she introduces with what "Many women are singing together," she has arrived at the centrality that prompts her own singing:

> Sweet weight,
> in celebration of the woman I am
> and the soul of the woman I am
> and of the central creature and its delight
> I sing for you. I dare to live.

Confirmed in her personal centering, the poet dares to universalize her feelings. She will extol science—"study the cardiovascular tissue, . . . examine the angular distance of meteors, . . . suck on the stems of flowers" if that is her part. She will embrace the humanities—"drum for the nineteen-year-olds, . . . carry bowls for the offering" if that is her part. She will contribute to the mythic—"make certain tribal figures" (perhaps physically, certainly metaphorically).

In poems like these three, "Live," "In Celebration of My Uterus," and "Hurry Up Please It's Time," Anne Sexton shows a growing concern for integration rather than division of parts. She develops the earlier negative of herself as the double image of her mother, as a woman caught in the other's life portrait, to a fuller image of herself as a woman participating in any number of chosen roles. In her personae she grows beyond the stage of demanding, "I want mother's milk" to that of celebrating, "let me sing / for the supper, / for the kissing, / for the correct / yes." She advances from "anointing myself daily / with my little poisons" to being "clothed in gold air with / one dozen halos glistening on my skin." Her poems record a woman's progress from a time when she gathered "guilt like a young intern / his symptoms, his certain evidence" to a new day when she realizes, "Each cell has a life. / There is enough here to please a nation." Anne Sexton, from her early poems to her late ones, does "come a long way" in understanding daughterhood and motherhood and in taking delight in a multiplicity of roles that celebrate womanhood and the woman she is.

NOTES

1. All of Anne Sexton's books of poetry have been published in the United States by Houghton Mifflin Co., Boston. In chronological order the volumes cited in this essay are as follows: *To Bedlam and Part Way Back* (1960), *All My Pretty Ones* (1962), *Live or Die* (1966), *Love Poems* (1969), *The Book of Folly* (1972), *The Death Notebooks* (1974), and *45 Mercy Street* (1976).

2. Patricia Marx, "Interview with Anne Sexton," *Hudson Review* 18 (Winter 1965–66): 563.

3. *Anne Sexton: A Self-Portrait in Letters*, ed. Linda Gray Sexton and Lois Ames (Boston: Houghton Mifflin Co., 1977).

STEPHANIE DEMETRAKOPOULOS

Goddess Manifestations as Stages in Feminine Metaphysics in the Poetry and Life of Anne Sexton

Throughout her poetry Anne Sexton's urge toward suicide is apparent, particularly in her first book and again in her last two. But her mid-career poetry mutes this dark tone, presenting rather an affirmation of life that is rooted in matrilineal or goddess values. I will examine in this essay her poems about her daughters and how she finds stability and worth in her relationship to them. When her daughters grow up, her death urge reemerges in grotesquely gigantic forms as Sexton attempts to find herself within a cosmos that she perceives then as managed by an alienating, brutal masculine godhead.

Women can realize an extended and broadly based metaphysical connection through the growth and unfolding of their children, especially daughters. For Anne Sexton maternity was her most positive experience of cosmic patterns as we apprehend them through the body. Her loss of the mother role was apparently a loss of connection to the body of her family, which for her was a link to cosmic and spiritual reality.

Any woman living in our Judeo-Christian, Western culture becomes at times overwhelmed with masculine values, especially as embodied in the official religions. In these contexts we lose a sense of significance, of selfhood. Perhaps Sexton, Plath, and Woolf are in some way symbolic of a larger casualty: women who embrace masculine values without a sufficient sense of feminine roots to keep their balance.[1] At the end of this essay, I will look briefly at Sexton's demise in the face of masculine godhead.

But the bulk of my study will examine Sexton's naming of positive feminine values. Her lifework was a heroic struggle to claim and redeem things previously held not worthy of name. Her earliest reviewers say, for instance, that her "diction is not poetical"—and their examples are of such terms as *aprons* and other artifacts of women's culture. But she went on naming as she saw things. I see this essay as a furthering of her task of defining the significance of the feminine self, a bringing to collective consciousness of both strong, positive feminine values and some especially powerful feminine sources of despair.

The Demeter-Kore Archetype

I will refer often in this study to a myth that strongly underlies the development of feminine consciousness in women, the Demeter-Kore configuration, especially as it was institutionalized in the religious ceremonies of the Eleusinian Mysteries, the mother-daughter religion that the classicist C. Kerényi calls the archetype of feminine destiny.[2] In connecting Sexton's matrilineal experiences to these ancient patterns, I establish a depth of time, a universality for the roots of feminine being she expresses. The term *Demeter-Kore* can be roughly interpreted as meaning mother-daughter; it refers to Demeter and her daughter Persephone, who was stolen from her mother by the underworld god Hades. Since Demeter is the goddess of grain and presides over bountiful harvest, her grieving for the loss of her daughter brings winter and desolation to the earth so that Zeus forces Hades to release Persephone back to her mother for part of each year. This is the mythological account of the seasons. It is a rich myth, and its intricacy and many versions are brilliantly treated by Jean Bolen in *Goddesses in Everywoman*; Bolen also shows how it applies to women's psychology.[3]

C. G. Jung describes the archetype this way:

> Demeter and Kore, mother and daughter, extend the feminine consciousness both upwards and downwards. They add an "older and younger," "stronger and weaker," dimension to it and widen out the narrowly limited conscious mind bound in space and time, giving it intimations of a greater and more comprehensive personality which has a share in the eternal course of things ... Every mother contains her daughter in herself and every daughter her mother, so that every woman extends backwards into her mother and forwards into her daughter. This participation and intermingling give rise to that peculiar uncertainty as regards *time*.... The conscious experience of these ties produces the feeling that her life is spread out over generations—the first step towards the immediate experience and conviction of being outside time, which

brings with it a feeling of *immortality*. . . . This leads to a restoration
. . . of the lives of her ancestors, who now, through the bridge of the
momentary individual, pass down into the generations of the future. An
experience of this kind gives the individual a place and a meaning in the
life of the generations, so that all unnecessary obstacles are cleared out
of the way of the life-stream that is to flow through her. At the same
time the individual is rescued from her isolation and restored to wholeness. . . .

It is immediately clear to the psychologist what cathartic and at
the same time rejuvenating effects must flow from the Demeter cult into
the feminine psyche, and what a lack of psychic hygiene characterizes
our culture, which no longer knows the kind of wholesome experience
afforded by Eleusinian emotions.[4]

Sexton's major images in developing her themes are typical of
the Demeter-Kore archetype, which Neumann calls the fruit-mother
to flower-child/maiden transition in the matriarchate.[5] Neumann has
shown that "the woman, too has to 'kill the parents' by overthrowing
the tyranny of the parental archetypes."[6] Only by killing the First
Parents can a way be found out of the conflict into personal life. He
traces the symbolic killing of the World Parents as the way to escape
the biological and familial entrapment of the ego and individuality; he
then examines the conscious coming to terms with those forces. The
World Mother is a far more looming and sometimes sinister archetype
for a woman than for a man. Sexton seldom writes of her father, but
she is obsessed with her mother. The young woman's female ancestry,
her personal experience of the matriarchy, can threaten and kill her
individuation process. These older women can embody an oppressive,
entrapping insistence on the insignificance of womanhood and its en-
slavement to patriarchy—for example, mothers with little sense of self
project this feeling of worthlessness onto their daughters and at the
same time try to bind those daughters to themselves as psychic hand-
maidens. The second deathblow to feminine individuation can also
come through matriarchal alliances; this second face of psychic death
is entrapment in the mother role itself. Sexton escapes both fixations
in stasis. She seems to be moving outside and beyond the cyclicality
of life that is almost solely dominated psychically and mythologically
by such figures as Demeter. She becomes a Sophia, powerful with
wisdom and transcendence over the natural world.

This transformation is worked out explicitly in *The Death Notebooks*, in which Sexton faces away from her family and begins to gaze

into the metaphysical depths that she explores in her next book, *The Awful Rowing Toward God.* The latter volume, significantly, contains no daughter poems; the poet loses touch with her matrilineal roots and her own feminine wisdom of the earth and relatedness as she moves toward the stifling yet spacelike, purely abstract spirituality of a male god. She embraces scatological images of herself that she remembers as a girl from her mother's disgust over the female body. Perhaps, like Plath, she wrote herself into the hands of death, but her experiments with consciousness and death are different from Plath's. *45 Mercy Street* reveals how Sexton's quest for God differs radically from Plath's.

As Sexton's development portrays, the Demeter role is not a simple one-step process; the role constantly reinitiates a woman into increasingly more complex psychic realms of consciousness, gradually leading her out of the earlier stages of mothering that entail immersion in the biological sphere into more spiritual tasks and higher consciousness, until Demeter becomes Sophia-Isis.[7] As a woman weans herself from mothering, she begins to act out more autonomous roles such as the Athena or Artemis who both move freely within, plumbing psychic depths, and also becomes more active in the social sphere, taking on more roles in the community. In her first book of poetry, Sexton writes her way out of Bedlam and out of the negative, pathological Kore role she has played vis-à-vis the devouring face of the matriarchate as embodied in her mother; she writes herself into the center of her young daughters' existence. In her next books, when the children are young, she enacts the role of Hestia, the goddess of the hearth, and Demeter, the mother and nursemaid. As she gains this foothold in reality, she grows steadier, more sure of her self-worth, and she continues to stand strong throughout her daughters' childhoods. As if to allay her own troubled development as a girl child, she participates in their more normal development and assimilates their growing consciousness into her own.

Finally, in her last books Sexton turns her back on the positive Demeter/Sophia/Isis plateau of feminine wisdom and maturity and becomes entangled psychically with patriarchal figures. She is in fact bedeviled with these figures, and her attention to them is a cause of the psychic distress that led to her suicide. But her earlier poetry portrays the power and profundity of her daughters as a ground of imagery for her metaphysics. This theme changes significantly as her daughters grow into different stages. Thus her chronological treatment of this theme presents the varieties of fulfillment and ambiguity women experience as both mother and daughter. The central spiritual strength in her life comes from the Demeter-Kore archetype as activated in her experience as mother.

Escape from the First Devouring Face of the Matriarchate: Fixation in the Kore

To Bedlam and Part Way Back (1960) is concerned much more with Sexton's relationship with her own mother than with her daughters; yet as she comes to terms with her role as a daughter, she moves more easily into her role as a mother. Part 7 of "The Double Image" explains how her sense of failure as a daughter checks her from fully embracing motherhood; she says to her daughter Joy, "You call me *mother* and I remember my mother again, / somewhere in greater Boston, dying." This turning back toward her own mother rather than toward her daughters reflects her initial inability to find her own place within the matrilineal generations. Yet she realizes that her daughters help her grope toward discovering herself:

> I didn't want a boy,
> only a girl, a small milky mouse
> of a girl, already loved, already loud in the house
> of herself. We named you Joy.
> I, who was never quite sure
> about being a girl, needed another
> life, another image to remind me.
> And this was my worst guilt; you could not cure
> nor soothe it. I made you to find me.
> (*CP*, 41–42)[8]

Her dis-ease in her own identity as a woman makes her unable to relate easily and naturally with her daughter. Although these are her last words in this book to her daughter, in the same poem a permanent relationship is nevertheless finally solidified: "For the last time I unpack / your things. We touch from habit. / The first visit you asked my name. / Now you stay for good" (*CP*, 41).

Time itself and a determined, deliberate immersion in her own life assuage the guilt that tied her to her mother. Along with beginning anew with her own daughter is a catharsis, one she will carry of pain and grief, and an acknowledgment of loving memories of her mother, as she accepts the mother role as her own.

First-Stage Demeter as Initial Adulthood

The arrangement of the sections of *All My Pretty Ones* (1962) reflects Sexton's adventures in the world of relatedness as opposed to the isolation of the insane in *Bedlam*. Her choice of "The Fortress," the single poem for section 3, the heart of her five-section book, is especially significant. Her relationship with her daughter stands at the core of her new experiences in life. The centrality in her life of that nestlike bed she shares with Linda reminds me of the bed in which John Donne celebrates the amorcentricity of the universe, as his beloved and he provide the center around which all else revolves. The solidity of her relationship with the child is poignantly emphasized:

> I press down my index finger—
> half in jest, half in dread—
> on the brown mole
> under your left eye, inherited
> from my right cheek: a spot of danger
> where a bewitched worm ate its way through our soul
> in search of beauty. . . .
>
> (CP, 66)

She looks in her daughter's face as in a mirror, her mole on the right cheek, reflected on the left side of Linda's face. The mole represents their shared soul and is in a way the transmission of original sin in the form of mutability. Muted anguish, too, resonates in the mother's knowledge that the child inherits from her a fallen life and all the pain that will grow out of that "spot of danger." The worm perhaps alludes to the apple of Eve, an apple passed on from mother to daughter in the form of their special beauty, which time will eat up.

The term *fortress* works two ways in this poem. First, the mother and daughter are in a fortress, taking refuge against the storm raging both outside and inside. Second, Anne recognizes that she is a fortress to the child, that her larger body gives the child a sense of protection, of comfort, that is (from the adult's perspective) all too fragile. Her child in bed with its mother experiences "the Feminine as the giver of shelter and protection."[9] Neumann remarks that this Great Mother is often represented as rounded and juglike, as a giver of fertility and riches, of abundance and stability; the poet evokes this cornucopian aspect of motherhood, describing the scene in vegetable and fruit terms (broccoli, beet-red, bittersweet, orange).

But the jarring complication that Sexton adds to this image contradicts the essence of the primordial Great Mother. Neumann says that such symbolic female forms are usually represented without mouths and often without eyes, as they are depersonalized, transpersonal forces.[10] Sexton insists that we be aware of her sense of hypocrisy in representing goodness and warmth and absolute safety to her child. She sees the falseness of all her daughter feels in the security of her mother as fortress: "Darling, life is not in my hands; / life with its terrible changes / will take you, bombs or glands. . . . I cannot promise very much. / I give you the images I know. . . . We laugh and we touch. / I promise you love. Time will not take away that" (CP, 67–68). And she does give her a special kind of love within the poem, a very personal love, by teaching the child to see with the poet's eye:

> Lie still with me and watch.
> A pheasant moves
> by like a seal, pulled through the mulch
> by his thick white collar. He's on show
> like a clown. He drags a beige feather that he removed,
> one time, from an old lady's hat.
>
> (CP, 67–68)

The emphasis on seeing and saying denies the depersonalization of the mother. Sexton moves back and forth from the child's sense of her as mother to her sense of herself as mother. And the fortress of motherhood is a comfort to her, too. She wishes she could give forever in this inarticulate, warm, natural way. This sort of nurturing is a form of comfort to all women as they enact the maternal protectress.[11]

In All My Pretty Ones, then, Sexton establishes a concrete knowledge of her own motherhood and a comprehension of the love and need her daughter has for her. She does evoke the memory of her own mother once, musing on the time they trimmed the trees. But it is a memory of good connections, reminiscent of the figures of Demeter and Kore/Persephone—two women, mother and daughter, shaping nature's fertility. In "The Fortress" Sexton herself becomes a first-stage Demeter figure, giving her daughter the special fruits of her own experience.[12]

This poem is a complex view of the responsibilities and rewards of mothering a small child, so unquestioningly dependent on its mother. What is especially striking is that Sexton has so consciously come to terms with the ambivalence of what she must do. She must adopt the stable and serene persona that her daughter needs while grieving internally and unobtrusively that she must ultimately give that child over into the cruel hands of fortune.

Most important, the poem celebrates in an oblique way the coming of age of a woman as mother. It illustrates the first and simple level of being a mother, a level that requires an unconscious, instinctual kind of love for the small animal the child still is at that age. It is important to see that the invulnerable resource of strength this role provides for the child gives strength to the mother herself as she reenters life in this volume. She is too self-aware not to see the ambiguity and irony of this role, but these tensions are kept within so as to shelter the child even from this uneasiness in the mother. The Demeter role inevitably becomes more complex as the child develops; the love grows complicated, thorny, and fearful as the daughter reaches adolescence.

Acceptance of Sexuality and Consciousness in the Kore/Daughters: The Assimilation of Venus to Demeter-Kore

In *Live or Die* (1966) the center of the earlier *All My Pretty Ones*, the fortress of early motherhood—that safe and known role of nurturing young children—crumbles, its surety dissolved both by her daughters' growing awareness and by her own troubled and expanding consciousness. *Live or Die* deals with the cycle of falling apart, as the consolidated psyche, having rested on the plateau described in the center of *All My Pretty Ones*, begins to stir again, seeking new levels and new experiences for the next cycle of expanding awareness. This is a typical pattern, one that is not neurotic but part of growth:

> There is a meeting point between containment and liberation and we can find it in the rites of initiation [that] can make it possible for individuals, or whole groups of people to unite the opposing forces within themselves and achieve an equilibrium in their lives. . . . Initiation [growth] is, essentially, a process that begins with a rite of submission, followed by a period of containment, and then by a further rite of liberation.[13]

For a woman the rites of initiation often have to do with unfolding roles of motherhood as the child's developing self demands new responses. *Bedlam* is a rite of submission, an attempt to contain and understand the forces of matriarchy from which she issued. *All My Pretty Ones* explores a period of containment, of newly won maturity, but ends with a sense of breaking up that signals the beginning of a new cycle.

In *Live or Die* there is a sense of moral disease and confusion that is healed in and by her daughter poems much as "The Fortress" holds together *All My Pretty Ones.* The last one-third of the poems in *Live or Die* contains all four of her daughter poems; these appear as oases of balance and stability with the mother reaching out into life, relating and nurturing. The other poems are primarily regressive and suicidal (except for one, "The Wedding Night," which, however, depicts a brutal deflowering). "The Addict" perhaps best distills a desire for the unconscious, painless euphoria of sedatives, an escape from the burgeoning of everyday reality. Her motherhood seems to pull her back into life, to face squarely its ongoing traumas.

One daughter poem, "A Little Uncomplicated Hymn" (dedicated to Joy), delineates the poet's guilt over earlier abdication of motherhood during her madness:

> In the naming of you I named
> all things you are . . .
> except the ditch
> where I left you once,
> like an old root that wouldn't take hold,
> that ditch where I left you
> while I sailed off in madness
>
> . . . .
> you were mine
> and I lent you out.
> I look for uncomplicated hymns
> but love has none.
>
> (*CP,* 150–52)

She projects onto the daughter's activities a "need not to grow" that reflects the mother perhaps as much as the child:

> little fetus, little snail
> carrying a rage, a leftover rage
> I cannot undo.

The fetal, curling up imagery suggests her desire for the womblike Ouroboros, the unconscious, rather than ever new and expanding reality. This helpless passivity must be overcome; her daughter's and her own locked-in psyche cohere into a refusal to touch or be touched— a myopic vision of life expanded in "Wanting to Die," in which she maintains that suicide is not a question of "why" but "how." How much of the pain over her daughter's refusal to grow is really her own pain? But "A Little Uncomplicated Hymn" ends in hope that her daughter will transcend, will "fly" above all the past, and shape her own life:

> After that you'll, quite simply, quite calmly
> make your own stones, your own floor plan,
> your own sound.
>
> (*CP*, 152)

The stone as self is a universal symbol of the strength and centrality of the ego. This hope for her children will blossom finally into hope for herself; and the psychic strength will carry over into her own life, buttressed by the maternal responsibilities she assumes and embraces.

In "The Fortress" and again in "A Little Uncomplicated Hymn," Sexton names through animal imagery the lower-level consciousness at which she sees her children:

> Joy, I call you
> and yet your eyes just here
> with their shades half-drawn over the gunsights,
> over your gigantic knowledge,
> over the little blue fish who dart back and forth. . . .
>
> (*CP*, 151)

She imagines her daughter gazing at her: "Or will your eyes lie in wait, / little field mice nestling on their paws?" ("Your Face on the Dog's Neck," *CP*, 154). The ego flickers out briefly at a world that it cannot yet understand; blessed still with an immersion in the fluid, easy world of childhood, like mice or fish, the children's minute identities gleam out briefly at the mother. In this image we see her understanding and compassion for their childish needs and dependencies. In a way, they are embodiments of the unconscious. Her tenderness and protectiveness will mother them forth to fuller identity, to help them be born into womanhood and adulthood. It seems that in facing this responsibility the poet can shoulder the burden of her own identity and growth. Through their juxtaposition to the other poems at the end of *Live or Die* and through their treatment of ideas troubling the poet herself, the love poems to her daughters become love poems to womanhood and to her new self.

In seeking to understand her daughters' worlds and feminine roles, Sexton learns to understand her own. The poems that best treat the poet's fear of sexuality and the metaphysical consciousness embodied in fuller sexuality are, respectively, "Little Girl, My String Bean, My Lovely Woman" and "Pain for a Daughter." In "Little Girl, My String Bean, My Lovely Woman," the Demeter-Kore relationship that provides the backdrop to "The Fortress" is again evoked through fruit and fertility allusions: "My daughter, at eleven / (almost twelve), is like a garden" (*CP*, 145). She sees her daughter under a "blueberry sky" and is reminded of "lemons as large as your desk-side globe," "market stalls of mushrooms," "garlic buds all engorged," "apples," and "yellow beans" (*CP*, 146). She describes the embryo of her daughter as fruit:

> if I could have seen through my magical transparent belly,
> there would have been such ripening within:
> your embryo,
> the seed taking on its own,
>
> . . . .
>
> the becoming—
> while it becomes!
>
> (*CP*, 147)

In the Aristotelian world of becoming and process, she and her daughter take their place. The fruit imagery that symbolizes the daughter's relationship to the mother foreshadows the natural womanhood into which the daughter will soon move into her own plenitudinous, fulsome transition "from maiden-flower to fruit-mother." The daughter is the mother's harvest and will bear fruit herself someday. The mother herself welcomes her new role of an aging Demeter as her daughter replaces her; she will now play a new role to her daughter, a role of stability: "I'm here, that somebody else, / an old tree in the background" (*CP*, 148). She's an old but steady tree.[14] The tree reflects a strength and permanence in nature that underlies its seasonal cyclicality. An old tree is stronger and withstands storms better; Demeter is always alive for her daughters to lean on.

Through embracing and celebrating her daughter's growth into sexuality, Sexton acknowledges her own developing womanhood, her own desire for fuller sexual consummation vividly treated in her next volume, *Love Poems* (1969). She recognizes her own sexuality and fertility, her own personal yet transpersonal eros, bursting out in her daughter's body. As she tries to move her daughter peacefully, without fear, into a new awareness, into womanhood with assurance, we gain insight into her own dilemmas as a girl:

> I hear
> as in a dream
> the conversation of the old wives
> speaking of *womanhood*.
> I remember that I heard nothing myself.
> I was alone.
> I waited like a target.
>
>   (*CP*, 146)

Considering her confusion about her own femininity and identity, her tenderness in this poem toward her daughter gains a lovely, almost heroic dimension. So many of her poems find her helpless, passive, facing mutilation; here, as she stands beside her daughter as mentor through the initiation rites, she perhaps mothers herself forth, too: "What I want to say, Linda, / is that women are born twice"; "What I want to say, Linda, / is that there is nothing in your body that lies" (*CP*, 147, 148). The poet herself is born again, too, into a new joy of motherhood, the giving of womanhood to daughters. There is no envy of the daughter's youth and beauty here, only joy and hope—an affirmation of the child's and poet's self in these puberty rites. The poet also celebrates her chthonic depths as an adult woman, noble and full in her ability to love, strong as an old tree, a force with which to be dealt.

The third to the last poem in *Live or Die*, "Pain for a Daughter," takes the mother as mentor to the threshold of the world that the daughter must enter alone. She observes her daughter's affinity for power as symbolized in horses; the horse suggests the powers of male sexuality, which Neumann says correspond to "the negative [and] masculine death principle as experienced by the matriarchate."[15] As she completes a series of feminine initiation rites, Psyche cuts the wool off the golden rams without being destroyed by their masculine force. When the daughter scours the boil of the horse, she, too, is ministering to and controlling a force that is yet too large for her, that lashes back with demoniac powers, mutilating her finally (the horse crushes her foot) as an initiation into the world of sexuality. She is playing with a sexual (erotic) and masculine principle that is yet beyond her:

> the swan-whipped thoroughbred
> that she tugs at and cajoles,
> thinking it will burn like a furnace
> under her small-hipped English seat.
>
> (CP, 164)

In the midst of the experiment with power and sexuality, the daughter is sundered from her mother by pain—a force that makes us each aware of our ultimate aloneness. The mother is alone, too, unable to nurture or even assist at this time:

> She bites on a towel, sucked in breath,
> sucked in and arched against the pain,
> her eyes glancing off me where
> I stand at the door, eyes locked
> on the ceiling, eyes of a stranger.
>
> (CP, 164)

Eye imagery often signifies transcendence; here both mother and child are blind with fear and blind to each other. Or perhaps they see too much to be able to look at each other. This emphasis on seeing and blindness permeates the whole poem and begins each stanza, almost liturgically emphasizing the visionary aspects of the poem: "Blind with love," "Blind with loss," "Blind with pain," and "Blind with fear." This is, of course, an Oedipal kind of blindness.

The mother and daughter share an epiphany that features the force that will finally sunder them: death. And death is understood in terms of birth, its pain, its irrevocability. Through birth we experience our inevitable death in the most direct, inarticulate, and natural way. We are made aware that our identities are caught in a cycle that will destroy us. Most terrible, in this poem the mother sees the impinging consciousness of death, the birth of death, in the child she bore. This consciousness, says Neumann, is an initiation into adulthood that is perhaps exclusively woman's:

> To experience maidenhood, womanhood, and
> nascent motherhood in one, and in this transformation

> to plumb the depths of her own existence: this is
> given only to the woman.[16]

Neumann also says that for a woman the birth of the daughter is a birth of the new self. In this poem the mother is driven into cognizance of even darker levels of consciousness and the courage requisite to face them; but perhaps by recognizing her daughter's new identity and perceptions, she, too, acquires new aspects of self.

Certainly the last poem in this volume, entitled "Live," answers finally the previous poem, "The Addict," which is about death through sedation. The major theme of "Live" is that the poet accepts joyously her role in her family, celebrating even the fertility of the dog. The daughter poems clustered at the end of the book resonate in the resolution of "Live" and force us to see the daughters (as in *All My Pretty Ones*) as life-giving forces. They are life-giving in that they demand a parental response and adaptation—perhaps children have more to do with moving parents along the path of adulthood, from one stage to another, than we suspect. Sexton's daughter poems seem also to be the most powerful and affirmative of all her poems, issuing from a depth of self that is universal and archetypal. Thus in this volume of poetry, she has affirmed her daughters' entry into pubescence and the force of sexuality with which they must now contend; she has also lived through with one of them the dawn of consciousness and consciousness of death, this latter through the Demeter-Kore paradox of birth as death and death as birth.

The Sacrifice and Outgrowing of the Demeter Role

Sexton's one daughter poem in *The Book of Folly* (1972) enacts the last phase of the maternal, which Harding says is both an "ordeal and deeper initiation" into selfhood. Harding discusses the "sacrifice of the son," which writers generally treat from the point of view of the (either male or female) child, "where the myth of his sacrifice refers to the need of each individual to sacrifice his own childishness and dependence."[17] Yet the mother, too, suffers a terrible ambivalence about weaning the child from her. There is the maternal in herself that craves fulfillment through the child; yet its dependency, softness, and clinging undermine her, and thus "in dark aspect she is fierce and terrible and will not tolerate the childish dependence of the child."[18] Harding points out that it is not truly maternal love that makes a mother hang on but rather her own selfness and selfishness; furthermore, society commends this self-indulgence, this possessiveness, as a virtue in the mother—the child is supposed to do the breaking away. Yet for her own psychological health, the mother also must break away.

This means a breaking out and away from a cyclical and generation-bound view of life into a transpersonal and far less sexually and relatedness-imbued role in life. And it means that, as far as her importance in the reproduction of her species is concerned, the woman must now accept that she is superfluous. Her death would be of negligible significance to the ongoing process of life itself. Death's chapped jaws draw nearer, perceptible now.

"Mother and Daughter" contains these ideas and more. Sexton experiences anger as well as a sense of poignancy about the now completely arrived womanhood of her daughter:

> Linda, you are leaving
> your old body now
>
> . . . .
>
> I reach out toward it but
> my fingers turn to cankers
> and I am motherwarm and used,
> just as your childhood is used.
>
> . . . .
>
> Linda, you are leaving
> your old body now.
> You've picked my pocket clean
> and you've racked up all my
> poker chips and left me empty.
>
> (CP, 305–6)

Besides this anger about being used up and left over, she also questions implicitly the sort of human beings young adults are. Linda's body at the peak of adolescence was "an old butterfly," the last and most beautiful stage of natural metamorphosis. Now Linda joins a heartless and militant army that mindlessly picks up the march of the species, carrying Homo sapiens forward, but where? She will now "pass by armies,"

> carrying keepsakes to the boys,
> carrying powders to the boys,

> carrying, my Linda, blood to
> the bloodletter.
>
> (*CP*, 306)

The male as bloodletter, a vampire that will prey on her daughter, recalls Plath's "Daddy"; but Sexton also labels as heartless, mechanistic, and mindless the young women who feed these armies. Linda's calisthenics become a "womanly leggy semaphore" that calls in the troops, soulless young men like the young Romans that lurk about for the crucifixion in "Little Girl, My String Bean, My Lovely Woman." But in that poem she had wished to protect her daughter and help prepare her for her entrance into sexuality. In "Mother and Daughter" there is a much darker maternal renunciation in her unflinching appraisal of her own daughter as a taker about to join an army of takers.

The Demeter-Kore relationship and matrilinearity underlie this poem as in her other daughter poems. The last lines reject the daughter in all her youthful callousness yet wryly and fondly comment on the daughter's place in the line of fertility and reproduction:

> Question you about this
> and you will see my death
> drooling at these gray lips
> while you, my burglar, will eat
> fruit and pass the time of day.
>
> (*CP*, 306–7)

Casual and unappreciative of her fertility, the daughter munches fruit, the emblem of reproduction. Yet in looking at her mother's death, Linda is unwittingly beholding the source of her own, for the poet with sinister irony bequeaths not only her own fertility and womanhood to Linda but also the cancer that strikes the women of her family:

> Now that you are eighteen
> I give you my booty, my spoils,
> my Mother & Co. and my ailments.
> Question you about this
> and you'll not know the answer—
> the muzzle at the mouth,
> the hopeful tent of oxygen,
> the tubes, the pathways,
> the war and the war's vomit.
>
> (*CP*, 306)

There is a suggestion that suicide ("muzzle at the mouth") and ob-
sessions with the mother ("Mother & Co.") are perhaps hereditary;
her daughter so certain, so filled with aplomb, will have her own
psychic battles, too.

In this poem, then, we see the Demeter-Kore theme that first
emerged in "The Fortress" with Sexton's own acceptance of herself as
a young Demeter figure; the motif underlies "My Little Girl, My String
Bean, My Lovely Woman" and "Pain for a Daughter," which feature
the mother older yet still a mentor; now the archetype is almost completely consummated with the mother symbolically dying as the
daughter steps into the initial fertility rites of the Demeter role. The
poem also completes the process and steps of active motherhood that
I have been tracing chronologically in Sexton's canon.

Thus Sexton's daughter poems reveal to the reader the degree and
quality of psychic consolidation with which she lives as she writes each
group of poems. Both *Bedlam* and *All My Pretty Ones* reflect a positive, groping sensibility, and both illustrate the poet coming to terms
with motherhood. *Live or Die,* the most complex of her books, embodies the fullest consolidation of her feminine life as she brings her
daughters to puberty and comes to terms (for a time, at least) with her
own sexuality through theirs. If these shifting roles of Demeter-Kore
are a universal pattern of evolving consciousness for women, as M.
Esther Harding insists, then the personal in Sexton's poems gains its
particular force from its universality.

Love Poems and *The Book of Folly* are less successful, less effective as works of art, perhaps because they do not carry the poet
into new stages of life and fuller identity. Yet they are a readying for
a surge of fuller and more intense creativity. *Love Poems* seems about
sexual exploration as much as a celebration of lovemaking. *The Book
of Folly* moves her out of the world of process, beyond domination
by the feminine principle; and the surreality of the poems represents
new reachings and trials, the experiments of a mind no longer so
entrapped by sex-determined roles. A new transformation is taking
place, for the daughter poem in this volume gives us the most explicit
statement I know on the process of a mother weaning *herself* from
motherhood. Sexton's first volume released her from her mother; now
she releases herself from being a mother. She has escaped two of the
faces of death in the matriarchate. She has weaned *herself* from motherhood but must still come to terms with her daughter as an adult

woman. This happens in *The Death Notebooks*. She and her daughter must *share* the Demeter role symbiotically as she and her mother did in "The Fortress," pruning trees together.

Transformation of Demeter into Sophia

Like the two preceding volumes, *The Death Notebooks* (1974) portrays at first a scatological, sadomasochistic terror in the face of death but moves through these forces to a transcendent, calm embracing of life-in-death and death-in-life that has the same effect as the closing scene of a great tragedy. A reader who has read all of Sexton's poems experiences a purging of pity and fear, a catharsis.

This volume is an unflinching appraisal of the dark forces of life. Sexuality is at first seen in terms of death in this book, and the poet readies herself with a "black necessary trousseau" ("For Mr. Death Who Stands with His Door Open," *CP*, 352). The book opens with a search for gods; then poem after poem dwells on the discovery of a dead baby.

But the persona/poet does finally encompass wisdom born of the sea and earth yet so transcendentally precious. Her last poem, "Tenth Psalm" (ED. "Ninth Psalm in *DN*), one of her best, is the only poem in this volume that treats her relationship with her daughters, and, as in her earlier volumes, her relationship with them is indicative of that to her own psyche, her own sense of balance and transformation. The biblical intonations are stirring and apocalyptic yet personal and intimate, gathering up and resolving her metaphysical questions, building to a fierce affirmation of life:

> For as the baby springs out like a starfish into her million light years Anne sees that she must climb her own mountain.
>
> For as she eats wisdom like the halves of a pear she puts one foot in front of the other. She climbs the dark wing.
>
> (*CP*, 411)

Neumann says of the highest level of the feminine principle: "The spiritual power of Sophia is living and saving; her overflowing heart is wisdom and food at once. The nourishing life that she communicates is a life of the spirit and transformation."[19] Sophia remains in touch with the earth; her wisdom never goes into abstract, unreal, immaterial regions like her counterpart in the masculine principle. To Sexton wisdom *is* fruit, thus spirit with nature conjoined. Yet her wisdom is transcendent as suggested by the ascent imagery. This imagery of food (pears as wisdom) as part of the poet's growth defines her voice as feminine in the way she gives of herself; as she gives, there is more for all, including herself:

> For as her child grows Anne grows and there is salt and canta-
> loupe and molasses for all.
>
> For as Anne walks, the music walks, and the family lies down
> in milk.
>
> > (*CP*, 411)

These stanzas seem to acknowledge the growth of the mother's consciousness with her child's maturation. The imagery of milk picks up the image of the nurturing universe as a milk giver in the "Eighth Psalm" (ED. "Seventh Psalm" in *DN*) and again emphasizes, as Neumann explains, the spiritual transformation of the poet:

> Just as in the elementary phase the nourishing stream of the earth flows into the animal and the phallic power of the breast flows into the receiving child, so on the level of spiritual transformation the adult human being receives the "virgin's milk" of Sophia. This Sophia is also the "spirit and the bride" of the Apocalypse, of whom it is written: "And let him that is athirst come. And whosoever will, let him take the water of life freely."[20]

Her family, in other words, is transformed through immersion in her beatific vision. She again blesses her husband's fertility:

> For the husband sells his rain to God and God is well pleased
> with His family.
>
> > (*CP*, 411)

Halfway through her last poem she delineates her relationship to her daughters and her sense of self in connection with them:

> For the child grows to a woman, her breasts coming up like
> the moon while Anne rubs the peace stone.
>
> For the child starts up her own mountain (not being locked
> in) and reaches the coastline of grapes.
>
> For Anne and her daughter master the mountain and again
> and again. Then the child finds a man who opens like the sea.

> For that daughter must build her own city and fill it with her
> own oranges, her own words.
>
> *(CP, 412)*

The poet's stone of peace is ground, rubbed down to a smooth inner ore of selfhood as the child grows. The grapes and oranges hark back to "Little Girl, My String Bean," which defines her daughter as a *hortus conclusus* (an enclosed garden) that will bear its own fruits. Yet Sexton and her now fully adult daughter are shoulder to shoulder in the quest, the pilgrimage of life. Again, Neumann sheds light on the archetypal aspects of this mother-daughter unity: "The well-known reliefs, finally, show Kore full grown and almost identical with her virgin-mother Demeter. Virgin and mother stand to one another as flower and fruit, and essentially belong together in their transformation from one to the other. . . . In the pictures where the two appear together one cannot make out at first which is mother and which is daughter."[21] Oranges have been used by Sexton earlier in this volume as the roundness a woman swallows that swells out her womb. So the oranges are children; the city, her daughter's home; and the man who opens like a sea, the beneficent and generous masculinity that Sexton desires for her daughter.

The poem ends affirmatively:

> For God was as large as a sunlamp and laughed his heat at us
> and therefore we did not cringe at the death hole.
>
> *(CP, 413)*

She and her brother/alter ego Christopher have washed clean a rat (born of Eve in an earlier poem) in the milk of the skies. The poem portrays a cleansing, cosmic vision far grander than "Live" of *Live or Die*, often considered the most positive poem in her canon.

This transformation, this pilgrimage, the quest through levels of consciousness, has been largely through female initiation rites. The link between sexual roles/knowledge and consciousness seems then to be borne out in Sexton's oeuvre. Her moon imagery in this last poem is important; after she leaves her daughter to her own "city," she tells us

> For Anne walked up and up and finally over the years until
> she was old as the moon and with its naggy voice.
>
> *(CP, 412)*

In discussing the necessity of the mother sacrificing her maternal urges as her children grow up, M. Esther Harding has said: "By facing her own emotion, love, fear, hate, whatever it may be, in stark reality, no longer camouflaged by the assumption of indulgence and maternal concern, she becomes once more one-in-herself, dependent only on the goddess, truly a Daughter of the Moon."[22] No longer resentful at all toward her daughter but rather assuming an adult woman-to-woman relationship with her, Sexton becomes her own wise old woman, her own mentor, proceeding on unflinchingly alone. She surveys the earth and all it contains from the height and scope of Sophia, a goddess of wisdom and love. No longer any part of cyclicality, though still in touch with nature, she faces death and transmutes it with her wisdom and her art.

Loss of Matrilineal Roots: The Devouring Masculine Principle

It is significant that Sexton's weakest volumes of poetry, *Love Poems* and *The Awful Rowing Toward God*, are both attempts to make authentic connections with the male world. Father, lover, husband, fantasied son ("Menstruation at Forty," *Live or Die*), and God—all are psychic vagaries that she tries to crystallize, to fix, that she may know them. But the most powerful and solid relationships in her life are those with the women in her family. Part of the fatality (and futility) in her search for God is her attaching all meaning in her life to contact with a male God. She seems to cast asunder all those matrilineal ties she so painfully forged earlier. Does she find herself adrift without her familiar foothold in the feminine principle to anchor her into life? Her central image of rowing suggests shipwreck and isolation.

Had she kept her sense of self as Demeter/Sophia—as the touchstone, the rudder—that identity may have guided her through the contradictory information about God with which we all struggle. She at times felt an alliance with other women even after her daughters left (see "The Child Bearers," *45 Mercy Street*), but this tie obviously becomes a minor force in her life. The resurgence of her mother as devourer of Sexton's selfhood is curious. Did her conscious acceptance of patriarchal versions of God push the good Earth Mother (incorporated before into her sense of self as Demeter/Sophia) into a repressed demon that demands a sacrifice of the child, of her? In connection with this, the poem "The Consecrating Mother," which ends *45 Mercy Street*, features a mother sea that calls Sexton to her depths.[23] The sea becomes for Sexton the same force that it is in Plath's *Ariel*—a soothing call to death. Unlike Plath, Sexton was a woman with intuitive, deep inner ties to the Mother Earth goddess of cyclical life and time, yet in her last years she strained to find a far away male God.

This desire for a father God must have been especially difficult for her, considering how isolated she apparently was from her father, whom she always speaks of as "on the road," as a salesman, drunk and faraway. No wonder she saw God as in a void, a helpless, ineffectual male who cannot reach her. She must be the active one, an unnatural state of being for a woman conditioned to passivity. *She must row toward God.*[24] Sexton comes from a tradition (New England Protestantism) espousing the nonrational Calvinistic God, a tradition that reinforces this sense of the faraway male. The rowboat becomes especially pitiful in view of the immense space between this inscrutable God and his depraved children. In Sexton's failure to find God, we find perhaps the confluence of a Calvinistic God and the removed father figure of the Industrial Revolution, a father figure who leaves the home and works at some inscrutable job all day, returning home a fearsome, unknown figure of authority.

In other words her sense of utter separateness from the whole male world clinches her inability to reach God. Instead of trying to redefine God in what Mary Daly calls an "ontological self-affirmation,"[25] instead of looking for God in a space and time she knew, she attempts to contact an inscrutable God whom she defines finally in Calvinistic terms. How much does this concept of God tie up with her father's absence in her childhood? There are special problems for the female artist in a separation from her father. Concomitant to the absence of the father is the closure of the mother upon the sensibility of the child, who is no longer able to bifurcate the possible modes of human being and personality, no longer able to posit alternative ways of handling the world's response to her. Especially if the mother is a hostile, negative figure, the father takes on an alluring potential of sympathy and nurture, if only one could reach him.

Especially for the creative, artistic daughter, the father becomes a necessary possible mode of independence to fight the mother role that she has incorporated as her future. To write poetry as compulsively and in such quantity as Sexton did was a heroic act, considering how it must have horrified her incorporated mother. She even doubts the validity of this act in a way few men suffer—consider her poem

"The Hoarder" in *The Book of Folly*, where she is afraid her poetry is only so much excrement.

Thus her father and God become emblems of potential comfort and belonging, but her background allows her to cast them only in terms of nothingness, great unknowns. As Daly points out, we must face nonbeing all the time to forge being. To this point in her life, Sexton's work reads like a series of fugues with the reassuring melody of Demeter and the emerging Sophia in the background as the one constant to stabilize her against the cacaphony of self-destruction and of loneliness that she allows finally to take over. She does not attempt to build the unknown out of the feminine roots of being that she has established. Nonbeing must be viewed from the boundaries of reality that give a solid foothold. Instead she tries to leap into the arms of an abstraction. She follows the masculine principle into its most danger-ous phase, which Neumann calls its tendency to psychic withdrawal, separateness from body and earth.[26] Patricia Berry has discussed the depressive trends of Demeter as a regression into the realm of man that makes her neglect her connections with the divine; she becomes caught up in an endless cycle of meaningless, fruitless emotions, an empty repetition.[27] This seems to describe well the poems and tone of *Love Poems* and *The Awful Rowing Toward God*. Perhaps Sexton neglected her own deepest particular and personal archetype in her sallies at God and lovers.

On the other hand, how much of Sexton's final opting for death was a refusal to transcend her Demeter persona by moving into a different and fuller aspect of womanhood? Are some individuals nat-urally more bound to their own sex in terms of identity? Certainly her move toward the masculine principle, as she understood it, proved disastrous. The current theories on the healthy arrival of androgynous personality to the mature person is belied by her canon. Her attempts to be genderless are exercises in passivity ("Consorting with Angels," *Live or Die*). The search for God turns into a search for being that sees personal essence contained in the great other. Annihilation of *her* self is the logical conclusion.

In a negative way she demonstrates the journey toward con-sciousness that Neumann describes in *The History of Consciousness*. In *The Awful Rowing Toward God*, God becomes the devouring Great Father in both her poetry and life. The early part of her canon reflects the slaying of the devouring Great Mother, the entrapment of the psyche by the biological sources of our being; at that time she could not seem to step forth into her own life as wife and mother. She ousts the negative force of the devouring Great Mother from her own being but is finally stymied and devoured by the World Father. Neumann discusses the devouring Great Father as that part of the psyche which accepts and incorporates without question the ideas of one's culture and traditions on both societal and ultimate reality. The last poem in 45 Mercy Street features her mother as a calling, drowning sea that suggests a resurfacing of the devouring Great Mother even as the devouring Great Father triumphs. This convergence of the Bestial Royal Couple suggests an inverse royal couple, a hideous pair, a duality that brings together two poles of horror into a wholeness of nothingness. They are like the twins in Spenser's Faerie Queene who committed incest in the womb and gallop about as adults, ravishing innocent victims. This sister/brother-husband/wife appears again in Milton's Sin and Death, who also gobble their victims. This archetype seems to partake of the apocalyptic Antichrist, and together this pair commands Sexton to self-destruct rather than self-fulfill and consolidate as she would have under the influence of a healthy metaphysical archetype of the Royal Couple. Jung's essay on the stages of life treats as innate the psyche's movement in the second stage of life toward a sense of metaphysical androgyny. To accomplish this each person tries to assimilate contrasexual psychic modes of being. June Singer sees the Royal Couple as symbolic of the primordial Androgyne; she sees it as perhaps "the oldest archetype of which we have any experience": "It derives from, and is second only to, the archetype of the Absolute, which is beyond the possibility of human experience and must remain forever unknowable."[28] Sexton, on the other hand, appears to construct a Royal Couple that preys on her, two vampires that finally devour her.

The Implications of Sexton's Quest

To summarize, Sexton's quest for higher and fuller consciousness begins with her first escaping the devouring Great Mother; she then moves into a Demeter role, incorporating only the positive aspects of the Great Mother. She attempts to move into the Venus or Juno archetype in her relationship to men but never seems to cope fully with that role, which perhaps requires an active, outgoing nature—somewhat antithetical to the more passive, protective, yet strong Demeter role with which she always appears more comfortable. In *The Death Notebooks* we see her ascension to a Sophia outlook, but all too briefly; she ends her canon and life with a fixation on connection with masculine archetypes. One can argue that this pattern is idiosyncratic to her, but the popularity of her poetry bespeaks the universal issues that she treats. Unafraid to face the deepest issues in her pilgrimage through life, bold enough to articulate her experience of the feminine, she speaks for many women.

Sexton's life demonstrates the richness and limitations of the Demeter archetype. (Perhaps more specifically, Sexton portrays the Demeter-Kore archetype with Sophia tendencies.) Men are not excluded from such a woman's life, but neither are they particularly necessary. It seems unlikely with what we know of her mother that Anne Sexton could have been enculturated toward the Demeter archetype. Are people naturally dominated more by one archetype than another? That is, are archetypes simply the naming of intrinsic integral tendencies of the personality? This, of course, flies in the face of the more popular theory that all gender behavior is conditioned, but is it not true that each woman relates to her own femininity/womanhood in a markedly characteristic fashion? Should we write off all possibility that modes of gender behavior are inborn? Sexton attempted other roles than the Demeter/Sophia, yet they seemed unnatural and finally even antithetical to her being.

With courage she has written of dim, inarticulate areas of feminine experience that many of us have felt afraid to acknowledge. Her voice is devastatingly authentic; she has made personal and lyrical many crucial experiences that before were shrouded in the language of treatises of feminine archetypes and depth psychology. She asserts feminine strength and its special ties and needs for matrilinearity. Her voice will make it more possible for modern woman to identify consciously with her own sex, instead of turning away to the alien models of patriarchy. She has written for the first time in an autobiographical mode of the bio-unity of three generations of mother and daughter.[29] She has written more graphically and movingly than any author hereto of how the child grows slowly beyond the vegetative principle of childhood, then bursts like a pupa into the full possession of a soul; she shows us the mother as a mentor, a Demeter figure that assists the child toward consciousness. She makes us see the mystical elements of motherhood. The mother is a Lady of our Plants that guides in the ascent toward the Sun of full being. We can even learn from Anne Sexton's failures; modern woman must forge her own deity. Most of all, women must learn to trust their own sense of reality, embrace it, articulate it, and celebrate it in a vision made flesh by language.

NOTES

1. Waltraud Mitgutsch writes compellingly of this: "Unlike the explicit feminist of the sixties and seventies, Sexton and Gluck share a female self-consciousness rather than a feminist consciousness. Their poetry . . . explores the danger zones of women's departure from patriarchal concepts. . . . Self-hatred is as frequent as self-assertion and this frequency of self-loathing creates an atmosphere of disgust and suffering. . . . Although they challenge the patriarchal order their world view is still dichotomized into the male versus the female poles . . . the loss of orientation in the universe and in society that has become acute in most contemporary literature intensifies the problematics women writers are faced with. . . . For a woman self-definition in a predominantly male-oriented culture still means non-acceptance, refusal, negation, before any affirmative stance can be achieved" ("Women in Transition: The Poetry of Anne Sexton and Luise Gluck," *Arbeiten aus Anglistik und Amerikanistik 9* [1984]: 131).

2. C. Kerényi, *Eleusis: Archetypal Image of Mother and Daughter*, trans. Ralph Manheim (New York: Schocken Books, 1977), xxxi.

3. Jean Shinoda Bolen, *Goddesses in Everywoman: A New Psychology of Women* (New York: Harper and Row, 1984). See also Nor Hall, *The Moon and the Virgin: Reflections on the Archetypal Feminine* (New York: Harper and Row, 1980).

4. Carl G. Jung and C. Kerényi, *Essays on a Science of Mythology: The Myth of the Divine Child and the Mysteries of Eleusis*, trans. R. F. C. Hull (New York: Bolligen Paperback, 1973), 162–63.

5. Erich Neumann, *The Great Mother: An Analysis of the Archetype*, trans. Ralph Manheim (New York: Princeton University Press, 1972), 307.

6. Erich Neumann, *The Origins and History of Consciousness*, trans. R. F. C. Hull (New York: Princeton University Press, 1954), 205.

7. Bolen says that this development of other goddess sides is what saves women with a primary Demeter identity from being stuck in depression when the children leave (*Goddesses*, 193).

8. All quotations of Sexton's poetry are from the standard edition, *The Complete Poems* [hereafter abbreviated *CP*], ed. Linda Gray Sexton (Boston: Houghton Mifflin Co., 1981).

9. Neumann, *The Great Mother*, 137.

10. Ibid., 96.

11. M. Esther Harding remarks on the maternal in woman "which craves for the contact with her infant." She further says that "a physical delight lurks in the relation to an infant, offspring of her own body, which is not far in its intensity and lure from the delight of an erotic contact, although different in its nature" (*Woman's Mysteries* [New York: Bantam Books, 1971], 36). It seems to me that this poem articulates an essential sacred space, a primordial mystery of motherhood, that all mothers feel in their physical relationship with small children. In *To the Lighthouse* Lily intuits this when she paints Mrs. Ramsey and her six-year-old son James as a purple triangle. Neumann has said that male mysteries take place in abstract spiritual space while "the primordial mysteries of the Feminine are connected more with the proximate realities of everyday life" (*The Great Mother*, 282). Significantly, my male students are generally surprised when they find out how much the women in the class identify with the mother in the poems; the men usually identify with the child.

12. As Diana Hume George remarks, "The mother-daughter poems in which she is a daughter are painfully ambivalent, but the ones in which she speaks as mother attempt to establish bodily integrity, wholeness, and dignity" (*Oedipus Anne: The Poetry of Anne Sexton* [Urbana: University of Illinois Press, 1987], 59). Diane Middlebrook offers incisive interpretations of Sexton's family background that explain her trouble with her own Kore identity: "The doctor's confidence in her intelligence conflicted with the family drama in which Sexton had been assigned the role of the dumb daughter. The sense of being rotten, purposeless, dumb was of course the issue in Sexton's therapy, where it was treated as a symptom" ("Becoming Anne Sexton," *Denver Quarterly* 18 [Winter 1984]: 27).

13. Joseph Henderson, "Ancient Myths and Modern Man," in *Man and His Symbols*, ed. Carl G. Jung (New York: Dell, 1964), 156.

14. I develop this image both in my *Listening to Our Bodies: The Rebirth of Feminine Wisdom* (Boston: Beacon Press, 1983), 131, and in a recent book coauthored with Karla Holloway, *New Dimensions of Spirituality: A Bi-Racial and Bi-Cultural Reading of the Novels of Toni Morrison* (Westport, Conn.: Greenwood Press, 1987). Morrison herself discusses old women as umbrella trees that protect the mothers and children.

15. Neumann, *Amor and Psyche*, 99.

16. Ibid., 64.

17. Harding, *Woman's Mysteries*, 266.

18. Ibid., 227.

19. Neumann, *The Great Mother*, 331.

20. Ibid., 329.

21. Ibid., 307.

22. Harding, *Woman's Mysteries*, 230.

23. It is important to note that Sexton did not arrange this book of poems; after Sexton's death her daughter arranged the remaining poems of her unpublished work, and it might have comforted the daughter as a survivor to think of her mother's death in this way. Although Sexton was not good with her children when they were young (see Middlebrook's analyses), she may have bonded with them more as they became older. Linda Wagner-Martin says: "Lost from even that maternal ancestry, searching as she honestly recounts, Sexton yet finds her strength in her kinship with her maturing daughters, and through them, with herself as woman. Her strength is, however, but fragile, tentative, a veil of bright motion, a daisy, which some eyes might consider ineffectual" ("45 Mercy Street and Other Vacant Houses," in *American Literature: The New England Heritage*, ed. James Nagel and Richard Astro [New York: Garland Publishing Co., 1981], 154, and *infra*, 227–47.).

24. For understanding the gentle, positive side of this God archetype, Diana Hume George's essay "Anne Sexton's Island God," in *Original Essays on the Poetry of Anne Sexton*, ed. Frances Bixler (Fayetteville: University of Arkansas Press, 1988), is definitive. She shows how Squirrel Island and Sexton's grandfather conflate into a comforting island of divinity, a kind of *omphalos*/navel that one reaches through the feminine sea.

25. Mary Daly, *Beyond God the Father: Toward a Philosophy of Women's Liberation* (Boston: Beacon Press, 1973), 32.

26. Neumann, *The Origins of History and Consciousness*, 187.

27. "The Rape of Demeter/Persephone and Neurosis," *Spring: An Annual of Archetypal Psychology and Jungian Thought* (1975): 191–93.

28. June Singer, *Androgyny* (New York: Anchor Press, 1976), 20.

29. At least two other sources treat this but more as a side issue: Margaret Mead's autobiography *Blackberry Winter* and Toni Morrison's novel *Sula*. But Sexton's is the first psychoanalytic-poetic rendition of this theme.

ESTELLA LAUTER

Anne Sexton's "Radical Discontent with the Awful Order of Things"[1]

Between 1970 and 1974 Anne Sexton[2] created an extraordinary, perhaps prophetic, body of poetry based upon images that have profound psychological and religious significance for our age. The brilliance of the images, her refusal to censor them no matter what kind of cultural challenge they contained, and her success in giving them significant form constitute a stunning achievement in poetry. This may come as a surprise to those who think of Sexton as a "confessional" poet who sought personal reconciliation with her parents and children, heterosexual love and psychological integration without concern for the larger issues of her time. Her poems show, however, that by 1963 she understood her personal predicament as an "exile from God" (WDY, 10) that would require a strenuous quest. Indeed, five of the six books containing poems she wrote after 1970[3] suggest that the original terms of her quest—the search for a viable relationship with the Father/Son/Holy Spirit promised by the Christian tradition—broke open under the pressure of her imaginative scrutiny. As she allowed her own images to matter, they began to "leak" from her pen "like a miscarriage" (BF, 32), and she began to inhabit a realm peopled by archetypal figures that could not be contained by the Christian story. Sexton was painfully aware that this new leg of her journey would be judged a folly by those who wanted her to "spill her guts" (DN, 65) but *not* to "unlock the Magi" or to "bolt for the sun like a diamond" (BF, 4). Yet she could not stop; her desire to "dig" remained insatiable even when she found that "people pop off and / muskrats float up backward" (BF, 34).

Sexton's quest is best understood, I think, in terms of archetypal psychology, as an act of "soul-making"—that is, the effort to find the connections between life and the fantasy images that are our "privi-

Reprinted from *Spring: An Annual of Archetypal Psychology and Jungian Thought* (1979): 77–92.

leged mode of access" to the soul and to those recurring worldwide figures who are tantamount to the gods.[4] Yet her search kept yielding unexpected results. Her poems, like the bricks of gold God left when he walked out (DN, 46), seem to have contained the treasure she sought without benefiting her. Despite her innumerable encounters with her figures from "the other world,"

> The soul was not cured,
> it was as full as a clothes closet
> of dresses that did not fit.
>
> (AR, 63)

Unfortunately for us all, she could not accord full value to her own visions. Apparently she persisted in seeing herself as the loser in a rigged game with God,[5] remaining oblivious to the fact that she had produced the richest body of God images to appear in some time.

I suggest that Sexton's difficulty in accepting the fruits of her soul-making had much to do with her inability to name them—particularly to know their feminine dimensions by name. I see her last five books, then, as a tragic part of the process of revisioning prescribed by Mary Daly for women who find it impossible to live with theologies designed to serve patriarchal ends.[6] Sexton's images raise questions about the premises of Christianity and show us one way to move beyond them; whether or not she understood the answers her images contained, she opened up a process of encountering the soul that others may use.

In this essay I sketch the contours of Sexton's later poetry to familiarize the reader with her medium and her world before I go on to uncover the psychological and religious dynamics of her imaginative pilgrimage. Finally, I will place her discontent with both the God of our culture and the alternative deities of her visionary imagination in the context of archetypal psychology and feminist theology to understand the implications her quest may have for our lives.

Poems of a World That Is "Up for Grabs"[7]

The shift from the personal to the transpersonal in Sexton's quest is reflected in her aesthetic decisions regarding her tone, her figuration, her use of a persona, and her formal principles of design in her last five books. Suzanne Juhasz has argued convincingly that *Transfor-*

mations, composed in 1970, marks a turning point in Sexton's poetry and has noted the increased boldness of her figures of association that accompanied her assumption of a "voice of power."[8] Sexton also rendered her new boldness in a stance that I call "impudent" because its most important feature is a refusal to observe decorum. In her case it was a refusal to cover up, gloss over, or withdraw from what she saw— a refusal to be shamed into silence. We hear it in the best-known phrases of all her later books: when she finds the gods "shut in the lavatory" (*DN,* 2), or remembers her mother's belly "big with another child, / cancer's baby, big as a football" (*DN,* 14), or gives her buttocks to both life and death (*DN,* 62). Impudence is not the only stance she assumed; in *The Awful Rowing Toward God,* it often gives way to a more defeated (p. 43), lost (p. 48), or deferential (p. 64) manner, and in *45 Mercy Street* it gives way to despair (p. 89) and fear (p. 96) as well. Yet even in these books her ability to create strong poems out of her most self-destructive feelings may be one of the fruits of impudence. I speculate that Sexton had to create an alternative to the image of the "good woman" (the one who softens the truth) before she could express what she saw.

This stance characterizes not only her use of language but also her level of imaginative activity.[9] For example, "The Boat" (*BF,* 44–45) is part of the sequence called "The Death of the Fathers," a subject that might have been handled in her earlier autobiographical manner, since the fathers are identified as her own biological and legal ones. But in this sequence Sexton keeps pushing beyond her memories and beyond her fantasies to an archetypal realm. In "The Boat" she begins in her familiar autobiographical manner, placing herself with her mother and father in a mahogany Chris-Craft and re-creating the scene as if it were happening now. This is an act of conscious imagination— graceful, authentic, and inherently controllable. At line 20 the character of the poem begins to shift as the poet-speaker delves more deeply into the fantasy life of her seven-year-old self wherein she is "riding / to Pemaquid or Spain" instead of just outside the harbor. The waves seem as high as buildings, and the child feels like a kumquat tumbling in the boat. The speaker allows herself to experience the wave washing over the boat as if it were engulfing her and sending her under water; she becomes an actor in a heroic journey that she imagines her father controls. But at line 33 another shift takes place: all the characters in the boat become like "scissors," and they dare the sea by "parting" it, as Moses did. They experience the sea as a green room filled with the dead where an angel warns them *"You have no business. / No business here."* The father cries for "a sign," and suddenly, as if by magic, there is sky and air once more. The poem returns to the level of fantasy where the act of bailing the boat is seen as "dividing our deaths" and then as "closing out / the cold wing that has clasped us." But in lines 33–45 we have inhabited an archetypal chamber, a nonhuman world where angels speak and humans are at the mercy of their signs. It is a world that Sexton dared to frequent during the last four years of her poetry.

Her courage also shows in her choice of masks and in her multipartite poetic form. Whereas in her earlier work the persona "Anne" bore the closest possible resemblance to herself, in her last books Sexton adopts the masks of taboo figures (an assassin, for example) and God figures (Jesus and Mary, among others) as a deliberate means of understanding experience that lies beyond her own. Her late persona "Ms. Dog" becomes a way of extending the parts of herself to and about whom she can speak. Likewise, her forms become more complex and resonant with cultural significance. As if it were not enough to rewrite the fairy tales, she tackles the Christian parables and the Hebrew Psalms, retells the creation and crucifixion stories, and adds a bestiary for good measure.

I am convinced that these artistic choices not only reflect but facilitate her quest. In her last books Sexton's journey continues in response to a force within her that she knows through her embodiment of it in her poems. As she moves from one stage of her journey to another, she personifies that force differently. At first she understands it as an "ambition bird" (*BF*, 3), and then as her alter ego or imaginary twin named Christopher (*DN*, 84). In *The Awful Rowing* it becomes a rat (p. 2), a jigsaw puzzle image of God (p. 3), a fallen angel (p. 23), a crab (p. 28), and a dead heart (p. 36).[10] In *45 Mercy Street* it is a demon (p. 106). Sexton is alternately attracted to and repelled by these figures; they are both her salvation and her cross. It is ironic that she could recognize such figures well enough to allow herself to be propelled by them but could *not* accord her more positive discoveries the same degree of validity, as I will show later in this essay.

Still, we can appreciate what her poems did allow Sexton to do. At the very least, they allowed her to inhabit every place she could imagine—from the interior of the earth (*AR*, 62) to "Floor six thousand" in the sky (AR, 18)—long enough to know that it did not contain what she sought. Luckily for us, her poems also allowed her to fulfill metaphorically some of the impossible demands of her vision, as when it required a destruction of the body, which is often more reminiscent of the dismemberment of Orpheus than of the Calvinist perspective that probably inspired it. This aspect of her journey seems to begin with her enumeration of body parts over which she takes control when she ousts the doctor, that "seasick grounded man" (BF, 6). In "The One-Legged Man" she assumes the persona of a man who has given away, planted, shipped off, and eaten his leg (BF, 16–17). In "Going Gone" she watches her loved one give an old crone her eyes, lips, and hands (BF, 20). In "The Red Shoes" she ties on the shoes of "All those girls" who tore off their ears, whose arms and heads fell off, and whose "feet could not stop" (BF, 28–29). In "Killing the Spring" she identifies with a spring that refuses to live by drowning her eyes and nailing her hands "in training for a crucifixion" (BF, 37). In her sister's dream she is laid out for the dogs and "loved" until she is gone (DN, 12). Indeed, the outcome of the dismemberment is a recognition of her kinship with Christ (AR, 41), when she eats herself and then receives mouth-to-mouth resuscitation from Jesus.

Her poems allowed her to proliferate her images of God in her exploration of the unsatisfactory aspects of his nature. The images are extraordinarily rich because they range across boundaries between inside and outside, female and male, animal, spirit and human forms, mythic and historical representations. In *The Book of Folly* we see God opening his teeth and saying "oh" like a witless old woman or a child (p. 8) or behaving like a magician, then a man, and finally a "pagan" demigod (BF, 98, 101, 105). In *The Death Notebooks* he is her grandfather (p. 21), but also a womb (p. 44), a casino owner who behaves like an unreliable washerwoman (p. 46), a dead fish (p. 53), and a mooner (p. 58). The poet boasts "I am God, la de dah" (p. 64). The lovers are God when they fuck (p. 37). Finally, in her psalms Sexton prays to a playful God who plugs up holes in the sky with his finger but who is also capable of digesting her (pp. 77, 81). In *45 Mercy Street* he is Falstaff (p. 19), a carrion (p. 107), and also the one who decrees the death of "centuries of our blue mothers" (p. 110). In *Words for Dr. Y.* he is a blue-faced tyrant (p. 47). The images she presents in *The Awful Rowing Toward God,* her clearest articulation of the "private God" she told her friends she found (*Letters,* 390), are no less diverse or heretical. Perhaps the difference between this book and the others lies in her determination to put the jigsaw pieces of God (the whore, the drunken old man, the man dressed up as a child "all na-ked / even without skin") together into a "whole nation of God" (AR, 3). Her vision of him as the winner in a crooked poker game at the end of that book is a sporting admission of her defeat rather than a decisive renewal of the Christian myth.

Sexton did not always stop short of mythmaking, although there are fewer full-fledged myths than one might expect in this mythic body of poetry.[11] Surely among the most important of her poetic achieve-ments is her image of death as an icy baby who has been with her from birth in the final part of "The Death Baby" (DN, 15–17). The cherub is one of those tiny nude angels, familiar from early Renaissance paintings, envisioned here as having the weight and size of the dough for a recipe of bread, soft golden hair, and glass eyes. In the act of rocking the cherub, chanting as she rocks, seeing in its glassy stare the essence of being, Sexton reenters that archetypal space she saw in "The Boat." As she rocks and her vision enlarges, she sees their image in stone, another pietà in the context of a world that is subdued and swallowed by war. Without breaking the rhythm of her rocking, she addresses us directly, admonishing us to beware of our tenderness for this "dumb traveler" who accompanies each of us through life.

The image is stunning in the context of Western iconography where death is often figured as an adult skeleton posing as lover or monk as if Lucifer were still engaged in the battle with God for souls. Sexton's image is an externalization of an ever-present, all-seeing eye within all human lives—an entity that is at once the most private aspect of one's life (one's smell) and the most universal aspect (primordial eye). It is an aspect of self and world within the person that never grows and can elicit tenderness in moments of despair, presented here as maternal self-sacrifice. This act of imagining death as a stillborn facet of life itself, rather than a power totally outside of life, belongs to a larger myth outside the Christian frame of reference, to which Sexton was drawn—as we shall see.

Sexton's Journey to the Sea

Ms. Dog stands on the shore
and the sea keeps rocking in
and she wants to talk with God.
                    (DN, 71)

Over and over again in the poems from 1970 to 1974, Sexton reenters the archetypal space we saw in "The Boat" (BF, 41), but often her encounters are not effectively mediated by the father figure of that poem. Indeed, the essential drama of her work in these years lies in her repeated discoveries of the Father-God's inadequacy coupled with her inability to give him up in favor of the many gods whose faces and voices appeared in her poetry but whose language she could not translate (DN, 73). I hope to set forth the terms of the conflict in my interpretation of "The Jesus Papers," Sexton's most ambitious attempt to work through her identification with Jesus,[12] before I uncover the alternative pattern that emerges in The Death Notebooks, 45 Mercy Street, and Words for Dr. Y., in her psalms, prayers, dreams, and visions that pulled her toward the gods in her lavatory (DN, 2).

The sequence of nine poems called "The Jesus Papers" (BF, 91–105) clearly derives from the modern desire to know who Jesus "really" was, intensified by Sexton's desire for face-to-face conversation with his father. The sequence expresses the fantastic quality of the New Testament parables on which it is based, while it preserves the vitality of the traditional cast of characters. Sexton achieves this delicate balance of mockery and belief by assuming different positions within the drama (the baby Jesus, the narrator, the dying Jesus, the poet-dreamer), by encountering the characters at several levels of imagination, and by envisioning them as presences rather than as historical figures or figments of an ancient imagination. In other words, she uses all the resources of her later poetic style to salvage what she can in Jesus' story.

Significantly, Sexton begins her exploration of Jesus in the sensory sphere of the mother in "Jesus Suckles" (BF, 93), speaking through the child directly to Mary about the experience of dozing, sucking, growing in her sealike domain. From the perspective of the first stanza, he can say, "I'm a kid in a rowboat and you're the sea, / the salt, you're every fish of importance" (BF, 93). But this Jesus "grows" at an astounding rate, so that in the second stanza he rejects his previous stance of adoration and assumes a more moderate stance of appreciation for his mother's milk. In the third stanza a still more truthful but less lovable Jesus says, "I am a truck. I run everything. / I own you." Here Sexton's artistry is at its peak; in twenty-three lines she runs the gamut of possible attitudes toward Mary. She draws at once on the myth of Jesus' impeccable honesty, on our common experience

of the growing child's struggle to dominate the mother, and our acknowledgment that our culture is run by the motor vehicle, dominated
by the masculine symbol of the truck. She undercuts any sympathy
we may have for the mother-child duo at the moment she reveals how
brutally the balance of power will be reversed.

In fact, "The Jesus Papers" can be read as a study of relationships
between love and power. Thus, in "Jesus Awake" (BF, 94), the narrator
reports that Jesus' penis is "sewn onto Him like a medal," all life and
feeling *departed* from it, implying both that his sex organ is a reward
and that he has *lost* his capacity for sexual feeling. Although he is
shrouded in gold, he is like a house emptied of people. Sexton's concern
with Jesus' sexuality does not stop here. In "Jesus Asleep" (BF, 95),
she understands the symbol of the pietà as a monument to his un-
fulfilled sexual desire for his mother. In her brilliant extension of Mary
Magdalene's story, "Jesus Raises Up the Harlot" (BF, 96), Sexton focuses on the negative outcome of Jesus' "healing" Mary by lancing
her breasts. He establishes a lifelong relationship of servitude. He "saves"
her from death by stoning; she is obliged to save his celibacy by giving
up her sexual desire.

When Sexton turns attention to Jesus' power in the next two
poems, she is no more reverent. In "Jesus Cooks" (BF, 98) she presents
Jesus as a substitute short order cook who is out of food. "The Lord"
in this comic revision of the parable of the loaves and the fishes is an
unskilled magician who has to supplement his one fish with advice
about opening sardine cans on the sly. Here, Sexton's vision of Jesus
as a human being applies to God as well. In "Jesus Summons Forth"
(BF, 99–100), her doubt about Jesus' capacity to raise Lazarus from
the dead (and about Lazarus's attitude toward his restoration) is mit-
igated by her vision of the tenderness Jesus feels for Lazarus in a
moment of artificial respiration. Here and in the next poem Sexton
brings us as close to understanding what she wanted from the New
Testament as we can get. Jesus is attractive to her in those moments
when he expresses love physically.

Her desire for human love from the Father-God is never clearer
than in "Jesus Dies" (BF, 101–2), where she assumes the persona of
Jesus once more—this time to envision what it is like for a real human
being to die on a cross surrounded by others who think he has a special
relationship with God. As Jesus, she desires the equality of a "man-

to-man" bond allowing affectionate teasing, the gift of heaven presented on a dinner plate, the enveloping kind of love that is most familiar to the child who is lifted out of a steaming bath by his mother, and privacy in death. This is the Jesus with whom Sexton identifies most clearly.

But not completely. She cannot forget Mary, even at the peak of her sympathy with Christ. Thus, in "Jesus Unborn" (BF, 103), she returns to the story of the immaculate conception and places us so close to Mary in the olive grove that we can see and feel the "pulse in her neck / beating" in animal anticipation of her transformation. She shows us Mary's physical lethargy that stops any active expression of sexual desire and yet makes her receptive to penetration. The "strange" being who comes to take advantage of the moment is neither swan nor bull nor angel but an "executioner" who deliberately "covers her like a heavy door / and shuts her lifetime up / into this dump-faced day." The poem shifts the responsibility for Mary's imprisonment from Jesus to God (or his henchman).

The final poem, "The Author of the Jesus Papers Speaks" (BF, 105), shows how the whole sequence is rooted in Sexton's struggle with God. She does "talk with God." She presents a dream in which she milked a cow, expecting "moon juice" or some magical mother-substance but receiving blood and shame instead, whereupon God appeared to reprimand her for saying bad things about Christ's birth. Without succumbing to either the shame or the reprimand, she "went to the well and drew a baby / out of the hollow water." Instead of punishing her, God gave her a "gingerbread lady" to sacrifice as a surrogate for the beautiful women who must be eaten "When the cow gives blood / and the Christ is born." God emerges as nothing more or less than a ruthless demigod.

"The Jesus Papers" is a wonderful act of *seeing through* God's power by means of her sympathy for Mary (and Jesus) and *seeing that* her own power lay in her ability to draw "babies" from the well of her own dreams. Although Sexton could identify with Jesus' need for his mother's nurturance and for his father's comradeship, sustenance, and warm support, she could not live comfortably with his celibacy or with his eradication of female sexual response in either Mary. Apparently her dissatisfaction with these aspects of Christianity, coupled with her attraction to Mary and her growing faith in her own powers,

led her into the realm of the archetypal mother often during the remaining years of her life. This was not a totally new direction for
Sexton. As Stephanie Demetrakopoulos has shown in her definitive
interpretations of Sexton's mother-daughter poems, she had long been
preoccupied with the Demeter-Kore archetype.[13] However, her concern with it became predominantly theological.

Thus "O Ye Tongues" (DN, 75–98) ostensibly belongs to the
worship of a male God at the same time it expresses Sexton's ecstatic
discovery of an alternative myth of creation and an alternative attitude
toward the trials of female experience. In the "Seventh Psalm" (ED.
"Eighth Psalm" in CP), for example, the poet sings the praises of a
woman who has survived her arduous voyage and is now giving birth
to a baby; by a subtle process of modulation, the mother takes on
more of the qualities of the Great Goddess until in the moment of
birth, she becomes the creator of a "new dawn" in the world.

> For the baby crowns and there is a people-dawn in the world.
>
> For the baby lies in its water and blood and there is a people-
> cry in the world.
>
> For the baby suckles and there is a people made of milk for
> her to use. There are milk trees to hiss her on. There are milk
> beds in which to lie and dream of a warm room. There are milk
> fingers to fold and unfold. There are milk bottoms that are
> wet and caressed and put into their cotton.
>
> For there are many worlds of milk to walk through under the
> moon.
>
> (DN, 92)

This psalm is part of a larger pattern of mother-female images in Sexton's later poetry of dreams, visions, and prayers that I can only refer
to here.

Perhaps the most revealing of these passionate poems is "The
Consecrating Mother," the poem Linda Gray Sexton chose to end 45
Mercy Street. The poet stands on the shore experiencing the rolling
sea as if it were a woman in labor giving birth to a handful of gods.
She wonders how the sea has borne all the ships of trade, slavery, and
war, and then without warning she slips from contemplation into
ecstasy:

> She should be entered skin to skin,
> and put on like one's first or last cloth,
> entered like kneeling your way into church,
> descending into that ascension,
> though she be slick as olive oil,
> as she climbs each wave like an embezzler of white.
>
> (45, 113–14)

The remainder of the poem is even more explicitly sexual, as the moonlight on the water suggests "flashing breasts made of milk-water, / flashing buttocks made of unkillable lust," and the poet wishes to participate in her "coming, coming, / going" as the lover in "The Song of Solomon." The poem is not as polished as the ones Sexton revised herself even in the galley stage of publication,[14] but it is clear enough. In it she desires sexual union with this woman/mother goddess/sea. Her image of worship is the antithesis of the procedure she urged in "The Wall," where her goal was to escape the paradox of death in life. There she had prescribed: "take off your life like trousers, . . . then take off your flesh. . . . In other words / take off the wall / that separates you from God" (AR, 47). By contrast, "The Consecrating Mother" would allow herself to be entered "skin to skin."

Toward an Interpretation of Sexton's Agon

> Yet I'd risk my life
> on that dilly dally buttercup
> called dreams. She of the origin,
> she of the primal crack, she of the boiling
> beginning, she of the riddle, she keeps me here,
> toiling and toiling.
>
> (WDY, 63)

At moments of affirmation such as the ones I have just presented—affirmations of female creativity and sexuality as principles "heavy" enough to counter death or God—it is difficult to remember that Sexton's images failed to save her life. Ironically, two contexts capable of illuminating her predicament were taking shape in January 1973 when she wrote The Awful Rowing Toward God. James Hillman was revising his Terry Lectures wherein he had sketched the contours of a theology based upon the encounter with archetypal images of the human psyche; his book Re-Visioning Psychology provides an alternative theory of human questing wherein Sexton's images are neither perverse nor grotesque but merely necessary. In the same year, Mary Daly argued in *Beyond God the Father* that the process of unfolding a God that was consonant with female being would require a painful exile to the "boundary of all that has been considered central."[15] Without these contexts it is all too easy to discount Sexton's achievements in her last books by questioning their aesthetic value and by diverting attention from the poems to her suicide.

In interpreting Sexton's work, I find Hillman's perspective illuminating. If the purpose of life is to "make psyche matter"[16] in order to gain access to the soul, Sexton lived out that purpose "to the hilt" (*Letters*, 424). Hillman removes the stigma from both "craziness" and suicide; either may be required in a genuine encounter with the archetypal figures that lie at the roots of the soul. "Falling apart" breaks the soul free from its identification with the ego and allows encounter with the deeper images. Other modes of soul-making are love, intellectual discipline, and death.[17] Apparently all these modes were necessary in Sexton's case; certainly she tried them all, substituting her imaginative discipline for the strictly intellectual kind.

Hillman also suggests a useful analytical procedure called "psychologizing" or "seeing through" one's images to locate the *idea* of psyche or soul that governs them. He points out, for example, that the "soul" has been variously defined as the life principle, as "love" in Christian theology, and as a "tabula rasa."[18] Unless we can see which idea frames our consciousness, we run the risk of being locked into one point of view, unaware that it is a point of view.

In this light Sexton's predicament was that her soul-making involved antithetical ideas of the soul. In the Demeter-Kore myth the soul is a life principle to be saved from death and developed anew in each fruitful season of life; in the myth of the crucifixion, the soul is attained in the sacrifice of the body and the identification with the Father. *The Awful Rowing Toward God* reveals that Sexton chose the second pattern uneasily, casting her die for the confidence man who "loafs around heaven" desiring a body to house his soul (p. 24), because he outwits her in their decisive poker game (pp. 85–86).

Nothing in Sexton's letters gives a more satisfactory reason for her choice.[19] As she cut herself off from her closest friends in the last two years of her life and spent virtually all her time writing (*Letters*, 390), her poems carried the entire burden of her soul-making. As she

said in a poem about pain as a medicine to "cure the soul / of its greed
for love,"

> One learns not to blab about all this
> except to yourself or the typewriter keys
> who tell no one until they get brave
> and crawl off onto the printed page.
>
> (45, 104)

At the peak of her belief in herself in "O Ye Tongues," she had said
heroically, "For I am placing fist over fist on rock and plunging into
the altitude of words" (DN, 96). Later poems, however, suggest that
her words were inadequate in the face of images she could not recognize.

Her choice of God, then, may have had less to do with the merit
of the Christian principle of soul than with her inability to *name* the
forces and figures she discovered in her images. She complains of this
often; for example, in "Demon":

> My demon,
> too often undressed,
> too often a crucifix I bring forth,
> too often a dead daisy I give water to
> too often the child I give birth to
> and then abort, nameless, nameless . . .
> earthless.
>
> (45, 106)

In another poem written at about the same time, she begs

> Mary, Mary, virgin forever,
> whore forever,
> give me your name,
> give me your mirror.
> Boils fester in my soul,
> so give me your name so I may kiss them,
> and they will fly off,
> nameless
> but named. . . .
>
> (45, 93)

The problem seems to have been most acute for her in relation to her
female deities. For years she had heard female voices in the leaves; by
1970 she had decided that they were a "sisterhood" associated with a

green God in whose belly she would lie down if she were to "die whole" (*WDY*, 29). In 1974 she is no longer sure who her "green girls" are. Although she loves them, she is bedeviled by their anonymous voices. Yet she awakens with a scream from a dream about their disappearance to find that they have left her (45, 96–97). Sexton had risked her life on the primal images in her dreams (*WDY*, 63), but no amount of toiling relieved her doubts about their nature and reliability.[20] In turn she herself becomes an unreliable worshiper. In another posthumously published poem, she dreams of a tall Nordic Aphrodite whom she asks to "inspect" her heart and "name its pictures." When the goddess becomes sick, however, her "children" leave, because she is "no one" (*WDY*, 38–39).[21]

Perhaps the most poignant of all the instances of Sexton's inability to name her visions is in "The Consecrating Mother," where her images of female nurturance and sexuality come together. The poet hears the drowned cry "*Deo Deo*," and sees the ocean offer up her gods to them:

> I wanted to share this
> but I stood alone like a pink scarecrow.
> The ocean steamed in and out,
> the ocean gasped upon the shore
> but I could not define her,
> I could not name her mood, her locked-up faces.
>
> (45, 113)

Sexton seems to have turned away from her ecstatic vision of female creativity because she could not name her imaginative "children" or because the most familiar name to her, "Mary," left her stranded inside the Christian story once again.[22] Although she could love the figures she knew in her dreams, she could not acknowledge them as gods.

Those of us who have internalized the perspective offered by Mary Daly in *Beyond God the Father* and who have struggled to name our own archetypal images cannot help but grieve at this sight. Sexton's poems reveal that she had lived on the boundaries of her culture for several years (at least from 1970). With all of her images of God, surely she was on the verge of seeing that the idea of God could not be contained by one name. Surely in *The Book of Folly* and in *The Death Notebooks* she was on the verge of believing that her own power to draw a "baby" out of the well of her own unconscious was her "saving" grace. But the possibility of reconceptualizing God as a verb[23] (or "seeing through" the nominalization of God, as Hillman suggests) did not exist for Sexton. Daly offers an explanation: She insists that the process of attaining psychic wholeness will involve for females an "exorcism of the internalized patriarchal presence, which carries with it feelings of guilt, inferiority, and self-hatred"; furthermore, she insists that it is "naive to think that healing can take place in isolation."[24] Only when women create a "counterworld to the prevailing sense of reality"[25] will we trust our visions.

I think we must be careful not to glamorize Sexton's struggle, not to deny her right to choose death over life, and not to inflate the aesthetic value of her poetry because of the difficulty of her quest. Yet I insist that many of her late poems approach greatness. I mourn her death. And I cannot help but wish that her nameless ocean deities had triumphed as Athena triumphed over Poseidon in the battle for Odysseus's life. Read in the context of archetypal psychology and feminist theology, Sexton's work is an urgent call to continue the process of soul-making until all the possible deities are named.

NOTES

1. The line comes from a poem written in 1971 and published in the posthumous collection *Words for Dr. Y.: Uncollected Poems with Three Stories,* ed. Linda Gray Sexton (Boston: Houghton Mifflin Co., 1978), 64. Hereafter page references to Sexton's oeuvre and writings will appear in the text abbreviated as follows:

BF: *The Book of Folly* (Boston: Houghton Mifflin Co., 1972)
DN: *The Death Notebooks* (Boston: Houghton Mifflin Co., 1974)
AR: *The Awful Rowing Toward God* (Boston: Houghton Mifflin Co., 1975)
45:     *45 Mercy Street* (Boston: Houghton Mifflin Co., 1976)
WDY: *Words for Dr. Y.*
Letters: *Anne Sexton: A Self-Portrait in Letters,* ed. Linda Gray Sexton and Lois Ames (Boston: Houghton Mifflin Co., 1977).

2. Anne Sexton was born in 1928 into an upper-middle-class family with roots in Massachusetts and Maine. She married "Kayo" Sexton in 1948 shortly after she graduated from private school, and she worked as a model in Boston while her husband served in the Korean War. She was first hospitalized for

suicidal depression after the birth of her first daughter in 1953, and her affliction continued for the rest of her life despite the help of at least eight therapists. She began writing poetry seriously in 1957 and achieved immediate success, publishing her first book in 1960 and winning the Pulitzer Prize for her third in 1967. She won grants from several foundations in the late 1960s, including a Guggenheim Fellowship; she was the recipient of honorary doctorates from several universities, and she became a professor herself at Boston University in 1971. Her fifth book, *Transformations* (Boston: Houghton Mifflin Co., 1971), written in 1970, containing ambitious revisions of seventeen fairy tales, marked a turning point in her career. In the next four years she wrote the five books of poems that are the subject of this essay (*BF, DN, AR, 45*, and most of *WDY*) and some additional poems published for the first time in *The Complete Poems*, ed. Linda Gray Sexton (Boston: Houghton Mifflin Co., 1981). Only two of those books were published in her lifetime: *BF* and *DN*; she proofread the galley sheets for *AR* on the day of her suicide, Oct. 4, 1974. All this biographical information comes from the editorial narrative provided in the *Letters*.

3. From the *Letters* and the editor's notes for her posthumous books, I have tentatively established the dates of composition as follows: *Transformations* was written in the winter of 1970; *BF* in early 1971; most of *DN* in 1972, although in 1970 she said it was the book she would work on all her life (*Letters*, 368); *AR* in Jan. 1973; most of *45* between Feb. 1973 and June 1974, although it charts the period from 1971. *WDY* spans her whole career, containing a poem sequence from 1960 to 1970, another from 1971, a group from 1971 to 1973, and three horror stories from 1974.

4. See James Hillman, *Re-Visioning Psychology* (New York: Harper and Row, 1975), iv, x, 89.

5. See *AR*, 2, 17, 22, 28, 35, 41, 47, 76, and 85–86, for the various dimensions of this choice. See also "The Bat; or, To Remember, to Remember" (*WDY*, 93–101) for her story of a female crucifixion.

6. Mary Daly, *Beyond God the Father: Toward a Philosophy of Women's Liberation* (Boston: Beacon Press, 1973).

7. The phrase comes from a section of *WDY* (p. 25), written Jan. 12, 1969.

8. Suzanne Juhasz, *Naked and Fiery Forms, Modern Poetry by American Women: A New Tradition* (New York: Harper and Row, 1976), 127.

9. I am indebted to Edward S. Casey, "Toward an Archetypal Imagination," *Spring: An Annual of Archetypal Psychology and Jungian Thought* (1974): 1–32, for the distinctions among conscious imagining, active imagination, and archetypal imagination.

10. James Hillman in his editorial comments on this essay notes that these are "important figures of a 'dying religion'; yet *rat*, for instance, is the New Year, the turning point, the survivor." Sexton's palindrome "Rats Live on No

Evil Star" (*DN*, 18, 19) should be read in this light. Sexton chose that palindrome for her tombstone.

11. Suzanne Juhasz contends that Sexton frequently makes myths (*Naked and Fiery Forms*, 133), but I do not agree. Sexton frequently encounters the archetypal images that are the stuff of myths, but she rarely offers them as structures in whose terms we might live our lives, as she does here.

12. Ralph J. Mills, Jr., *Contemporary American Poetry* (New York: Random House, 1966), 231–33, noticed Sexton's identification with Christ as early as 1962 in "For God while Sleeping," *All My Pretty Ones* (Boston: Houghton Mifflin Co., 1962), 24.

13. In her fine essay "Goddess Manifestations as Stages in Feminine Metaphysics in the Poetry and Life of Anne Sexton," *supra*, 117–44.

14. See Linda Gray Sexton's editorial notes in *45* and *WDY*.

15. Daly, *Beyond God the Father*, 41.

16. Hillman, in his address "Concrete Psychology," C. G. Jung Conference, Notre Dame, Apr. 1977.

17. See Hillman, *Re-Visioning Psychology*, 89, 111.

18. Ibid., 123–26.

19. Her decision to seek a divorce followed rather than precipitated the composition of the poems in *AR*. Her break with her last psychiatrist also came after the poems in question. See *Letters*, 389, 400.

20. See also *45*, 10, 110, and 76, for related poems.

21. Cf. "The Poet of Ignorance," where the poet fears "Perhaps I am no one" (*AR*, 28), and "The Bat; or, To Remember, to Remember" (*WDY*, 99), where "Miss No-Name" is brutally crucified at the direction of a mysterious all-powerful director.

22. There were other problems as well: that her mother's name was Mary may have led her to personalize her archetypal images too readily, as in *45*, 92, and *DN*, 52, 53. It is also possible that her visions of sexual union with a goddess may have seemed beyond the pale in spite of her brave words about accepting her demon, "If it be man . . . or if it be woman I love" (*45*, 107). Obviously I have another essay to write. In it I also hope to clarify the relationship between the pattern of female imagery I have traced and another pattern of the "woman clothed in the sun" (See *DN*, 18–19).

23. Daly, *Beyond God the Father*, 45. Daly's notion of God as a "form-destroying, form-creating, transforming power that makes all things new" is not very different from Sexton's image of the mother in the "Seventh Psalm" (*DN*, 93–94—Ed. "Eighth Psalm" in *CP*) cited above.

24. Daly, *Beyond God the Father*, 50.

25. Ibid., 51.

THE AWFUL ROWING
TOWARD GOD

KATHLEEN L. NICHOLS

The Hungry Beast Rowing Toward God: Anne Sexton's Later Religious Poetry

Although Anne Sexton began writing religious poems early in her career, her last volumes of poetry—*The Death Notebooks, The Awful Rowing Toward God,* and *45 Mercy Street*—reflect her growing awareness of the imminence of death, an awareness that seemed to cut her off from the conventional world of suburbia and the marriage in which she would formerly "lose [her] frightened self."[1] Instead, with increasing absorption, she turned to a private, self-contained mythology of God and self that would compensate for the sense of a lost self that had plagued her all of her life. The compensatory function of religious myth is especially apparent in Sexton's posthumously published volume *The Awful Rowing Toward God.* Although this volume is controlled by the religious frame of the journey toward God, the archetypal patterns evoked by her poetic descents into the unconscious reveal her increasing need to find in death the ideal mother and father—the male and female archetypes of the united self—from which she had felt severely dissociated by her birth and, even more so, by their deaths. In *The Awful Rowing,* these underlying psychological patterns transform her sea journey toward God into a regressive journey back to the all-embracing womb of the mythic mother and, contained within, the lost aspect of self—the archetypal father-soul.

The consciously imposed religious pattern is readily perceived in the opening and closing "frame" poems that set up the sea-journey analogy. The opening poem entitled "Rowing" records the poet's retrospective awareness that for most of her life "God was there like an island I had not rowed to." The change of focus in middle age is shown by the rowing refrain: "I am rowing, I am rowing / though the oarlocks stick and are rusty . . . I am rowing, I am rowing, / though the wind

Reprinted from *Notes on Modern American Literature* 3 (Summer 1979), item 21.

pushes me back."[2] This poem "ends with me still rowing," but as the title of the last poem indicates, "the rowing endeth" when she moors "at the dock of the island called God," where she finds laughter and "lucky love" (pp. 85–86). Given Sexton's poetic progress from Bedlam in her first volume of poetry to the island of God in this one, the reader might almost be tempted to see a "divine comedy" pattern informing the entire Sexton canon.

Yet the sense of progress that this frame should provide is missing within the poetic sequence. In poem after poem the animal and scatological images evoked from the unconscious vividly express the poet's sense of being overwhelmed by some inner, negative force against which she has no defenses. As in earlier volumes, Sexton thinks of herself as "Ms. Dog" (p. 50), as well as a "pig in a trenchcoat" (p. 1). Even more grotesquely, inside her is a "gnawing pestilential rat" (p. 2) and elsewhere, "clutching fast to my heart, / a huge crab," which not even modern surgery can remove (p. 28). These images of disgust become even more intense when Sexton returns to a metaphor found in her earlier poetry: man is "an outhouse" (p. 27); "I . . . was a house full of bowel movement" (p. 41). The "shit" with which she feels constipated "right into the fingers" is the "evil that permeates"—it is "Poison / and the poison was all of me" (p. 55). She feels "a pain in my bowels" because "the devil has crawled / in and out of me" (p. 48), and this evil is so insidious and ubiquitous that "even in a telephone booth / evil can seep out of the receiver" (p. 45); it "comes oozing / out of flowers at night," and she warns the reader that "It comes into your mouth while you sleep. . . . Beware. Beware" (p. 34). Overwhelmed by this evil that "climbed into me," she wishes to "pour gasoline over my evil body / and light it" (p. 50).

Although Sexton had struggled in her earlier poetry to find herself through a painful analysis of her family relationships, one of the unusual features of this volume is the limited number of direct references to those most problematic forces in her life—namely, to her mother and father. Yet these dominating figures, as abstract principles or idealized archetypes, still hover in the background, defining her life and transforming the meaning of her religious journey. The poet's sense of dissociation and self-loathing, for instance, is attributed to the loss of a controlling, godlike essence—a divine father who could love and "feed" the seemingly insatiable primal hungers. Sexton maintains that "To be without God is to be a snake / who wants to swallow an elephant" (pp. 38–39), and elsewhere she thinks that she can get rid of the hungry rat "gnawing" inside of her only if she can find God, who will "embrace" the starving creature (p. 2). Male and female are viewed as conflicting forces that have created the dissociative problem of a sexually restricted identity. In one of the few autobiographical references, Sexton defines "Mother" as the repressive force that surgically fragmented the daughter's bond with the father principle. "Ms. Dog," for instance, speculated that "Maybe my mother cut God out of me" (p. 50), leaving only the "evil" flesh—the incestuous instincts— that "separates you from God" (p. 47). But, when "God went out of me . . . My body became a side of mutton" (p. 40).

This instinctual appetite to find the safely distanced father is especially reflected in the sexual act that symbolically, like a rite of sympathetic magic, unites the male-female aspects of self; the sexual instincts are man and woman's "double hunger" bringing them together and driving them "to reach through / the curtain of God" (p. 19). This ravenous hunger for the sexually complementary self can assume hyperbolic, indeed, nearly mythic proportions: "man is eating the earth up / like a candy bar / and not one of them can be left alone with the ocean / for it is known he will gulp it all down. / The stars (possibly) are safe" (pp. 13–14). When the priest asks "whose God are you looking for?" the poet's reply is again in a hunger metaphor: "a starving man doesn't ask what the meal is" (p. 50). Her "God" is obviously the male principle—the lost and idealized father who could provide recognition and meaningful transformation of the primal instincts.

To express her sense of psychic dissociation or loss of "soul," Sexton frequently externalizes this lost "god," but the lost self has, in actuality, been buried under the repressed and distorted instincts that often break out with dangerous intensity. However, through poetry she can "cut out the beggar" and "pry out the broken / pieces of God in me," an agonizing process that will enable her to "build a whole nation of God / in me—but united" (pp. 3–4). Her poems can become Whitmanesque "song[s] of myself" (p. 4) or "anthems" when the controlling poetic process succeeds, as it sometimes does, in integrating the hidden and conscious selves: "my books anoint me" (p. 11) when the inner objects inside "the room of my life" begin to "dream and wear new costumes, / compelled to, it seems, by all the words in my hands" (p. 10). These "miraculous" words (p. 71) are also "fallen angels" that she "shove[s]" around "till something comes" (p. 22). The importance of this poetic process of integration is suggested by the image of her typewriter as "my church / with an altar of keys" (p. 51), yet even when she rejoices in the power of poetic control— "I carol with what the typewriter gives, / with what God gives" (p. 80)—the same image simultaneously expresses her sense of an only partially assimilated self, for the God or male principle she writes about is the one that her *typewriter* "believes in" (p. 76).

When this poetic integration does work, her discovery of the hidden "God" or repressed self transforms, by "caging" or controlling in poetic forms, the hungry beasts that threaten her,[3] but a sense of only minimally fulfilled hungers or of precariousness is still implied. In several poems her search for God leads her to "gravy" and "water," a meal, however, of bare survival (pp. 63, 65), and elsewhere God "fills" her even though "there are times of doubt / as hollow as the Grand Canyon" (p. 70). On the other hand, the hungers of dissociation are satisfied by a falling, mannalike "snow," which she calls God's "blessed" milk—"Today God gives milk / and I have the pail" (p. 77)— while a positively joyful note is sounded in "Welcome Morning," a poem of thankfulness for the "God / right here in my pea-green house" (p. 58)—that is, as she phrased it earlier, in the "room of my life." But even in the exquisitely controlled poem "Small Wire," which asserts a calm, confident faith, the reader senses the precarious balance and security of a "faith" that is "a great weight / hung on a small wire." The ease with which she claims "He will enter your hands" lies in an uneasy tension with her surprising, past tense analogy—"as easily as ten cents used to / bring forth a Coke" (p. 78).

According to Sexton each poetic descent into the unconscious brought a sense of wholeness—a "rebirth" that, however, lasted only a couple days[4]—which is precisely the problem, for in her poetry the integrating process must also be attempted over and over again, establishing an exhausting cycle that finally can be stopped only by death. Although Sexton externalizes her "voyage / onto the surgical and-iron / of God" (p. 82), the archetypal sea-womb images change the meanings of the surface Christian patterns. Sexton, for instance, refers to the "sea without which there is no mother, / the earth without which there is no father" (p. 56); in her version of the Genesis story, man and woman's origins are the sea (p. 7), and the sea is called the "mother" of God himself (p. 68). This sea-womb association is also

apparent in the many mother-child poems in which the image of the
archetypal sea-mother transforms the poet's imaginative journey toward
death into a fetal journey back to primal sources and an undifferentiated preconsciousness that encompasses both male and female principles. In "Mothers," for instance, a "suckling child" views the nursing
breast as the "sea wrapped in skin" and the mother's legs "that bounce
me up and down" as the "horses I will ride / into eternity" (p. 72).
Even Jesus, the male principle of divorced consciousness and suffering
with which she identifies frequently in all of her poetry, begs to be
allowed to reenter the primordial world of the virgin mother's "belly,"
where he can "float . . . like a fish" and perhaps be reborn "into something true," something he has not become in his previous "rebirths"—
a real "Messiah" (p. 61).

This image of Jesus arouses in the poet feelings of pity and abhorr-
ence because it fuses the ideas of continual rebirth and of eternal suffering. Therefore, when Jesus "comes with his eggful of miracles"
(promises of renewal), what the poet envisions is "his guts drooping
like a sea worm"—his unrelieved suffering because he "lives on, lives
on" in the "awful death" (p. 57)—which is actually his life and the
consciousness of dissociation. Her distrust of the efficacy of a Christian
renewal and her horror at the idea of an endless series of "rebirths"
that never quite "take" are echoed in the grotesque image of the "Lord"
contained within a womblike "oven" in which "He is boiled, / but He
never dies, never dies" (p. 33). Therefore, when she sees the amphibious
"fish that walked" out of the sea (separated from his maternal origins),
this Christ-fish that unites so awkwardly both sea and land functions
only revives in the poet a "misplaced" or prenatal memory of her
mother and the "salt of God's belly / where I floated in a cup of darkness." She "longs" for the "country" of the fish's origins (pp. 20–21)—
for a cessation of postpartum consciousness.

Despite the religious frame of *The Awful Rowing Toward God*,
Sexton's poetic descents into the unconscious release archetypal images
and patterns that alter the meaning of her journey. What she imaginatively attains at the end of the volume is a wish-fulfilling "re-union"
with her lost soul or "divine" father on a "fish-shaped" island floating
in and surrounded by the archetypal amniotic fluid of her preconscious,
maternal origins. Her final goal is the delivery unto death and the lost,
archetypally distanced parents who define the missing aspects of self.

NOTES

1. *Anne Sexton: A Self-Portrait in Letters,* ed. Linda Gray Sexton and Lois Ames (Boston: Houghton Mifflin Co., 1977), 24. Two typical studies of Sexton's religious poetry are A. R. Jones, "Necessity and Freedom: The Poetry of Robert Lowell, Sylvia Plath and Anne Sexton," *Critical Quarterly* 7 (1965): 11–30; and Paul A. Lacey, *The Inner War* (Philadelphia: Fortress, 1972), 25–30.

2. Anne Sexton, *The Awful Rowing Toward God* (Boston: Houghton Mifflin Co., 1975), 1–2. All further references to this edition will be included in the text.

3. Patricia Marx, "Interview with Anne Sexton," *Hudson Review* 18 (Winter 1965–66): 586.

4. Ibid., 570.

WILLIAM H. SHURR

Mysticism and Suicide: Anne Sexton's Last Poetry

Schweigen. Wer inniger schwieg rührt an die Wurzeln der Rede.
—Rilke

And Rilke, think of Rilke with his terrible pain.
—Anne Sexton[1]

When Anne Sexton died in 1974, she had just produced what she intended to be her final book of poems, *The Awful Rowing Toward God*.[2] Before that volume the direction of her work was unclear. There had been seven earlier books of poetry, beginning with the forceful and unsettling poems of *To Bedlam and Part Way Back* (1960). Her signature was the clear line of personal narrative, but it was frequently not clear whether the narratives were true biography or a kind of artistically manipulated pseudo-biography. She became famous, winning a Pulitzer Prize in 1966, and the reader became familiar with such frequently anthologized poems as "Unknown Girl in the Maternity Ward," "The Truth the Dead Know," "The Farmer's Wife," and "The Abortion." We knew her voice, but each poem seemed an unrelated victory. Her early classification among the "confessional poets" never seemed to confer the insights it had promised.[3] One fellow poet dismissed her work as garbage;[4] at the other pole Sandra Gilbert canonized her divine madness in an essay entitled "Jubilate Anne."[5]

The reader's reward was finally *The Awful Rowing Toward God*, the book of a mature poet whose dedication to art was single-minded and supreme, who could finally declare with utter simplicity, "I am in love with words" (p. 71). Sexton had prepared and intended *The Awful Rowing Toward God* as a posthumous publication. A year before she died she told an interviewer that she had written the first drafts of these poems in two and a half weeks, that she would continue

Reprinted from *Soundings: An Interdisciplinary Journal* 68 (Fall 1985): 335–56.

to polish them, but that she would allow publication only after her death.[6] Her published letters add the chilling information that she had then sent the manuscript to her publisher and was actually reading the galley proofs on the day she took her own life.[7]

The volume gains authority as Anne Sexton's intended final work. The shape and direction of her poetic career finally becomes clear. Certain also is the grim fact that the suicide is a consciously intended part of the book. We miss her meaning, the total program she provided for her reader to experience, without this stark fact.

As the "Rowing" of the title suggests, the image of the sea pervades this collection; and it soon becomes obvious that this metaphorical sea is the carrier for one of the most profound and pervasive ideas of Western culture.

One of Sexton's earliest reviewers noticed the prominence of the sea in her work,[8] and when a later interviewer asked her about it, she affirmed its personal importance to her. She was a New Englander: the sea was in her history and in her daily experience.[9] The imagery aligns her, also, with some of the most prominent American writers. Emily Dickinson was another virtually landlocked lady in whose poetry the sea is pervasive. The New England tradition was remembered as having begun with a dangerous adventure across the unknown ocean; the culture was supported throughout its history by commerce on the sea. For Sexton personally the sea was escape and renewal, where the family had vacationed since her childhood. It is both a danger and life-support system. In most of her poetry it is also the setting for the journey of the soul. The phrase most often quoted from her early books by reviewers was the one she retrieved from Kafka and used as epigraph for *All My Pretty Ones:* "A book should serve as the ax for the frozen sea within us."[10]

In her final volume this sea becomes warm with swarming life. The two poems that begin and end the collection, "Rowing" and "The Rowing Endeth," set up a framework of sea exploration, and there are overt references to the sea in two-thirds of the poems. The sea is quite literally the fluid medium in which the mental life of this poetry takes place. The first poem begins with the emergence of the self from nonbeing; the child is gradually able to do more human things but feels itself still "undersea all the time." We are only seven pages into the collection when the perception becomes clear that the sea is the source of all life:

> From the sea came up a hand,
> ignorant as a penny,
> troubled with the salt of its mother,
> mute with the silence of the fishes,
> quick with the altars of the tides,
> and God reached out of His mouth
> and called it man.
> Up came the other hand
> and God called it woman.
> The hands applauded.
> And this was no sin.
> It was as it was meant to be.

There is a calm rightness carrying this statement along, a sense of order, and—new for Sexton—an untroubled account of the invention of sexuality. The poem achieves dignity and authority by its imitation of biblical diction.

But the sea is not only origin; it is also metaphor for the continuing flow of life within the human being. Sexton, for example, perceives the pulse that beats in her arteries as "the sea that bangs in my throat" (p. 10). The figure is extended a few pages later, where "the heart . . . swallows the tides / and spits them out cleansed" (p. 25). The sea is simultaneously within and without. Even the ears are "conch shells," fashioned to bring in the sound of the sea constantly to human consciousness. This seems to intimate that human beings live in a Sea of Life, but if one knows that the conch shell really amplifies the rush of the blood within the hearer, then this line also indicates that the Sea of Life is within.

There are negative elements in this massive symbolic sea world. On the margin between sea and land, between spirit and matter, are the crab who causes painful cancer (p. 28), the sand flea who might enter the ear and cause madness in the brain (pp. 34–35), the turtle who furnishes an image of human sloth and insensitivity (p. 36). There is also the land itself, which supports human iniquity (p. 44) and furnishes images for spiritual dryness and desolation (pp. 42, 44, 62). But in this world the margin between sea and land is also creative; it is the area where "the sea places its many fingers on the shore" and opposites can interact. The sea is necessary "mother," as the earth is necessary "father," and without interaction between the two there is no life (p. 56).

Still another perception unfolds as Sexton explores her sea subject: "Perhaps the earth is floating" on the sea (p. 28). The world of matter floats on the sea of spirit and life; and so that sea is never far off from any of us. Even the earthbound can dig wells in the middle of the desert, and tap into that sea, as the Sphinx advises the poet to do in another poem:

> I found the well [of God],
>
> . . . .
>
> and there was water,
> and I drank.
>
> Then the well spoke to me.
> It said: Abundance is scooped from abundance,
> yet abundance remains.
>
> (Pp. 64–65)

The appreciative reader has now arrived, at this point in the book, at the ancient literary perception of a metaphoric sea that surrounds and animates all life with a creative vitality, the fluid medium in which things live and move and have their being, a creative "Abundance" prodigal of its forms. This is the same perception that is behind much literature that can be described as "romantic," "enthusiastic," or in any way "mystical."

These figures and tropes carry us to one of Sexton's most moving poems, the only one in the collection in which the obvious and awaited word "Logos" appears:

> When man
> enters woman,
> like the surf biting the shore,
> again and again,
> and the woman opens her mouth in pleasure
> and her teeth gleam
> like the alphabet,
> Logos appears milking a star,
> and the man
> inside of woman
> ties a knot
> so that they will
> never again be separate
> and the woman

> climbs into a flower
> and swallows its stem
> and Logos appears
> and unleashes their rivers.

(P. 19)

Sexton recapitulates twenty-five centuries of Western erotic mysticism here, where the imagery of the Song of Solomon merged early with the worship of the Torah and then developed through the writings of Saint John the Divine into the Logos Christology of the Greek Fathers, who were themselves influenced by Plato's lovely idea, in the *Timaeus*, of the world as divine creative body. Divine creative energy, which unleashes itself in permanent joyous activity, has—according to the poem—its momentary analogue in human ecstasy: the human being can, at least briefly during intercourse, "reach through / the curtain of God" to participate by immediate contact in the creative flow of life.

Image carries idea. The most important function of the sea images in *The Awful Rowing Toward God* is to carry the items that produce this Logos mysticism as Sexton's final achievement, the final life-conferring idea her work came to embody.

Among the most important poems in this personal synthesis then becomes the strange one called "The Fish That Walked" (pp. 20–21). The title introduces the scenario: a fish enters the human element for a period, finds the place "awkward" and "without grace." "There is no rhythm / in this country of dirt," he says. But the experience stimulates deep memories in the poet-observer, of her own vague preexistence in the sea, floating in "the salt of God's belly," with deep longings "for your country, fish." In view of the Logos poem that immediately precedes it, this poem is not so strange. With its allusions to grace and to the traditional symbol of fish as Christ, this is Anne Sexton's highly personal version of the Logos made flesh and dwelling among men. Sexton asserts that she herself has enjoyed the mystical experience of living in the flowing life of the divine: the poem ends with conversation between the lady-poet and the fish-Logos.

Sexton's Logos intuition is itself creative, generating further imaginative work. More developments follow, and more connections are made. God is incomplete without a body, for example: according to a poem called "The Earth,"

> God owns heaven,
> but He craves the earth,
>
>   . . . .
>
> but most of all He envies the bodies,
> He who has no body.
>
>   (P. 24)

And in a later poem in the collection, the Logos would like to be incarnated more than once:

> I have been born many times, a false Messiah,
> but let me be born again
> into something true.
>
>   (P. 61)

Such a world, in which the Logos is the sea where the poet lives, is charged with personality or personhood. Near the end of the collection a poem begins

> I cannot walk an inch
> without trying to walk to God.
> I cannot move a finger
> without trying to touch God.
>
>   (P. 83)

The grounds here are those of mystics and theologians who have perceived the Logos as eternally existing, responsible for the creation of the physical world and responsible also for preventing its lapse back into nonbeing.[11]

The image of the sea, as it merges into the idea of the Logos, is thus the underlying metaphor that gives *The Awful Rowing Toward God* its largest meaning and its undeniable power: the sea-Logos gives life initially, sustains and supports it, and finally receives it back. It is the personalized arena for the struggle of the human mind as well as the goal of the human mind and affections. And the poet's consciousness is at the center of this world. Her genius comes alive in this vital connection with its source. With this collection Anne Sexton's work creates a highly personal synthesis of the mystical potential in Western civilization.

It is startling to find such traditional piety in the sophisticated lady whose conversation was sprinkled with conventional obscenities, whose trademark was the ever-present pack of Salems. In the photographs that accompany her works, she is immaculately groomed, expensively dressed, posing against a glassed-in sun porch amid wicker furniture and potted plants. If this is the setting of anguish, it seems mockingly ironic. On the evidence of the photographs, one might almost accuse Anne Sexton of self-indulgence; we might almost agree with one of her early critics that she is "a poet without mystical inclinations."[12] But her voice is deeply formed from layers of authentic experience. Style in this last volume has grown lean and precise, the presentation of a personal idiom.

It is surprising, also, to find the lady so learned in the tradition. She despised her formal education: "I'm not an intellectual of any sort I know of. . . . I had never gone to college, I absolutely was a flunk-out in any schooling I had, I laughed my way through exams. . . . And until I started at twenty-seven, hadn't done much reading."[13] Her comments led one sympathetic friend to write (mistakenly, I think): "Nor was Sexton a particularly reflective or intellectual person. She came to poetry late, to learning even later, and though she worked hard to educate herself, she never acquired a vocabulary to discuss her ideas on a level of enduring interest or value."[14] But the reader emerges from *The Awful Rowing Toward God* with the sense of having been put deeply in touch with the tradition of letters and religious sensibility; she embodies both the length and the richness of that tradition.

For example, the title, *The Awful Rowing Toward God*, seems to arrest the reader with its overtones from Emily Dickinson, some of whose love poems feature images of rowing to safe harbor.[15] And, indeed, among the first impressions that the book makes is that it recapitulates the American experience in literature. The myth from Poe's *Eureka* is reflected in these lines: "I will take a crowbar / and pry out the broken / pieces of God in me" (p. 3). Sexton repeats Whitman in calling her poems "a song of myself" (p. 4). The later voice of T. S. Eliot can surely be heard in these lines:

> Listen.
> We must all stop dying in the little ways,
> in the craters of hate,
> in the potholes of indifference—
> a murder in the temple.
> The place I live in
> is a kind of maze
> and I keep seeking
> the exit or the home.

> Yet if I could listen
> to the bulldog courage of those children
> and turn inward into the plague of my soul
> with more eyes than the stars
> I could melt the darkness. . . .
>
> (P. 6)

There must be a nod to Thoreau's personified pond as she notices "the pond wearing its mustache of frost" (p. 13). There is direct engagement with one of Emily Dickinson's poems when she says, "Perhaps I am no one" (p. 28). The American Indian legacy is briefly regarded as she imagines a reservation with "their plastic feathers, / the dead dream" (p. 44) and tries herself to revitalize those Indian dreams of fire, vulture, coyote, and wren (p. 66). The great American writers are also apparent in the sea imagery on almost every page of *The Awful Rowing Toward God*. She extends as well an American writer's interest in evolution: the two themes emerge in one poem, where "the sea . . . is the kitchen of God" (p. 46).

But she can be found even more intensely among the modernist concerns of the century. She sounds like Yeats early in her collection: "[The children] are writing down their life / on a century fallen to ruin" (p. 5). She has learned the modern temper from Kierkegaard, and in one poem gives her own personal version of "The Sickness unto Death" (p. 40). She has learned from Beckett to construct scenarios of the absurd with her own life as the text (p. 38). She has learned the metaphysical seriousness of *The Seventh Seal* of Ingmar Bergman: the last poem of this collection imagines Sexton playing her royal flush against the lyrically wild cards of God (p. 86). She has learned from Lowell, Berryman, and Snodgrass so to liberate her writing as to match the tones and concerns of modern inner speech. The language taboos are broken through: the banal reductions of ordinary speech are as telling, in context, as were the flights of fancy in former times. Formal structures of versification in her final work are valid only for the individual poem—each poem has its own form.

The Awful Rowing Toward God embodies a stratum of even deeper and longer historical traditions. What will make the poetry of Anne Sexton permanently valid is her modernization of the perennial meditative wisdom of the West. C. S. Lewis said many years ago that "humanity does not pass through phases as a train passes through stations: being alive, it has the privilege of always moving yet never leaving anything behind."[16] Heaven and hell remain useful for the mind to locate itself, even for a population without the "faith" to regard them as actual places. Anne Sexton's last volume presents a very personalized compendium of the permanent wisdom of the West, of those questions that frame our inquiry, those values that are constantly meditated on in our solitude. She has written her own psalm sequences, her own proverbs of wisdom. She can look at traces of evil within and strike a playful explanation from the first text of Western literature: "(not meaning to be [evil], you understand, / just something I ate)" (p. 49). The fabric is densely woven by a woman of "little education."

The Awful Rowing Toward God describes not only perception of the Logos but also the traditional journey of the ascetic soul toward encounter. A voice present from the earliest volumes reiterates the neurotic intensity of her perceptions, the hypersensitivity produced by inner disorder. But in this final book the voice that had earlier spoken her madness now seems cultivated for insight. The room where she writes has become sacred and magical: the electric wall sockets are perhaps "a cave of bees" (p. 9), the phone takes root and flowers (p. 9), "birds explode" outside the window (p. 10); her typewriter is at the center, with forty-eight eyeballs that never shut (p. 9); it holds carols for the "dance of Joy," songs that come from God (pp. 80–81). This room of the writer becomes the geographical center of her poems, as her writing becomes the one passion that has mercilessly excluded all others—the lover who had been celebrated in Love Poems, the recently divorced husband, the growing daughters, and the friends who have been alienated or abandoned have all dropped beneath the mental horizon of this collection. Perhaps there is the ruthless egotism that Perry Miller believed he saw in Thoreau, the violent simplification to gain her writer's solitude. But perhaps it is the last instinct of the ascetic, ruthlessly to exclude everything from one's life that suggests this world, that does not furnish essential baggage for the next.

The journey within this room begins with savage emptying. Sexton imagines herself as the Witch, a figure from earlier poems now assumed as a personal identity. She goes to her window only to shout, "Get out of my life!" (p. 11). She imagines herself as old and ridiculous to look at.

> I am shoveling the children out,
> scoop after scoop.
>
> . . . .
>
> Maybe I am becoming a hermit,
> opening the door for only
> a few special animals?
>
> . . . .
>
> Maybe I have plugged up my sockets
> to keep the gods in?

But it is all required, she says in a magnificent phrase, for "climbing the primordial climb" (pp. 11–12).

In the earliest stages of the climb, the power of evil intrudes and impedes. She senses "the bomb of an alien God":

> The children are all crying in their pens
>
> . . . .
>
> They are old men who have seen too much,
> their mouths are full of dirty clothes,
> the tongues poverty, tears like pus.
>
>   (P. 5)

She takes this evil upon herself and sings the lament of the ancient psalmist:

> God went out of me
> as if the sea dried up like sandpaper,
> as if the sun became a latrine.
> God went out of my fingers.
> They became stone.
> My body became a side of mutton
> and despair roamed the slaughterhouse.
>
>   (P. 40)

As a sufferer herself her compassion expands to all of humanity caught in the hell of a bad dream:

> They are mute.
> They do not cry help
> except inside
> where their hearts are covered with grubs.
>
>   (Pp. 42–43)

And insight arrives with compassion. She senses that her heart is dead, but only because she called it EVIL (pp. 36–37). And further light appears when she sees that physical isolation is an aspect of human misery; in a poem called "Locked Doors" she looks into the human hell: "The people inside have no water / and are never allowed to touch" (p. 42). In the earliest poem in this collection, she had already started this theme of isolation:

> Then there was life
> with its cruel houses
> and people who seldom touched—
> though touch is all.
>
> (P. 1)

Three poems that appear near the center of the collection recapitulate aspects of the journey toward perception of the Logos. The most historically based poem of the collection is called "The Sickness unto Death," and it is a Kierkegaardian meditation on the human sense of loss and isolation, of estrangement from the Sea of Life. What is left is evil, excremental; it must be eaten slowly and bitterly. The poem stands as a pivot at the center of the book, and it ends with a turn upwards, with a catharsis:

> tears washed me,
> wave after cowardly wave,
>
> . . . .
>
> and Jesus stood over me looking down
> and He laughed to find me gone,
> and put His mouth to mine
> and gave me His air.
>
> (P. 41)

The next poem in this series follows a few pages later and continues this upward development. "The Wall" begins with the paradox that over the millions of years of evolution the only thing that has not changed in nature is the phenomenon of change; mutability is the only constant. It is a part of wisdom to participate consciously in this reality. At the end the poet's voice assumes great authority and formality. She is now the seer who has lived close enough to her experience to emerge with wisdom worth imparting:

> For all you who are going,
> and there are many who are climbing their pain,
> many who will be painted out with a black ink
> suddenly and before it is time,
> for those many I say,

> awkwardly, clumsily,
> take off your life like trousers,
> your shoes, your underwear,
> then take off your flesh,
> unpick the lock of your bones.
> In other words
> take off the wall
> that separates you from God.
>
> (P. 47)

The road upwards, the journey of affirmation, contains moments of joy and vision. The grounding insight, which regulates the rest of the ascent, comes in a third poem called "Is It True?" the longest poem in the collection and also located near the book's center. It is a poem of occupations and blessings for ordinary things, which become transparent and holy. But in the midst of these the poet still senses herself "in this country of black mud" (p. 51) and can see herself as animal, filled with excrement, living in a country that still prosecuted the Vietnam War. The poem begins with the natural instinct of the human to stop his work and look up at the sun occasionally; it ends with looking up to find Christ in the figure of the wounded seagull:

> For I look up,
> and in a blaze of butter is
> Christ,
> soiled with my sour tears,
> Christ,
> a lamb that has been slain,
> his guts drooping like a sea worm,
> but who lives on, lives on
> like the wings of an Atlantic seagull.
> Though he has stopped flying,
> the wings go on flapping
> despite it all,
> despite it all.
>
> (P. 57)

The next poem records moments of pure ecstasy, where daily chores and ordinary occupations are permeated with the presence of the divine: "There is joy / in all" (p. 58). She is transported by the impulse "to faint down by the kitchen table / in a prayer of rejoicing" (p. 58). She expands in a poem called "The Big Heart" a few pages later, accepting a new repose at a higher level of reconciliation:

> And God is filling me,
> though there are times of doubt
> as hollow as the Grand Canyon,
> still God is filling me.
> He is giving me the thoughts of dogs,
> the spider in its intricate web,
> the sun
> in all its amazement,
> and the slain ram
> that is the glory,
> the mystery of great cost,
> and my heart,
> which is very big,
> I promise it is very large,
> a monster of sorts,
> takes it all in—
> and in comes the fury of love.
>
> (P. 70)

This leads, in the poems that follow, to multiple reconciliations. Friends are gathered around her, valued for their "abundance" (p. 69). Words sometimes fail the poet, but they are "miraculous" nevertheless.

> I am in love with words.
> They are doves falling out of the ceiling.
> They are six holy oranges sitting in my lap.
> They are the trees, the legs of summer,
> and the sun, its passionate face.
>
> (P. 71)

She becomes reconciled with the mother who had been a harsh presence in earlier volumes; she relives life at the breast, life at the knee, and now feels the strength necessary to face what she calls "the big people's world" (p. 73). The whole of the mystical tradition now becomes her personal domain, and she can speak of the Jesus of Christianity as "the Christ who walked for me" (p. 76).

We must, then, come down to Anne Sexton as a *religious* poet; critics have found this aspect of her poetry more difficult than her shocking language or her revelation of family secrets. It is quite obvious in the later collections that she becomes progressively more interested in exploring aspects of the Western religious tradition. Barbara Kevles was the interviewer who was able to probe most deeply into this aspect of Sexton's experience. In the *Paris Review* interview of 1971, her gently persistent questions led Sexton to reveal a great deal about her religious experiences. She protested initially that she was not "a lapsed Catholic" as some had conjectured; she was religious on her own Protestant terms. The most startling revelation of this interview was her experience with visions: "I have visions—sometimes ritualized visions—that come of me of God, or of Christ, or of the Saints, and I feel that I can touch them almost . . . that they are a part of me. . . . If you want to know the truth, the leaves talk to me every June. . . . I feel very much in touch with things after I've had a vision. It's somewhat like the beginning of writing a poem; the whole world is very sharp and well defined, and I'm intensely alive. . . ." One recalls the story that Hilda Doolittle told on herself—it was only after she mentioned to Sigmund Freud that she had religious visions that Freud felt she was sufficiently interesting, and sufficiently sick, for him to take her on as a patient. But in this interview Sexton was able to keep religion and mental illness separated at least to her own satisfaction: "When you're mad, [the visions are] silly and out of place, whereas if it's so-called mystical experience, you've put everything in its proper place." She protested that speaking of these things to the interviewer caused her some discomfort and she would prefer to move on to other subjects. But the line of questioning produced this final insight: "I think in time to come people will be more shocked by my mystical poetry than by my so-called confessional poetry."[17]

The mystical poetry has not been universally appreciated. For one hostile critic the religious poems read like "verbal comicstrips . . . the pathetic figure of 'Mrs. Sexton' reminds one less of St. Theresa than of Charlie Brown."[18] Another critic, though, could recognize in her the "sacerdotal . . . a priestess celebrating mysteries," and could use such words as "hieratic . . . sibyl . . . vatic."[19]

It may be that Sexton herself was somewhat surprised or even embarrassed by this turn of her interests, this direction of her own growth. At least this seems a possible explanation for her decision to leave the poems for posthumous publication—though the careful reader can already discern seeds of this book, hints of this evolution, in her earlier collections.

We come then finally to deal with Saint Anne, who found the Western tradition of spirituality anything but bankrupt. Toward the end of this collection we find that she has been reading the lives of the saints (p. 79) and that she even has meditations on the three theological virtues of faith, hope, and charity. Faith is initially described as a great weight of information hung on a small wire. The small wire then becomes a thin vein with love pulsing back and forth through it, sustaining the believer with a higher life. The relation is life-giving and life-sustaining, as the twig feeds life to the grape, from another figure in the poem. The ending is dramatically modern, with one of Sexton's reductive similes: the pulsing vein of faith is man's contract with God, who "will enter your hands / as easily as ten cents used to / bring forth a Coke" (p. 78). The poem is remarkable for its intelligence and its compactness, as well as for its historical sweep.

Two rowing poems bracket this collection and give its title. They are the only ones to use the rowing metaphor. The first is a poem of beginnings: recollections of the crib, dolls, early school years, the gradual recognition of inner pain and loneliness. Consciousness emerges from all of these experiences as if rising from under a sea, gradually discerning God as an island goal. The rower as in a dream fights absurd obstacles but has the hope of possible calm and resolution at journey's end.

The last poem is full of joy. The rowing has ended; the struggle is over. The surprise in the poem is the game of poker that God requires of the newcomer. He deals her a royal flush, the complete family of cards. But he has tricked her—with wild cards he holds five aces. The game and the trickery serve to release the final tensions of the volume. Laughter spills out, and the hoop of his laughter rolls into her mouth, joining God and the rower in intimate union.

> Then I laugh, the fishy dock laughs
> the sea laughs. The Island laughs.
> The Absurd laughs.
>
> (P. 86)

The poem and the volume end with love for the wild card, the "Dearest dealer," the "eternal . . . and lucky love."

The Awful Rowing Toward God seems a complex harmonium, a radical simplification achieved at great personal expense. Anaïs Nin once described her own work as a writer in the following way: "Why one writes is a question I can answer easily, having so often asked it of myself. I believe one writes because one has to create a world in which one can live. I could not live in any of the worlds offered to me—the world of my parents, the world of war, the world of politics. I had to create a world of my own, like a climate, a country, an atmosphere in which I could breathe, reign, and recreate myself when destroyed by living. That, I believe, is the reason for every work of art."[20]

The Awful Rowing Toward God is a polished and completed "alternative world," inevitable like every great work of art. It is the personal embodiment of one of the oldest and most invigorating ideas in the Western tradition, the idea of the Logos. She does not die as does Henry James's character Dencombe, in *The Middle Years*, feeling that he had never completed the artistic work for which his whole life has been a preparation. But her achievement in this book of poems is penultimate; the final action, the suicide, remains to be pondered.

There is a body of scientific theory on suicide. One sociopsychological theorist begins with questions such as "Why does man induce so fearful a thing as death when nothing so terrifying as death is imminent?"[21] His assumption is that death is always and in every case "fearful" and "terrifying." Sexton's final work is contrary evidence. "Exhilaration" would be a more appropriate word.

It may be that we are closer to the reality with A. Alvarez. In his extraordinary study of literature and suicide, Alvarez writes that "each suicide is a closed world with its own irresistible logic."[22] Each suicide is special, wrapped in its own individual mystery. We must then build a theory for each case, and for a start we may cull a brief anthology of Sexton's comments on death, from several different letters to friends:[23]

> Killing yourself is merely a way to avoid pain.
>
> Suicide is the opposite of a poem.
>
> Once I thought God didn't want me up there in the sky. Now I'm convinced he does.
>
> In my opinion Hemingway did the right thing.
>
> One writes to forestall being blotted out.
>
> I'm so God damned sure I'm going to die soon.

The list is chronological, and though the statements are in ragged prose, unsupported by the framework of a poem, they show progression, from a conventional and guilt-ridden attitude toward suicide to a more open understanding of it. Sexton's ideas on suicide obviously changed as she came closer to her own death.

Much of Sexton's artistic speculation on suicide she herself gathered in her third book of poems, *Live or Die* (1966), and a full account of the genesis of her thought would have to deal extensively with these explorations. A brief tour through that book produces several direct statements about "the almost unnameable lust" for self-destruction:

> But suicides have a special language.
> Like carpenters they want to know *which tools.*
> They never ask *why build.*
>
> (P. 59)

Her voyage has already set in that direction. But so in a more general sense has everyone's:

> But surely you know that everyone has a death,
> his own death,
> waiting for him.
> So I will go now
> without old age or disease. . . .
>
> (P. 77)

The last poem of *Live or Die* was actually called a "hokey" ending to the collection by an unsympathetic reader.[24] But it can be seen as strongly defining the collection. The decision not to take one's life is "a sort of human statement" (p. 87), a celebration

> of the sun,
> the dream, the excitable gift.
> (P. 90)

It was about this time that Sexton recorded her psychiatrist's plea, "Don't kill yourself. Your poems might mean something to someone else some day."[25] It was as if she sensed a mission still to be completed.

But what may be the most powerful poem in the 1966 volume comes in the center, "To Lose the Earth." The reader is arrested by the epigraph, from Thomas Wolfe: "To lose the earth you know, for greater knowing; to lose the life you have, for greater life; to leave the friends you loved, for greater loving; to find a land more kind than home, more large than earth" (p. 35). The poem itself goes on to conduct the reader's entry into a work of art, and it is a remarkably moving experience. It is an entry into the world of timeless beauty, which is elevating and utterly mind-altering. But introduced as it is by the quotation from Wolfe, the poem is ambivalent: it is, equally, the experience of death into which she conducts us. The poem is Sexton's "Ode on a Grecian Urn" and "Ode to a Nightingale" stated simultaneously: the lure of death merges with the idea of timeless beauty. It is the escape of the ego, with its imagination, into the eternal stasis of beauty and truth. Joyce Carol Oates wrote, much more sympathetically, that "Sexton yearned for that larger experience, that rush of near divine certainty that the self *is* immortal."[26] Freud had already generalized on this phenomenon: "Our unconscious . . . does not believe in its own death; it behaves as if it were immortal."[27] We need, then, a broader set of categories for suicide.

As a young man Ralph Waldo Emerson speculated quite generously on the variety of motivations leading to suicide, and provided this listing:

> It is wrong to say generally that the suicide is a hero or that he is a coward. . . . The merit of the action must obviously depend in all cases upon the particular condition of the individual. It may be in one the effect of despair, in one of madness, in one of fear, in one of magnanimity, in one of ardent curiosity to know the wonders of the other world.[28]

Emerson's last two categories, startling for a young clergyman, carry us farther toward meanings latent in *The Awful Rowing Toward God*.

One accomplishment of the collection is an enormous expansion of awareness, of consciousness. As Sexton grows from inner disorder to inner harmony, from madness to poetry, the themes and images of the mystical tradition provide rungs for that "primordial climb." A vast inwardness develops: silence and introspection sculpt the inner world until it matches the larger lineaments of the common tradition of Western mysticism. The journey is the dangerous work of solitude:

> one must listen hard to the animal within,
> one must walk like a sleepwalker
> on the edge of the roof,
> one must throw some part of her body
> into the devil's mouth.
>
> (P. 44)

The flight from multiplicity, in the search for "the realm of purity, and eternity, and unchangeableness," which Plato described in *The*

Phaedo, results in a sense of accomplishment, of self-control and rest, of "being in communion with the unchanging."[29] Sexton comes to embody one form of the long tradition of liberal inquiry and inward search for concepts and values that, as Socrates observed, make human life worth living. There results a sense, as in Poe's *Eureka*, of the return from fragmentation to unity, to the primordial paradise, the home of life, beauty, intelligence. The preliminary report of this world can now be tendered by one "in love with words," but the reality itself is fully experienced only when one takes the final step into the Great Silence that climaxes Thoreau's journey in *A Week on the Concord and Merrimack Rivers*. To borrow a phrase from Rilke, Sexton "steps, festively clothed, out of the great darkness" of her solitude. She has achieved, in her climactic work, exactly what Emerson called "magnanimity."

It is not enough to say that literature is an imitation of life. It is rather an abstract of life and a forced patterning of life. Time, in art, is stopped, repeatable, arranged, enriched, reversible—as it is not in life. The events that befall a person in a drama or a narrative may be the experiences of a real person in real life. But there is an important difference. In real life the experience is part of a flow; significant experiences are merged with experiences of entirely different meaning or of no apparent meaning at all. The pattern of significance is clouded over by other events. Even the profoundest introspection may not uncover the exact beginning or the final end of the reverberations of an experience. In art, on the other hand, even the most abstract art, there is selectivity and conscious pattern. Art and the life experience are rarely identical. There are cases where life becomes significant when it tries to imitate art, as closely as possible, as when one might try to live up to a code or an ideal.

Sexton became totally an artist, to the exclusion of any other role, an artist whose medium, in the final event, was her own life. The major actions of her final months seem deliberate attempts at denouement: the final book was shaped to its final order; the final task was to act the finis. How else guarantee the permanence of the accomplishment; how else act authentically on the present state of insight?

The most famous twentieth-century comment on suicide was Albert Camus's in *The Myth of Sisyphus:* "There is but one truly serious philosophical problem, and that is suicide. Judging whether life is or is not worth living amounts to answering the fundamental question of philosophy."[30] It is generally assumed, in the context of Camus's thought, that suicide would be a negative judgment of the "worth" of life. In Sexton's case the contrary is true.

For Sexton one can see suicide as grounded in "magnanimity," as the result of "ardent curiosity," the self-chosen final capstone to a structure of life and art now satisfactorily completed. Suicide becomes a version of Kierkegaard's leap of faith, a step into what the imagination had seemed, by its harmonizings, to authenticate. Should there be no light beyond, at least the adventurer has left behind a vision of sublime light. Sexton's way is not evèryone's, but it has its own rationale and, as artistic vision, its own extraordinary beauty.

NOTES

1. Patricia Marx, "Interview with Anne Sexton," *Hudson Review* 18 (Winter 1965–66): 562.

2. Anne Sexton, *The Awful Rowing Toward God* (Boston: Houghton Mifflin Co., 1975). (All references to poems from this collection will be cited in the text.) At the time of her death, Sexton was working on still more poems, but she does not seem to have prized them as highly; they appear to be more of a miscellany. They were edited by her daughter Linda Gray Sexton and published as *45 Mercy Street* (Boston: Houghton Mifflin Co., 1976).

3. M. L. Rosenthal, who invented the phrase, says, "The term 'confessional poetry' naturally came to mind when I reviewed Robert Lowell's *Life Studies* in 1959"; see *The New Poets: American and British Poetry since World War II* (New York: Oxford University Press, 1967), 25. Robert Phillip's book, *The Confessional Poets* (Carbondale: Southern Illinois University Press, 1973), places Anne Sexton as a member of this "school" and discusses the themes of her early poetry at some length. Sexton showed herself to be interested in the designation: in an interview with Patricia Berg in the *New York Times* for Nov. 9, 1969, she said: "About a year ago I decided I was the only confessional poet around. Well . . . Allen Ginsberg too. He holds back nothing and I hold back nothing." But such a statement puts the reader off balance for at least two reasons: Ginsberg has never been suggested as belonging to the confessional school of poetry, nor has any one else ever thought to compare Ginsberg with Sexton.

4. James Dickey, in a review of Sexton's volume *All My Pretty Ones*, in the *New York Times* Book Review section, Apr. 28, 1963. Dickey reprinted the remarks, thus appearing to reconfirm them, in *Babel to Byzantium: Poets and Poetry Now* (New York: Grosset and Dunlap, 1971), 133–34. Other early reviewers also showed considerable animus in their initial responses to Sexton.

Peggy Rizza, for example, felt Sexton to be "excessively personal," a devotee of "the feminine stereotype of Hysteria," "obsessive"; for Rizza, "we feel like voyeurs, as though we have read something we hadn't quite intended to read, something which is revealing or embarrassing but in no way instructive." See "Another Side of This Life: Women as Poets," in *American Poetry since 1960,* ed. Robert B. Shaw (Cheshire, England: Carcanet Press, 1973), 169–79, passim. Such snarling from reviewers is almost always a sign that something significant and new is happening in literature.

5. Sandra Gilbert, a review of *The Death Notebooks,* in *Nation* 219 (Sept. 14, 1974): 214–16. Margaret Ferrari, though somewhat uneasy about the theological orthodoxy of the poems, also concentrated on Sexton's religious intensity throughout her poetic career. See "Anne Sexton: Between Death and God," *America* 131 (Nov. 9, 1974): 281–84.

6. "From 1928 to Whenever: A Conversation with Anne Sexton," in *The American Poets in 1976,* ed. William Heyen (Indianapolis: Bobbs-Merrill, 1976), 316–17.

7. *Anne Sexton: A Self-Portrait in Letters,* ed. Linda Gray Sexton and Lois Ames (Boston: Houghton Mifflin Co., 1977), 423.

8. Melvin Maddocks, in a review of *To Bedlam and Part Way Back, Christian Science Monitor,* Sept. 1, 1960, 1.

9. An interview with Anne Sexton, Apr. 13, 1964, in *Talks with Authors,* ed. Charles F. Madden (Carbondale: Southern Illinois University Press, 1968), 178: "I . . . live right near the sea and love it. Your region becomes imbedded in you."

10. Anne Sexton, *All My Pretty Ones* (Boston: Houghton Mifflin Co., 1962), vii.

11. A few samples from the tradition may suffice. Origin, in his commentary on Psalm 36, writes of the Logos "of whom all human kind and, maybe, the whole universe of creation, is the body." Maximus the Confessor, one of the major sources of Western mysticism, wrote that "the mystery of the Incarnation of the Logos contains in itself the meaning of the whole of creation." An Easter sermon attributed to a disciple of Saint Hippolytus, speaks of the cross of Jesus, after the Resurrection, as "strong bulwark of the universe, bond that holds all things together, foundation of the world we live upon, framework of the cosmos. . . . It maintains that which exists, preserves that which lives, animates that which feels, enlightens that which thinks." Saint Gregory of Nyssa, in his first homily on the Resurrection, stated that the Logos "unites firmly and fits to himself the whole universe, bringing back into one single concord and one single harmony, through his own person, the different natures of the world." More expansively, Saint Bonaventura wrote at the end of chap. 5 of his famous treatise *The Mind's Road to God:*

> Because, then, Being is most pure and absolute, that which is Being simply is first and last and, therefore, the origin and the final cause of

all. Because eternal and most present, therefore it encompasses and pen-
etrates all duration, existing at once as their center and circumference.
Because most simple and greatest, therefore it is entirely within and
entirely without all things and, therefore, is an intelligible sphere whose
center is everywhere and whose circumference nowhere. Because most
actual and most immutable, then "remaining stable it causes the universe
to move," as Boethius says. Because most perfect and immense, therefore
within all, though not included in them; beyond all, but not excluded
from them; above all, but not transported beyond them; below all, yet
not cast down beneath them. Because most highly one and all-inclusive,
therefore all in all, although all things are many and it is only one. And
this is so since through most simple unity, clearest truth, and most
sincere goodness there is in it all power, all exemplary causality, and all
communicability. And therefore from it and by it and in it are all things.
And this is so since it is omnipotent, omniscient, and all-good. And to
see this perfectly is to be blessed.

For the notion of the personification and divinization of the Torah, see, for
example, the *Pirke Aboth* (3:23). "There was given to [Israel] a precious instrument [i.e., Torah] whereby the world was created." I do not wish to suggest,
by any means, that Sexton knew all of these texts, but rather to assert that
she did have a full intuitive grasp of the meaning of Logos in the mystical and
theological tradition.

12. Ralph J. Mills, Jr., *Contemporary American Poetry* (New York: Random
House, 1966), 232.

13. "From 1928 to Whenever," 315. On her lack of formal education, see
also Barbara Kevles's interview with Anne Sexton in *Writers at Work: The
Paris Review Interviews*, ed. George Plimpton, 4th ser. (New York: Viking,
1976), 399–400; the interview was originally published in the *Paris Review*
[13], no. 52 (Summer 1971): 159–91.

14. This remark was published in a review of *Anne Sexton: A Self-Portrait
in Letters* and perhaps was intended to apply only to the diction of the letters
and to the writer's recollection of conversations with Sexton. The topic of
Sexton's lack of education also finds a place in the mystical tradition in which
I have been placing her. Richard Rolle, for example, in the *Incendium Amoris*
(bk. 2, chap. 3) says, "Those taught by wisdom acquired, not inshed, and those
swollen with folded arguments, will disdain him [the humble contemplative]
saying, 'Where did he learn? Under what doctor did he sit?' For they do not
admit that the lovers of eternity are taught by a doctor from within to speak
more eloquently than they themselves, who have learned from men, and studied all the time for empty honors."

15. See, for example, no. 249 ("Wild Nights") and no. 368 ("How sick . . . to wait . . .") in *The Complete Poems of Emily Dickinson*, ed. Thomas H. Johnson (Boston: Little Brown and Co., 1960), 114, 175.

16. C. S. Lewis, *The Allegory of Love: A Study in Medieval Tradition* (London: Oxford University Press, 1936), 1.

17. Kevles, interview with Anne Sexton, in *Writers at Work*, 418–21.

18. Ben Howard, in a review of *The Book of Folly, The Death Notebooks*, and *The Awful Rowing Toward God*, in *Poetry* 127 (Feb. 1976): 286–92.

19. Richard Howard, *Alone with America: Essays on the Art of Poetry in the United States since 1950* (New York: Atheneum, 1969), 442, 450.

20. Anaïs Nin, *In Favor of the Sensitive Man and Other Essays* (New York: Harcourt Brace Jovanovich, 1976), 12.

21. Maurice L. Farber, *Theory of Suicide* (New York: Funk and Wagnalls, 1968), 3.

22. A. Alvarez, *The Savage God: A Study of Suicide* (New York: Random House, 1972), 120. Alvarez remarks, and I think his narrative proves it, that the suicide of Sylvia Plath "adds nothing at all to the poetry" (p. 40); Sexton's case, I feel, is quite different.

23. *Anne Sexton: A Self-Portrait in Letters*, 209, 246, 257, 282, 326, 336.

24. Rizza, "Another Side of This Life, 175.

25. Kevles, interview with Anne Sexton, in *Writers at Work*, 400.

26. Joyce Carol Oates, a review of *The Awful Rowing Toward God*, in the *New York Times* Book Review section, Mar. 23, 1975, 3–4.

27. Quoted in A. Alvarez, *The Savage God*, 210.

28. Ralph Waldo Emerson, *Journals and Miscellaneous Notebooks*, ed. William H. Gilman et al. (Cambridge: Belknap Press of Harvard University Press, 1960), 2:257.

29. *The Dialogues of Plato*, trans. B. Jowett (Oxford: Clarendon Press, 1953), 1:434.

30. Albert Camus, *The Myth of Sisyphus and Other Essays*, trans. Justin O'Brien (New York: Vintage Books, 1955), 3.

ON THE POETIC BIOGRAPHY

How It Was: Maxine Kumin
on Anne Sexton

Anne Sexton as I remember her on our first meeting in the late winter of 1957, tall, blue-eyed, stunningly slim, her carefully coifed dark hair decorated with flowers, her face skillfully made up, looked every inch the fashion model. And indeed she had briefly modeled for the Hart Agency in Boston. Earrings and bracelets, French perfume, high heels, matching lip and fingernail gloss bedecked her, all intimidating sophistications in the chalk-and-wet-overshoes atmosphere of the Boston Center for Adult Education, where we were enrolled in John Holmes's poetry workshop. Poetry—we were both ambitious beginners—and proximity—we lived in the same suburb—brought us together. As intimate friends and professional allies, we remained intensely committed to one another's writing and well-being to the day of her death in the fall of 1974.

The facts of Anne Sexton's troubled and chaotic life are well known; no other American poet in our time has cried aloud publicly so many private details. While the frankness of these revelations attracted many readers, especially women, who identified strongly with the female aspect of the poems, a number of poets and critics—for the most part, although not exclusively, male—took offense. For Louis Simpson, writing in *Harper's Magazine*, "Menstruation at Forty" was "the straw that broke this camel's back." And years before he wrote his best-selling novel, *Deliverance*, which centers on a graphic scene of homosexual rape, James Dickey, writing in the *New York Times Book Review*, excoriated the poems in *All My Pretty Ones*, saying, "It would be hard to find a writer who dwells more insistently on the pathetic and disgusting aspects of bodily experience. . . ." In a terse eulogy Robert Lowell declared, with considerable ambivalence it would seem, "For a book or two, she grew more powerful. Then writing was

Reprinted from "How It Was" by Maxine Kumin, foreword to *Anne Sexton: The Complete Poems*. Foreword copyright © 1981 by Maxine Kumin. Reprinted by permission of Houghton Mifflin Company.

too easy or too hard for her. She became meager and exaggerated. Many
of her most embarrassing poems would have been fascinating if someone had put them in quotes, as the presentation of some character,
not the author." Sexton's work rapidly became a point of contention
over which opposing factions dueled in print, at literary gatherings,
and in the fastnesses of the college classroom.

And yet the ground for Sexton's confessional poems had been
well prepared. In 1956 Allen Ginsberg's *Howl* had declaimed:

> I saw the best minds of my generation destroyed by madness,
>   starving hysterical naked
>
>   . . . .
>
>   on the granite steps of
>   the madhouse with shaven heads and harlequin speech of
>   suicide, demanding instantaneous lobotomy,
> and who were given instead the concrete void of insulin metrasol
>   electricity hydrotherapy psychotherapy occupational therapy
>   pingpong & amnesia . . .

At the time Sexton began to work in the confessional mode, W.
D. Snodgrass had already published his prize-winning collection *Heart's
Needle*, which included details of his divorce and custody struggle.
Sylvia Plath and Robert Lowell were hammering out their own autobiographical accounts of alienation, despair, anomie, and madness.
John Berryman, deceiving no one, charmingly protested in a prefatory
note that the Henry of *The Dream Songs* "is essentially about an
imaginary character (not the poet, not me) . . . who has suffered an
irreversible loss and talks about himself sometimes in the first person,
sometimes in the third, sometimes even in the second. . . ." The use
of *le moi* was being cultivated in fashionable literary journals everywhere. It seems curious that the major and by far most vitriolic expressions of outrage were reserved for Sexton.

Someone once said that we have art in order not to die of the
truth, a dictum we might neatly apply to Sexton's perspectives. To
Hayden Carruth the poems "raise the never-solved problem of what
literature really is, where you draw the line between art and docu-
mentary."

While Louise Bogan and Joyce Carol Oates for the most part
appraise Sexton favorably, Mona Van Duyn finds Sexton's "delineation
of femaleness so fanatical that it makes one wonder, even after many
years of being one, what a woman is. . . ." Muriel Rukeyser, who sees

the issue as "survival, piece by piece of the body, step by step of poetic experience, and even more the life entire . . .," finds much to praise, for instance singling out "In Celebration of My Uterus" as "one of the few poems in which a woman has come to the fact as symbol, the center after many years of silence and taboo."

Over and over in the critical literature dealing with the body of Sexton's work, we find these diametrical oppositions. The intimate details divulged in Sexton's poetry enchanted or repelled with equal passion. In addition to the strong feelings Anne's work aroused, there was the undeniable fact of her physical beauty. Her presence on the platform dazzled with its staginess, its props of water glass, cigarettes, and ashtray. She used pregnant pauses, husky whispers, pseudoshouts to calculated effect. A Sexton audience might hiss its displeasure or deliver a standing ovation. It did not doze off during a reading.

Anne basked in the attention she attracted, partly because it was antithetical to an earlier generation's view of the woman writer as "poetess," and partly because she was flattered by and enjoyed the adoration of her public. But behind the glamorously garbed woman lurked a terrified and homely child, cowed from the cradle onward, it seemed, by the indifference and cruelties of her world. Her parents, she was convinced, had not wanted her to be born. Her sisters, she alleged, competed against and won out over her. Her teachers, unable to rouse the slumbering intelligence from its hiding place, treated her with impatience and anger. Anne's counterphobic response to rejection and admonishment was always to defy, dare, press, contravene. Thus the frightened little girl became a flamboyant and provocative woman; the timid child who skulked in closets burst forth as an exhibitionist declaiming with her own rock group; the intensely private individual bared her liver to the eagle in public readings where almost invariably there was standing room only.

Born Anne Gray Harvey in 1928, she attended public school in Wellesley, Massachusetts, spent two years at Rogers Hall preparatory school, and then one year at Garland Junior College in Boston. A few months shy of her twentieth birthday, she eloped with Alfred Muller Sexton II (nicknamed Kayo), enrolled in a Hart Agency modeling course, and lived briefly in Baltimore and San Francisco while her husband served in the Navy. In 1953 she returned to Massachusetts, where Linda Gray Sexton was born.

The first breakdown, diagnosed as postpartum depression, occurred in 1954, the same year her beloved great-aunt Anna Ladd Dingley, the Nana of the poems, died. She took refuge in Westwood Lodge, a private neuropsychiatric hospital that was frequently to serve as her sanctuary when the voices that urged her to die reached an insistent pitch. Its director, Dr. Martha Brunner-Orne, figured in Anne's life as a benevolent but disciplinary mother, who would not permit this troubled daughter to kill herself.

Nevertheless, seven months after her second child, Joyce Ladd Sexton, was born in 1955, Anne suffered a second crisis and was hospitalized. The children were sent to live with her husband's parents; and while they were separated from her, she attempted suicide on her birthday, November 9, 1956. This was the first of several episodes, or at least the first that was openly acknowledged. Frequently, these attempts occurred around Anne's birthday, a time of year she came increasingly to dread. Dr. Martin Orne, Brunner-Orne's son, was the young psychiatrist at Glenside Hospital who attended Anne during this siege and treated her for the next seven years. After administering a series of diagnostic tests, he presented his patient with her scores, objective evidence that, despite the disapproving naysayers from her past, she was highly intelligent. Her associative gifts suggested that she ought to return to the writing of poetry, something she had shown a deft talent for during secondary school. It was at Orne's insistence that Anne enrolled in the Holmes workshop.

"You, Doctor Martin" came directly out of that experience, as did so many of the poems in her first collection, *To Bedlam and Part Way Back*. On a snowy Sunday afternoon early in 1957, she drove to my house to ask me to look at "something." Did she dare present it in class? Could it be called a poem? It was "Music Swims Back to Me," her first breakaway from adolescent lyrics in rhyming iambic pentameter.

Years later, when it seemed to her that all else in her life had failed—marriage, the succor of children, the grace of friendship, the promised land to which psychotherapy held the key—she turned to God, with a kind of stubborn absolutism that was missing from the Protestantism of her inheritance. The God she wanted was a sure thing, an Old Testament avenger admonishing his Chosen People, an authoritarian yet forgiving father decked out in sacrament and ceremony. An elderly, sympathetic priest she called on—"accosted" might be a better word—patiently explained that he could not make her a Catholic by fiat, nor could he administer the sacrament (the last rites) she longed for. But in his native wisdom he said a saving thing to her, said the magic and simple words that kept her alive at least a year beyond her time and made *The Awful Rowing Toward God* a possibility. "God is in your typewriter," he told her.

I cite these two examples to indicate the influence that figures of authority had over Anne's life in the most elemental sense; first the psychiatrist and then the priest put an imprimatur on poetry as salvation, as a worthy goal in itself. I am convinced that poetry kept Anne alive for the eighteen years of her creative endeavors. When everything else soured; when a succession of therapists deserted her for whatever good, poor, or personal reasons; when intimates lost interest or could not fulfill all the roles they were asked to play; when a series of catastrophes and physical illnesses assaulted her, the making of poems remained her one constant. To use her own metaphor, "out of used furniture [she made] a tree." Without this rich, rescuing obsession I feel certain she would have succeeded in committing suicide in response to one of the dozen impulses that beset her during the period between 1957 and 1974.

Sexton's progress in Holmes's workshop in 1957 was meteoric. In short order her poems were accepted for publication in the *New Yorker, Harper's Magazine,* and the *Saturday Review.* Sam Albert was in that class, and Ruth Soter, the friend to whom "With Mercy for the Greedy" is dedicated. Through Holmes we met George Starbuck at the New England Poetry Club. A year later, five of us joined together to form a workshop of our own—an arrangement that lasted until Holmes's untimely death from cancer in 1962. During this period all of us wrote and revised prolifically, competitively, as if all the wolves of the world were at our backs. Our sessions were jagged, intense, often angry, but also loving. As Holmes's letters from this period make abundantly clear, he decried the confessional direction Anne's poems were taking, while at the same time acknowledging her talent. Her compulsion to deal with such then-taboo material as suicide, madness, and abortion assaulted his sensibilities and triggered his own defenses. Convinced that the relationship would harm my own work, he warned me to resist becoming involved with Anne. It was the only advice he gave me that I rejected, and at some psychic cost. Anne and I both regarded Holmes as an academic father. In desperate rebuttal Anne wrote "For John, Who Begs Me Not to Enquire Further." A hesitant, sensitive exploration of their differences, the poem seeks to make peace between them.

Virtually every poem in the *Bedlam* book came under scrutiny during this period, as did many of the poems in *All My Pretty Ones.* There was no more determined reviser than Sexton, who would willingly push a poem through twenty or more drafts. She had an unparalleled tenacity in those early days and only abandoned a "failed" poem with regret, if not downright anger, after dozens of attempts to make it come right. It was awesome the way she could arrive at our bimonthly sessions with three, four, even five new and complicated poems. She was never meek about it, but she did listen, and she did respect the counsel of others. She gave generous help to her colleagues, and she required, demanded, insisted on generous response.

As a result of this experience, Anne came to believe in the value of the workshop. She loved growing in this way, and she urged the method on her students at Boston University, Colgate, Oberlin, and in other workshops she conducted from time to time.

During the workshop years we began to communicate more and more frequently by telephone. Since there were no message units involved in the basic monthly phone company fee—the figure I remember is seven dollars—we had a second phone line installed in our suburban homes so that we could talk at will. For years we conducted our own miniworkshops by phone, a working method that does much to train the ear to hear line breaks, internal rhymes, intentional or unwanted musical devices, and so forth. We did this so comfortably and over such an extended period of time that indeed when we met we were somewhat shy of each other's poems as they appeared on the page. I can remember often saying "Oh, so *that's* what it looks like," of a poem I had heard and visualized through half-a-dozen revisions.

Over the years, Anne's lines shortened, her line breaks became, I think, more unpredictable, and her imagery grew increasingly surreal. Initially, however, she worked quite strictly in traditional forms, believing in the value of their rigor as a forcing agent, believing that the hardest truths would come to light if they were made to fit a stanzaic pattern, a rhyme scheme, a prevailing meter. She strove to use rhyme unexpectedly but always aptly. Even the most unusual rhyme, she felt, must never obtrude on the sense of the line, nor must the normal word order, the easy tone of vernacular speech, be wrenched solely to save a rhyme.

The impetus for creation usually came when Anne directly invoked the muse at her desk. Here, she read favorite poems of other poets—most frequently Neruda—and played certain evocative records over and over. One I remember for its throaty string section was Respighi's *Pines of Rome.* Music acted in some way to free her to create, and she often turned the volume up loud enough to drown out all other sounds.

But for all the sought-after and hard-won poems Anne wrote—in this connection I recall the arduous struggle to complete "The Operation," "All My Pretty Ones," "Flee on Your Donkey"—a number were almost totally "given" ones. "Riding the Elevator into the Sky," in *The Awful Rowing,* is an example. The newspaper article referred to in the opening stanza suggested the poem; the poem itself came quite cleanly and easily, as if written out in the air beforehand and then transcribed onto the page with very few alterations. Similarly arrived at, "Letter Written on a Ferry while Crossing Long Island Sound" began at the instant Anne sighted the nuns on an actual crossing. The poem was written much as it now appears on the page, except for minor skirmishes required to effect the closure in each stanza. "Young" and "I Remember" were also achieved almost without effort. But because Anne wanted to open *All My Pretty Ones* with a terse elegy for her parents, one shorn of all autobiographical detail, "The Truth the Dead Know" went through innumerable revisions before arriving at its final form, an *a b a b* rhyme scheme that allows little room for pyrotechnics.

For a time it seemed that psychiatrists all over the country were referring their patients to Anne's work, as if it could provide the balm in Gilead for every troubled person. Even though it comforted and nurtured her to know that her poems reached beyond the usual sphere of belles lettres, she felt considerable ambivalence about her subject matter. Accused of exhibitionism, she was determined only to be more flamboyant; nevertheless, the strict Puritan hiding inside her suffered and grieved over the label of "confessional poet." For instance, when she wrote "Cripples and Other Stories" (*Live or Die*), a poem that almost totally "occurred" on the page in an hour's time, she crumpled it up and tossed it into the wastebasket as if in embarrassment. Together we fished it out and saved it, working to make the tone more consistent and to smooth out some of the rhythmically crude spots. Into this sort of mechanical task Anne always flung herself gladly.

The results were often doubly effective. I remember, for instance, how in "The Operation" she worked to achieve through rhyme and the shaping of the poem's three parts a direct rendition of the actual experience. The retardation of rhyming sounds in those short, rather sharply end-stopped lines, in the first section, for example (*leaf, straw, lawn: car, thief, house, upon*), add to the force of metaphor in the poem—the "historic thief," the "Humpty-Dumpty," and so on. Or, to take another poem, "Faustus and I," in *The Death Notebooks*, was headed for the discard pile. It was a free verse poem at the outset and had what seemed to me a malevolently flippant tone. Often when stymied for a more articulate response to one of her poems I disliked, I suggested, "Why don't you pound it into form?" And often the experiment worked. In the case of the Faustus poem, the suggestion was useful because the rhyme scheme gave the subject a dignity it demanded and because the repetitive "pounding" elicited a level of language, of metaphor, that Anne had not quite reached in the earlier version.

Sexton had an almost mystical faith in the "found" word image, as well as in metaphor by mistake, by typo, or by misapprehension. She would fight hard to keep an image, a line, a word usage, but if I was just as dogged in my conviction that the line didn't work, was sentimental or mawkish, that the word was ill-suited or the image trite, she would capitulate—unless she was totally convinced of her own rightness. Then there was no shaking her. Trusting each other's critical sense, we learned not to go past the unshakable core, not to trespass on style or voice.

Untrammeled by a traditional education in Donne, Milton, Yeats, Eliot, and Pound, Anne was able to strike out alone, like Conrad's secret sharer, for a new destiny. She was grim about her lost years, her lack of a college degree; she read omnivorously and quite innocently whatever came to hand and enticed her, forming her own independent, quirky, and incisive judgments.

Searching for solutions to the depressive episodes that beset her with dismaying periodicity, Anne read widely in the popular psychiatric texts of the time: interpretations of Freud, Theodore Reik, Philip Rieff, Helena Deutsch, Erik Erikson, Bruno Bettelheim. During a summer school course with Philip Rahv, she encountered the works of

Dostoevski, Kafka, and Thomas Mann. These were succeeded by the novels of Saul Bellow, Philip Roth, and Kurt Vonnegut. But above all else she was attracted to the fairy tales of Andersen and Grimm, which her beloved Nana had read to her when she was a child. They were for her, perhaps, what Bible stories and Greek myths had been for other writers. At the same time that she was being entertained and drawn into closer contact with a kind of collective unconscious, she was searching the fairy tales for psychological parallels. Quite unaware at first of the direction she was taking, she composed the first few "transformations" that comprise the book of that name. The book evolved very much at my urging and gathered momentum as it grew. It struck me that Anne's poems based on fairy tales went one step further than contemporary poets' translations from languages they did not themselves read but apprehended through a third party. Their poems were *adaptations;* hers were *transformations.*

Thematically, Anne's concern in *Transformations* was a logical extension of the material she dealt with in the confessional genre, but this time with a society-mocking overlay. Her attention focuses on women cast in a variety of fictive roles: the dutiful princess daughter, the wicked witch, the stepmother. We see the same family constellations in a fairy tale setting, ranging from the Oedipal explorations of "The Frog Prince" to the stage-set adultery of "The Little Peasant." The poems are replete with anachronisms from pop culture: the Queen in "Rumpelstiltskin" is "as persistent / as a Jehovah's witness"; Snow White "opened her eyes as wide as Orphan Annie"; and Cinderella in her sooty rags looks like Al Jolson. Moreover, the conventional happily-ever-after endings receive their share of sardonic jibes. Cinderella and her prince end up as "Regular Bobbsey Twins. / That story." And the princess and her husband in "The White Snake" are condemned by way of a happy ending to "a kind of coffin, / a kind of blue funk."

Despite Houghton Mifflin's initial misgivings about publishing it, *Transformations* was widely acclaimed for its balance between the confessional and the fable. It was a new lode to mine. I hoped that by encouraging Anne to continue to look outside her own psyche for material, she might develop new enthusiasms to match the one she felt for the Brothers Grimm.

And indeed her impulse to work in fable continued in *The Book of Folly,* where, in addition to three prose inventions, Sexton created the sequence of poems she called "The Jesus Papers." These are more searching, more daring than the early Jesus poems ("In the Deep Museum," "For God while Sleeping," "With Mercy for the Greedy") from *All My Pretty Ones,* in which it seemed to be the cruelty of the crucifixion itself that fascinated her. Now we have a different voice and a different Jesus, however humanized, however modernized—a Jesus who still suffers knowingly in order to endure.

Jesus, Mary, angels as good as the good fairy, and a personal, fatherly God to love and forgive her figure ever more prominently in the late poems. Always Sexton explores relentlessly the eternal themes that obsess her: love, loss, madness, the nature of the father-daughter compact, and death—the "death baby" we carry with us from the moment of birth. In my view the sequence entitled "The Death of the Fathers," a stunning investigation of the last two themes, is the most successful part of *The Book of Folly.* It would be simplistic to suggest that the Oedipal theme overrides all other considerations in Sexton's work, but a good case might be made for viewing her poems in terms of their quest for a male authority figure to love and trust. Yeats once said that "one poem lights up another," and in Sexton's poetry the reader can find the poet again identifying herself through her relationship with the male other, whether in the person of a lover or—in the last, hasty, and often brilliant poems in *The Awful Rowing,* which make a final effort to land on "the island called God"—in the person of the patriarchal final arbiter.

The poems in *Transformations* mark the beginning of a shift in Sexton's work, from the intensely confessional to what Estella Lauter, in a fascinating essay, "Anne Sexton's 'Radical Discontent with the Awful Order of Things,' " has termed the "transpersonal." In retrospect it seems to me that the broad acceptance *Transformations* eventually earned in the marketplace (after hesitant beginnings) reinforced Sexton's deeply rooted conviction that poems not only could but had to be made out of the detritus of her life. Her work took on a new imaginative boldness. She experimented with a variety of persona/ poems, particularly involving God figures, revisited the crucifixion stories, reworked the creation myth and ancient psalms, and even planned a book-length bestiary, which was only partially realized. Her perception of her place in the canon of American letters was enhanced, too, by the success of *Transformations.* Inscribing a copy of *The Book of Folly* for me in 1972, she wrote: "Dear Max—From now on it's OUR world."

She began to speak of herself as Ms. Dog, an appellation that is ironic in two contexts. We were both increasingly aware of the women's movement. To shuck the earlier designations of Miss and Mrs. was only a token signal of where we stood, but a signal nonetheless. Dog, of course, is God in reverse. The fact that the word worked both ways delighted Sexton, much as her favorite palindrome, "rats live on no evil star," did. There was a wonderful impudence in naming herself a kind of liberated female deity, one who is "out fighting the dollars."

In the collections that followed *Transformations*, images of God proliferate, crossing all boundaries between man and woman, human and animal; between inner and outer histories of behavior. It was slippery material, difficult to control. Not all the poems Anne arrived at in this pursuit of self-definition and salvation succeed; of this she was well aware. Whenever it came down to a question of what to include or what to drop from a forthcoming collection, Anne agonized at length. It was our practice over the years to sit quietly with each other on the occasion of the arranging of a book, sorting through groups of poems, trying out a variety of formats, voting on which poems to save and which to discard. In a kind of despondency of the moment, suffering the bitter foretaste of reviews to come, Anne frequently wanted to jettison half the book. But I suspect this was a way she had of taking the sting out of the selection process, secure in the knowledge that she and I would always rescue each other's better poems; even, for the right reasons, rescue those flawed ones that were important psychically or developmentally. We took comfort from Yeats's "lighting-up," allowing the poems to gain meaning and perspective from one another.

When Anne was writing *The Awful Rowing* at white heat in January and February 1973, and the poems were coming at the rate of two, three, even four a day, the awesome pace terrified me. I was poet-in-residence at Centre College in Danville, Kentucky; we had agreed in advance to split the phone bill. Fearing a manic break, I did everything I could to retard the process, long-distance, during our daily hour-long calls. The Sexton who had so defiantly boasted, in her Ms. Dog phase, "I am God la de dah," had now given way to a ravaged, obsessed poet fighting to put the jigsaw pieces of the puzzle together into a coherence that would save her—into "a whole nation of God." Estella Lauter states that "her vision of Him as the winner in a crooked poker game at the end of that book is a sporting admission of her defeat rather than a decisive renewal of the Christian myth." At one level, I agree. But at another, even more primitive level, God the poker player was the one living and constant Daddy left to Sexton out of "The Death of the Fathers." Of course he held the crooked, winning hand.

Though the reviewers were not always kind to Anne's work, honors and awards mounted piggyback on one another almost from the moment of the publication in 1960 of her first book, *To Bedlam and Part Way Back*. The American Academy of Letters Traveling Fellowship in 1963, which she was awarded shortly after *All My Pretty Ones* was published and nominated for the National Book Award, was followed by a Ford Foundation grant as resident playwright at the Charles Playhouse in Boston. In 1965 Anne Sexton was elected a fellow of the Royal Society of Literature in Great Britain. *Live or Die* won the Pulitzer Prize in poetry in 1967. She was named Phi Beta Kappa poet at Harvard in 1968 and was accorded a number of honorary doctoral degrees.

Twice in the 1960s, and twice more in the 1970s, Anne and I collaborated to write books for children. *Eggs of Things* and *More Eggs of Things* were constructed within the constraints of a limited vocabulary. *Joey and the Birthday Present* and *The Wizard's Tears* were more fanciful excursions into the realm of talking animals and magical spells. Our work sessions were lighthearted, even casual. We took turns sitting at the typewriter; whoever typed had the privilege of recording or censoring the dialogue or description as it occurred to us. Three or four afternoon workouts sufficed for a book. We were full of generous praise for each other's contributions to the story line and to the exchanges of conversation. It was usually summer. We drank a lot of iced tea and squabbled amiably about how to turn the *Wizard*'s townspeople into frogs, or about which of us actually first spoke the key line in *Joey:* "And they both agreed a birthday present cannot run away." Sometimes we explored plans for future collaborations. We would do a new collection of animal fables, modeled on Aesop. We would fish out the rejected sequel to *More Eggs*, entitled *Cowboy and Pest and the Runaway Goat*, and refurbish it for another publisher. Sexton enthusiastically entertained these notions, as did I. Working together on children's books when our own children were the age of our projected readership kept us in good rapport with each other's offspring. It provided a welcome breathing space in which nothing mattered but the sheer verbal play involved in developing the story. Indeed, we regressed cheerfully to whatever age level the text required and lost ourselves in the confabulation.

But between the publication of new books and the bestowal of honors fell all too frequently the shadow of mental illness. One psychiatrist left. His successor at first succumbed to Sexton's charm, then terminated his treatment of her. She promptly fell downstairs and broke her hip—on her birthday. With the next doctor her hostility grew. Intermediary psychiatrists and psychologists came and went. There seemed to be no standard for dealing with this gifted, ghosted woman. On Thorazine, she gained weight, became intensely sun-sensitive, and complained that she was so overwhelmed with lassitude that she could not write. Without medication, the voices returned. As she grew increasingly dependent on alcohol, sedatives, and sleeping pills, her depressive bouts grew more frequent. Convinced that her marriage was beyond salvage, she demanded and won a divorce, only to learn that living alone created an unbearable level of anxiety. She returned to Westwood Lodge, later spent time at McLean's Hospital in Belmont, Massachusetts, and finally went to the Human Resources Institute in Brookline, Massachusetts. But none of these interludes stemmed her downward course. In the spring of 1974 she took an overdose of sleeping pills and later remonstrated bitterly with me for aborting this suicide attempt. On that occasion she vowed that when she next undertook to die, she would telegraph her intent to no one. A little more than six months later, this indeed proved to be the case.

It seems presumptuous, only seven years after her death, to talk about Anne Sexton's place in the history of poetry. We must first acknowledge the appearance in the twentieth century of women writing poetry that confronts the issues of gender, social role, and female life and lives viewed subjectively from the female perspective. The earlier worldview of the poet as "the masculine chief of state in charge of dispensing universal spiritual truths" (Diane Middlebrook, *The World into Words*) has eroded since World War II, as have earlier notions about the existence of universal truths themselves. Freed by that cataclysm from their clichéd roles as goddesses of hearth and bedroom, women began to write openly out of their own experiences. Before there was a women's movement, the underground river was already flowing, carrying such diverse cargoes as the poems of Bogan, Levertov, Rukeyser, Swenson, Plath, Rich, and Sexton.*

The stuff of Anne's life, mercilessly dissected, is here in the poems. Of all the confessional poets, none has had quite Sexton's "courage to make a clean breast of it." Nor has any displayed quite her brilliance, her verve, her headlong metaphoric leaps. As with any body of work, some of the later poems display only ragged, intermittent control, as compared with "The Double Image," "The Operation," and "Some Foreign Letters," to choose three arbitrary examples. The later work takes more chances, crosses more boundaries between the rational and the surreal; and time after time it evokes in the reader that sought-after shiver of recognition.

Women poets in particular owe a debt to Anne Sexton, who broke new ground, shattered taboos, and endured a barrage of attacks along the way because of the flamboyance of her subject matter, which, twenty years later, seems far less daring. She wrote openly about menstruation, abortion, masturbation, incest, adultery, and drug addiction at a time when the proprieties embraced none of these as proper topics for poetry. Today, the remonstrances seem almost quaint. Anne delineated the problematic position of women—the neurotic reality of the time—though she was not able to cope in her own life with the personal trouble it created. If it is true that she attracted the worshipful attention of a cult group pruriently interested in her suicidal impulses, her psychotic breakdowns, her frequent hospitalizations, it must equally be acknowledged that her very frankness succored many who clung to her poems as to the Holy Grail. Time will sort out the dross among these poems and burnish the gold. Anne Sexton has earned her place in the canon.

*I have omitted from this list Elizabeth Bishop, who chose not to have her work included in anthologies of women poets.

Anne Sexton at the Radcliffe Institute

On November 20, 1960, the Sunday *New York Times* carried a long story announcing an experimental new program directed at women in mid-life whose careers had been interrupted. The program was to be called the Radcliffe Institute; its founder was Mary Ingraham Bunting, the recently inaugurated president of Radcliffe, the women's college affiliated with Harvard University.

A biologist, as well as a canny administrator, Mary Bunting privately looked upon the institute as a kind of laboratory where she could test a thesis that many well-educated married women in the Boston area were ready, after raising families, to return to full-time intellectual or artistic work but were struggling for opportunity in a "climate of unexpectation."[1] Unlike men, who were already hooked into the system of professional development and recognition, women had to break through firmly held cultural beliefs that a woman's choices were either marriage or career. The Radcliffe Institute was to be a place where women could make up for lost time, using the facilities of the Harvard libraries and laboratories, and where the prestige of renewed recognition of their accomplishments might nudge them into the path of further opportunities.

Mary Bunting's idea was radical, but not *too* radical: she had targeted a group that represented the probable destinies of current Radcliffe undergraduates. And her proposal touched a nerve in the middle class. Even Mary Bunting was amazed at the response: the first requests for applications arrived in two days.[2] Among the first to apply was Anne Sexton, who called Radcliffe for information the morning after the story appeared in the *New York Times*.[3] Eventually, 1,700 women applied for the twenty available fellowships.[4] A few were designated for working artists.

Sexton's letter of application reflects a characteristic mix of meekness and hubris. "I know my academic background looks anemic and

From *Anne Sexton: A Biography* (forthcoming).

without interest. However it seems to me that I have come a long way alone," she commented. She added that she thought the fellowship would "pave the road I am walking on" and thus make her seem less strange to the academic communities where she was frequently invited to read her poems. As a well-reviewed, prize-winning poet already, she said she wanted to get beyond the values of the marketplace, to write poetry, stories, and plays that would still be read in a hundred years. "I feel that I am already an accomplished poet. What I ask for now is the opportunity to be a lasting one."[5] Letters from Philip Rahv, Dudley Fitts, Louis Untermeyer, and John Sweeney supported her application.[6] "Wow!" was the response of the Harvard committeeman who interviewed her. "We'll know she's around. She has enormous vitality and zest! Her comments on writing are fascinating."[7]

Sexton's best friend Maxine Kumin, a Radcliffe graduate, also applied. When Kumin received her letter of appointment a few days before Sexton's arrived, Sexton felt an acute pang of envy. All the shortcomings in her own patchy education made it seem perfectly reasonable that Maxine would be chosen over her. Despite her astonishingly rapid professional success, Sexton had never studied literature nor anything else systematically. Her preferred educational environment was the writer's workshop, where free-for-all discussion could have immediate practical results. "With literary people I'm nervous," she confided to her doctor. "I have strong feelings but no critical theories—there is no 'real' place for me. As a poet I want to con people and be a prophet and be great—I feel as if I have a whole mouthful of truth and I can't spit it out."[8] She had felt this limitation acutely at Brandeis the preceding summer, attending seminars on modern fiction led by Irving Howe and Philip Rahv. "I can't analyze a novel; I don't know how to be objective," she lamented. "Either I love something and it's mine, I'm existing in it, or I don't. I don't retain it. All I can do is be emotional about it."[9]

When Sexton's letter of appointment finally arrived, she capered through the neighborhood with joy, "running into the neighbors' houses, leaping up on their counters. I got it, I got it!"[10] She and Maxine were the only two creative writers in the group of twenty.[11]

As a Radcliffe Scholar Sexton was awarded an honorarium of $2,000, paid in two installments. Immediately after the grant was announced, Anne and Kayo decided to make some additions to the family home. They converted a back porch into a study for Anne and built a swimming pool. This apparently frivolous use of the Radcliffe money scandalized the director of the institute, and it is still one of the stories told in Boston circles about Anne Sexton: that she used her Radcliffe fellowship to build a swimming pool.[12] For Sexton, of course, this decision made perfect sense. She hated to leave her house—that was one of the debilitating symptoms of her illness. "I can meet my goals if they are *writing* goals," she commented once, "because writing does not involve going out into the frightening world."[13] Her home was her workplace; and her swimming pool was an extension of her study.

Since most of the fellowship recipients were married women supported by husbands, the issue of what the money was actually *for* became a major source of commentary in the national press. *Newsweek* was typical in reporting that most of the women had used the grant to hire additional help around the house, although one "sent her willing children to summer camp," while another bought a new washing machine and dishwasher "to ease her household chores."[14] The message seemed to be that the Radcliffe Scholars had no intention of slighting their womanly duties: family came first.

Sexton did not mention the swimming pool to *Newsweek* when she was interviewed for their story on the Radcliffe Institute. But it was her picture they chose to run, showing her at home, feet propped against a bookcase, with an open book in her lap and a wide smile on her face. Although she went to Cambridge for regular gatherings with the other Radcliffe Scholars, she did not use office space there, preferring to work at home surrounded by her own books and notes. "My books make me happy," she told an interviewer. "They sit there and say, 'Well, we got written and you can too.' "[15]

Nor did she enroll in courses at Harvard, which the appointment permitted. "It didn't suddenly give me guts, just because I was a member of the Institute," she explained. "I was still reluctant to push my way into these courses. I couldn't bring myself to it. It wasn't that I didn't feel like it."[16] To her doctor, who chided her for this decision, Sexton gave another explanation: "You have to be careful who you study with—I want to be great. . . . If Saul Bellow was teaching around here I'd be in his class— . . . I have to be great, I want it to last—I don't have time to start over—I want to leave the imprint of my personality carved in marble."[17]

In fact, she had arrived at what was for her an effective work routine, which didn't change much that autumn. She continued working on poems for *All My Pretty Ones;* she began teaching a weekly writing seminar to Radcliffe and Harvard undergraduates; she and Maxine began compiling a poetry anthology for high school students.[18]

For Sexton the appointment as a Radcliffe Scholar was important not because it gave her access to Harvard but because it gave her Harvard credentials. Anne Sexton had already established herself as a professional, before coming to the institute; many of the other Radcliffe Scholars had not. But she was the only scholar that year who had no college degree; most of the others had advanced degrees. "I used to go around saying 'I didn't go to college—I don't know anything—I'm very dumb and have a big mouth,' " she told her interviewer. "Now I say, 'I'm at the Radcliffe Institute.' It's just like I'd graduated."[19] This made some difference to her standing in the literary world based in Boston, and it sometimes eased her relations with the literary people she met at social gatherings before and after her readings at various colleges. But the biggest difference, she claimed, was in her relations with her family. "It's a status symbol," she observed.

> It immediately made what I was doing more respectable, to my husband. I wasn't taking so much from my family; I gave more back. You see, you always have a guilty feeling that it's selfish, because everyone says "Why isn't it enough to be a wife and mother?" I still remember my mother-in-law saying "Why aren't your husband and children enough? Why must you do this? Why don't you just do it a little bit—why don't you make it a hobby." You have this guilt. But if you get this amount of money, then everyone immediately thinks you're respected, and beyond that, you're contributing. . . .
>
> You have to go back into the psychology of it as far as I'm concerned. It's the final approval of the institute that's important in my case.—I started educating myself. And it was like it opened a whole new world. I'd been all alone and I didn't know why. Well, I broke into it. I gained momentum and continued to gain it and getting the grant was certainly a great mark of approval from the world. You could say that Radcliffe was an approving mother. And this was certainly very important to me.
>
> I want to write something that matters. I want to reach people. I don't want to be powerless against life and death and the whole thing dying and it all seems hopeless. I know you can't put all of that into children; it's too much for them to drag through their lives.

But it's very, very chancy to find yourself later on. You've got one thing that's for you: you've matured some, you've lived longer and you're just naturally more intelligent, and you care more. You've fulfilled the need of getting married, which every woman has, and of having children. Now you can look at yourself and say "Now what?" But everything is against you doing it, you know. I mean society isn't set up for somebody realizing yourself at 28. I really only started to live when I was 29.

But I couldn't have lived this long without being married. I mean, this is for me. To be married and have children. There's one more thing I have asked of life. That is, they've got to let me off to be a writer. And that's asking quite a bit of them.[20]

The Radcliffe Scholars began meeting weekly for lunch in September at a small house on Mt. Auburn Street in Cambridge that had been set aside for them. The lunch meetings gave them a chance to become acquainted and to take on the feeling of a group. Early in the new year 1962, they began holding afternoon seminars, to present portions of their work. Sexton and Maxine Kumin were scheduled to open the series in February with discussions of their own poetry.

The tape made that afternoon at Radcliffe shows better than any testimonial the complementary nature of the public personae Kumin and Sexton had developed as poets. Maxine Kumin approached the occasion with self-professed stage fright but a firm pedagogical manner. In her reading she dovetailed poems from her children's books and from her "adult" books, emphasizing the techniques involved in varying meter, in forming and distributing rhyme. She supplied epigraphs and cited intellectual sources from Thoreau to Sartre, and poetic models from Belloc to Starbuck. Despite her emphatic intellectualism and formality, the effect is warm and gracious—but she gives the impression of not wanting to waste anyone's time.

Sexton, on the other hand, opens with a claim that she is not very well prepared, that she usually gives formal readings where the audience is seated at a distance, that she has simply thrown together some pages of notes "torn from a couple of readings." Between readings of poems she apologizes that her poems are "so serious." Yet planted among her nervous and effusive comments are well-considered and astute observations about her practice as a writer.

Maxine and she were much alike, she observed; they had the same ambitions, many of the same thoughts and feelings. "But we write with different intent." In her presentation she intended to comment not on the techniques she used—"these are just tricks I throw in"—but on her intent as a poet. "Every poem has its own voice, like an actor," she claimed. "I can be deeply personal, but often I'm not being personal about myself." As a prime example she read "In the Deep Museum," where she had adopted the voice of Christ in the tomb.

Sexton ended her presentation with a reading of "The Fortress," a poem written during the past fall. Here she commented amply on the sources of the poem: taking an after-dinner nap with her daughter Linda, lazily making up images. She had written the images down as the game progressed—"I knew I was onto a good thing." But the images, she commented, were not the poem. "I had an emotion but I didn't know what the emotion was" until many drafts later. Her first shaping had been to design a stanza of ten lines of varying length, elaborately rhymed. She installed the imagery, so to speak, in this machinery; but as she did so, the emotion began to clarify. It was an old emotion working its way to the surface of the poem like the leaves in the poem, "fed / secretly from a pool of beet-red dye." Like her earlier poem "The Double Image," addressed to Joy, "The Fortress" muses on hidden connections between mother and daughter:

> I press down my index finger—
> half in jest, half in dread—
> on the brown mole
> under your left eye, inherited
> from my right cheek: a spot of danger
> where a bewitched worm ate its way through our soul. . . .

In "The Fortress" the disease dreaded is not madness, as in "The Double Image," but inevitable death—for which the cobbling of images becomes a defense, a kind of cure.

> I cannot promise very much.
> I give you the images I know.
> Lie still with me and watch.
> A pheasant moves
> by like a seal, pulled through the mulch
> by his thick white collar. He's on show
> like a clown. He drags a beige feather that he removed,
> one time, from an old lady's hat.
> We laugh and we touch.
> I promise you love. Time will not take away that.

An old lady has been mentioned two stanzas above:

> Outside the bittersweet turns orange.
> Before she died, my mother and I picked those fat
> branches, finding orange nipples
> on the gray wire strands.
> We weeded the forest, curing trees like cripples.

The bittersweet of memory colors the poem and then inspires its rhymes: the New England weeds survive the mother's death; the mother's joke survives her, the form of love time can't take away. So the plumage is restored to the bird by wit, the daughter's childhood commemorated in the mother's imagery once and for all.

"Radcliffe was like a good mother," Sexton said in retrospect of her two years at the institute. There were two mothers in Sexton's psyche: "Nana," her spinster aunt, and her biological mother, Mary Gray. In "The Double Image," addressed to Joy, Sexton had accounted for the "bad" or witchy side of her own mothering, associated with Mary Gray; the poem expresses hope of finding another way of mothering: protective, nurturing, touching, responsible—like Nana, whose middle name Joy also bore.[21] Yet Nana, for all her kindness, was a figure of powerlessness in the family, and Sexton knew that "preferring" her was in some sense dangerous to her own growth as a woman, certainly as an artist.

In "The Fortress" Sexton for the first, probably the only, time wrote about the side of herself associated with Mary Gray. This poem, significantly, is addressed to Linda Gray: is addressed, in short, to the legacy of Writer in the family, the name that weaves (like the mole on the mother's face and the daughter's) down through the family from grandfather Arthur Gray Staples (a newspaper editor) through Mary to Anne and on to Linda.

The writer is possessor of the magic power to heal and cure through the creation of images. Lying side by side with her in bed, the mother begins mothering the daughter by transforming the world outside the shelter of their room into amusing metaphors that reduce it to domestic scale and suffuse it with feeling, the mother's desire for the daughter's security and joy. Desire does not alter the harshness of a world of death and contingency, but the expression of desire does bridge the space between two people and the space between generations as well. In making images for the child, the mother expresses her love in a form mnemonically powerful, a form that has the power to contain and convey her love even after death.

So does the daughter in Anne renew her mother's love in metaphor that makes the fruit of the bittersweet plant into "orange nipples." The dead mother, deprived by cancer of her breasts, glows along the fence bordering the family property in a radiant afterimage of herself, feeding the daughter's needy heart. So in writing the poem Sexton deposits a legacy for Linda that will affirm her creative power and her maternal love even if—even when—she dies by her own intention sometime in the perhaps immediate future. Among Sexton's daughters Linda Gray is the chosen auditor of this effort because her name is a reference to the magic continuity made possible by writing. And made possible by "alma mater," Radcliffe, the home of writing and its dissemination to generations of women.

NOTES

1. Dr. Mary Ingraham Bunting, interview with Diane Middlebrook, Dec. 2, 1982, Cambridge, Mass.

2. Ibid.

3. The Radcliffe College Archives note a phone call from Sexton on Nov. 21, 1960. Writing for the application, she added her "Hurrah! for your creative and highly stimulating project. I know it will succeed" (Anne Sexton to Rene Kuhn Bryant, special assistant to the president, Jan. 13, 1961, Radcliffe College Archives).

4. Arline Grimes, "Scholars Praise Radcliffe Institute," *Boston Herald*, Oct. 8, 1961.

5. Application to the Radcliffe Institute, Mar. 7, 1961, Radcliffe College Archives.

6. It was an impressive and savvily selected group of referees: a blend of literary talents well known to the Harvard academics in charge of selecting the Radcliffe Scholars; and all regarded themselves as "discoverers" of Sexton, to some degree. Rahv, Sexton's teacher at the Brandeis Summer Institute of Modern Literature the previous summer, was editor of the respected journal *Partisan Review*; Fitts, instructor in classics at Phillips Academy, Andover, Mass., and currently judge of the Yale Younger Poets competition, was an acquaintance through John Holmes; the ubiquitous Untermeyer had offered himself as referee in all her grant applications that year; John Sweeney was in charge of the prestigious Morris Gray poetry readings at Harvard, one of which he had invited Sexton to give, in 1959.

7. Attachment to Sexton application from Harvard Department of English, Radcliffe College Archives.

8. Anne Sexton, therapy notebook, Nov. 24, 1962, restricted collection, Anne Sexton Archive, Harry Ransom Humanities Research Center, University of Texas, Austin; quoted by permission of Linda Gray Sexton.

9. Anne Sexton, therapy notebook, Jan. 16, 1962, restricted collection, Anne Sexton Archive.

10. Anne Sexton, interview with Alice Ryerson, Radcliffe Institute, Jan. 1962, Radcliffe College Archives.

11. The other Radcliffe Scholars, 1961–62, were Elizabeth Barker, Elizabeth Clarke, Carol McCormick Crosswell, Carmen Goldings, Nancy Hendire, Vilma Hunt, Shirley Robin Letwin, Denah Lida, Lily Macrakis, Ursula Niebuhr, Emiliana Noether, Lillian Randall, Brita Stendahl, Barbara Swan, Lois Swirnoff, Atarah Twersky, Anna-Teresa Tymieniecka, and Alma Wittlin. Memo to Anne Sexton from the Radcliffe Institute, Jan. 19, 1962, Anne Sexton Archive.

12. Sexton told her doctor that the pool was paid for with a combination of Radcliffe money and Sexton's advance for *All My Pretty Ones:* "The pool cost $1,300—Radcliffe $1,000, $300 from Houghton Mifflin" (therapy notebook, Apr. 21, 1962, restricted collection, Anne Sexton Archive).

13. Anne Sexton, interview with Dr. Martha White, Radcliffe Institute, July 1963, Radcliffe College Archives.

14. *Newsweek,* Oct. 23, 1961, 97.

15. Anne Sexton, interview with Alice Ryerson. A few of the Radcliffe Scholars had desks in small rooms that served as offices, but most worked in the Harvard libraries or at home. Sexton and Kumin were granted access to the Poetry Room at Lamont Library, which was ordinarily closed to women. (Constance E. Smith, director of the Radcliffe Institute, wrote Sexton informing her about this special privilege, Sept. 25, 1961, Anne Sexton Archive.)

16. Anne Sexton, interview with Dr. Martha White, Radcliffe College Archives.

17. Anne Sexton, therapy notebook, Nov. 7, 1961, restricted collection, Anne Sexton Archive.

18. In Dec., writing up a progress report requested by the institute's director, Sexton greatly exaggerated her output for the months from Sept. through the end of the year: "I have written about fourteen new poems, rewritten four old poems, put them together and submitted them to Houghton Mifflin for their consideration" (Anne Sexton to Constance Smith, Dec. 15, 1961, Radcliffe College Archives). Dates on worksheets suggest that Sexton had written about four or five new poems and revised one (works: *All My Pretty Ones,* Anne Sexton Archive). As she said in an interview, she found the group demand upsetting. "You know, they want to make sure you're going to do something. I've always said my ambition is a hell of a lot bigger than theirs. No one need

worry, my ambition is that big" (Anne Sexton, interview with Dr. Martha White, Radcliffe College Archives).

19. Anne Sexton, interview with Dr. Martha White, Radcliffe College Archives.

20. Anne Sexton, condensed from interview with Dr. Martha White, Radcliffe College Archives.

21. Nana's name was Anna Ladd Dingley; Joy was Joyce Ladd Sexton.

INFLUENCES AND CONNECTIONS

"Daddy": Sylvia Plath's Debt to Anne Sexton

"Daddy" is one of Sylvia Plath's most anthologized poems, and, some might say, one of her most quintessential; yet this seemingly original and idiosyncratic work is deeply indebted to an early, virtually unknown, confessional poem by Anne Sexton:

> "My Friend, My Friend"
> *For M. W. K. who hesitates each time she sees*
> *a young girl wearing The Cross.*
>
> Who will forgive me for the things I do?
> With no special legend or God to refer to,
> With my calm white pedigree, my yankee kin,
> I think it would be better to be a Jew.
>
> I forgive you for what you did not do,
> I am impossibly guilty. Unlike you,
> My friend, I can not blame my origin
> With no special legend or God to refer to.
>
> They wear The Crucifix as they are meant to do.
> Why do their little crosses trouble you?
> The effigies that I have made are genuine,
> (I think it would be better to be a Jew).
>
> Watching my mother slowly die I knew
> My first release. I wish some ancient bugaboo
> Followed me. But my sin is always my sin.
> With no special legend or God to refer to.
>
> Who will forgive me for the things I do?
> To have your reasonable hurt to belong to
> Might ease my trouble like liquor or aspirin.
> I think it would be better to be a Jew.
>
> And if I lie, I lie because I love you,
> Because I am bothered by the things I do,
> Because your hurt invades my calm white skin:

> With no special legend or God to refer to,
> I think it would be better to be a Jew.[1]

"My Friend, My Friend" appeared in the *Antioch Review* during the summer of 1959. Plath, however, may have seen the poem some months earlier, in late 1958 or early 1959, during one of Robert Lowell's workshops at Boston University or after one of his classes when Plath, Sexton, and George Starbuck customarily retired to the Ritz Bar to continue their discussion of poetry informally over martinis.[2]

During this time Sexton was assembling her first book of poems, *To Bedlam and Part Way Back* (1960). She set Plath an example by tackling private and deeply personal material in an outspoken and colloquial fashion in the first person. Plath later acknowledged the liberating influence that Sexton and Lowell had on her poetic development:

> I've been very excited by what I feel is the new breakthrough that came with, say, Robert Lowell's *Life Studies* [1959], this intense breakthrough into very serious, very personal, emotional experience which I feel has been partly taboo. . . . I think particularly . . . Ann Saxton [*sic*] . . . is an extremely emotional and feeling young woman and her poems are wonderfully craftsman-like poems and yet they have a kind of emotional and psychological depth which I think is something perhaps quite new, quite exciting.[3]

Both this statement, made in the course of a BBC interview on October 30, 1962, and "Daddy," written on the twelfth of that month, date from the most intensely creative period of Plath's brief life. During October and November 1962 she wrote over half of *Winter Trees* (1971) and *Ariel* (1965). It is for the poems of this period that she is best remembered, and perhaps for none better than "Daddy," the work that draws so extensively upon "My Friend, My Friend."

Sexton's poem is dedicated to M. W. K., making it plausible to say that it is addressed to Sexton's friend Maxine Winokur Kumin. This is reinforced by the fact that, like Kumin, the friend in the poem is Jewish. The speaker claims to be without religion, "With no special legend or God to refer to," yet she is burdened by her sense of guilt. It pervades her life, coming to its fullest expression in her account of her mother's death, and crucially in the speaker's attendant feelings of liberation and "release." It is the awareness of her inescapable guilt that creates the poem's focus and accounts for the speaker's deep need to forgive and in turn to be forgiven.

"Daddy" is also addressed in the first person to someone close to the speaker. Undoubtedly Otto Plath and Ted Hughes inspired "Daddy," but they are no more a Nazi Daddy or "a man in black with a Meinkampf look" than Plath is a gypsy tarot mistress who feels herself to be Jewish. Plath used and distorted autobiographical facts to portray a sadomasochistic and, ultimately, mutually destructive relationship. In so doing, she found Sexton's model useful.

For its own purposes "Daddy" borrows and slightly alters rhythms, rhymes, words, and lines from the early Sexton poem. "My Friend, My Friend" has an *a a b a* rhyme scheme throughout its six stanzas, with the exception of the last stanza, which adds a line with an *a* rhyme to the basic quatrain. These *a* rhymes repeat and echo in "Daddy." Plath borrows Sexton's "do," "you," and "Jew," adding ingenious variants of her own: "shoe," "Achoo," "blue," "du," "true," "through," "who," and "glue." Of particular note is Plath's "gobbledygoo" to Sexton's "bugaboo."

Sexton's quatrains end in alternate refrains, the second and fourth lines of the opening stanza: "With no special legend or God to refer to" and "I think it would be better to be a Jew." The second of these refrains is twice reworked by Plath, becoming in "Daddy": "I think I may well be a Jew" and "I may be a bit of a Jew." Furthermore, the lines "With my calm white pedigree, my yankee kin, / I think it would be better to be a Jew," from the first quatrain of "My Friend, My Friend," clearly serve as the model for the lines leading into Plath's second variation on the "Jewish" refrain:

> With my gypsy ancestress and my weird luck
> And my Taroc pack and my Taroc pack
> I may be a bit of a Jew.

Here Plath's alterations are exotic and expansive, allowing the speaker to chant about her dark arts.

Another similarity is the concern with the death of, and subsequent release from, a parent. In "Daddy," however, it takes twenty years of suffocating suffering and finally an exorcism and an elaborate ritual—the stake in the heart of vampire-like Daddy—to make him lie still enough, the persona hopes, to allow her to get "through" to personal freedom. Daddy's death is far more drawn out, dramatic, tortuous, and sinister than that of the mother in Sexton's poem. The death brings Plath's poem to its close, as the persona gasps her valediction, "Daddy, daddy, you bastard, I'm through," and collapses, exhausted by her efforts, into a world without Daddy. On this disturbing threshold the poem ends, leaving the reader teetering and searching for a foothold on the final and troubling word "through." In contrast, Sexton's poem turns back on itself, taking the reader back through the poem's closed circuit of guilt. This process is nicely captured in the closing couplet, which brings together the poem's alternating refrains.

In such differences in treatment Plath reveals her true artistry. Clearly she drew upon her former classmate's poem as she wrote "Daddy," and her debt to Sexton is considerable. Acknowledging the debt, however, is not to detract from Plath's achievement. Whereas "My Friend, My Friend" is an unexceptional, early example of Sexton's confessional poetry, "Daddy" is a brilliant act of exorcism from Plath's glittering late period. Despite Plath's use of a source in the composition of "Daddy," the poem remains distinctly and uniquely hers.

NOTES

1. Anne Sexton, "My Friend, My Friend," *Antioch Review* 19 (1959): 150. (Copyright © 1959 by Anne Sexton. Reprinted by permission of the Sterling Lord Agency, Inc.)

2. See Anne Sexton, "The Barfly Ought to Sing," in *The Art of Sylvia Plath: A Symposium*, ed. Charles Newman (London: Faber and Faber, 1970), 174–81.

3. Sylvia Plath, *The Poet Speaks*, ed. Peter Orr (London: Routledge and Kegan Paul, 1966), 167–68.

LINDA WAGNER-MARTIN

45 *Mercy Street* and Other Vacant Houses

It would be a gross oversimplification to attempt to define the "New England tradition" in poetry as intellectual, instructive, patriarchal, British, and somewhat imitative. To use that sense of tradition would be to force such nineteenth-century poets as Emily Dickinson, Ralph Waldo Emerson, Henry David Thoreau, and—to stretch the boundaries a bit—Walt Whitman far outside the accepted patterns: too innovative, too American, too emotional, and certainly too personal—these poets were already working toward achieving a distinctly unique poetic voice, a concept we today regard as "modern." To illustrate, what a difference between the well-known lines of a poet who represents the formal New England poetic tradition, William Cullen Bryant, and those of Dickinson, Emerson, and Whitman:

> To him who in the love of Nature holds
> Communion with her visible forms, she speaks
> A various language; for his gayer hours
> She has a voice of gladness, and a smile
> And eloquence of beauty, and she glides
> Into his darker musings, with a mild
> And gentle sympathy. . . .
>
> "Thanatopsis"

> I celebrate myself, and sing myself,
> And what I assume you shall assume,
> For every atom belonging to me as good belongs
>   to you
> I loafe and invite my soul,
> I lean and loafe at my ease observing a spear
>   of summer grass.
> My tongue, every atom of my blood, form'd from
>   this soil, this air,

Reprinted from *American Literature: The New England Heritage*, ed. James Nagel and Richard Astro (New York: Garland Publishing Co., 1981), 144–65.

> Born here of parents born here from parents the
>   same, and their parents the same,
> I, now thirty-seven years old in perfect
>   health begin,
> Hoping to cease not till death.[1]

When Whitman shares with us his biography (and nickname)—the fact that he is thirty-seven, a loafer, an American, and expansive in his American confidence—we respond to that identity, that reaching out. "Camerado, this is no book," he writes in "So Long"; "Who touches this touches a man. . . . From behind the screen where I hid I advance personally solely to you" (p. 391). A new definition of the poem as a means of speaking intimately evolves here, not only with Whitman but with Emerson in "The Problem":

> I like a church; I like a cowl;
> I love a prophet of the soul;
> And on my heart monastic aisles
> Fall like sweet strains, or pensive smiles;
> Yet not for all his faith can see
> Would I that cowled churchman be.[2]

Simultaneously but very separately, in her timid yet strangely assertive voice, Emily Dickinson began the same process of using personal speech in poems that defied both classification and publication:

> I tie my Hat—I crease my Shawl—
> Life's little duties do—precisely. . . .[3]

> I am alive—I guess
> The branches on my Hand
> Are full of Morning Glory—
>   (Pp. 225–26)

> This is my letter to the World
> That never wrote to Me—
>   (P. 211)

> I was the slightest in the House—
> I took the smallest Room—
> At night, my little Lamp, and Book—
> And one Geranium—
>   (P. 234)

These are hardly poems marked by any tones of imitation, any deference toward the mother country and its poetics, or any attempt to set forth large statements of intellectual weight. They are beginnings rather than culminations, forerunners of modern poetry rather than inheritors of an eighteenth-century mode. And they are strangely ungeographical, placed much more directly in the province of the heart than in any New England location. The conflict that must have existed between poetic convention—the use of place, landscape, to reveal larger ideas; the absence of the personal; the use of poetic diction rather than normal speech rhythms—and the interiority of these poems probably accounted for much of the poets' satisfaction with them.

From Dickinson's room in the family home in Amherst, Massachusetts, to Anne Sexton's lost family home on Mercy Street is only a brief walk. The wallpaper may be different, given the century that divides the houses, but the atmosphere is distressingly similar: both Sexton's and Dickinson's poems speak of the need for an identity as a writer and of their search for a male authority figure—father, brother, editor, analyst, husband, minister, critic, fellow writer—to support that writing process. The poems share a tone of apology for their emotional, feminine subject matter (as contrasted with supposedly "intellectual" themes) and an awareness on the part of each poet that this work is innovative, unconventional, and that it exists almost as a flight from accepted traditions. Both Sexton's and Dickinson's poems are marked with exuberance, anger, guilt, frustration, and, finally, self-acceptance. The best account of these dichotomies between a woman's trying to come, aggressively, to art while simultaneously trying to survive in a social context that demands passivity is *The Madwoman in the Attic* by Susan Gubar and Sandra M. Gilbert. Their readings of Dickinson's poems explain full well her reclusive, questioning, unsure yet dramatic poetic persona; and the extensions one can make from Dickinson to some of the best-known New England poets of this century are clear.[4]

Without benefit of criticism or sociology, Anne Sexton captures these contradictions in the title poem from 45 *Mercy Street*. Published posthumously in 1976, this collection creates a paradigm of the non-traditional poet's journey, the movement from the need for a place in the accepted mainstream to the strength to stand outside. The hegira that begins the book is, tellingly, a female hegira, and Sexton defines the journey as "a means of escaping from an undesirable or dangerous environment" as well as "a means of arriving at a highly desirable destination." Where are the models, in the canon of American liter-

ature, for a woman's initiation story? Where are the portraits of the
young woman as artist? Here.

With "45 Mercy Street" Sexton creates that story, that portrait.
She gives us Mercy and other subtle echoes of the "Twenty-third Psalm"
throughout the collection: "Surely goodness and mercy shall / follow
me all the days of my life; / and I will dwell in the house of the / Lord
for ever." Sexton plays with *surely*, the female expectation of living a
good, modest, loving life and being rewarded; with *goodness*, in both
a social and sexual sense; and she sets those words against a recurring
theme of *mercy*, the particularly female capacity for compassion that
is nonjudgmental. Inherent in Sexton's portrayal is the female ability
to accept, to forgive; not surprisingly, the characters of these last Sexton
poems are almost entirely female—her daughters Linda and Joy, her
mother, grandmother, great-aunt Nana, friends.

> In my dream,
> drilling into the marrow
> of my entire bone,
> my real dream,
> I'm walking up and down Beacon Hill
> searching for a street sign—
> namely MERCY STREET.
> Not there.
>
> I try the Back Bay.
> Not there.
> Not there.
> And yet I know the number.
> 45 Mercy Street.
> I know the stained-glass window
> of the foyer,
> the three flights of the house
> with its parquet floors.
> I know the furniture and
> mother, grandmother, great-grandmother,
> the servants.
> I know the cupboard of Spode,
> the boat of ice, solid silver,
> where the butter sits in neat squares
> like strange giant's teeth
> on the big mahogany table.
> I know it well.[5]

Sexton here accepts both the reality of dream, "real dream," and her need to find sources, home—and how maternal a home; she is also in her refrain affirming her own knowledge—"I know," "I know." Reality hits her with its contradictions, however, for no matter that she knows this house, knows it with the acute memories of the child, she cannot find it.

What she does find, in the next two stanzas, are the dichotomies inherent in being the female child: "When she was good, she was very, very good":

> Where did you go?
> 45 Mercy Street,
> with great-grandmother
> kneeling in her whale-bone corset
> and praying gently but fiercely
> to the wash basin,
> at five A.M.
> at noon
> dozing in her wiggy rocker,
> grandfather taking a nip in the pantry,
> grandmother pushing the bell for the downstairs maid,
> and Nana rocking Mother with an oversized flower
> on her forehead to cover the curl
> of when she was good and when she was . . .
> And where she was begat
> and in a generation
> the third she will beget,
> me,
> with the stranger's seed blooming
> into the flower called *Horrid*.
>
> I walk in a yellow dress
> and a white pocketbook stuffed with cigarettes,
> enough pills, my wallet, my keys,
> and being twenty-eight, or is it forty-five?
> I walk. I walk.
> I hold matches at the street signs
> for it is dark,
> as dark as the leathery dead
> and I have lost my green Ford,
> my house in the suburbs,
>   . . . .
> and I am walking and looking

> and this is no dream
> just my oily life
> where the people are alibis
> and the street is unfindable for an
> entire lifetime.

(Pp. 4–5)

The significance of the poem's being titled "45 Mercy Street" instead of just "Mercy Street," as was her earlier play, now becomes clear. Sexton is forty-five. She will die at forty-five, just a scant month before turning forty-six. These chronological markings are as important to Sexton as is her astrological profile—Scorpios both, she and Plath, marked, she thought, by violence, unkindness, will.[6] Married at seventeen, Sexton found herself in her poetry at twenty-eight. That age, then, is important to her; it represents the myth that people *do* find themselves, do mature, do become independent. Even after her divorce from the man who had husbanded her since she was seventeen, Sexton could not find that independence she seemed to prize so highly, and her anger, her disillusion, at this recognition leads to the stanza of withdrawal, denial, and finally a return to her own womanliness as her chief identity:

> Pull the shades down—
> I don't care!
> Bolt the door, mercy,
> erase the number,
> rip down my street sign,
> what can it matter,
> what can it matter to this cheapskate
> who wants to own the past
>
>   . . . .
>
> Not there.
>
> I open my pocketbook,
> as women do,
>
>   . . . .
>
> Next I pull the dream off
> and slam into the cement wall
> of the clumsy calendar
> I live in,
> my life,

and its hauled up
notebooks.

(Pp. 5–6)

Sexton as poet (Dickinson as poet, Plath as poet)—can we accept the
persona as writer only, unmoored, lost, admittedly searching, unlo-
cateable, certainly NOT New England bound. We can hear Sexton laugh
as she writes to Jon Stallworthy in 1967, "I adore being called the
Nefertiti of New England."[7] In 1963, to Robert Lowell, she had admitted, "One of these days, I will learn to bear to be myself."[8] The
poems of *45 Mercy Street* show that bearing, that becoming, and the
anger in having to remain outside an accepted tradition, both geo-
graphic and poetic.

Always "confessional," usually "hysterical," always maligned for
poems written to menstruation, lovers, abortions, her uterus, Sexton
turns to apology for that personal element, as in "Talking to Sheep,"
or to questioning her multiple roles, as in "The Falling Dolls":

> Dolls,
> by the thousands,
> are falling out of the sky
> and I look up in fear
> and wonder who will catch them?

Guilt—why are you a poet? Who's taking care of your children (daughters)?

> I dream, awake, I dream of falling dolls
> who need cribs and blankets and pajamas
> with real feet in them.
> Why is there no mother?
> Why are all these dolls falling out of the sky?
> Was there a father?
> Or have the planets cut holes in their nets
> and let our childhood out,
> or are we the dolls themselves,
> born but never fed?

(Pp. 10–11)

As with her earlier collections, some of the best poems in *45 Mercy
Street* are Sexton's poems to her children, but here the simple sense
of love and responsibility—an awesome responsibility—is coupled with
an anguish of lost identity, of lost place: *are we the dolls themselves!*

Parallel with that sense of loss, increasing because of that disorientation, runs a terrible, oppressive responsibility. Even the animal poems are marked with the maternal guilt, as when Sexton laments to a dead animal, "Mole dog, / I wish your mother would wake you up." The divorce poems carry similar guilt. Whether the wife is reattaching her husband's severed hands and feet or worrying about her teenage daughters ("we, mothers, crumpled and flyspotted / with bringing them this far / can do nothing now but pray"), the female persona bears the responsibility. Not easily. Undeniably. She is born to it. As Sexton writes in "The Big Boots of Pain":

> I would sell my life to avoid
> the pain that begins in the crib
>
> . . . .
>
> when the planets drill
> your future into you
> for better or worse
> as you marry life
> and the love that gets doled out
> or doesn't.
>
> (P. 103)

The gamble of the traditional woman's life, be she Cinderella or Sexton, is her marriage, and that marriage is her primary responsibility. That such a single responsibility, carried singly, may wear into madness is the image of the poet's crucifixion in "The Passion of the Mad Rabbit":

> Next it was bad Friday and they nailed me up
> like a scarecrow and many gathered eating popcorn, carrying
> hymnals or balloons. There were three of us there,
> though *they* appeared normal. My ears, so pink like powder,
> were nailed. My paws, sweet as baby mittens, were nailed.
> And my two fuzzy ankles. I said, "Pay no attention. I am
>   crazy."
> But some giggled and some knelt. My oxygen became tiny
> and blood rang over and over in my head like a bell.
> The others died, the luck of it blurting through them.
> I could not. I was a silly broken umbrella
> and oblivion would not kiss me. For three days it
> was thus.
>
> Then they took me down and had a conference.
> It is Easter, they said, and you are the Easter Bunny.

Then they built a great pyre of kindling and laid me on top
and just before the match they handed me a pink basket
of eggs the color of the circus.
Fire lit, I tossed the eggs to them, *Hallelujah* I sang
    to the eggs,
singing as I burned to nothing in the tremor of the flames.
My blood came to a boil as I looked down the throat of
    madness,
but singing yellow egg, blue egg, pink egg, red egg, green
    egg,
Hallelujah, to each hard-boiled-colored egg.

(Pp. 90–91)

Poor lost Alice in Wonderland; poor mother, responsible for any ritual, tradition, food, spirit; poor woman lost in sexuality, fertility, the flames of lust and madness—here as in *Transformations* Sexton makes use of our common heritage of fairy tale, myth, and archetype of sex goddess/ mother and poises it against that other set of opposites, sanity/insanity. She similarly uses the image of angel food in her poem about the virgin/whore identity, wishing to change her name from Anne to Mary (her mother's name); wishing for purity, for grace, and finally—pervasively—for mercy:

I kneel once more,
in case mercy should come. . . .

(P. 89)

finding my Mercy Street,
kissing it and tenderly gift-wrapping my love. . . .

(P. 105)

Much as she hopes for mercy, tired and resentful as she is of life's nonacceptance and its demands, still Sexton comes in these last poems to the confidence of her own self-possession. There is contentment of a sort in *45 Mercy Street*. There are images throughout the collection of houses, shelters gained through love, homes. The ultimate image of place occurs in her poem "Keeping the City." Lost from even that maternal ancestry, searching as she honestly recounts, Sexton yet finds her strength in her kinship with her maturing daughters and, through them, with herself as woman. Her strength is, however, but fragile, tentative, a veil of bright motion, a daisy, which some eyes might consider ineffectual:

> The city
> of my choice
> that I guard
> like a butterfly, useless, useless
> in her yellow costume, swirling
> swirling around the gates.
> The city shifts, falls, rebuilds. . . .
>
> (P. 24)

That place, unnamed as it is, that city, is, finally, of Sexton's *choice*— and her ability to make that choice is crucial. And while it is not a New England city but a much more interior and specifically female city, it does, finally, "rebuild."

The same sense of alienation, of being dis- or mislocated, permeates the poetry of Sylvia Plath as well. The torture of attempting to create a safe home anguishes her late poems, particularly those of *Ariel* and *Crossing the Water*, when the poet/persona, like that of Sexton, bears the responsibility for not only her own children but the world's lost souls. As Plath promises in her poem to her son, "Nick and the Candlestick,"

> Love, love,
> I have hung our cave with roses.
> With soft rugs—
>
> The last of Victoriana.[9]

In this safe room Plath can contend bravely,

> Let the stars
> Plummet to their dark address,
>
> Let the mercuric
> Atoms that cripple drip
> Into the terrible well. . . .

She has found her solidity—her children, her sense of self, her work. As her poem to her friend and nurse, "Kindness," declares:

> Kindness glides about my house.
> Dame Kindness, she is so nice!
> The blue and red jewels of her rings smoke
> In the windows, the mirrors
> Are filling with smiles

. . . .

And here you come, with a cup of tea
Wreathed in steam.
The blood jet is poetry,
There is no stopping it.
You hand me two children, two roses.

(P. 82)

These are hardly the typical Plath poems so often anthologized. Plath's more common poems, throughout her career, are those of search. Even as a young poet, she images herself as alienated, different. Displaced at home, displaced at Smith, displaced in New York in the fashionable offices of *Mademoiselle,* she finally seems to have found a sympathetic locale in England. She loved its tranquility, its traditions, during her years at Oxford; and once she and Ted Hughes had decided to live in England rather than America, she wrote her mother:

> I am growing very pleased with the idea of living in England. The speed and expense of America is just about 50 years ahead of me. I could be as fond of London as of any other city in the world, and plays, books, and all these things are so much more within one's means. . . . I want Ted to take me on a trip around England, especially to Wales and to little fishing villages. When you come, we should go on a jaunt of some sort, staying at old inns and taking country walks.[10]

Throughout her late poems it becomes clear that Plath saw herself as old-fashioned, virtuous, pure. Set against her husband's adultery, his betrayal of what she had found to be a perfect marriage, one that combined satisfaction in work with satisfaction in love, her sense of place and tradition becomes wound into her sense of self and even of morality.

Given Plath's personal situation in 1963, separated from Hughes, living in the house Yeats once inhabited, entirely responsible for the children, Frieda and Nicholas, her feelings of personal bitterness may have colored her view of her country. In her 1963 essay "America! America!" Plath faults her superficial American education for its emphasis on conformity. "Eccentricities, the perils of being *too* special, were reasoned and cooed from us like sucked thumbs."[11] Because there is no place in America for "the embryo rebel, the artist, the odd," Plath happily relinquishes her identity as American. As she muses in "Three Women":

I shall meditate upon normality.
I shall meditate upon my little son.

. . . .

I do not will him to be exceptional.
It is the exception that interests the devil.
It is the exception that climbs the sorrowful hill
Or sits in the desert and hurts his mother's heart.
I will him to be common,
To love me as I love him,
And to marry what he wants and where he will.[12]

The contradictions inherent in saying one is more or less British or more or less American (and Plath's poetry implies that Hughes was certainly more American than she—in a negative sense—just as he was also German, Nazi, Panzer-man) surface again in a 1962 essay titled "Ocean 1212-W." Plath speaks here of her passionate love for the sea:

> My childhood landscape was not land but the end of the land—the cold, salt, running hills of the Atlantic. I sometimes think my vision of the sea is the clearest thing I own. I pick it up, exile that I am, like the purple "lucky stones" I used to collect with a white ring all the way round, or the shell of a blue mussel with its rainbowy angel's fingernail interior; and in one wash of memory the colors deepen and gleam, the early world draws breath.
>
> Breath, that is the first thing. Something is breathing. My own breath? The breath of my mother? No, something else, something larger, farther, more serious, more weary.[13]

Replacing identity, replacing the mother as source of life and breath, the sea became Plath's alter ego. She refers to herself in this essay as both "an exile" and a "reject"; yet she had found solace and an essential part of her person—"my love of change and wildness"—in these early years by the sea, living in the "sea-bitten house" that was lost with her father's death. Plath mourns, "Those nine first years of my life sealed themselves off like a ship in a bottle—beautiful, inaccessible, obsolete, a fine, white flying myth."

It is not accidental that, in Plath's beautifully tranquil poem "Morning Song," her hymn to her newborn son, his cry returns her to that beloved seaside:

> All night your moth-breath
> Flickers among the flat pink roses. I wake to listen:
> A far sea moves in my ear.

> One cry, and I stumble from bed, cow-heavy and floral
> In my Victorian nightgown.
> Your mouth opens clean as a cat's. The window square
>
> Whitens and swallows its dull stars. And now you try
> Your handful of notes;
> The clear vowels rise like balloons.
>
> (*Ariel*, 1)

The poet's yearning for a like tranquility is the theme of Plath's masterful "Tulips." The old man's death in "Berck-Plage" is imaged to be like the sea, "a green sea . . . fold upon fold far off, concealing hollows" (p. 23). The woman on horseback in "Ariel" reaches her moment of climax in a similar sea image: "And now I / Foam to wheat, a glitter of seas" (p. 26).

Plath's recognition of the central importance of primal themes in poetry in some ways explicates this recurrence of the sea image. The 1962 comment to follow is written with that tinge of defiance that shows Plath's defensiveness and reminds us of the true alienation of Dickinson, Sexton, and Plath from both the world of the traditional poet and, similarly—because of their poetry—from the world of the traditional woman:

> My poems do not turn out to be about Hiroshima, but about a child forming itself finger by finger in the dark. They are not about the terrors of mass extinction, but about the bleakness of the moon over a yew tree in a neighboring graveyard. Not about the testaments of tortured Algerians, but about the night thoughts of a tired surgeon.
>
> In a sense, these poems are deflections. I do not think they are an escape. For me, the real issues of our time are the issues of every time—the hurt and wonder of loving; making in all its forms—children, loaves of bread, paintings, buildings; and the conservation of life of all people in all places. . . .[14]

Plath's mention of her yew tree poem sends us to one of the most central poems in *Ariel*. Unrelieved anguish is its tone, imaged in the "blackness and silence" of the closing, the "complete despair" of the shut, starkly white moon. What the scene of the yew tree in the graveyard, pointing up through the bluish light toward the moon, does, in effect, is to convince the poet/persona that all her beliefs are in error. She searches for a mother, a spirit of tenderness, and finds nothing—either in the moon, in the Virgin, or in her own mother. Church bells, nature, human relations have all disappointed her. Of herself the poet tells us only "I have fallen a long way," "How I would like to believe in tenderness," "I simply cannot see where there is to get to" (p. 41).

If vacillation marks many of Plath's late poems, a pulling between affirmation and negation, then "The Moon and the Yew Tree" is striking in its outright denial. It parallels "Medusa," in which Plath asks of her mother's presence, "Did I escape, I wonder?" (p. 39) and "Getting There," the most forbidding of Plath's journey poems, in which life is pictured as a war and the poet/persona described as a struggling refugee "dragging my body / Quietly through the straw of the boxcars."

> It is Adam's side,
> This earth I rise from, and I in agony.
> (P. 37)

All the refugee wants is a place, a destination: "It is so small / The place I am getting to, why are there these obstacles." Yet she despairs repeatedly

> Is there no still place
> Turning and turning in the middle air,
> Untouched and untouchable. . . .
> (P. 37)

Even in the midst of her anguished search, however, she bears responsibility for the other despairing travelers: "I shall bury the wounded like pupas, / I shall bury and count the dead." Here again, and throughout Plath's late poems, are the themes of the Sexton poems: the search for place and support, the disassociation from the expected, the assumption of grave responsibilities, and finally the acceptance of both the self and its place—always partial, disappointing, dismaying: "No where." "I do not fear it: I have been there." "Starless and fatherless, a dark water."

One of Plath's most direct poems to deal with the loss of place—and, accordingly, with the loss of the myth that women are to be cared for, protected, and housed by men—is "Letter in November." One assumes a final letter from her estranged husband, close to the time of her thirtieth birthday—Plath, like Sexton, was a Scorpio and, more important, believed that she was plagued with the Scorpian doubleness[15]—for the poem opens addressing him:

> Love, the world
> Suddenly turns, turns colour. The streetlight
> Splits through the rat's-tail
> Pods of the laburnum at nine in the morning.
> It is the Arctic,
>
> This little black
> Circle. . . .
>
> (P. 46)

This is the world Plath was born to, one of a man's building, now only a "little black circle, the Arctic." Instead, as the world suddenly turns, the poet has found her *own* world; most of the poem gives us her possession of that world, through a simple life-affirming subject-verb structure. And, as often in Plath's late poetry, the subject is *I:*

> I am flushed and warm.
> I think I may be enormous,
> I am so stupidly happy,
> My Wellingtons
> Squelching and squelching through the beautiful red.
>
> This is my property.
> Two times a day
> I pace it, sniffing
> The barbarous holly with its viridian
> Scallops, pure iron,
>
> And the wall of old corpses.
> I love them.
> I love them like history.
> The apples are golden,
> Imagine it—
>
> My seventy trees
> Holding their gold-ruddy balls. . . .
>
> (P. 46)

The tone changes abruptly, whether with some reference to the chilling Midas touch, that gold like this is unnatural, or more directly with reference to the letter of the title: outwardly the persona has won; she has her place; she has created it. Inwardly, however, the victory of possession—alone—is hollow. The poem closes:

> My seventy trees
> Holding their gold-ruddy balls

> In a thick grey death-soup,
> Their million
> Gold leaves metal and breathless.
>
> O love, O celibate.
> Nobody but me
> Walks the waist-high wet.
> The irreplaceable
> Golds bleed and deepen, the mouths of Thermopylae.
>
>   (P. 47)

The same duality—pride in survival, dismay at abandonment—dominates the marvelous sequence of bee poems, "The Bee Meeting," "The Arrival of the Bee Box," "Stings," "The Swarm," and "Wintering." The identity of the old queen seems to represent Plath—as old wife, old poet, soon to be displaced by Hughes's new lover:

> They are hunting the queen.
> Is she hiding, is she eating honey? She is very clever.
> She is old, old, old, she must live another year, and she knows it.
>
>   (P. 57)

Yet for all her endurance and cleverness, the old queen is "exhausted . . . exhausted. . . . The magician's girl who does not flinch" (p. 58). All the knives of pain do not, finally, hurt as much as they might because the poet/persona sees herself as being in control: "I ordered this, this clean wood box" (p. 59). "Bare-handed, I hand the combs" (p. 61).

In the poem "Stings" Plath shifts from identity as queen bee to identity as woman-observer robbed of her uniqueness in the process of domesticity:

> I stand in a column
>
> Of winged, unmiraculous women,
> Honey-drudgers.
> I am no drudge
> Though for years I have eaten dust
> And dried plates with my dense hair.
>
> And seen my strangeness evaporate,
> Blue dew from dangerous skin.
> Will they hate me,
> These women who only scurry,
> Whose news is the open cherry, the open clover?

> It is almost over.
> I am in control.
>
> (Pp. 61–62)

Fearful that other women will not accept her, the persona yet refuses to deny her power, her strangeness; and at the end of "Stings" the identities fuse so that the final image—of powerful femaleness turned to destruction against male confinement—parallels the ending of "Lady Lazarus." In that poem the woman persona rises from death by fire:

> Ash, ash—
> You poke and stir.
> Flesh, bone, there is nothing there—
>
> A cake of soap,
> A wedding ring,
> A gold filling.
>
> Herr God, Herr Lucifer,
> Beware
> Beware.
>
> Out of the ash
> I rise with my red hair
> And I eat men like air.
>
> (Pp. 8–9)

In "Stings" the rebirth depends less on anger against a single male prosecution or betrayal than it does on the woman's self-awareness. Rebirth is as much a personal discovery as it is a vindication:

> They thought death was worth it, but I
> Have a self to recover, a queen.
> Is she dead, is she sleeping?
> Where has she been,
> With her lion-red body, her wings of glass?
>
> Now she is flying
> More terrible than she ever was, red
> Scar in the sky, red comet
> Over the engine that killed her—
> The mausoleum, the wax house.
>
> (Pp. 62–63)

Place as house, wax house, mausoleum, confinement, death—Plath's images of would-be triumph are almost unbearable, but she softens the impact of "house" in the last poem of the bee sequence, "Wintering."

> This is the easy time, there is nothing doing.
> I have whirled the midwife's extractor,
> I have my honey,
> Six jars of it,
> Six cat's eyes in the wine cellar,
>
> Wintering in a dark without window
> At the heart of the house. . . .
>
> (P. 67)

Somnolent, peaceful, woman in possession of spoils—rather than being a possession herself—there is a calm here, an acceptance, first in the direct statement,

> The bees are all women,
> Maids and the long royal lady.
> They have got rid of the men,
>
> The blunt, clumsy stumblers, the boors.
> Winter is for women—

and finally in the affirmation of the last stanza:

> Will the hive survive, will the gladiolas
> Succeed in banking their fires
> To enter another year?
> What will they taste of, the Christmas roses?
> The bees are flying. They taste the spring.
>
> (P. 68)

For all her emphasis on endurance, Plath's poems leave us rather with the anguish, the sense of displacement, the search for place, the terrible weight of responsibility. In Plath as in Sexton, in Dickinson as in Rich, the themes recur, pointing repeatedly to the double disenfranchisement, the double disorientation of being both writer and woman. I had intended to include two other poets, the vibrant and strangely androgynous E. E. Cummings and the divided but responsive Robert Lowell. Reminiscent as many of their poems are of the New England heritage, their poems differ greatly from those of Dickinson, Plath, and Sexton: the defiance against tradition is more often intellectualized, controllable. The refusal to conform is itself a pose and, in that, more acceptable. As Richard Kennedy points out in his fine biography of Cummings: "Despite his hostility to American culture, he is as American as Concord Bridge and the Statue of Liberty. 'The tradition, after all, in this nation is bucking the tradition. . . .' "[16]

Acceptance of attitudes, an intellectual understanding of defiance—our male writers feel secure enough in their roles as artists, and the cultural expectations of those roles, that they can deal with alienation and even with loss of place, parents, and love. There is much less sense of torture, much less search imagery in the poems of Cummings and Lowell, and more of a tendency to offer wisdom, panacea, and achieved knowledge. Just as in "Thanatopsis" Bryant's view of that final search, that final definition of place—death—is highly intellectualized:

> When thoughts
> Of the last bitter hour come like a blight
> Over thy spirit, and sad images
> Of the stern agony, and shroud, and pall,
> And breathless darkness, and the narrow house,
> Make thee to shudder, and grow sick at heart;—
> Go forth under the open sky, and list
> To Nature's teachings. . . .

Death as "pleasant dreams" in the Bryant poem has no echo in the work of Dickinson, Sexton, or Plath. The fact of actual death is the price we have all paid for their great alienation: the loss of place, the hostility of nonacceptance becomes the image throughout the poems so that Sexton may write, in *Words for Dr. Y,*

> Home is my Bethlehem,
> my succoring shelter[17]

but just as quickly admit "Houses haunt me. . . ."

> I am alone here in my own mind.
> There is no map
> and there is no road.
>
> (P. 63)

Lest we be tempted to read the pervasive images of Sexton's and Plath's poems as only contemporary, striking evidence of the interiority of the modern poetic focus, we must return to the poems of Emily Dickinson:

> One need not be a Chamber—to be Haunted—
> One need not be a House—
> The Brain has corridors—surpassing
> Material Place. . . .[18]

Isolation, loss of place, responsibility, guilt, the creation of a new world—alone, alone as both artist and woman. The New England tradition seems far removed from these poets, who are, perhaps, among our greatest. We should reach this recognition, I think, with less anger than with lament, for, as Dickinson wrote in 1863, one hundred years before Plath's suicide:

> Victory comes late—
> And is held low to freezing lips—
> Too rapt with frost
> To take it—
> How sweet it would have tasted—
> Just a drop. . . .
> Crumbs—fit such little mouths—[19]

NOTES

1. Walt Whitman, *Leaves of Grass and Selected Prose*, ed. John Kouwenhoven (New York: Modern Library, 1950), 23–24. Subsequent references are cited in the text.

2. Ralph Waldo Emerson, "The Problem," in *The Norton Anthology of American Literature*, vol. 1, ed. Ronald Gottesman et al. (New York: W. W. Norton, 1979), 833.

3. *The Complete Poems of Emily Dickinson*, ed. Thomas H. Johnson (Boston: Little, Brown and Co., 1960), 212. Subsequent references are cited in the text.

4. Sandra M. Gilbert and Susan Gubar, *The Madwoman in the Attic: The Woman Writer and the Nineteenth-Century Literary Imagination* (New Haven: Yale University Press, 1979). That there still exists a sense of the modern "New England" poet seems clear from looking at the table of contents in Donald Hall's anthology *Contemporary American Poetry* (New York: Penguin Books, 1972). Nearly 75 percent of the thirty-nine poets included are either from New England or were educated there. Of the thirty-nine poets, only four—Sexton, Plath, Rich, and Denise Levertov—are women; and of those four, Levertov is British, and the other three are all New Englanders.

5. Anne Sexton, *45 Mercy Street*, ed. Linda Gray Sexton (Boston: Houghton Mifflin Co., 1976), 3. Subsequent references are cited in the text.

6. Sexton's sequence of poems "Scorpio, Bad Spider, Die: The Horoscope Poems" was published in 1978 in the collection *Words for Dr. Y.: Uncollected Poems with Three Stories*, ed. Linda Gray Sexton (Boston: Houghton Mifflin Co.). There are frequent references in both Sexton's and Plath's poetry and letters to astrology.

7. Included in *Anne Sexton: A Self-Portrait in Letters*, ed. Linda Gray Sexton and Lois Ames (Boston: Houghton Mifflin Co., 1977), 318.

8. Quoted in ibid., 170.

9. Sylvia Plath, *Ariel* (New York: Harper and Row, 1965), 34. Subsequent references are cited in the text.

10. *Letters Home by Sylvia Plath: Correspondence, 1950–1963*, ed. Aurelia Schober Plath (New York: Harper and Row, 1975), 356.

11. Included in Sylvia Plath, *Johnny Panic and the Bible of Dreams: Short Stories, Prose, and Diary Excerpts* (New York: Harper and Row, 1979), 54.

12. Sylvia Plath, "Three Women: A Poem for Three Voices," *Winter Trees* (New York: Harper and Row, 1972), 62.

13. Plath, *Johnny Panic*, 20.

14. Ibid., 64.

15. Many references to astrology pepper Plath's work, perhaps the most effective being the ending of "Words" (*Ariel*, 85): "While / From the bottom of the pool, fixed stars / Govern a life."

16. Richard S. Kennedy, *Dreams in the Mirror: A Biography of E. E. Cummings* (New York: Liveright, 1980), 7.

17. *Words for Dr. Y.*, 61. Subsequent references are cited in the text.

18. Dickinson, *Complete Poems*, 333.

19. Ibid., 340.

PERSONAL AND PUBLIC: CONTROLLING THE MATERIAL

ALICIA OSTRIKER

That Story: Anne Sexton and Her Transformations

I

Anne Sexton is the easiest poet in the world to condescend to. Critics get in line for the pleasure of filing her under N for *narcissist* and announcing that she lacks reticence. A recent example: "She indulges in self-revelation without stint, telling all in an *exposé* of her innermost workings that amounts to literary *seppuku.*" The critic wonders whether "such messy preoccupations will remain to stain the linen of the culture for long or whether good taste bleaches out even the most stubborn stain eventually."[1]

In letters as in life, to expose a personal fragility is to invite attack. Cruelty and contempt follow vulnerability, just as respect follows snobbishness; it is a law of human nature. Having been on both sides of this reflex, I suspect that the sneer derives from fear—a fear of being stung into imaginative sympathy—and in Anne Sexton's case I suspect that the fear is threefold.

First of all, Sexton's material is heavily female and biological. She gives us full helpings of her breasts, her uterus, her menstruation, her abortion, her "tiny jail" of a vagina, her love life, her mother's and daughters' breasts, everyone's operations, the act of eating, the way her father's "serpent, that mocker, woke up and pressed against me / like a great god" when she danced with him after much champagne at a wedding, even the trauma of her childhood enemas. Preoccupied with the flesh, she swings between experiencing it as sacred and fertile and experiencing it as filthy and defiled. This distinguishes her from Plath, for whom the body is mainly an emblem of pain and mutilation. But the distinction will not be an interesting one to the timid reader.

Reprinted from Alicia Ostriker, *Writing Like a Woman* (Ann Arbor: University of Michigan Press, 1983), 59–85.

Far more than Plath, Sexton challenges our residual certainties that the life of the body should be private and not public, and that women especially should be seen and not heard, except among each other, talking about their messy anatomies. We believe, I think, that civilization will fall if it is otherwise.

Second, Sexton is assertively emotional. A love junkie who believes "touch" is "the kingdom and the kingdom come," she is driven by an unquenchable need for acceptance and caresses, and by bottomless guilt that she herself has been insufficiently loving to others. Simultaneously, the poetry presses intimately toward its audience. Feel what I feel, it says. Accept me, love me, love everything about me, my strength, my weakness. This of course is very much a feminine sort of demand, or rather it is a demand we discourage men from making explicitly (disguised versions are acceptable) and encourage women to make, with predictable results. Remember Marilyn Monroe? The egotistical sublime we tolerate, not the egotistical pathetic. The demand for love is narcissistic and childish. It is usually self-defeating, since most of us respond to another's need for love with aversion. Insofar as we manage (barely) to keep the upper lip stiff in our own lives, we judge neediness (in excess of our own) to be immoral. In the same way, wealth judges poverty and success perceives failure to be a consequence of low character. We understand that beggars and cripples exist, but do they have to put themselves where we can see them?

But what is most distressing about Sexton, I think, is her quality of unresignedness. She writes more fiercely than any poet in our time about physical and mental bliss and the holiness of the heart's affections. Her explorations of pathology are feverish attempts to "gnaw at the barrier" dividing us from one another and from the "weird abundance" of our creative capacities. She is sure not only that poetry saved her own life but that it can save others' lives. Many of her poems are gestures of rather pure human generosity. "For My Lover, Returning to His Wife" and "December 12th" in *Love Poems* are two examples. Typically her work enacts a pitched battle between Thanatos and Eros, self-loathing and self-love, suicide and survival. This, too, is irritating. "The mass of men lead lives of quiet desperation," wrote Thoreau more than a century ago, trying to twit them out of it. "We think of the key, each in his prison, / Thinking of the key, each confirms a prison," wrote Eliot a half-century back, on the way to his conversion to Christianity. But consider how much of our literature, our high literature especially, and most especially our high poetry, confirms the prison. We are instructed perhaps in its interior decoration, but not encouraged to seek escape. John Fowles's Daniel Martin muses "how all through his writing life, he had avoided the happy ending, as if it were somehow in bad taste . . . offensive, in an intellectually privileged caste, to suggest publicly that anything might turn out well." If each in his cell believes himself locked up forever, the last thing he wants to hear from a neighboring cell is the noise of scratching, poundings, screamings for the jailer.

Antipathy to a writer like Sexton makes sense if we assume that poetry must somehow be decorous. Obviously a great deal of poetry, both great and trivial, is so. But I see no real reason why poetry should be limited to tasteful confirmations of my psychic *status quo ante,* or indeed why it should be limited in any way. Reticence and good taste are excellent things, but unscrewing the doors from their jambs is a good thing too. Our original sin as humanists is a tendency to forget that nothing human is alien to any of us. This means that the crazy suicidal lady is not to be condescended to by me. It also means that she is one of the inhabitants of my own proper attic, whom I deny at my peril. A poem does not have to be, yet may legitimately be, "an axe for the frozen sea" of sympathy and self-recognition "within us," provided only that its language be living and its form just.

This brings me to the vexed question of Anne Sexton's artistry, where I must say immediately and with regret that she is not a *fine* artist. At her best she is coarse. Musically her instrument is the kazoo. If Plath, say, is porcelain, and Robert Lowell bronze, Sexton is brightly painted earthenware. Reading every book of hers but *Transformations,* I burn with the desire to edit. She repeats herself without noticing. Her early poems before she hits her stride tend to be too stiff, her late ones tend to be shapeless. Her phrasing is sometimes sentimental, her endings sometimes flat.

And yet the writing dazzles. Sexton's colloquial line, vigorous, flexible, and earthy, is not only a standing rebuke to every sort of false dignity but a strategy for redeeming the common life. Her organic and domestic imagery captures species of phenomena for poetry that were never there before. Her metaphors, breathtaking as ski jumps, direct attention both to the play of the language and to the writer's intelligence—which is not the same as bookishness—and sheer capacity to describe. One does not rapidly exhaust the significance of a poem about the mad that says "what large children we are" and mentions the night nurse who "walks on two erasers," or a poem about a hospital stay concluding with the lines "and run along, Anne, and run along now, / my stomach laced up like a football / for the game." Is one's body really a toy? To others, to the self? Consider a fantasy of dying that says, "I moved like a lobster, / slower and slower," or a quick allegory of the poet's life in which Jonah, finding he cannot escape the whale, "cocked his head attentively / like a defendant at his own trial," or the simile of "tears falling down like mud," or the story of Eve giving birth to a rat "with its bellyful of dirt / and its hair seven inches long" that she did not realize was ugly. It is writerliness and nothing else that enables Sexton to re-create the child-self more keenly than Roethke, to define inner demons more clearly than Lowell, and to evoke the complicated tensile strands of intimate relationships, which include physical need and revulsion, affection and fear, pride and guilt, resentment, jealousy and admiration, better than most novelists. As to the primitive style, anyone who thinks it is easier to write "raw" than "cooked" should try it.

Often Sexton's best poems in the early books are not the harrowing accounts of private trauma that understandably most gripped her first readers, but poems where self-knowledge makes possible the verbal crystallization of some larger piece of the human condition. "Housewife," a ten-line poem with four hairpin turns and a final two lines that are as important as the first two of "The Red Wheel Barrow," is a good example. It is this that brings me to my main subject. Though Sexton is always a strong poet of the subjective self, in the middle of her career her center of gravity shifted. Beginning with *Transformations,* which was a sort of poetic self-initiation, she set the uninhibited self to work interpreting prior, external, shared cultural traditions. The texts I want to examine are *Transformations,* which is her most successful single book because of its brilliant fusion of public with personal matter; "The Jesus Papers" in *The Book of Folly,* which is her most shocking and subversive work; and the poetry of spiritual quest in *The Death Notebooks* and *The Awful Rowing Toward God,* which is her most tragic. I believe that "confessional" or not, all these poems change the way we must look at our shared past. As their themes are increasingly ambitious, their conclusions are increasingly significant culturally. Obviously they also change the way we must look at Sexton.

II

In the winter of 1969–70, with four volumes of intimately personal poems behind her, Anne Sexton embarked on a new sort of venture. The early work dealt with the poet's family, her struggles against madness, her loves, her terrors, her desires. "That narrow diary of my mind" was laid publicly bare both as a personal necessity and in the faith that to reveal rather than conceal one's private nightmares was to perform a poetic service. The orientation of her poetry was psychoanalytic, as befitted a poet who began writing as a form of therapy following mental breakdown, who enacted in her poems the analysand's self-probing through examination of relationships with others, and who explained the vitality of her images by saying that "poetry, after all, milks the unconscious." Of all the poets subsequently labeled confessional or extremist—Snodgrass, Lowell, Berryman, Plath—she was the least reticent personally and the most eager to have her poems "mean something to someone else." Public popularity had spectacularly confirmed Sexton's convictions. For much of 1969 the poet immersed herself with the aid of a Guggenheim grant in the autobiographical drama *Mercy Street,* a work of extreme self-saturation that played for some weeks in the fall at the American Place Theater to mixed but respectful reviews. Until this point Sexton had not tried "to give you something else, / something outside of myself."[2] Self was the center, self the perimeter, of her vision.

Concerning the new series of poems that retold sixteen fairy tales from the Brothers Grimm, neither the poet nor her publishers expressed great confidence. Houghton Mifflin wondered whether she should publish them at all and wanted to consult an outside reader. Sexton was defensive and apologetic, worrying that "many of my former fans are going to be disappointed that these poems do not hover on the brink of insanity," and acknowledging that they were "a departure from my usual style . . . they lack the intensity and confessional force of my previous work." To persuade herself and her publishers that the work was good, she solicited an opinion from Stanley Kunitz. To boost it with the public, she arranged for an admiring preface by Kurt Vonnegut, Jr.

Transformations breaks the confined circle of a poetic mode Sexton had needed but outgrown, that of the purely personal. That folktales carry a heavy cultural burden has been understood since they were first collected. Mircea Eliade tells us they represent "an infinitely serious and responsible adventure" that he identifies with the universal ordeal of initiation, "passing by way of a symbolic death and resurrection from ignorance and immaturity to the spiritual age of the adult." Bruno Bettelheim believes they provide children with models for the mastery of psychological problems, teach them the necessity of struggle, and embody through fantasy "the process of healthy human development." We see these tales, in other words, as the expression of a social mandate favoring individual growth.

Sexton does not alter Grimm's plots. Her fidelity to the stories preserves what Eliade calls the "initiatory scenario," and this may partially explain why a poet who was perennially torn between remaining a child and assuming adulthood was attracted to these tales in the first place. Formally, the plot lines give her what she never had before: something nominally outside of her personal history to write about. What she does with this material is to seize it, crack it open, and *make* it personal. The result is at once a brilliant interpretation and a valid continuation of folktale tradition—and a piece of poetic subversion, whereby the "healthy" meanings we expect to enjoy are held up to icy scrutiny.

Syntax and diction in *Transformations* are conspicuously and brazenly twentieth-century American, stripped to the colloquial bone, in a mode probably generated for American poetry by Eliot's "Journey of the Magi." The technique brings us closer to the unsentimental pre-Christian origins of these stories, much as the language of Eliot's "Magi" intends not to deflate the significance of Christ's nativity but to force the reader to confront it more nakedly. But unlike Eliot (or Pound, or their imitators), far from being interested in the past for its own sake, Sexton makes the time of the tales our own. In her "Snow White and the Seven Dwarfs":

> the virgin is a lovely number:
> cheeks as fragile as cigarette paper,
> arms and legs made of Limoges,
> lips like Vin Du Rhône,
> rolling her china-blue doll eyes
> open and shut.

This is the opening tale and sets the tone. Of the miller's daughter in "Rumpelstiltskin," threatened with extinction if she does not spin straw into gold, the narrator condoles, "Poor thing. / To die and never see Brooklyn." In "Cinderella" the heroine

> slept on the sooty hearth each night
> and walked around looking like Al Jolson.

The reader's initial response to these anachronisms may be one of delighted shock—Cinderella and Al Jolson, yes, of course, think of the parallels—it is like a blue volt leaping a gap. We need to remember that just such modernization and adaptation, making the tales locally meaningful, is what peasants and poets have done with traditional lore for millennia. The stories would never survive without it. But Sexton's telescoping of past and present is also a surface manifestation of a more profound interpretive activity.

The poet's effort to understand her stories on her own terms precipitates a transformed view of traditional social values, particularly those associated with feminine life patterns: love and marriage, beauty, family, and most radically, the idea of goodness and moral responsibility, all of which she slices through like butter. The fairy tale ending of marriage, supposed to represent romantic and financial security ever after, becomes, ironically, "That story"—incredible in the first place and, were it credible, pathetically dull:

> Cinderella and the prince
> lived, they say, happily ever after,
> like two dolls in a museum case
> never bothered by diapers or dust,
> never arguing over the timing of an egg,
> never telling the same story twice,
> never getting a middle-aged spread,
> their darling smiles pasted on for eternity.
> Regular Bobbsey Twins.
> That story.

Half of Sexton's tales end in marriage, and most of these marriages are seen as some form of either selfishness or captivity. Regarding the value of beauty, we learn in "Snow White" that an innocent virgin's unconscious beauty makes her a stupid doll, a commodity, while an experienced woman's conscious beauty makes her not only cruel but doomed. "Beauty is a simple passion, / but, oh my friends, in the end / you will dance the fire dance in iron shoes." Moreover, since "a woman *is* her mother," at the wedding celebration during which the step-

mother gets tortured to death in those iron shoes, Snow White chill-
ingly begins "referring to her mirror / as women do." Describing the
sacred emotion of mother love, Sexton in "Rumpelstiltskin" remarks
with pure contempt:

> He was like most new babies,
> as ugly as an artichoke
> but the queen thought him a pearl.
> She gave him her dumb lactation,
> delicate, trembling, hidden,
> warm, etc.

While none of the protagonists in Sexton's versions is described
in terms of his or her virtue, which is Grimm's as it should be, pre-
Disney and amoral, "evil" characters and deviant behavior commonly
receive her sympathy. The witch in "Hansel and Gretel" is cannibalistic
and terrifying, as in the original, and her death is represented as poetic
justice. But the poem's prologue has been a fantasia on the theme of
a normally affectionate mother's desire to "eat up" her son, and the
epilogue provocatively suggests that in a world governed by eating or
being eaten, the witch in "the woe of the oven" has been a sacrifice
"like something religious." Does Sexton mean that the witch is a Christ
figure? Is this a reference to the subduing of the mother-goddess by a
civilized daughter allied with the patriarchy? (Louise Glück's "Gretel
in Darkness," by the way, raises similar questions.) In "Rapunzel"
Sexton sees the witch as a lesbian in love with her imprisoned girl, and
the poem stresses the emotional poignancy of the older woman's loss,
while perfunctorily dismissing the normality of the heterosexual lovers. "Rumpelstiltskin" and other stories follow a similar pattern, prod-
ding us toward identification with antagonist-loser instead of protag-
onist-winner.

By the same token a number of characters we have conventionally
accepted as good are made repellent. In "The Maiden without Hands"
the king who weds the mutilated girl is motivated by "A desire to own
the maiming / so that not one of us butchers / will come to him with
crowbars." So long as the queen is a cripple, the king will feel secure
in his own wholeness. (This, by the way, is one of the few occasions
when Sexton writes, albeit allegorically, about her own marriage. Asked
in an interview whether she was not afraid of hurting others by her
intimate revelations of family life, she explained that she wrote mainly

about the dead who could not be hurt and avoided saying painful
things about the living.) In "The Twelve Dancing Princesses," which
is transformed to an Eros versus Logos, or pleasure principle versus
superego parable, Logos unfortunately wins, in the person of the clever
young man who finds out where the irresponsible princesses do their
dancing. His mean-minded success brings an end to their enjoyable
nightlife. The shocking final poem, "Briar Rose (Sleeping Beauty),"
eliminates the heroine's mother and makes the father not merely the
possessive maintainer of his daughter's prepubescent purity—"He forced
every male in the court / to scour his tongue with Bab-o"—but its
incestuous exploiter. Sleep in this poem brings "a voyage" into regressive infantilism. Wakened after her hundred-years' sleep, Briar Rose
cries "Daddy! Daddy!" What she will see for the rest of her life when
she wakens from the nightmares that plague her is

> another kind of prison.
> It's not the prince at all,
> but my father
> drunkenly bent over my bed,
> circling the abyss like a shark,
> my father thick upon me
> like some sleeping jellyfish.

Here and everywhere Sexton's interpretations discover and release elements already implicit in the stories. Over and over one thinks "of
course." Were we to look at these poems as moral texts, we would
have to see in them a demand for some transvaluation of social values.

But the appeal of the tales is primarily neither moral nor immoral.
They are, as the central fact of magic in them partially indicates, rooted
in and addressed to something less rational in our natures than the
impulse toward social reform. Joseph Campbell makes the obvious
point that folktale, like dream and myth, derives ultimately from the
individual psyche, modified by the successions of cultures it travels
through, and that its images are not simply relics of religious or su-
perstitious periods in cultural history but projections of universal and
primitive human desires and fears. It is proper, therefore, that Sexton's
handling of these tales, while unconventionally personal and morally
skeptical, is nevertheless designed to maintain, not reduce, their psychic
impact. The poet does not rationalize or explain. She narrates, and
with great swiftness and skill. She is funny, which makes sense since

comedy is a major element in the traditional stories. She is intensely vivid. Her style excites, rather than soothes, the senses. Her imagery, to borrow a term from tabloids and horror movies, is sensational, full of food and feeding, sexuality, greed, and death—often fused, in a kind of synesthesia of appetites.

"Snow White," the first story in the volume, is sensationally and gratuitously oral. It tells us that the virgin is "unsoiled . . . white as a bonefish," and a few lines later that her stepmother has been "eaten, of course, by age." Where in Grimm the evil queen wants Snow White's heart merely as proof of her death, Sexton's stepmother expresses a cruder longing: "Bring me her heart . . . and I will salt it and eat it." Brought a boar's heart by the compassionate hunter, "the queen chewed it up like a cube steak."

Proceeding with the story, Sexton embroiders. Snow White on entering the strange cottage eats "seven chicken livers" before sleeping, and then we meet what I and most of my students regard as the best single metaphor in the book, "The dwarfs, those little hot dogs." Revived after her first coma, Sexton's heroine is "as full of life as soda pop." When she bites the poison apple, the dwarfs "washed her with wine / and rubbed her with butter," though to no avail. "She lay as still as a gold piece." The passive coin, recalling Plath's "I am your jewel, I am your valuable, / The pure gold baby," parallels food in its appeal to greed.

Other poems similarly ply us with images of the tactile, the expensive, the devourable. The girl in "Rumpelstiltskin" is "lovely as a grape." The dwarf commits suicide by tearing himself in two, "somewhat like a split broiler." Feeding and sexuality are cheerfully identified in the bawdy poem "The Little Peasant," tragically identified in "Rapunzel," where women in love "feed off each other." In "Red Riding Hood" and "Hansel and Gretel," Sexton again implies the interchangeability of feeding and being fed on, in dramas of death and rebirth.

Where the Grimm stories are violent, Sexton does not skimp on pain and gore but describes with inventive detail:

> First your toes will smoke
> and then your heels will turn black
> and you will fry upwards like a frog. . . .
>   ("Snow White")

When Cinderella's sister cuts a toe off to fit the shoe, we see

> the blood pouring forth.
> That is the way with amputations.
> They don't just heal up like a wish.

And both sisters at Cinderella's wedding have their eyes pecked out, leaving "Two hollow spots . . . like soup spoons." Well over half the tales include death or mutilation, and both in the individual poems and cumulatively, Sexton's images of killing and eating in *Transformations* seem not merely childish but infantile.

That, I think, is the point. The evocation of these desires and terrors reminds us of powers we can scarcely control even as adults, in our lives and world. We are reminded of the helpless Ur-self whose whole world is touch and taste, who fantasizes omnipotence, who dreads annihilation in a thousand ways. And it is this self, we understand when reading *Transformations*, that generates fairy tales.

III

Although Sexton did not again write in the manner of *Transformations*, the volume marks a turning point. She had learned how to interpret the impersonal by means of the personal, the symbol belonging to a culture by experience belonging to the self. She had exercised for the first time a gift of iconoclasm regarding social and moral conventions. She had acquired, as her later work shows, a taste for the quasi-mythic narrative. Her final finished books, *The Book of Folly* (1972), *The Death Notebooks* (1974), and *The Awful Rowing Toward God* (1974), return to a predominantly autobiographical mode. But they are bolder in language, formally more experimental, and readier to challenge convention than any of her earlier work. In them the poet increasingly sees herself not as merely a private person, certainly not as a psychoanalytic case study, but as the heroine in a spiritual quest. At the same time, the question of what it means to be feminine—not simply to the self but to the culture and within the religion created by that culture—deepens and darkens. In an early (1965) *Hudson Review* interview, Sexton says: "It's very hard to reveal yourself. . . . I'm hunting for the truth. . . . Behind everything that happens to you, every act, there is another truth, a secret life." What the late books reveal is that behind the "live or die" struggle in Sexton's life was another struggle, which led her first to a reenvisioning of Christian myth, then to a reimagining of God the Father. I am tempted to say that Sexton's final wrestling was between loving and loathing God, and that she lost it because she knew too much.

The Book of Folly makes us think about gender in a way that moves a step past the deflating techniques of Transformations. It includes a group of personal pieces that enable the poet to imagine the violent personalities of one-legged man, assassin, wife beater—all of them castrated figures for whom woman is enemy, all of them evidently animus figures for Sexton, as are "the ambition bird" in the finely sardonic and self-critical opening poem, and the destructive doppelgänger in "The Other." In "The Red Shoes," a spinoff from Transformations, ambition is secretly and shamefully handed down from mother to daughter, is uncontrollable, and destroys them. "Anna Who Was Mad" and "The Hex" are secular salvation and damnation poems struggling with the poet's guilty fear that her ongoing life is responsible for the madness and death of the beloved aunt whose namesake she is. In "Mother and Daughter" Sexton's tone is glad and proud as she relinquishes "my booty, my spoils, / my Mother & Co." and celebrates the daughter's growth to womanhood, but what womanhood means is:

> carrying keepsakes to the boys,
> carrying powders to the boys,
> carrying, my Linda, blood to
> the bloodletter.

There is a figure in the carpet here.[3] In all these poems self-sacrifice is the condition of self-acceptance, and to be feminine is to be either powerless or punished. The "Angels of the Love Affair" sonnet sequence, inspired by Rilke, challenges a set of elemental angels to know and exorcise what the poet knows of shame, defilement, paralysis, despair, and solitude. In the one poem where the poet remembers herself taking a pleasurable initiative (stealing grandfather's forbidden raspberries), the angel is a punitive lady "of blizzards and blackouts." The three prose narratives in The Book of Folly still more clearly identify passive feminine roles (daughter, wife, erotic object) with victimization and self-victimization. The one figure who seems to escape passivity, the protagonist's adventurous friend Ruth in "The Letting Down of the Hair," finally finds Christ—and kills herself. Sexton does not tell us why. But the series of seven short poems entitled "The Jesus Papers" may explain.

Before *The Book of Folly*, in occasional poems dealing with Christ, Sexton had evidently identified with him as sufferer and public performer. "When I was Christ, I felt like Christ," she said of "In the Deep Museum." "My arms hurt, I desperately wanted to pull them in off the Cross. When I was taken down off the Cross, and buried alive, I sought solutions; I hoped they were Christian solutions." "That ragged Christ, that sufferer, performed the greatest act of confession." In "The Exorcists," an early poem about abortion, the title implies ironically that an aborted fetus is being cast out like a demon, but the poem's text, with its "I know you not" refrain, implies that on the contrary it is a Christ whom the speaker is betraying. Many of Sexton's letters depict an intense need for faith undermined by solid skepticism: "In case it's true, I tell my Catholic friend . . . in case it's true, I tell myself, and plead with it to be true, after all. No matter what I write, I plead with it to be true!"[4] "God? spend half time wooing R. Catholics who will pray *for* you in case it's true. Spend other half knowing there is certainly no God. Spend fantasy time thinking that there is a life after death, because surely my parents, for instance, are not dead, they are, good god!, just buried" (*Letters*, 235). "Oh, I really believe in God—it's Christ that boggles the mind" (*Letters*, 346). "Yes, it is time to think about Christ again. I keep putting it off. If he is the God/man, I would feel a hell of a lot better. If there is a God . . . how do you explain him swallowing all those people up in Pakistan? Of course there's a God, but what kind is he?" (*Letters*, 368–69). Sexton also experienced visions, of varied duration and of great physical urgency, of Christ, Mary, God, the martyred saints, and the devil, in which "I feel that I can touch them almost . . . that they are part of me. . . . I believed that I was talking to Mary, that her lips were upon my lips," she said in an interview. None of this data, however, explains the radical vision of "The Jesus Papers," which is a systematic and structured—if miniature—reinterpretation of Christian myth, as *Transformations* is of Grimm. The subject is of course far more audacious; indeed, only two other poets in English have attempted it, Milton in *Paradise Regained* and Blake in *The Everlasting Gospel*. Was Jesus a man? Very well then, let the poet imagine what manner of man. Let her begin, since much Christian iconography dwells on his infancy, by imagining what manner of infant, and take it from there. Allowing for the vast difference in scale, Sexton's Jesus is as disagreeable as Milton's in *Paradise Regained*—and perhaps as unintentionally so.

The opening poem, "Jesus Suckles," consists of three sections of dwindling length. As so often in Sexton we are in the mind of someone utterly dependent on love. The language at first is erotic-playful, rich, organic, unstructured—one of Sexton's catalogs in which the condition of happiness is expressed through images of fertility. There is a tone of amplified gratification, rather like that of "In Celebration of My Uterus," and for the same reason. It is the mental effect of physical bliss:

> Mary, your great
> white apples make me glad.
>
> . . . .
>
> I'm a jelly-baby and you're my wife.
> You're a rock and I the fringy algae.
> You're a lily and I'm the bee that gets inside.
>
> . . . .
>
> I'm a kid in a rowboat and you're the sea,
> the salt, you're every fish of importance.

But then:

> No. No.
> All lies.
> I am small
> and you hold me.
> You give me milk
> and we are the same
> and I am glad.
>
> No. No.
> All lies.
> I am a truck. I run everything.
> I own you.

First metaphor is killed, then the love, joy, and sense of universal connection that generated the metaphor. We have a tidy drama of pleasure principle succumbing to reality principle, with both natural and supernatural implications. The poem reminds us that to a god, or a boy child, grateful love and helplessness are "all lies," and that reality—assuming the dualistic universe that Christianity does assume—means power, repugnance toward the flesh, and rejection of the mother. The relevant biblical text attributes this moment of brutality to Jesus' adolescence: "Woman, what have I to do with thee?" Sexton merely pushes the time back. Blake's "To Tirzah" is a comparably cruel poem on the same text. The initial imagery implies that Mary is Mother Nature, or the pre-Christian goddesses who represent her divine fertility. Man and God are her privileged superiors and historical conquerors. The modern technological outcome of the split between Flesh and Logos that Christianity sacralizes is modestly accommodated by the synecdoche "truck."[5]

The succeeding poems trace what follows from the initial willed division of Jesus from Mary, boy child from mother, the will to control from the willingness to fondle and nurture. While the rest of the human and animal kingdom frolics and propagates, Jesus fasts. "His penis no longer arched with sorrow over Him"—the rainbow image recalling God's forgiving covenant with Noah and mankind—but "was sewn onto Him like a medal," an outrageous metaphor that not only disparages Jesus' celibacy but calls into question that Christian replacement of sexual love by *caritas*. Though he still desires Mary when asleep, he subdues his need, uses his penis as a chisel à la Rodin, and produces a pietà so that they will be united in his death. *Civilization and Its Discontents* is the necessary gloss for this poem. For the next one de Sade's *Justine* might do. When Jesus encounters the harlot Mary Magdalen being stoned ("Stones came at her like bees to candy / and sweet redheaded harlot that she was / she screamed out, *I never, I never*"), he raises her up and efficiently heals her "terrible sickness" then and there by lancing with his thumbs her breasts, "those two boils of whoredom," until the milk runs out. Sexton's deadpan combination of biblical and contemporary language here is typical:

> The harlot followed Jesus around like a puppy
> for He had raised her up.
> Now she forsook her fornications
> and became His pet.

In "Jesus Cooks" and "Jesus Summons Forth," we get the miracle of the loaves and fishes as a sleight-of-hand act and the raising of Lazarus by assembling his bones as if he were a model airplane kit. "Tenderness" appears in a single line and appears to be part of the instructions. As with the poems on Jesus' sexuality, the poet's wry self-projection is important here. The roles of food provider and healer were Sexton's, as was the role of public performer for whom feeling was part of the act. In the bitterly comic "Jesus Dies," the crucifixion is like an ultimate Sexton poetry reading, where Jesus' self-revelation of his sore need for God—a "man-to-man thing" that is half-competitive, half-desperate—is mingled with furious irritation at his audience's sensation seeking.

From crucifixion Sexton does not move on to resurrection but drops back to another woman poem, "Jesus Unborn," which turns out to be, like "Jesus Suckles," a judgment of the Virgin's role in Christianity. It is the moment before the Annunciation, and again the imagery is lushly natural. Mary sits among olive trees, feels lethargic as an animal, wants to settle down like a camel or doze like a dog:

> Instead a strange being leans over her
> and lifts her chin firmly
> and gazes at her with executioner's eyes.

So much for how many centuries of Mariolatry? How many centuries of sacred iconography? But in case Sexton has not made herself clear, she appends to "The Jesus Papers" a final poem entitled "The Author of the Jesus Papers Speaks," which defines the place not only of Mary but of all womankind in Western religion. It is a dream poem in three tiny episodes. First, Sexton milks a great cow, but instead of "the moon juice . . . the white mother," blood spurts "and covered me with shame." Several related readings are possible here: blood may be menstrual blood, shameful because taboo, sign of female pollutedness; or blood as sign that mothers surrender their own lives for others' lives, like beasts; or a reminder that all life leads to death. The cow might be Nature, or Mother-goddess, or Sexton's own mother, who shamed and blamed her and whose "double image" she was. We have the beginnings of a rich female drama, but there is no development, for at this point God speaks to Sexton and says, "People say only good things about Christmas. / If they want to say something bad, / they whisper."

This is a change in tone as well as a non sequitur; it is funny, and it gives us a God who, like a boss or an earthly father, is half-uncomfortable with the way his governing role divides him from those he governs. God seems to be interrupting a mother-daughter interview, making a bid for attention—and sympathy—for his own concerns. But why should anyone say bad things about Christmas? Is God paranoid? Or guilty? Or, if this dream is taking place in the twentieth century, might we say that he doesn't know the half of it? In any case, Sexton's response is to go to the well and draw a baby out, which in her own drama means she moves from daughter role to mother role, and in God's terms means she produces the Christ. Judging by the poem's final seven lines, this is the submissive gesture God was looking for.

> Then God spoke to me and said:
> Here. Take this gingerbread lady
> and put her in your oven.
> When the cow gives blood
> and the Christ is born
> we must all eat sacrifices.
> We must all eat beautiful women.

Now the changed tone tells us that God has been, as it were, reassured and confirmed in his godliness by Sexton's feminine compliance, much as a man tired and complaining after work will have his dignity renewed by a wife or daughter laying out a perfect dinner. This final speech is authoritative not only in the sense of issuing commands but in the sense of assuming verbal command over the poem's prior structure of symbols. Nature and femaleness (cow, moon, milk, blood), at first large and powerful, are reduced to domesticity and powerlessness. Dream-cow becomes cookie. "We" must at the advent of Christianity not *make* sacrifices but eat them, and God's pseudo-cozy "we" is the velvet glove of paternal imperative. The substitution of gingerbread lady for the bread that is Christ's body reminds us that the Christ cult (and the Passover feast it builds on) takes its symbolism from earlier Middle Eastern religions in which the object of primary worship was the fertile and nourishing mother. Perhaps it implies that the misogyny of the Church and its need to subordinate ("sacrifice") women derive ultimately from a forgotten time of usurpation and a dread lest the "cow" move again to the forefront of our dream.

As a comment on "The Jesus Papers" sequence, the epilogue is a recapitulation of the theme of divine male power and mortal female submission. But it also fixes the position of its author as one who is by no means protesting the images of herself and other women within Christianity. On the contrary, she complies, she obeys, in this final dream, just as Mary and the harlot comply within the sequence. For herself, and on behalf of all beautiful women, she accepts humiliation. We may even say, since after all the dream is her invention, that she requires it.

IV

I need some such explanation to understand Sexton's religious poetry in *The Death Notebooks* and *The Awful Rowing Toward God*. For in these books, like a defeated athlete, she hurls herself again and again into a contest that her own poetry should have showed her she could not win, trying to imagine—trying to experience—a God she could both believe in and be loved by. The decisive intelligence that dismantles religious myth is no match for the child-woman's ferocious need for cosmic love, and so what we see in the last two books is a poet attempting to give imaginative birth to an adequate godhead. But since her need is no match for her doubt, what we see is heroic failure. Or rather, perhaps, her need is no match for her sense of the significance of divine power, which is the power of the parent writ very large.

The Death Notebooks begins with a seriocomic quest poem, one of Sexton's funniest and best. It also contains "The Furies" series; the cycle of "Psalms" written in the manner of Christopher Smart, who becomes her imaginary twin and ally; and two semisurreal figures for the omnipresent Thanatos and the frustrated Eros of the poet's soul: the icy "death baby" and the despairing yet smart-aleck "Ms. Dog." *The Awful Rowing* is a series of quest poems written at breakneck speed "in a frenzy of despair and hope" shortly after her divorce in November 1973, and scarcely revised. "I cannot walk an inch / without trying to walk to God. / I cannot move a finger / without trying to reach God" is the burden of these poems. Both books are attempts to locate the self in a context of the objectively sacred, but with Sexton implicitly insisting that the realm of the sacred must answer to her private experience of reality, that the objective and subjective must be one, as she was able to make them one in *Transformations*. She is once again working through a prior tradition (God is no post-Tillich moral abstraction but an omnipotent male person), but now as if her life depended on it. Poems like "The Civil War" and "Frenzy" imply, in fact, that only by an unremitting effort to create a God coextensive with her own imagination can the poet hope to be saved. This is strenuously antinomian religion, an American specialty, and a risky business in any case, riskier when the worshiper's ego is as frail as Sexton's.

"Let there be a God as large as a sunlamp to laugh his heat at you," begins the "First Psalm" of "O Ye Tongues." She prays in the course of the psalms that "God will digest me" and at the end declares "for God was as large as a sunlamp and laughed his heat at us [i.e., Anne and Christopher] and therefore we did not cringe at the death hole." Sexton wants to imagine God as simultaneously transcendent and immanent within all flesh. He is a jigsaw with thousands of pieces, "dressed up" like a whore, an old man, a naked child, present within all domestic routines and especially present within human sexuality:

> When they fuck they are God.
> When they break away they are God.
> When they snore they are God.
> In the morning they butter the toast.
> They don't say much.
> They are still God.
>   ("The Fury of Cocks")

Such a God is necessarily benevolent. The sustaining of even a small faith will bring him into one's hands the way a dime used to bring forth a Coke. He has no body but wishes he had one, envying humans their bodies as we envy him his soul. If Sexton can reach him he will remove and embrace the "gnawing pestilential rat," which represents her sense of inner vileness. On good days he gives milk (cf. the cow in "The Jesus Papers" and Isaiah 66:12) and she has the pail. Salvation depends on her ability to keep "typing out the God / my typewriter believes in. / Very quick. Very intense, / like a wolf at a live heart. / Not lazy" ("Frenzy").

Sexton is full of startlingly "right" modern analogues for traditional images in Christian writing. Her lifelong rowing against the wind is the emotional equivalent of the journey in *Pilgrim's Progress.* Her "sunlamp" God emits an eerie charge that the word *sun* no longer has in our language. Her infinitely multiple jigsaw or typewriter God is oddly like Milton's figure in *Areopagitica* of the scattered body of Truth, whose form all true men must be engaged in gathering up limb by limb throughout human history, until the Second Coming "shall bring together every joint and member." Almost every poem has something like this.

What defeats Sexton is in part a sense of her own evil, the "rat" or "bowel movement" her mother tried to force out of her child-self but that still fills her to the fingertips. Hers is not a conventional sin divisible from her bodily being, and priests are unable to shrive or even comprehend it. In the long sequence of faith-doubt poems beginning with "The Dead Heart" and ending with "Is It True?" a mocking self-disgust is inextricably mingled with God's unbearable departure. The tone strongly resembles that of Hopkins in the Terrible Sonnets, and Sexton's habitual oral imagery touches close on Hopkins's "I am gall. I am heartburn. God's most deep decree / Bitter would have me taste; my taste was me." There are hints that the problem is insoluble because Sexton cannot or will not deny her identification with the flesh that divides her from God:

> We are all earthworms
> digging into our wrinkles.
> We live beneath the ground
> and if Christ should come in the form of a plow
> and dig a furrow and push us up into the day
> we earthworms would be blinded by the sudden light
> and writhe in our distress.
> As I write this sentence I too writhe.
>
> ("The Wall," *The Awful Rowing*)

Logically, theologically, it is inconsistent to imagine a God immanent in all bodies and a body unable to tolerate God's blinding presence. But immanence in Western religion is a heresy, and for the image of God as blinding glory there are precedents going back at least to Dante, while Christ with his plow is one of the most forceful images of Revelation. What I earlier called an "adequate" godhead—one powerful enough to love and accept Sexton and all of us ratlike "cursed ones falling out after"—must also be powerful enough to reject and annihilate. It is such a God, closer to Scripture than Sexton's hopeful fantasies desire, who dominates *The Awful Rowing*. Through most of the volume the tone is frenzied and agonized. God is distant, indifferent. Near the close God is "surgical andiron." In the penultimate poem, when the poet trembles to utter her faith that God is in all matter, "heaven smashes my words."

The final poem of *The Awful Rowing* was, I think, intended to be a happy ending. When the poet finally arrives at her island, God challenges her to a game of poker. She thinks she wins because she holds a royal straight flush. God wins because he holds five aces. Here is the end of the poem and the book:

> As He plunks down His five aces
> and I sit grinning at my royal flush,
> He starts to laugh,
> the laughter rolling like a hoop out of His mouth
> and into mine,
> and such laughter that He doubles right over me
> laughing a Rejoice-Chorus at our two triumphs.
> Then I laugh, the fishy dock laughs
> the sea laughs. The Island laughs.
> The Absurd laughs.
>
> Dearest dealer,
> I with my royal straight flush,
> love you so for your wild card,
> that untamable, eternal gut-driven *ha-ha*
> and lucky love.
>
>   ("The Rowing Endeth")

To my ear there is something appalling in such an ending. Is the "lucky love" of that dreadfully lame last line supposed to be the wild card with which God triumphs? What I hear sounds like a grotesque attempt to placate and conciliate a God of our Fathers who is being experienced as atrocious, brutal, a betrayer.

"Out of His mouth / and into mine . . . He doubles right over me." Is God conceivably a rapist? This power figure, who also inhabits the last poem of "The Jesus Papers" and the last poem of *The Death Notebooks*—is he also the father-lover of the last poem in *Transformations?* John Donne, too, wanted to be raped by God; yet "Batter My Heart" and "The Rowing Endeth," comparable in their yearning for divine union expressed in this shared metaphor, are utterly different in emotional resonance. Reading Donne, I am able to believe the paradox of Christian surrender: "for I / except you enthrall me, never shall be free, / Nor ever chaste except you ravish me." Perhaps the reason there are so many excellent devotional writers who are men, so few who are women, is that the feminine experience of submission is for a man a rounding out of his usual personality, hence truly a fulfillment and kind of freedom. "Absolute sovereignty is what I love to ascribe to God," Jonathan Edwards announces, and he convinces us that this is "not only a conviction, but a delightful conviction." For a woman it merely reinforces her usual social role.

On October 14, 1974, after reading galleys of *The Awful Rowing*, Sexton killed herself. In the same year, Mary Daly published *Beyond*

God the Father, an attack on patriarchal religion. Among feminist theologians and historians of ideas, it has subsequently become a commonplace assumption that the passive-female imagery of Western religion is inadequate for women's spiritual needs, and a countercultural women's search for goddess figures has become something of a cultural brushfire in England and France as well as America. Sexton has no part in that search. She is not a protest poet. Her religion is determinedly patriarchal. Her God is not self but other.

There is a precedent for Sexton's painful ambivalence in this matter of God the Father. Emily Dickinson, a poet aesthetically poles removed from Sexton, seems also to have modeled her God on the image of a father. One of her roles with him is that of coy little girl, a pose that makes modern audiences twitch. But girlishness was an approved tone in Dickinson's own time, especially for unmarried women, as we know by its ubiquitous titter in many of her letters. (There is a similar aggravated girlishness in Plath's letters to her mother.) Behind anything so ostentatiously agreeable, we feel, something disagreeable must lurk. Dickinson's portrait of God, when she does not draw him flatteringly as nice daddy, is, like Sexton's, the portrait of an indifferent brute ("Of course I cried! And did God care?"), a bully, an "Inquisitor" who may or may not grant one "the liberty to die," a foe whom one must love because defiance is impossible. "Burglar! Banker—Father!" is only the most famous of her tense portrayals. And like Sexton, Dickinson seems genuinely to have adored and needed this divine antagonist. Ancestress of rebels, she is none herself. At times it is difficult to distinguish Lord from Lover in both poets. Sexton's "rowing" figure itself has an antecedent, coincidentally or not, in Dickinson's most erotic poem, addressed to an unknown love:

> Wild Nights—Wild Nights!
> Were I with thee
> Wild nights should be
> Our luxury!
>
> Futile—the winds—
> to a Heart in port—
> Done with the Compass—
> Done with the Chart!
>
> Rowing in Eden—
> Ah, the Sea!

> Might I but moor—Tonight—
> In Thee!

The range, the demands, and the risks of Sexton's poetry increased throughout her lifetime. If she failed to achieve "a Heart in port," she was not alone in that.

NOTES

1. Rosemary Johnson, "The Woman of Private (but Published) Hungers," *Parnassus* (Fall/Winter 1979): 92.

2. The early volumes, all published by Houghton Mifflin Co., Boston, are *To Bedlam and Part Way Back* (1960), in which the apologia poem "For John, Who Begs Me Not to Enquire Further" appears; *All My Pretty Ones* (1962), *Live or Die* (1966), for which she received the Pulitzer Prize, and *Love Poems* (1969). Sexton's *Complete Poems*, with an excellent introduction by Maxine Kumin, was published by Houghton Mifflin Co. in 1981. The interviews I quote are in J. D. McClatchy, ed., *Anne Sexton: The Artist and Her Critics* (Bloomington: Indiana University Press, 1978).

3. I mention this, I must confess, in specific irritation with W. H. Pritchard's authoritative pronouncement that "there is no figure in the poetry's carpet to worry about discovering—it's all smack on the surface," and that the late Sexton jettisoned "whatever modest technical accomplishment she possessed in favor of getting down the excitingly grotesque meanings" ("The Anne Sexton Show," *Hudson Review* 31 [Summer 1978]: 389, 391). He does not specify *what* meanings. But we do not see what we do not look for.

4. *Anne Sexton: A Self-Portrait in Letters*, ed. Linda Gray Sexton and Lois Ames (Boston: Houghton Mifflin Co., 1977), 125. Subsequent page references to the *Letters* appear in the text.

5. This image appears also in "Those Times . . ." of *Live or Die*, where Sexton writes of childhood humiliations inflicted by her mother and says, "I did not know that my life, in the end, / would run over my mother's like a truck." The distance between earlier and later poems makes a good index of Sexton's development. The earlier poem is private and familial; the later one locates the private scenario within a mythic context. The earlier poem is strictly autobiographical and describes the self as passive; in the later "Jesus" becomes, among other things, a figure for active and aggressive (i.e., "male") elements in her character that she was reluctant to acknowledge while writing as a woman.

JEANNE KAMMER NEFF

The Witch's Life: Confession and Control in the Early Poetry of Anne Sexton

With her death in 1974, Anne Sexton confirmed for many readers her place among the group of confessional, suicidal poets (Berryman, Plath, and Lowell, for example) who inhabit and invest with their prophetic presence the troubled decades of the middle century. Approaches to her poetry are often correspondingly handicapped by the voyeuristic interest that followed her last volumes toward their inevitable outcome. There is more interest in the substance of her writing, it seems, than in its craft—and the limbo area where art touches life appears more ill-defined than ever. To see more clearly what she became as a poet, it is helpful to return to the place where she began—to the first collections, whose strongest poetry has settled securely into the American tradition and by which she was first known to the current generation of students and scholars.

The most striking aspect of her first book, *To Bedlam and Part Way Back*, is the regularity of form that characterizes most of the poems in it. In a sequence marked by recurrent themes of grief and loss, explicit in its depiction of physical and emotional distress, the horror of the institutional experience, Sexton's use of reiterated stanza patterns and complex rhyme schemes comes as a surprise to the reader expecting a "free" confessional narrative. Some of this may indeed be therapeutic; "the ingenuity of shape," says Richard Howard, "has something of the basket-weaver's patience about it, it is the work of a *patient*."[1] But it is also true that, like her literary predecessors and with her strongest contemporaries, Sexton perceived the general dilemma of the woman artist as characterized by the culture ("A woman who writes feels too much . . ."), along with her personal vulnerability as a poet inclined to the confessional mode. She responded to both conditions, in the early years of apprenticeship and reputation building,

Reprinted from *Language and Style* 13 (Fall 1980): 29–35.

by imposing upon the stuff of her experience the boundary and counterpoint of intense poetic control.

"You, Doctor Martin," the opening poem of the collection and
one of the strongest, is a good example of her technique and can stand
critical scrutiny. The voice of the "queen of this summer hotel" is full
of the gleeful, murderous, placating tones of the inmate/patient, held
in check by an orderly visual pattern. Sexton's habit is to allow an
initial stanza to take its own shape, then to repeat that form in the
ones that follow. Here, the visual enclosure is tidy and symmetrical:

> You, Doctor Martin, walk
>   from breakfast to madness. Late August,
> I speed through the antiseptic tunnel
>   where the moving dead still talk
>   of pushing their bones against the thrust
> of cure. And I am queen of this summer hotel
>   or the laughing bee on a stalk
>
>   of death. . . .

The apparent symmetry of the stanza is opposed, however, by the run-
on lines and the failure of the whole to be, in the end, self-contained.
The form is both an ironic extension and a contradiction of the content:
it swings, like Doctor Martin and his patients, "from breakfast to
madness," a ritual pacing, a pushing of the "bones against the thrust
of cure." At the same time, there is a denial of motion; the "moving
dead" only *talk* of resistance, and the final pun on "stalk" (contrasting
with Dr. Martin's free "walk" in the first line) conveys the speaker's
double sense of herself as aggressor and victim, "queen" and prisoner.

"Walk"/"talk"/"stalk"—rhyme is an important element in Sexton's early poetry, because it is a game played against visual uniformity
even as the appearance of regularity is maintained: the patient's riddle
and the witch's web. While the shape of the stanzas may remain consistent throughout a poem as an element of visual control, the rhyme
scheme shifts, doubles back, deceives the eye. In the later stanzas of
"You, Doctor Martin," for example, the dominant "walk"/"talk" of
the first is moved to a secondary position, then buried in syntax and
masked by spelling variations and half-rhyme. It persists, nevertheless,
as a reminder of the poem's main axis: the attempt of the individual
to move, to speak, and to escape, opposed by the immobility, silence,
inexorable sameness, and containment of the institutional group.

By the end of the poem the same rhyme is acting (like Denise Levertov's "horizon note") as a constant in the background that centers theme and tone. "Doctor," after all, has sounded the initial note, which becomes "god of our block" in stanza 4, to be echoed again in "foxes"/ "boxes" and the "foxy children." Near the end of the poem, the "block"/"smock" sound softens to "frost"/"lost," but we find "talking," "forgotten," and "moccasins" reflecting and repeating earlier terms. It is a painful sound, repeated over and over, sometimes sharp and sometimes muffled, cut off even as it begins—an appropriate vehicle for the speech and the feeling of Bedlam.

Other patterns of internal rhyme support the poem's core of control and feeling: the sequence, for example, of "moving"/"pushing"/"laughing"/"cutting"/"breaking"/"talking" emphasizes the contradictory doubleness of the human-but-confined; the repetition of "moving"/"move"/"moves" is poignantly linked to "love" in the fourth stanza; there is a humorously punning opposition of "I" and "eye" (patient to doctor) stretched to a painful edge in the echoes of "lines"/ "smiles"/"whine"/"knives"/"lives"/"sky"/"lights"/"cry"/"*life*"; the casual "breakfast"/"thrust" of the first stanza reappears sarcastically, desperately in the last ones as "most"/"best"/"nest"/"twist"/"frost"/ "*lost*." The total effect, says Richard Howard, is of rhyme slightly off-balance, "roughed-up, abandoned when inconvenient, psychologically convincing."[2]

Howard's last phrase is important to an understanding of Sexton's poetic choices, where matters of form and style are involved. Control, for Sexton, is not simply an antidote to autobiography but also a vehicle for communicating the individual experience. It is a means of making strong poems—sturdy baskets—while telling the truth. Nearly all the pieces in this first collection exhibit a similar use of set, visually repetitive stanza forms with varying sorts of contrapuntal, expressive sound activity. They range from the self-generated shape and patterns of "You, Doctor Martin" to a thick, sixteen-line unit with heavy end rhyme in "Some Foreign Letters" to the childlike litany of "Ringing the Bells." "Elizabeth Gone" is composed of two sonnets, and "Her Kind" employs a rhythmic, incantatory stanza and refrain. The poet's technical concern, in all of these, deflects the imagination from the pain of direct confrontation and denies the temptation to self-pity, even as the experience is relived and named. In her later work, even as she moves beyond the visual security of the reiterated stanza form and loosens her grip on meter and syntax, Sexton preserves this early discipline of internal control.

The *Bedlam* poems, after all, do not simply represent the therapy of intricate weaving, the "counting of moccasins," although that element is certainly present. Rather, the riddle—the game of order in disorder, structure in chaos—is an important aspect of their peculiar stance: dramatically unstable but determined to have an authority that form and style alone do not create. One source of that authority is found in another aspect of control in Sexton's work, a feature more difficult to dismiss as therapeutic in origin or mechanical in nature. By the time of her second volume, *All My Pretty Ones*, her instinctive sense of the striking opening phrase is matched by her knack for a closure that is powerful and precise. In both cases the principles of understatement and economy are uppermost and rooted in the placement of sharp images within tight, often minimal sentences.

Here is the first stanza of "The Operation":

> After the sweet promise,
> the summer's mild retreat
> from mother's cancer, the winter months of her death,
> I come to this white office, its sterile sheet,
> its hard tablet, its stirrups, to hold my breath
> while I, who must, allow the glove its oily rape,
> to hear the almost mighty doctor over me equate
> my ills with hers
> and decide to operate.

"Recall if you can," says Peter Davison, "the opening of any recent poem to match that for economy, fullness, and power in setting a scene."[3] We may notice once again the strong presence of rhyme; the most painful or shocking words are saved for the ends of lines and joined firmly, faced up to. At the same time, they comment ironically on one another: "Sweet . . . sheet," "rape . . . equate . . . operate." The play of the long line against the short, the enclosure of present details within a hazier past and future, intensify the emotional stress. From the deceptively "sweet promise, / the summer's mild retreat," we come quickly to a catalog of horrors: "this white office, its sterile sheet, / its hard tablet, its stirrups. . . ." "To hold my breath," in the center, is a temporary death, imaging the mother's even as it is an ironic acting out, in a hostile setting, of the "little death" of sexual fulfillment ("the glove's oily rape"). "My ills," in line 8, is more than a literal, physical

term—encompassing as it does a span of seasons, generations of fear
and grief. The effect of the stanza's shape and movement is to focus
all our attention on the last word: "operate" is both abstraction and
image, familiar and ominous, flat and charged with emotion. The patient is exposed in her vulnerability even as the artist remains supreme
in her control.

Other poems demonstrate the same capacity in Sexton to sum-
mon to opening lines the emotional core of an experience while economically setting forth its key images and issues. In "The Truth the
Dead Know," she provides a headnote with the dates of her parents,
who died within months of each other, then begins with these blunt
lines:

> Gone, I say and walk from church,
> refusing the stiff procession to the grave,
> letting the dead ride alone in the hearse,
> It is June. I am tired of being brave.

"Letter Written on a Ferry while Crossing Long Island Sound"
opens with the sarcastic, understated strength of this declaration:

> I am surprised to see
> that the ocean is still going on.

"The Starry Night" in swift strokes recalls to mind the painting
that occasions the poem and at the same time recasts it in the speaker's
private images and emotional landscape:

> The town does not exist
> except where one black-haired tree slips
> up like a drowned woman into the hot sky.

Sexton's impulse to crisp, direct statement is a way of not appearing overemotional, where the subject is highly personal and intensely felt. It is also a tactic that invites the reader's recognition and
curiosity and demands a close attention. So, too, in her endings. The
effectiveness of poetic closure is often a means of distinguishing between the gifted and the merely competent writers, the interesting
poetry and the great. In the *Bedlam* volume the endings of Sexton's
poems are for the most part unmemorable, except for the few that set
up a complex resonance and mark the best pieces:

> A woman like that is not ashamed to die.
> I have been her kind.
>
> ("Her Kind")
>
> Go child, who is my sin and nothing more.
> ("Unknown Girl in the Maternity Ward")
>
> Allah will not see
> how I hold my daddy
> like an old stone tree.
>
> ("The Moss of His Skin")

By the time of *All My Pretty Ones,* however, she is hitting the mark more consistently; many poems end with phrases that strike us as singularly appropriate, collecting the poem's force in few well-placed final words. There is humor in "Woman with Girdle":

> straightway from God you have come
> into your redeeming skin.

tenderness in "I Remember":

> and what
> I remember best is that
> the door to your room was
> the door to mine.

Death and pain are met with characteristic understatement and irony:

> The supper dishes are over and the sun
> unaccustomed to anything else
> goes all the way down.
>
> ("Lament")
>
> and run along, Anne, and run along now,
> my stomach laced up like a football
> for the game.
>
> ("The Operation")

Rhyme remains a strong element in Sexton's closure, even if camouflaged or postponed; the last phrases are kept deliberately minimal, isolated carefully—apparently artless but powerful in their simplicity. Again, the structure of lines and sentences causes us to focus on the final image each time, which provides the testimony of the senses for what has been said.

It should be apparent by now that the structural means by which Sexton maintains a firm command over material that is nakedly personal are consistently supported, in these volumes, by a texture of language often as lean and cryptic as that of an Emily Dickinson. Yet James Dickey, in reviewing the *Bedlam* poems, comments that "they lack concentration, and above all the profound, individual linguistic suggestibility and accuracy that poems must have to be good."[4] And Barbara Howes, from the opposite corner, complains that Sexton "has a habit, which may be mere carelessness, of using verbs ungrammatically or of wrenching them away from their usual meaning, and sometimes she twists words cruelly. . . ."[5] Some of this critical scoring may be explained in its context; Sexton suffered in the early 1960s from competition (almost book for book) with Denise Levertov, a more widely recognized and experienced poet, and with such "delicate" poets as Katherine Hoskins, noted for her coolness and restraint.[6]

Nevertheless, carelessness and lack of concentration are hardly terms that can apply to Sexton in these volumes, particularly where language is concerned. She employs a diction that is characteristically simple, strong, and colloquial, in what Richard Howard accurately terms a "lucid obstruction to sentimentality."[7] A good example is found in "The Operation":

> There was snow everywhere.
> Each day I grueled through
> its sloppy peak, its blue-struck days, my boots
> slapping into hospital halls, past the retinue
> of nurses at the desk, to murmur in cahoots
> with hers outside her door, to enter with the outside
> air stuck on my skin, to enter smelling her pride,
> her upkeep, and to lie
> as all who love have lied.

The "ungrammatical" use of "grueled," the coinage of "blue-struck," the unusual sense of "upkeep" are all part of the effort to portray accurately the distorted hospital world, to preserve the delicate balance of feeling and saying required of patients, staff, and visitors.

Language in general for Sexton appears bound up with the act of *seeing*, of accurate observation and naming—truth sought out and confronted, reflected in the solidity of the printed word, the appropriate image. "Perception," says the poet Marvin Bell in a recent essay on the art, "has two meanings: sight and insight. I believe that both sight and insight derive from fierce consciousness, whether it begins in looking at a small object or in paying attention to all of the implications and resonances of an idea or image."[8] For Sexton a "fierce consciousness" of the real world as well as of the individual word was inextricably linked with self-consciousness as we find it in her literary ancestors: Dickinson, H. D., Marianne Moore.

"*See* how she sits on her knees all day," she says in "Housewife"; "Let us consider the *view*," in "From the Garden"; "*see* them rise on black wings" in "Letter Written on a Ferry. . . ." And the loon (crazy, ridiculous among birds) landing awkwardly in "Water" goes under "calling, / I have *seen*, I have *seen*." (Italics mine.) The contemporary need, of which Bell speaks, to *get closer to* rather than to accumulate more of poetic detail[9] is strong in Sexton and in the peculiar sort of confessional tradition associated with poets like Dickinson: the self revealed in the craft of the poem even more than in its content. It is also an effort to escape both self and outer world by getting *through* the image in the word—the same attempt described in Gerard Manley Hopkins's process of "inscape" and celebrated by Denise Levertov in the poetry of H. D.—to a still place of clarity and peace.

In these early books, however, the habit of seeing and of finding the precise words to articulate insight is primarily another means of control in a world that otherwise appears subjective, inchoate. In her later books sight intensifies to vision and is coupled with an increasingly oracular persona and images that take on archetypal mythic dimensions. With *Live or Die*, unity of volume becomes the most apparent controlling factor in Sexton's poetry; the individual poem begins to be subsumed in the larger movement of which it is a part. And with *Transformations*, Suzanne Juhasz argues, Sexton is able to abandon her tight control of meter, rhyme, and syntax because she is in command of the poem at a different level.[10]

Without denying the effect of these developments in Sexton's poetry (longer, more prosaic poems and the use of poem sequences, for example), we may still pay attention to the means of its technical success—and find that the early discipline hangs on in the continuing love of the challenge of set forms (the sonnet sequence "Angels of the Love Affair," in *The Book of Folly*); the subtle internal control of rhyme ("Doctors," in *The Awful Rowing Toward God*, may be profitably compared with "You, Doctor Martin"); and the urgent effort to approach and enter the image/word that, at its best, allows us to see as she sees.

The outspoken, confessional poet of "The Abortion," "Menstruation at Forty," and "The Fury of Cocks" remains throughout her
career a determined and beguiling shaper of words in the best tradition
of the art. To see that her work, in Philip Legler's words, is in fact
"crazily sane and beautifully controlled,"[11] is to understand that the
witch's life has more solidity to it than fetishes and spells, and that
the exploration of the self does not preclude the mastery of speech. It
is an important lesson for those who read and teach Anne Sexton's
poetry; it is even more important for those others who would practice
that black art.

NOTES

1. Richard Howard, "Some Tribal Female Who Is Known but Forbidden,"
in *Alone with America: Essays on the Art of Poetry in the U.S. since 1950*
(New York: Atheneum, 1969), 444.

2. Ibid., 445.

3. "The New Poetry," *Atlantic,* Nov. 1962, 88.

4. "Five First Books," *Poetry* 97, no. 5 (Feb. 1961): 319.

5. Review of *Bedlam* poetry, *New York Herald Tribune* Lively Arts section,
Dec. 11, 1960, 37.

6. See, for example, Louis Simpson, "The New Books," *Harper's,* Aug.
1967, 91.

7. Howard, "Some Tribal Female," 447.

8. Marvin Bell, "Homage to the Runner," *American Poetry Review* 7, no.
1 (Jan.-Feb. 1978): 38.

9. Ibid.

10. Suzanne Juhasz, *Naked and Fiery Forms: Modern American Poetry by
Women, a New Tradition* (New York: Harper and Row, 1976), 127.

11. Philip Legler, "O Yellow Eye," *Poetry* 110, no. 2 (May 1967): 127.

STEVEN E. COLBURN

The Troubled Life of the Artist

A story, a story!
(Let it go. Let it come.)
—Anne Sexton, "Rowing"

Anne Sexton's poetry, like the creative productions of many other artists, is the public record of the activities of a skillful and dedicated storyteller. The reader reflecting upon the distinctive artistic qualities of Sexton's work soon comes to realize the degree to which the thoroughgoing *dramatization* of human experience in her poetry is responsible for the highly charged emotional reaction it is capable of eliciting.

Sexton's presentation of material in her poetic narratives is always a carefully controlled, highly self-conscious activity that takes into account the presence of her audience. One need only think of a poem such as "The Gold Key," whose prologue captures the storyteller in the very act of beginning a story, or "Rowing," where the poet frames her tale with the traditional narrative formulas of the West African folktale, thus reminding her reader of the time-honored nature of her enterprise. Her awareness of what a story is and, consequently, what it means to be a storyteller are two of the most important elements of Sexton's mythopoeic activity and take us to the heart of the poet's relation to her audience.

Among the most frequently recurring subjects in Sexton's poetry is the artist herself. That she should have, as a basic ontological concern, a desire to explore her own creativity is understandable, since the individual artist's conception of his or her own creative powers— their source, mode of operation, purpose, and goal—is one of the most potent forces that shape artistic production, whether it be the ritual mask of a Dogon woodcarver, the painting of a Soviet realist, or the poem of a contemporary American poet.

Although the poems in which Sexton focuses on the artist appear throughout her career, we can only consider a few of the best and most representative examples here. In these poems about the life of the artist, the central character makes her way through a babble of competing discourses, variously identified as the voices of religious orthodoxy, literary tradition, media exploitation, and depth psychology.[1] Her stories are both a response to and an appropriation of these competing voices of cultural authority, challenging the assumptions, methods, and intellectual structures upon which they are based and employing their characteristic means and forms of elaboration to undermine the structures from within. In the four poems discussed below—"With Mercy for the Greedy" (*All My Pretty Ones*), "For John, Who Begs Me Not to Enquire Further" (*To Bedlam and Part Way Back*), "Making a Living" (*The Death Notebooks*), and "Said the Poet to the Analyst" (*To Bedlam and Part Way Back*)—we see some of the challenges faced by the creative artist as she struggles against forces that impinge upon her activity. We also observe some of the ways in which Sexton the storyteller transforms the perceptions and actions of her fictional characters into a shared form of communication. Her focus on the experience of the artist and her portrayal of the artist through fictional means go beyond autobiographical "confession" and enter the realm of cultural myth.

"With Mercy for the Greedy"

"With Mercy for the Greedy"[2] is one of Sexton's best-known poems. Although it displays Sexton's early poetic style at its best, "With Mercy" is generally anthologized not so much for its technical mastery as for its content, for of all her poems it refers most explicitly to the relation between poetry and confession. The statements made by Sexton's persona in the poem are often repeated as evidence of the author's own opinion on the matter by commentators who, in seeking confirmation for the critical theory of confessionalism and the historical notion of a "confessional school," deny the fictional nature of Sexton's work. "With Mercy," nevertheless, is not a polemical essay—however much one might want it to be—but an imaginative work of art in dramatic form. As Kay Capo points out, the poem has a dramatic occasion as well as a persuasive message, and a proper understanding of its meaning must take into account both of these elements.[3]

In "With Mercy" the poet's struggle to answer the challenge of religious orthodoxy is expressed in dramatized form. The speaker's response to the requests of a pious friend, who urges her to submit to the authority of church doctrine, stimulates the artist to clarify for herself the nature, purpose, and goal of her creative enterprise—and, in the process, to find an effective way of communicating this understanding to her audience. The dramatic context into which the reader is drawn is the personal correspondence between two friends—a most intimate form of human communication usually closed to outside observers. This drawing of the readers into situations from which they are normally excluded is not unique to this poem, as those familiar with Sexton's poetry are well aware. Sexton's reader is frequently invited to peruse the personal letters and private journals and to listen in on the prayers, psychoanalytic interviews, and confessions of her characters. One need only think of such poems as "Letter Written on a Ferry while Crossing Long Island Sound," "Letter Written during a January Northeaster," the "Letters to Dr. Y." and "Scorpio, Bad Spider, Die" sequences, "Love Letter Written in a Burning Building," "Suicide Note," "Eighteen Days without You," "For the Year of the Insane," and "Praying to Big Jack," among others. Thus the poet's choice of situation and viewpoint in "With Mercy" is not an accidental, unimportant feature of the poem but one that is vitally important for understanding the powerful emotional effect of Sexton's work.

In "With Mercy" an unnamed speaker, who later identifies herself as a poet, is responding to a letter she has received from a friend named Ruth. The text of the poem itself, with its discontinuous, conversational style, resembles the rambling, informal presentation of a letter. This epistolary impression is reinforced by the opening phrase, which echoes the conventional opening formula of a reply to previous correspondence, as well as by the speaker's reference to the correspondent's enclosure.

Although these last two features of the poem provide expository information needed by the reader to understand the dramatic occasion of the poem, they also serve to establish a curiously formal and impersonal tone at the outset that conflicts with the highly personal subject matter and with the informal manner of presentation that predominates throughout the remainder of the poem. One way of resolving this apparent conflict of tone is to see it as a reflection (whether deliberate or unconscious is not particularly important) of the speaker's

contradictory attitude toward her friend Ruth and the subject of her
letter.

What, then, do we know about Ruth's letter to her friend? It
contains a number of requests—some explicit, some implied, and all
of which concern the subject of sacramental confession—which are
echoed in the speaker's reply. Ruth has written to her poet-friend
urging her "to call a priest," "to wear The Cross" she has enclosed,
and "to make an appointment for the Sacrament of Confession." Although she does at first wear the cross her friend has sent her, the
speaker does not even attempt to fulfill the other two requests, both
of which would require a more tangible commitment. Despite this
refusal the poet indicates her affection for Ruth by reflecting on her
friend's act. Ruth has made a sacrifice, has indicated her love for the
speaker, by sending her own cross to the poet. Although small and
unassumingly "dog-bitten" as it lies now, "no larger than a thumb,"
on the page of Ruth's letter open before her, this is a gift the speaker
cannot accept. The cross is now simply an "enclosure" to be cour-
teously returned, for although she "cherishes" the letter Ruth has
written, she cannot fulfill her friend's requests, just as she cannot wear
the cross that symbolizes acceptance of her friend's plea for her to seek
absolution.

What, specifically, does the speaker tell us about herself in attempting to respond to Ruth's requests? First, she is caught between
two contradictory impulses. It is obvious she wants desperately to
believe in the cross and accept the saving mercy it represents for her:
"How desperately he wanted to pull his arms in! / How desperately I
touch his vertical and horizontal axes!" This impression is reinforced
by the warmth and intimacy with which she addresses her friend, by
her initial act of acceptance in wearing the cross "All morning long,"
and by her attempt to bring herself to contrition through prayer: "I
detest my sins and I try to believe / in The Cross." Although the cross
is reassuring and comforts her, tapping her "lightly as a child's heart
might, / tapping secondhand, softly waiting to be born," and although
she can imagine "a beautiful Jesus," all she feels is "Need"—which,
she admits, "is not quite belief."

The final stanza explores the careful distinction the speaker is
making here between need and belief. Addressing herself affectionately
to her friend, she compares herself to the confessor, and her poems to
the confessions of the penitent: "My friend, my friend, I was born /

doing reference work in sin, and born / confessing it." "This is what poems are," she tells Ruth, a sacramental gift of the poet to her audience—no different from Christ's act of mercy in sacrificing himself for the sake of those "greedy" for salvation. To reinforce her argument further, she concludes in the characteristic fashion of a poet, offering Ruth three imaginative metaphors that attempt to define more clearly the essential nature of her enterprise. She tells Ruth that poems are "the tongue's wrangle, / the world's pottage, the rat's star."

The first of these figurative expressions makes explicit the conflict we have seen the poet struggling with throughout the course of the poem, for here she suggests that poetry, as "the tongue's wrangle," is the verbal record of the poet's internal argument. The second metaphor indicates the seriousness with which the poet has taken her friend's requests by answering Ruth on her own terms. Alluding to Genesis 25:29–34, she invites her pious friend to consider the cautionary tale of Esau, who sold his birthright to Jacob for a worthless mess of pottage to satisfy a momentary hunger. This appropriation of her petitioner's own means of argument is a gentle reminder to Ruth that she does know what is at stake in her rejection of the authority of priest and church as a means of access to the sacrament of confession. The final metaphor, perhaps the most difficult of the three, identifies her poetry with "the rat's star," an imagined place of refuge from the fallen state of the world, referring to a private symbol to which Sexton returned in many subsequent poems—most especially in "Rats Live on No Evil Star," where the importance she attached to the symbolism of this palindrome is explored in further detail.

Although in the end the poet denies her friend's requests, her struggle to answer Ruth does have a positive outcome, for in the process of trying to find a solution to her dilemma, she manages to clarify for herself the purpose and goal of the creative act and finds a way to communicate this understanding to her friend Ruth, just as Sexton the storyteller is able to communicate with her readers through the dramatic medium of the story into which she has placed her characters.

Like the work of many storytellers, Sexton's tales are often related to one another in various ways and frequently incorporate within them certain details of the author's own experience. Ten years after the publication of "With Mercy," Sexton returned to the subject of Ruth's letter in a short story entitled "The Letting Down of the Hair," which was collected in *The Book of Folly*, her sixth published volume.[4] Here

the account of Ruth's letter to her friend is merged into Sexton's retelling of the traditional fairy tale "Rapunzel," which—apart from its
prose form—closely resembles Sexton's treatment of other fairy tales
from the Brothers Grimm collection in *Transformations*, her fifth volume.[5] The story of Ruth's letter also reappears in Sexton's correspondence, where the poet describes the incident upon which the poem
and the story are based.[6] This confirmation of the factual background
does not, however, change the fact that Sexton has transformed the
incident into literature, just as her retelling of the story of Ruth's letter
in "The Letting Down of the Hair" does not mitigate the concrete
dramatic immediacy of its presentation in "With Mercy." These three
versions of the story reveal, instead, the degree to which Sexton's work
goes beyond confession and how the factual incident of Ruth's letter
becomes, in the hands of a skillful storyteller, an imaginative, fictional
dramatization of the artist's confrontation with the difficult nature of
the creative enterprise.

"For John, Who Begs Me Not to Enquire Further"

Not all of the stories told in Sexton's poems use such private
forms of narrative as "With Mercy for the Greedy." "For John, Who
Begs Me Not to Enquire Further" (*CP*, 34), although largely main-
taining the intimacy of situation present in Sexton's letter poems, is
given a formal rhetorical structure based on the classical apologia.[7]

In "For John" the speaker struggles against the authority of literary tradition in the guise of a beloved teacher, whose challenge moves
her to make a formal apologia for her art. By appropriating the means
and methods handed down to her by that same rhetorical tradition,
she communicates her discovery that the artist's fear of self-exploration
only serves to perpetuate and intensify his or her sense of separation
from the world and from others, and she effectively undermines the
authority of her teacher's argument from within.

The poem presents us with a simple dramatic situation: the
speaker, a young writer, is addressing her teacher, who is older and
more experienced. The unnamed student-speaker of the poem attempts
to defend her work from the criticisms her teacher, whom she affectionately addresses as "John," has levied against it. Judging from the
counterarguments she presents, his objections center on three points
of criticism: that the subjects of her poems are unconventional or at

least unfashionable, that the manner of their presentation is indeco-
rous, and that the subjects they deal with evoke fear and revulsion in
her audience instead of inducing aesthetic pleasure. These three charges
are all answered effectively during the course of the poem. Then, having completed her formal defense, she makes a direct appeal to John,
pleading with him, against all reasonable hope, to understand and
accept her enterprise, drawing on the personal bond they share as
friends, setting aside the hierarchy of teacher and student for a more
equal relationship.

Together with "With Mercy for the Greedy," "For John" is among
the most frequently anthologized of Sexton's poems, and its autobiographical background is well known: "John" is the poet John Holmes,
with whom Sexton studied in two poetry workshops between 1957
and 1958.[8] To many editors and commentators, such confirmation of
the poem's autobiographical basis is an irresistible opportunity to validate the critical theory of confessionalism. The usual fate of "For
John" is therefore similar to that of "With Mercy for the Greedy":
claiming them as grist for the critical mills, the literary theorist and
historian cease to consider the poems as works of imaginative art and
disregard their fictional autonomy from the poet's biography.[9]

Let us consider, then, what Sexton tells us about the experience
of the artist in this apologia for her art. The life of the artist is a troubled
one; the title of the poem reminds us of this in alluding to the statement
by Schopenhauer that serves as epigraph for *To Bedlam and Part Way
Back*, the volume in which this poem appears. This epigraph contrasts
two types of personalities, distinguished, according to Schopenhauer,
by their differing attitude toward misfortune: one must either be like
"Sophocles's Oedipus, who, seeking enlightenment concerning his terrible fate, pursues his indefatigable enquiry, even when he divines that
appalling horror awaits him in the answer," or be like "the Jocasta
who begs Oedipus for God's sake not to inquire further."[10]

It is obvious which attitude Schopenhauer favors and presumably
Sexton as well. It is also clear from the allusion to this epigraph in the
title of "For John" how she associates the characters in her poem with
this same distinction. The speaker, who exemplifies the Oedipal character, pursues her enterprise, "seeking enlightenment" about her fate
as an artist, displaying the "courage" necessary "to make a clean breast
of it in face of every question" raised by her auditor. The speaker
addresses her apologia to John, who, in begging her "not to enquire

further," assumes the role of Jocasta to her Oedipus when he counsels her to forsake her enterprise, fearful of the "appalling horror" that he believes her investigation might bring to light.

For Sexton's Oedipus, however, no appalling horror attends the speaker's "enquiry" into the "narrow diary" of her mind. What she discovers there is, perhaps, "not . . . beautiful," she says, but it does create "a certain sense of order." This is, perhaps, the greatest point of divergence between the speaker's aesthetic values and those of her teacher, for while he sees the purpose of art as the creation of beauty, she emphasizes its ability to give order and meaning to experience, even to suffering, madness, and death. Moreover, her relentless "enquiry" brings useful knowledge, "something worth learning," about herself, and although the discoveries she makes seem at first to be "narrow," like the private truths of the diary, she later finds the same lessons "in the commonplaces of the asylum." This is the first of her answers to John's entreaty: by looking within, by combating the natural fear of the Jocasta "most of us carry in our heart" with "courage," the artist works through personal misfortunes to discover universal truths. She tells him: "At first it was private. / Then it was more than myself." It is this quality of perseverance, the speaker concludes with Schopenhauer, "that makes the philosopher" or the artist.

What has happened to the speaker of Sexton's poem to effect this conviction in her so strongly? She tells us of "a small thing," her experiences in the asylum, "where the cracked mirror / or my own selfish death / outstared me." It is the engagement of the speaker with such painful subjects as madness and death that has apparently elicited the criticisms of her teacher. There is a danger that lies in the avoidance of the truth, however painful, as we are reminded by the story of Oedipus and Jocasta. Oedipus survives and learns from his ordeal; Jocasta ends in despair and suicide. This same lesson is behind the conviction expressed in the speaker's response to her reluctant teacher, with his Jocastalike nature: "And if I tried / to give you something else, / something outside of myself, / you would not know / that the worst of anyone / can be, finally, / an accident of hope." Here the speaker argues from the example of her own personal experience. The thrust of her assertion is that we cannot let our fear of misfortune lead us to reject the opportunities given us for working out and overcoming inner conflicts, for, as she reminds him, "the worst of anyone" can become, paradoxically, the best—that unforeseen "accident of hope." Being thus resolved, she turns within: "I tapped my own head; / it was glass, an inverted bowl," and finds ample confirmation of the rightness of her decision in the fact that her mind is neither opaque nor restrictingly enclosed to influences from outside.

In line 19, nearly halfway through her apologia, the speaker begins shifting her rhetorical strategy from that of counterargument, exception, and counterexample to a more subtle form of rhetorical persuasion. After having argued in a discursive, rational manner, the speaker abandons her attempt to convince through logic and simply embraces her opponent, using a strongly emotional appeal as she tells him: "It is a small thing / to rage in your own bowl," humbling herself before his authority in this self-effacing verbal gesture. Following the advice of Cicero, the poet-speaker has reserved the use of the emotional appeal for the conclusion where—having answered all her teacher's objections with logical argument—it can be used as a means of gaining sympathy from her opponent so that a reconciliation may be reached. In "How It Was," the biographical memoir that prefaces Sexton's *Complete Poems*, Maxine Kumin describes her friend's relationship to John Holmes during this period in terms that have a particular relevance to the dilemma of the speaker in "For John":

> As Holmes's letters from this period make abundantly clear, he decried the confessional direction Anne's poems were taking, while at the same time acknowledging her talent. Her compulsion to deal with such then-taboo material as suicide, madness, and abortion assaulted his sensibilities and triggered his own defenses. . . . Anne and I both regarded Holmes as an academic father. In desperate rebuttal, Anne wrote "For John, Who Begs Me Not to Enquire Further." A hesitant, sensitive exploration of their differences, the poem seeks to make peace between them. (P. xxiv)

In Sexton's poem this strategic move from the rational to the emotional appeal is signaled by the increasing frequency of direct, second-person address in the latter half of the poem, as the speaker willfully equates her own experience with that of her reticent teacher, overriding his implicit denial of this fact: "At first it was private. / Then it was more than myself; / it was you, or your house / or your kitchen." Sexton often uses the second-person form of address in this manner—to draw the detached reader, or in this case an unwilling participant, into the experience presented in the poem. Anticipating his reaction, the speaker moves to prevent it and, by taking the initiative, is able to weaken the objectifying potential of his denial, calling its validity into question:

"And if you turn away / because there is no lesson here / I will hold my awkward bowl, / with all its cracked stars shining / like a complicated lie, / and fasten a new skin around it." Dressed in a new skin, it is still the same bowl, the same self, however disguised; its concrete reality cannot be avoided, no more than Jocasta can disguise the truth about Oedipus, regardless of the intensity of her desire to do so.

The final movement of the artist's apologia begins with a reprise that echoes the opening lines of the poem, gently reaffirming the reasons why she must reject her teacher's entreaty "not to enquire further": "There ought to be something special / for someone / in this kind of hope. / This is something I would never find / in a lovelier place, my dear." This last phrase of the passage once again enfolds the reluctant auditor into an affectionate embrace, and the emotional appeal it employs makes it difficult to reject.

She strengthens her emotional appeal by rationalizing her teacher's action, associating it with a universal human failure of nerve— "your fear is anyone's fear"—attempting to soften the impact of this painful truth upon her auditor. Although she understands his fear, the speaker firmly rejects it, for it is, she says, "like an invisible veil between us all." Here the poet argues, echoing the argument of Schopenhauer's letter to his friend Goethe, that the fear of self-exploration only serves to perpetuate our state of separation from each other, preventing our discovery of that "accident of hope" through which, perhaps, the troubled life of the Oedipuslike artist can be made more meaningful and productive.

In "For John" we see the persuasive artistry of Sexton's rhetorical design as she recounts the story of an artist's encounter with a formidable critic. In the process of working out a reply, she explores and clarifies, through the concrete, dramatic situation of the story she has created, her own conception of the essential nature of the artist's enterprise. Moreover, in Sexton's imaginative use of the Oedipus and Jocasta figures to explore humanity's inner conflicts, she presents us with a powerful symbolic key to a theme that reappears frequently during the course of her career, in poems such as "Her Kind," "Ringing the Bells," "Old," "Flee on Your Donkey," "The Earth Falls Down," and "Riding the Elevator into the Sky."

"Making a Living"

One of Sexton's most interesting poems about the life of the artist, considered from the perspective of her activity as a storyteller, is "Making a Living" (*CP*, 350). Like much of Sexton's later poetry, this poem has received little attention from critics and is rarely anthologized. In "Making a Living" Sexton's artistry as a storyteller is manifested by the narrative design of the poem itself. Like her poetic reworkings of Grimm's fairy tales in *Transformations*, Sexton's retelling of the Old Testament story of Jonah transforms the received material of the source into a contemporary story about the fate of the artist, extending the symbolic implications of the original account while appropriating its moral authority.

"Making a Living" is different from the other poems we are considering in that Sexton is working here with a ready-made plot, complete with characters, one not autobiographical in the sense that many of her stories are. The story of the reluctant prophet Jonah is applied to and equated with the life of the creative artist, whose suffering and sacrifice are exploited by the media to satisfy the hunger of a public greedy for some sort of miracle. The storyteller reminds us of this at the beginning and the end of the poem, inviting us to draw out the comparison.

What is there about the biblical story of Jonah that has led the poet to employ it in this way? First, the legend will already be familiar to most of her audience, and she can thus build her transformation on the cultural authority of shared experience. Second, her readers are already likely to be predisposed to think of the story of Jonah as a symbolic tale, laden with allegorical meaning, that can be appropriated to the poet's own purposes. This is attested to by its use as a typological example in the New Testament gospels (Matthew 12:38–41 and Luke 11:29–32). Third, the emphasis placed in the original tale upon Jonah's trying experience as an unwilling servant of the Lord, his act of self-sacrifice for the salvation of his shipmates, and his final reconciliation to the inescapable necessity of his role as prophet provide Sexton with a story that approximates the general outlines of her portrayal of the artist's experience at the hands of an uncomprehending audience, who can only be reached by the extraordinary measure of allowing them to witness the artist's suffering. The connection between the reluctant prophet Jonah and the literary artist is also seen through the poem's title, which alludes to Hemingway's admonition to the writer, that "con man," to "make a living" out of his death—referring specifically to the passage from *A Moveable Feast* that serves as the epigraph to *The Death Notebooks*, the volume in which "Making a Living" appears. This admonition, moreover, applies not only to this individual poem but, by implication, to the very enterprise of *The Death Notebooks* itself, which amply demonstrates Sexton's ability to "make a living" out of her "death."

That Sexton does not follow the details of the biblical account of Jonah very closely in constructing her own version of the tale is not an unusual or even surprising aspect of the poem for readers familiar with Sexton's earlier work, for she often diverges quite widely from her source material; consider her treatment of the traditional fairy tale in *Transformations*, her retelling of Christ's resurrection in "In the Deep Museum," or her account of Eve's temptation in "Rats Live on No Evil Star."

"Making a Living" is of a kind with these "transformed" stories, as Sexton makes clear in the opening sentence of the poem, where the speaker asserts, "Jonah made his living / inside the belly." This bold summary of the plot serves to indicate the storyteller's interpretive slant, suggesting a specific context of meaning in which the reader is to place the symbolic actions, events, and characters. What does the narrator's opening statement tell us about this context? First, that this version of the story of Jonah is about "making a living"—about finding a means of survival, of getting along in the world. Second, it specifies that Jonah's living is made "inside the belly," an ambiguous echo of the original source that leaves the reader wondering whether the referent of the article here is Jonah or the whale. This ambiguity is further compounded by the subsequent line where the speaker boldly equates her own situation with that of Jonah: "Mine comes from the exact same place." For both of them making a living entails (as Hemingway suggested) an inner sacrifice that draws upon the core of the self— whether this is imaged in corporeal or psychological terms. This impression is reinforced by the conclusion of stanza 1, where the storyteller recounts Jonah's willingness to sacrifice himself to the forces of destruction. The inconsistency with which Jonah behaves at this point in the biblical source is transformed, in Sexton's version, into the fearless cheerful demeanor with which Jonah goes to face his punishment: "Jonah opened the door of his stateroom / and said, 'Here I am!' and the whale liked this / and thought to take him in."

In the second stanza Sexton's storyteller lets her imagination go to work on the source story, providing her audience with a fanciful account of Jonah's sojourn in the whale's belly. It is here, where the narrator strikes out on her own, that we see Sexton's imaginative art. The speaker's description of Jonah's experiences is, of course, entirely absent from the biblical account—where this portion of the plot is occupied by a psalm of thanksgiving in which Jonah prophesies his deliverance. In place of this Sexton's storyteller traces the hero's changing response to his misfortune by dramatizing his reaction to a number of puzzling encounters, a process that helps clarify the universality of his experience.[11]

Describing the way down into the whale, the speaker informs us: "At the mouth Jonah cried out," protesting his misfortune before it has even begun. By the time he has reached the belly of the whale, however, "he was humbled." Having resigned himself to his fate, "He did not beat on the walls. / Nor did he suck his thumb." Instead, "He cocked his head attentively / like a defendant at his own trial," attempting, like the writer to whom Hemingway addresses his admonition in *A Moveable Feast*, to "profit" from his fate.

In stanza 3, however, Jonah makes a series of painful discoveries about the dangers and conditions such a self-sacrifice entails. As he progresses through the stages of his journey, he discovers his fundamental isolation from others: "Jonah took out the wallet of his father / and tried to count the money / and it was all washed away." Having lost the inheritance of his father, Jonah tries once again to establish contact, with similar results: "Jonah took out the picture of his mother / and tried to kiss the eyes / and it was all washed away." Finally, realizing that he has no other authority to refer to, he acquiesces, stripping himself down to the essential core of self as he abandons coat, trousers, tie, watch fob, and cuff links. Fully cognizant at last of the absoluteness of his isolation, Jonah asserts boldly at the beginning of stanza 4: "This is my death, . . . and it will profit me to understand it." As he resolves to "make a mental note of each detail," the storyteller intrudes to tell her reader, "His whole past was there with him."

Jonah's announcement of his death is premature, however, for having made his discovery, he is abruptly released from his ordeal: "At this point the whale / vomited him back out into the sea." Following the ironically appropriate directive of Hemingway to "make a living" out of his death, Jonah tells "the news media / the strange details of his death / and they hammered him up in the marketplace / and sold him and sold him and sold him." This, then, is the bitter reward of the reluctant prophet who, having been stripped down to the core of self by his suffering, tells the public of his troubled fate. His story, turned into some sort of broadside ballad suitable for popular entertainment, is hammered up and sold in the marketplace. In the concluding line of the poem, Sexton's speaker reminds the readers of the contemporary application of the story by reasserting the identity between herself and Jonah—"My death the same"—thereby directing them to interpret her story as a parable about the fate of the artist at the hands of her audience. Here Jonah's own fate and the story he tells about it are so closely equated by the speaker that, as her figurative expression suggests, it is really Jonah himself, not his tale, that is hammered up for public inspection like the body of some Christlike martyr. Where the narrator diverges most widely from her source material in "Making a Living," we see the degree to which Sexton is shaping the material to suit her own purposes; where she abides by its basic plot details, characterization, and symbolism, we see the degree to which she is appropriating its moral authority to instill her own convictions into the traditionally accepted meaning of the tale.

"Said the Poet to the Analyst"

Sexton tells the story of the artist as egotist in "Said the Poet to the Analyst" (CP, 12), a little-known poem from To Bedlam and Part Way Back, her first published volume. Here Sexton's character struggles to justify the imaginative, impersonal source of her artistic materials before the analytic challenge of modern psychoanalysis, which attempts to equate her artistic productions with the symptoms of neurosis.[12] The title itself, as is the case with many of Sexton's other poems, establishes the dramatic situation; already identified in the title, the two participants in the plot are presented to the reader one at a time. The formal structure of the poem reinforces this simple dramatic opposition; its eighteen lines of verse are neatly divided into two stanzas of equal length, providing an effective means for contrasting the two characters.

In stanza 1 the poet-speaker presents her case to the reader first, gaining the advantage of precedence. The poet—whose "business is words"—speaks to her analyst—whose "business" is "watching" her words. This repeated emphasis on the poet's businesslike enterprise may seem surprising at first, although in fact the metaphor is carefully developed as the speaker proceeds. First, she suggests, words are not things but "labels" for things. Attempting to dignify her creative act, she borrows the language of commerce to describe the currency of words in which she deals. Words are like "coins," whose printed inscription indicates their value as currency. Finally, they are "like swarming bees," and working by a sort of chain reaction, they tend to attract one another and settle together in a collective mass, resulting perhaps in a poem such as this one.

Having carefully defined the nature of words, the material with which she works, the poet tells her analyst that she is "only broken by the *sources* of things" (italics mine), a phrase that reiterates the idea, expressed in her figurative definition of language, that words have a parabolic relationship to actual experience, that they only approach reality indirectly. Here the poet uses figurative language to appeal to her analyst's imagination, suggesting to him that her inner conflicts are not accessible through words—the essence of the talking cure he is trying to employ in repairing her "broken" state.

Sexton herself often commented in interviews about this separation of words from their inner sources or *affects* and seemed to recognize quite clearly the relationship this had to a proper understanding of her own work. In an interview with James Day, conducted shortly before her death, she told him: "I remember a psychiatrist once saying: 'Well, you've forgiven your father; it *says* so right here.' And I said: 'Yes, I *tried* to forgive my father.' It's each time an attempt at mastery."[13] Speaking in more general terms in a 1970 interview with William Packard, Sexton said: "You don't solve problems in writing. They're still there. I've heard psychiatrists say, 'See, you've forgiven your father. There it is in your poem.' But I haven't forgiven my father. I just wrote that I did."[14]

Yet it is only the words that can be "counted" and recorded by the analyst, "like dead bees in the attic." These words, however, are "unbuckled" from "the sources of things." Concluding her defense, the speaker reaffirms the self-containment of words, noting "how one word is able to pick / out another, to manner another, until I have got / something I might have said . . . / but did not." This fundamental rift between the "business" of words and the emotional realities to which they refer, she finally asserts, is at the heart of the poet's and analyst's antithetical attitudes toward the meaning and value of her work.

In the second stanza the poet-speaker turns and addresses her analyst directly, pointing out that although she realizes it is his "business" to watch her words, she feels obligated to warn him that "I / admit nothing" by writing poems, and that he would be wise to look elsewhere for the sources of her conflict. This is the point at which the self-directed irony of the poem begins to become apparent. She provides her auditor with a specific example: "I work with my best, for instance, / when I can write my praise for a nickel machine, / that one night in Nevada." In her state of ecstatic abandonment over an unexpected windfall, she pours out a litany of praise, "telling how the magic jackpot / came clacking three bells out, over the lucky screen."

The poet has chosen her hypothetical example carefully to illustrate for the analyst the differences between their attitudes toward her creativity, for she knows that he is bound by his method of analysis to see a symbolic meaning in the act of gambling. Fully aware of this, the poet concludes, "But if you should say this is something it is not, / then I grow weak, remembering how my hands felt funny / and ridiculous and crowded with all / the believing money," warning him that his paralyzing analysis will only cause her to become introspective and silent, robbing her of the ecstatic abandonment she needs in order to create.

In the poems discussed here, we have seen some of the challenges faced by the creative artist struggling against various forms of orthodoxy. The sense of alienation—from self, from others, from society—produced by this struggle is one of the central features of the stories Sexton tells about the troubled life of the artist. Yet it is this very experience that can also lead, as Sexton demonstrates, through suffering to truth, that unforeseen "accident of hope." Appropriating the lessons of our shared past, she parallels the experiences of her fictional characters with figures of legendary and mythic proportions: Oedipus, Jocasta, Rapunzel, Esau, and Jonah. Drawing upon the familiar forms, events, language, characters, and symbols of these sources, she uses the traditional tools of the storyteller to express her discoveries in a way that transcends the bounds of autobiographical "confession" and becomes a shared form of experience.

NOTES

1. I am indebted to the suggestions of an anonymous reader for some of the wording in this sentence.

2. Anne Sexton, *The Complete Poems*, ed. Linda Gray Sexton (Boston: Houghton Mifflin Co., 1981), 62; all subsequent references to this volume (hereafter abbreviated *CP*) will be given in the text.

3. Kay Ellen Merriman Capo, "Redeeming Words: A Study of Confessional Rhetoric in the Poetry of Anne Sexton" (Ph.D. diss., Northwestern University, 1978), 227–28.

4. Anne Sexton, *The Book of Folly* (Boston: Houghton Mifflin Co., 1972), 82–90; this story, like Sexton's other prose fiction, is not included in *The Complete Poems*.

5. Sexton's poetic version of "Rapunzel" in *Transformations* (*CP*, 244) is quite different from "The Letting Down of the Hair" and does not refer to the incident of Ruth's letter.

6. *Anne Sexton: A Self-Portrait in Letters*, ed. Linda Gray Sexton and Lois Ames (Boston: Houghton Mifflin Co., 1977), 129–30.

7. See Capo, "Redeeming Words," 201–19, for a detailed technical exposition of Sexton's rhetoric in this poem.

8. See, for example, *Letters*, 29, 58–60.

9. This practice has been challenged by more recent critics such as Diane Wood Middlebrook and Diana Hume George.

10. Sandor Ferenczi comments on this same letter in his *Contributions to Psycho-Analysis*, trans. Ernest Jones (New York: Institute for Psycho-Analysis, 1916), 214–27, where he explores "the symbolic representation of the Pleasure and Reality Principles in the Oedipus Myth," associating Jocasta with the former and Oedipus with the latter as he focuses upon the myth's demonstration of the dynamic interaction of these two opposing forces in human nature.

11. In "The Belly of the Whale: The Night Journey," *The Act of Creation* (New York: Macmillan, 1964), 358–62, Arthur Koestler comments about the mythic qualities of the story of Jonah, which, he claims, manifests an archetype "of special significance for the act of creation. It is variously known as the Night Journey, or the Death-and-Rebirth motif; but one might as well call it the meeting of the Tragic and the Trivial Planes"; he concludes that "the Night Journey is the antipode of Promethean striving."

12. For three widely differing psychoanalytic views of the relation of creativity to neurosis, see Lawrence S. Kubie, *Neurotic Distortion of the Creative Processes* (Lawrence: University of Kansas Press, 1958); Rollo May, "The Nature of Creativity," in *The Courage to Create* (New York: W. W. Norton, 1975), 29–49; and Jay Harris and Jean Harris, *The Roots of Artifice: On the Origin and Development of Literary Creativity* (New York: Human Sciences Press, 1981).

13. James Day, *A Conversation with Anne Sexton* (North Hollywood: Center for Cassette Studies, 1974), sound cassette.

14. William Packard, "Craft Interview with Anne Sexton," in *Anne Sexton: The Artist and Her Critics*, ed. J. D. McClatchy (Bloomington: Indiana University Press, 1978), 46.

WHAT POETRY CAN AND CANNOT DO

SUZANNE JUHASZ

Seeking the Exit or the Home: Poetry and Salvation in the Career of Anne Sexton

If you are brought up to be a proper little girl in Boston, a little wild and boy crazy, a little less of a student and more of a flirt, and you run away from home to elope and become a proper Boston bride, a little given to extravagance and a little less to casseroles, but a proper bride nonetheless who turns into a proper housewife and mother, and if all along you know that there lives inside you a rat, a "gnawing pestilential rat,"[1] what will happen to you when you grow up? If you are Anne Sexton, you will keep on paying too much attention to the rat, will try to kill it, and yourself, become hospitalized, be called crazy. You will keep struggling to forget the rat and be the proper Boston housewife and mother you were raised to be. And into this struggle will come, as an act of grace, poetry, to save your life by giving you a role, a mission, a craft: an act, poetry, that is you but is not you, outside yourself. Words, that you can work and shape and that will stay there, black and true, while you do this, turn them into a poem, that you can send away to the world, a testimony of yourself. Words that will change the lives of those who read them and your own life, too. So that you can know that you are not only the wife and mother, not only the rat, but that you are the poet, a person who matters, who has money and fame and prizes and students and admirers and a name, Anne Sexton.

But what about the mother and wife, and what about the rat, when Anne Sexton becomes a poet? This essay is about the end of Sexton's career and poetry, and it looks at the role that her poems played in her life and in ours. It is a tale for our times, because it is also about what poetry can do for women and what it cannot do for women. Something we need to know.

Reprinted from *Shakespeare's Sisters: Feminist Essays on Women Poets*, ed. Sandra M. Gilbert and Susan Gubar (Bloomington: Indiana University Press, 1979), 261–68.

Since the recent publication of Sexton's letters, there is now no doubt how conscious she was of the craft of poetry, of the work that it is, and how devoted she was to doing that work. "You will make it if you learn to revise," she wrote to an aspiring poet in 1965,

> if you take your time, if you work your guts out on one poem for four months instead of just letting the miracle (as you must feel it) flow from the pen and then just leave it with the excuse that you are undisciplined.
>
> Hell! I'm undisciplined too, in everything but my work . . . and the discipline the reworking the forging into being is the stuff of poetry. . . .[2]

In fact, for Sexton the poem existed as a measure of control, of discipline, for one whom she defined as "given to excess." "I have found that I can control it best in a poem," she says. "If the poem is good then it will have the excess under control . . . it is the core of the poem . . . there like stunted fruit, unseen but actual."[3]

Yet the poem had another function in her life, the one which gives rise to that label "confessional," which has always dogged her work and is not usually complimentary. Her poetry is highly personal. She is either the overt or the implicit subject of her poem, and the she as subject is the person who anguishes, who struggles, who seems mired in the primary soil of living: the love/hate conflict with mother and father, the trauma of sex, the guilt of motherhood. The person in the poem is not the proper lady and mother and wife who is always trying her best to tidy up messes and cover them with a coating of polish and wax. Rather, it is the rat, a creature of nature rather than culture, who is crude and rude, "with its bellyful of dirt / and its hair seven inches long"; with its "two eyes full of poison / and routine pointed teeth."[4] The rat person, with her "evil mouth" and "worried eyes,"[5] knows that living is something about which to worry: she sees and tells. In form her poem often follows a psychoanalytic model, as I have pointed out in an earlier essay,[6] beginning in a present of immediate experience and probing into a past of personal relationships in order to understand the growth (and the damaging) of personality. As such, the poem for Sexton is an important agent in her quest for salvation: for a way out of the madness that the rat's vision engenders, a way that is not suicide.

Very early in her career, in "For John, Who Begs Me Not to Enquire Further," she presents an aesthetics of personal poetry which is conscious that the poem, because it is an object that communicates and mediates between person and person, can offer "something special" for others as well as oneself.

> I tapped my own head;
> it was glass, an inverted bowl.
> It is a small thing
> to rage in your own bowl.
> At first it was private.
> Then it was more than myself;
> it was you, or your house
> or your kitchen.
> And if you turn away
> because there is no lesson here
> I will hold my awkward bowl,
> with all its cracked stars shining
> like a complicated lie,
> and fasten a new skin around it
> as if I were dressing an orange
> or a strange sun.
> Not that it was beautiful,
> but that I found some order there.
> There ought to be something special
> for someone
> in this kind of hope.[7]

In such poetry, she warns, there is no "lesson," no universal truth. What there is is the poem of herself, which, as she has made it, has achieved an order; that very order a kind of hope (a belief in salvation) that might be shared. The poem of herself is, however, not herself but a poem. The imagery of this poem attests to that fact, as it turns self into object, a bowl, an orange, a sun, while it turns the poem about self into a coating or covering that surrounds the self. The bowl is like a planet in a heaven of "cracked stars shining / like a complicated lie"; if he should turn from this poem, she promises to "fasten a new skin around" or "dress" her orange, that strange sun.

Of course Sexton was right when she said that there ought to be something special in that gesture her poems made toward others. People responded to her poetry because she had the courage to speak publicly of the most intimate of personal experiences, the ones so many share. She became a spokesperson for the secret domestic world and its pain. And her audience responded as strongly as it did, not only because of what she said but because of how she said it. She was often, although not always, a good poet, a skilled poet, whose words worked insight upon her subject matter and irradiated it with vision.

But what about herself, in the process? What did her poems do for her?

In a letter she speaks of the necessity for the writer to engage in a vulnerable way with experience.

> I think that writers . . . must try *not* to avoid knowing what is happening. Everyone has somewhere the ability to mask the events of pain and sorrow, call it shock . . . when someone dies for instance you have this shock that carries you over it, makes it bearable. But the creative person must not use this mechanism anymore than they have to in order to keep breathing. Other people may. But not you, not us. Writing is "life" in capsule and the writer must feel every bump edge scratch ouch in order to know the real furniture of his capsule. . . . I, myself, alternate between hiding behind my own hands protecting myself anyway possible, and this other, this seeing ouching other. I guess I mean that creative people must not avoid the pain that they get dealt. I say to myself, sometimes repeatedly "I've got to get the hell out of this hurt" . . . But no. Hurt must be examined like a plague.[8]

The result of this program, as she says in a letter to W. D. Snodgrass, is writing "real." "Because that is the one thing that will save (and I do mean save) other people."[9]

And yet the program is not only altruistic in intent. Personal salvation remains for her an equally urgent goal. As she writes in "The Children," from one of her last books, *The Awful Rowing Toward God* (1975):

> The place I live in
> is a kind of maze
> and I keep seeking
> the exit or the home.
> (P. 6)

In describing this position of vulnerability necessary for poetry, she tells Snodgrass that a poet must remain "the alien." In her vocabulary for herself, that alien is of course the rat. But there is a serious problem here, because Anne Sexton the woman (who is nonetheless the poet, too) does not like the rat. The existence of the rat obstructs salvation. In "Rowing," the opening poem of *The Awful Rowing*

Toward God, salvation is described as an island toward which she journeys. This island, her goal, is "not perfect," having "the flaws of life, / the absurdities of the dinner table, / but there will be a door":

> and I will open it
> and I will get rid of the rat inside me,
> the gnawing pestilential rat.
>
> (P. 2)

In the "Ninth Psalm" (ED. "Tenth Psalm" in *CP*) of her long poem "O Ye Tongues" (*The Death Notebooks*), an extended description of the state of salvation includes this vision: "For the rat was blessed on that mountain. He was given a white bath" (p. 97).

In other words, Sexton, recognizing at the age of twenty-eight her possession of a talent, turned her mad self to good work (and works): into a writer, an active rather than a passive agent. For she had defined madness as fundamentally passive and destructive in nature. "Madness is a waste of time. It creates nothing . . . Nothing grows from it and you, meanwhile, only grow into it like a snail."[10] Yet the rat who is the mad lady is also the poet. To have become a poet was surely an act toward salvation for Sexton. It gave her something to do with the knowledge that the rat possessed. Left to her silence, the rat kept seeing too much and therefore kept seeking "the exit." Words brought with them power, power to reach others. They gave her as well a social role, "the poet," that was liberating. Being the poet, who could make money with her poetry, who could be somebody of consequence in the public world, was an act that helped to alleviate some of the frustration, the impotence, the self-hatred that Sexton the woman experienced so powerfully in her life. The poet was good: how good she was Sexton, as teacher and reader and mentor, made a point of demonstrating.

But the rat was not good; in yet another image of self-identification, Sexton called that hated, evil, inner self a demon.

> My demon,
> too often undressed,
> too often a crucifix I bring forth,
> too often a dead daisy I give water to
> too often the child I give birth to
> and then abort, nameless, nameless . . .
> earthless.

> Oh demon within,
> I am afraid and seldom put my hand up
> to my mouth and stitch it up
> covering you, smothering you
> from the public voyeury eyes
> of my typewriter keys.

These lines are from "Demon," which appears in her posthumous volume, *45 Mercy Street*.[11] The poem begins with an epigraph from D. H. Lawrence: "A young man is afraid of his demon and puts his hand over the demon's mouth sometimes." It goes on to show why the demon, though frightening, cannot be covered, smothered, or denied speech; because the demon, exposed, is at the center of her poetry. At the same time the poem, with its bitter repetition of "too often," reveals a hatred, not only of the demon but of the act of uncovering and parading it, an act that is nonetheless essential to making the poem.

Finally, the poem's imagery points to a further aspect of the demon that is for Sexton perhaps the most terrible of all. The demon is crucifix, icon of salvation through death; is dead daisy for which the poem alone provides water; is child that, through the act of the poem, is both birthed and aborted. The demon may begin as something that lives within and is a part (albeit frightening and nasty) of herself; but the poem, in being written, turns the demon into an object separate and alien from herself. This disassociation, this conversion of self into other, is as distressing to Sexton as the self-hatred that she must experience each time she acknowledges the existence of the demon or the rat. Because, as "Demon" makes clear, the self as object, the self in the poem, is dead. To use the self in making poems is to lose the self, for the poem is never the experience that produces it. The poem is always an artifice, as she herself observes in another poem from *45 Mercy Street*, "Talking to Sheep":

> Now,
> in my middle age,
> I'm well aware
> I keep making statues
> of my acts, carving them with my sleep. . . .
>   (P. 7)

The poems can never offer personal salvation for their poet, and she has come to understand why. First, because she defines salvation as a life freed at last from the rat and her pain ("I would sell my life to avoid / the pain that begins in the crib / with its bars or perhaps / with your first breath"[12]), and yet she cannot kill the rat without killing the vision that is the source of her poetry. Second, because the poems themselves are a kind of suicide. She knows that poetry must be craft as well as vision; that the very act of crafting objectifies the poem's content. What has lived within her, externalized and formalized by art, becomes something other than herself; it is form but not flesh.

She expresses this new knowledge in the only way she knows, by making poetry of it. In poems like those quoted, or in the following lines from "Cigarettes and Whiskey and Wild, Wild Women" (45 Mercy Street), the other side of "For John, Who Begs Me Not to Enquire Further" is revealed: the implications of this aesthetic of personal poetry for the poet herself.

> Now that I have written many words,
> and let out so many loves, for so many,
> and been altogether what I always was—
> a woman of excess, of zeal and greed,
> I find the effort useless.
> Do I not look in the mirror,
> these days,
> and see a drunken rat avert her eyes?
> Do I not feel the hunger so acutely
> that I would rather die than look
> into its face?
> I kneel once more,
> in case mercy should come
> in the nick of time.
>
> (P. 89)

In an earlier essay on Sexton, I maintained that poetry had saved her from suicide. It did, for the years in which she wrote and was the poet. But it is equally true that poetry could not prevent her death, "the exit," because it could not bring her to salvation, "the home."

For Sexton salvation would have meant sanity: peace rather than perpetual conflict, integration rather than perpetual fragmentation. Sanity would have meant vanquishing at last her crazy bad evil gnawing self, the rat, the demon. Yet the rat was, at the same time, the source of her art. Its anxious visions needed to be nurtured so that she might be a poet. Sanity might bring peace to the woman, but it would destroy the poet. And it was not the woman, who made the peanut butter sandwiches and the marriage bed, whom Sexton liked. It was the poet. The discipline of her craft and the admiration, respect, and power that it brought allowed her to feel good about herself. That the woman and the poet were different "selves," and in conflict with each other, she was well aware. "I do not live a poet's life. I look and act like a housewife," she wrote. "I live the wrong life for the person I am."[13] Although this fragmentation of roles wrought conflict and confusion, it nonetheless made possible the kind of poetry that Sexton wrote. But more and more in her final years she seemed to have come to despise the balancing act itself, demanding all or, finally, nothing.

Perhaps the kind of salvation that Sexton sought was unattainable, because its very terms had become so contradictory. Certainly, her poetry could not offer it. In poetry she could make verbal and public what she knew about her private self; she could shape this knowledge, control it, give it a form that made it accessible to others. But she could not write what she did not know, so that while her poems document all the rat has seen, they never offer an alternative vision. They are always too "close" to herself for that. And they are at the same time too far from her. By creating through externalization and formalization yet another self with which to deal, her poetry increased her sense of self-fragmentation in the midst of her struggle toward wholeness.

Yet Sexton's poetry has offered salvation to others. Personal poetry of this kind, a genre that many women, in their search for self-understanding and that same elusive wholeness, have recently adopted, must be understood to have a different function for its readers and for its writers. Art as therapy appears less profitable for the artist, who gives the gift of herself, than for its recipients. I think that I can learn from Sexton's poems as she never could. They project a life that is like my own in important ways; I associate my feelings with hers, and the sense of a shared privacy is illuminating. At the same time, they are not my life; their distance from me permits a degree of objectivity, the ability to analyze as well as empathize. Possibly I can use the insights produced by such a process to further change in my own life. For the artist, however, because the distance between herself and the poem is at once much closer and much greater, it is more difficult, perhaps impossible, to use the poem in this way. Salvation for the artist must come, ultimately, from developing a life that operates out of creative rather than destructive tensions. Sexton's life, art, and death exemplify some of the difficulties faced by women artists in achieving this goal and also dramatically underline the necessity of overcoming them.

NOTES

1. "Rowing," *The Awful Rowing Toward God* (Boston: Houghton Mifflin Co., 1975), 2. Subsequent references to this volume appear in the text.

2. *Anne Sexton: A Self-Portrait in Letters,* ed. Linda Gray Sexton and Lois Ames (Boston: Houghton Mifflin Co., 1977), 266–67.

3. Ibid., 144.

4. "Rats Live on No Evil Star," *The Death Notebooks* (Boston: Houghton Mifflin Co., 1974), 19. Subsequent references to this volume appear in the text.

5. Ibid.

6. Suzanne Juhasz, " 'The Excitable Gift': The Poetry of Anne Sexton," in *Naked and Fiery Forms: Modern American Poetry by Women, a New Tradition* (New York: Harper and Row, 1976), 117–43.

7. "For John, Who Begs Me Not to Enquire Further," *To Bedlam and Part Way Back* (Boston: Houghton Mifflin Co., 1960), 51–52.

8. *Letters,* 105.

9. Ibid., 110.

10. Ibid., 267.

11. *45 Mercy Street,* ed. Linda Gray Sexton (Boston: Houghton Mifflin Co., 1976), 106–8, lines quoted, 106–7. Subsequent references to this volume appear in the text.

12. "The Big Boots of Pain," *45 Mercy Street,* 103.

13. *Letters,* 270, 271.

Not That It Was Beautiful

Last year I was asked by a professor at Penn State at Erie, The Behrend College, to do some work involving the poetry of Anne Sexton. And who is that, my mother asked over the phone, trying not to sound suspicious. Oh, well, I found myself saying, Sexton is this poet who killed herself. But she's really good, Mom, she's really very good. And so we proceeded, a mother and daughter, apologizing to each other for life's innate nastiness, for what Sexton would call, toward the end of her life, the awful order of things.

Anne Sexton: that poet who killed herself. It's true that I was introduced to Sexton this way, but since then my understanding of her and her work has deepened, grown more complex. Or has it? I am still tempted to use the easy label "suicidal poet," partly because it provides a shortcut to "explaining" a difficult artist. But there's more to it, I think. Although my intellectual response to Sexton has changed over time, my emotional response is deeply rooted in my first reaction to her: I will not, I must not let her take her own life.

My initial reaction was predictable. I was one of those normal people who struggle to be passionately in love with, if not their own lives, then at least with living. The alternative was unspeakable and freakish; even to consider it was at the very least bad luck. I wanted to be able to dismiss this suicidal poet out of hand. The courageous ones stick it out. Therefore, I thought, she can't be any good. The gods wouldn't have it any other way. Ironically, the first Sexton poem I read was "For John, Who Begs Me Not to Enquire Further." The poem spoke to my resistance to that kind of art, that kind of truth:

> And if you turn away
> because there is no lesson here
> I will hold my awkward bowl,
> with all its cracked stars shining
> like a complicated lie,
> and fasten a new skin around it
> as if I were dressing an orange

or a strange sun.
Not that it was beautiful,
but that I found some order there.

From the beginning, reading Anne Sexton was for me less like a process of discovering than of admitting: yes, I want that, I know that, and although I don't want to, I've always known that. Sexton's poems are like the dreams we've had that we will not share with anyone. We are attracted by the power of the poems but are frightened by the vulnerability of the speakers. In Sexton's work strength and vulnerability are the two hands that lift the cracked bowl for the stars to shine through, the hands that beckon us to look.

What is the truth that the dead know, the truth that drives women to the asylum and men to God? A fellow traveler, the suicide is blessed and cursed with the knowledge of where the journey ends. "Yes," she said, "when death comes with its hood / we won't be polite."

"So," my mother, and the mother in me, asks, "how is it that this great poet of yours kills herself? She knew she was going to die, so she kills herself? Makes no sense." Of course, it makes little sense to those who believe in, and desire, the affirmation of life in art. I struggled with Sexton's suicide because her relationship to death was central to her poetic vision. I felt that she owed me some kind of explanation, because as a writer Sexton was one touched by that special burning power and was one from whom I had the right to expect to learn something worth knowing. It is something we demand of our artists: if you can't make it better, at least make it make sense. And so, more than a decade after her death, I played "mother-me-do" with Sexton's ghost.

Through her poetry I came to see Sexton as one who was intensely aware of her undeniable aloneness, and of her life's frailty and shortness. To a suicide, perhaps, any finality is better than this vulnerable not knowing. This is how I began to understand Sexton: But understanding is not quite forgiving. Need, Sexton said, is not quite belief. A friend told me recently that he has no doubt that Sexton is a brilliant poet, but that he finds her worldview so dark and menacing that he turns away from it. So the question becomes, what's in it for us? I responded, at first, by pointing out the joy in Sexton's poetry. The sly wit of *Transformations* and the reverent eroticism of *Love Poems* reveal a poet who glorifies what she can. But I realized that in the best of her poetry, death is waiting and hungry. I stopped apologizing.

The fury of Sexton is the fury of the acutely mortal. Her poetry both touches and chills us, affirming what we share in common: the pain of life's brevity, the wonder that we've been gifted with life at all. Sexton uses a quote from Van Gogh to open her poem "The Starry Night": "That does not keep me from having a terrible need of—shall I say the word—religion. Then I go out at night to paint the stars."

"There ought to be something special for someone in this kind of hope," Sexton says, in the struggle to become brutally honest about this brutal world. Sexton is no Pandora; she is not the one responsible for pain and death. She only echoes, like a doomed nymph, the truth she cannot help but see. The writer is a foolish spy who wants to "warn the stars" and a crook who can only hope to make a tree with the "used furniture" of her short life. Hope lies in this building, even though the process is slow, painful, and doomed from the start. Still, we create, as Camus put it, in the midst of the desert, not in spite of it. We create because we are dying.

Light and dark coexist in Sexton's world but not as neat dualities. Light enlightens or blinds; dark conceals to comfort or to threaten. In the family drama male power, as Father-God, is punishing and accusing; it is also careless and blind. The awful rowing toward the Father-God is coupled with continual separation from him: "I am divorcing daddy—Dybbuk! Dybbuk!" Similarly, female power consecrates and devours and is itself devoured. The self of the poems, aware of the forces raging around her, becomes diminished in stature, "consumed with that which it was nourished by."

In Annie Dillard's *Pilgrim at Tinker Creek*, the author quotes a woman who mused, "Seem like we're just set down here, and don't nobody know why." Sexton, in a voice that is similarly conversational and sad, asks the first star: "Why am I here? / why do I live in this house? / who's responsible? / eh?" The lines are both sad and funny: the world is horrible and it is beautiful. Searching for angels, Sexton found only creatures, mortal like herself. She came to identify with the rats, bats, and moles of the earth, angels muddied and bloodied by whoever it is that's "responsible."

"Rats live on no evil star" was Sexton's favorite palindrome, and she wanted it to be her epitaph. The palindromes that delighted Sexton as a lover of language also speak to us of the hidden quality of the world, the mirror image that we can see if we dare to look: the rats become the transcendent star, the evil becomes the live, and our god just may be the lowly dog of our imagination and need. We must not say so. Our fear begs us not to inquire further.

For Sexton there seems to have been little choice. She needed to know. Courage, hope, and a chilling honesty are her legacies. In the brilliant "Death Baby" poems, the poet uses the fetus as symbol of life and embodiment of death. We can recoil from this awful vision, or we can embrace it for the truth it contains. Sexton, the gifted seer, could not help but see more than is comfortable for us. The world offers comfort, and it devours.

One of the most memorable scenes in Jim Jarmusch's film *Down by Law* introduces the character of Roberto, an Italian immigrant. In broken English he addresses a drunken man lying in an alley by saying, hopefully, "It is a sad and beautiful world." The man shoos Roberto away and is left alone, drunkenly singing the line over and over to himself.

After reading a Sexton poem, I am left feeling a similar pang of contact, bittersweet and familiar. I must now admit it: I could not have saved Anne Sexton. She could not save us. Not that it was beautiful, she said, only that she found some order there. This order demands awe, invites tenderness, if we are courageous enough to face it. In Sexton's vision awareness of the end makes the present possible; like a bowstring pulled taut, each moment becomes more intense, more precious. Death motions to us, wordlessly. Powerfully, in the voice she had been given, Sexton motioned back, each word a gift to the living.

Notes on the Contributors

HEATHER CAM teaches contemporary and modern literature and creative writing at Macquarie University, Sydney, New South Wales, Australia. Her Ph.D. thesis, "The Confessor's Art," examined the work of Anne Sexton, Sylvia Plath, Robert Lowell, John Berryman, and W. D. Snodgrass.

STEVEN E. COLBURN is an independent scholar and poet whose publications include essays on the work of Jean Arp, André Breton, Fernando Pessoa, Tristan Tzara, William Golding, Doris Lessing, Eugene O'Neill, Cesare Pavese, Alberto Moravia, and Pär Lagerkvist. Cofounder of *White Mule: A Poetry Journal*, he has published poetry in *Alabama Alumni News, Aura, Kaleidoscope, Kraken, Maryland Poetry Review*, and *Omnibus II*. The editor of Anne Sexton's *No Evil Star: Selected Essays, Interviews and Prose* and *Anne Sexton: Telling the Tale*, his most recent projects include a study of Sexton's uncollected poetry and a critical monograph on the theological backgrounds of her work.

STEPHANIE DEMETRAKOPOULOS is professor of English at Western Michigan University, where she teaches Renaissance literature, women's studies, archetypal criticism, and film. She is author of *Listening to Our Bodies: The Rebirth of Feminine Wisdom* and coauthor of *New Dimensions of Spirituality: A Biracial and Bicultural Reading of the Novels of Toni Morrison* (with Karla F. C. Holloway). Demetrakopoulos is now working on a book on the spiritual dimensions of women and addiction.

DIANA HUME GEORGE is professor of English at Penn State at Erie, The Behrend College, where she teaches poetry, creative writing, and women's studies. Her books include *Blake and Freud, Epitaph and Icon* (with M. A. Nelson), and *Oedipus Anne: The Poetry of Anne Sexton*. With Diane Wood Middlebrook, she is the editor of *Selected Poems of Anne Sexton*. George is currently writing a book on Maxine Kumin and Anne Sexton.

MARGARET HONTON is a poet and poetry therapist based in Columbus, Ohio. She is also the editor of Sophia Books. Her last publication was *The Poets' Job: To Go Too Far*. Ms. Honton gives workshops on investing dream images in poetry. She has been an active participant in the Poets-in-the-Schools program of the Ohio Arts Council for the past ten years.

SUZANNE JUHASZ is professor of English at the University of Colorado, Boulder, where she teaches women's literature and American literature. She is the author of *The Undiscovered Continent: Emily Dickinson and the Space of the Mind, Naked and Fiery Forms: Modern American Poetry by Women, a New Tradition*, and *Metaphor and the Poetry of Williams, Pound, and Stevens* and is the editor of *Feminist Critics Read Emily Dickinson*. She is presently writing a book on Jane Austen and women's romance fiction.

KIM KRYNOCK is a recent graduate of Penn State at Erie, The Behrend College, where she majored in English. She won the 1986 Lehman Creative Writing Award in poetry.

MAXINE KUMIN has published eight books of poetry, one of which, *Up Country*, won the Pulitzer Prize in 1973. Viking will publish her new collection, *Nurture*, late in 1988. A collection of her country essays, *In Deep*, was published by Viking in 1987. She has taught at Columbia, Princeton, Brandeis, and MIT and was Consultant in Poetry to the Library of Congress in 1981–82.

ESTELLA LAUTER is professor of humanistic studies, literature and language at the University of Wisconsin-Green Bay, where she teaches courses in women's studies, poetry, criticism, and American Indian studies. Her books include *Women as Mythmakers: Poetry and Visual Art by Twentieth-Century Women, Feminist Archetypal Theory: Interdisciplinary Re-Visions of Jungian Thought* (coauthored and coedited with Carol Schreier Rupprecht), and *Teaching Literature and Other Arts* (coedited with Joseph Gibaldi and Jean-Pierre Barricelli, forthcoming). Her interdisciplinary studies continue in book-length projects on feminist aesthetics and female creativity. In 1984 she received her university's award for excellence in scholarship, and in 1985 *Women as Mythmakers* received the Chicago Women in Publishing Award for Excellence. She is a contributing editor to *Women's Studies Quarterly* and serves on the editorial broad of *Soundings*.

J. D. McCLATCHY has published two collection of poems, *Scenes from Another Life* and *Stars Principal*, and has edited several books, including *Anne Sexton: The Artist and Her Critics*. The recipient of both Guggenheim and NEA fellowships, he has been awarded the Witter Bynner Poetry Prize by the American Academy of Arts and Letters, the Eunice Tietjens Memorial Prize from *Poetry* magazine, and the Gordon Barber Memorial Award from the Poetry Society of America. His work appears regularly in the *New York Times Book Review, New Yorker, New Republic, Poetry, Paris Review,* and elsewhere. He has taught at Yale and Princeton and is poetry editor of the *Yale Review*.

DIANE WOOD MIDDLEBROOK is the Howard H. & Jessie T. Watkins University Professor in English and Feminist Studies at Stanford University. Her books include *Walt Whitman and Wallace Stevens, Worlds into Words, Coming to Light: American Women Poets in the 20th Century,* (edited with Marilyn Yalom), and *Gin Considered as a Demon,* a chapbook of poems. With Diana Hume George, she is editor of *Selected Poems of Anne Sexton.* Her biography of Anne Sexton will be published by Houghton Mifflin Co. in 1990.

JEANNE KAMMER NEFF is Vice President of Academic Affairs at Susquehanna University, Pa. Following an early career as a teacher and scholar in the areas of poetry, creative writing, and women's studies, she chose to bring that experience to bear upon the work of academic administration. In 1987 she served as chair of the American Conference of Academic Deans.

KATHLEEN L. NICHOLS is associate professor of English and coordinator of women's studies at Pittsburg State University in Kansas, where she teaches American literature, women writers, and interdisciplinary women's studies courses. She has published articles on women's poetry and American fiction and is presently working on a study of Willa Cather's fiction.

ALICIA OSTRIKER is the author of six volumes of poetry, most recently *A Woman under the Surface, The Mother/Child Papers,* and *The Imaginary Lover,* which won the 1986 William Carlos Williams Award from the Poetry Society of America. As a critic she is the author of *Vision and Verse in William Blake* and editor of Blake's *Complete Poems.* Her writing on women poets includes the essays published in *Writing Like a Woman* and *Stealing the Language: The Emergence of Women's Poetry in America.* Alicia Ostriker has received awards from the National Endowment for the Arts, the Rockefeller Foundation, and the Guggenheim Foundation. She lives in Princeton, N.J., and is professor of English at Rutgers University.

WILLIAM H. SHURR is Distinguished Humanities Professor at the University of Tennessee, Knoxville, and is a specialist in nineteenth-century American literature. He has written *The Mystery of Iniquity: Melville as Poet* (winner of the SAMLA award), *Rappaccini's Children: American Writers in a Calvinist World,* and *The Marriage of Emily Dickinson: A Study of the Fascicles,* in addition to many articles and reviews. His book on Marx and Melville will appear shortly, and he is currently at work on a book entitled *Walt Whitman: The Sexual Manifesto.*

LINDA WAGNER-MARTIN has recently assumed the Hanes Chair in English at the University of North Carolina, Chapel Hill. Recent publications are *Sylvia Plath, a Biography, Sylvia Plath: The Critical Heritage,* and *Ernest Hemingway: Six Decades of Criticism.* She is presently working on a study of American women's poetry since the 1950s.

Index

"Abortion, The" (*Complete Poems*), 171, 282

"Addict, The" (*Complete Poems*), 125, 130

"All My Pretty Ones" (*All My Pretty Ones*), 203

All My Pretty Ones, xviii, 47, 48, 122–25, 130, 133, 172, 197, 202, 203, 208, 214, 277, 279

"Ambition Bird, The " (*Book of Folly*), 60

Amor and Psyche (Neumann), 128, 129–30, 143

Anal stage, 106

"Angels of the Love Affair" (*Book of Folly*), xix, 60, 67, 262, 281

"Anna Who Was Mad" (*Book of Folly*), 62–63, 262

Anne Sexton: A Self-Portrait in Letters (Sexton and Ames), 8, 18

Anne Sexton: Telling the Tale (Colburn), x

Archetypes, xi, xiv, xv, 99–161; Demeter-Kore, 118–21, 123, 130, 141–46; Devouring Father, 137–40; Devouring Mother, 100, 120, 140; Father-God, xiv, xv, 119–22, 137–41, 149–53, 155–59, 165–69, 184, 200–201, 206, 207, 261–73, 314; Mother-Goddess, xiv, xv, 119, 122–23, 139, 154, 157–59, 165–69, 267, 272; Sea, 168–69, 172–74; Sophia, 119–20, 134–37, 140–41; World Parents, 119, 165–69

Ariel (Plath), 236, 239

"Assassin, The" (*Book of Folly*), 60

"Author of the Jesus Papers Speaks, The" (*Book of Folly*), 153, 266

Awful Rowing Toward God, The, xiv, xx, 47, 68, 69, 120, 137, 139, 146–49, 155, 156, 165, 169, 171–90, 201, 206–7, 254, 261, 268, 270–71

"Baby" (*Death Notebooks*), 67, 88–94

Becker, Ernest: *The Denial of Death*, 74–77, 80

"Begat" (*Book of Folly*), 65–66

"Bells, The" (*Complete Poems*), 41

Berryman, John, 30, 178, 198, 253, 274; *The Dream Songs*, 198

"Bestiary U.S.A." (*45 Mercy Street*), 67

Bettelheim, Bruno, xix, 256

Beyond God the Father (Daly), 138, 144, 146, 156, 158, 160, 161, 271–72

"Big Boots of Pain, The" (*Complete Poems*), 234

"Big Heart, The" (*Awful Rowing Toward God*), 70, 182–83

Blake, William, 263, 265

"Boat, The" (*Book of Folly*), 64–65, 147, 151

Bolen, Jean: *Goddesses and Everywoman*, 118

Book of Folly, The, xix, 60–66, 69, 145, 148, 149, 158, 205, 206, 261, 262

"Breast, The" (*Love Poems*), 8, 57

"Briar Rose (Sleeping Beauty)" (*Transformations*), 59–60, 259

Bryant, William Cullen, 227, 245

Camus, Albert, 189–90, 314

"Child Bearers, The" (*45 Mercy Street*), 112, 137

"Children, The" (*Awful Rowing Toward God*), 306

Christ, xix, 11, 20, 25–26, 47–48, 101–3, 149, 169, 182, 183, 184, 262, 263, 267, 270

Christianity: Sexton and, 145–46, 261–67

"Christmas Eve" (*Live or Die*), 104

Christopher, of "O Ye Tongues," 136, 148, 268, 269

"Cigarettes, Whiskey and Wild, Wild Women" (*45 Mercy Street*), 309

"Cinderella" (*Transformations*), 205, 257, 260–61

Colburn, Steve: *Anne Sexton: Telling the Tale*, x; *No Evil Star: Selected Essays, Interviews and Prose*, 10, 18

Complete Poems, The, ix, 7, 8, 9, 11, 12, 18, 121, 122, 123, 125, 126, 127, 128, 129, 131, 132, 134, 135, 136, 159

Compulsion to Confess, The (Reik), 31–32

Confessionalism, ix–x, xii, xiv, xvii, xviii, 29–40, 99–100, 145, 171, 184, 201, 203, 210, 251–54, 255; in early poetry, 274–81; and Freud's definition of poetry, 31; and psychotherapy, 33–36; Reik's definition of, 31–32; and Sexton's form, 35–36, 39–40. *See also* Berryman; Lowell; Plath

"Consecrating Mother, The" (*45 Mercy Street*), 137, 154–55, 158

"Consorting with Angels" (*Live or Die*), 53, 139

Consumption: fear of, 78–81, 83, 95n11, 108

"Cripples and Other Stories" (*Live or Die*), 55, 61, 203

"Daddy" (Plath), 32, 132, 223, 224, 225–26

Daly, Mary: *Beyond God the Father*, 138, 144, 146, 156, 158, 160, 161, 271–72

"Dancing the Jig'" (*Book of Folly*), 107

"Dead Heart, The" (*Complete Poems*), 270

Death, 73–94, 165–69; fear of/wish for, xiii, xix–xx, 73–94, 95n17, 165–69; repressed knowledge of, 73–94; sex and, 74–77, 134; Sexton's parents', 49, 165

—symbolism of: as death baby, 78, 81–84, 86–88, 89, 107–8, 206; as doll, 77–94; as "green girls," 93; as ice baby, 78–80, 150; as Mr. Death, 93, 134

Death Baby, xix–xx, 77–94, 107–8, 150, 315; as ice baby, 78–80, 108, 150; and Madonna, 84, 86–87, 89

"Death Baby, The" (*Death Notebooks*), xiii, xix–xx, 77–94, 107–8, 150, 315

Death Notebooks, The, xiii, xix, 66–69, 73–94, 119, 134, 140, 145–49, 154, 158, 165, 261, 268, 271, 294

"Death of the Fathers, The" (*Book of Folly*), xix, 12, 32, 63–66, 68, 147, 206

"December 10th" (*Love Poems*), 57

"December 12th" (*Love Poems*), 252

Demeter-Kore, 118–21, 123, 130, 141–56. *See also* Archetypes

Demetrakopoulos, Stephanie, 154

"Demon" (*45 Mercy Street*), 307–8

Denial of Death, The (Becker), 74–77, 80

Devouring Father, 137–40

Devouring Mother, 100, 120, 140

Dickey, James, 17, 197, 280

Dickinson, Emily, xvi, 54, 172, 177, 178, 227, 228, 229, 233, 239, 240, 245–46, 272–73, 280, 281

Dillard, Annie: *Pilgrim at Tinker Creek*, 314

Dingley, Anna Ladd ("Nana"), 42–43, 54–55, 59, 63, 200, 205, 217, 230

"Division of Parts, The" (*To Bedlam and Part Way Back*), 46–47, 67, 101–3

"Divorce Papers, The" (*45 Mercy Street*), 32, 68

"Divorce, Thy Name Is Woman" (*45 Mercy Street*), 42

"Doctor of the Heart, The" (*Book of Folly*), 61–62

"Doctors" (*Awful Rowing Toward God*), 281

Doll: as death symbol, 77–94

"Double Image, The" (*To Bedlam and Part Way Back*), 8, 30, 32, 34, 43–46, 48, 50, 54, 55, 100–101, 108–9, 121, 210, 216, 217

"Dreaming the Breasts" (*Book of Folly*), 105

Dream Songs, The (Berryman), 198

"Dreams" (*Death Notebooks*), 78–81, 82, 83, 84

"Dy-dee Doll, The" (*Death Notebooks*), 81–84, 88

"Earth, The" (*Complete Poems*), 175–76

"18 Days Without You" (*Complete Poems*), 9

Eleusinian Mysteries, 118, 119
Eliot, T. S., 177, 252, 256
"Elizabeth Gone" (*Complete Poems*), 42, 276
Emerson, Ralph Waldo, 188, 227, 228
Erikson, Erik, 32
Eros and Thanatos, xx, 73–94, 252, 259, 268. *See also* Death
Eroticism, 3–17, 20–26, 133, 167
Eureka (Poe), 177, 189
"Exorcists, The" (*Complete Poems*), 263
"Expatriates, The" (*Complete Poems*), 41

Fairy tales, xviii, 57–60, 205, 255–61. *See also Transformations*
"Falling Dolls, The" (*Complete Poems*), 233
Father-God, xiv, xv, 119–22, 137–41, 149–53, 155–59, 165–69, 184, 200–201, 206, 207, 261–73, 314
Fathers, 17, 23, 65–66, 147
"Fish That Walked, The" (*Awful Rowing Toward God*), 175
"Flee on Your Donkey" (*Live or Die*), 29, 53, 55–56, 203
"For God While Sleeping" (*All My Pretty Ones*), 47, 206
"For John, Who Begs Me Not to Enquire Further" (*To Bedlam and Part Way Back*), xviii, 37–38, 202, 284, 288–91, 304–6, 309, 312–13
"For My Lover, Returning to His Wife" (*Love Poems*), 9, 252
"Fortress" (*All My Pretty Ones*), 51–52, 109, 122–23, 125, 126, 127, 133–34, 216–17
"45 Mercy Street" (*45 Mercy Street*), 68–69, 230–33
45 Mercy Street, xx, 68, 78, 120, 140, 147–49, 157, 165, 229, 233, 235
"Frenzy" (*Awful Rowing Toward God*), 69, 268, 269
Freud, Sigmund, xix, 33, 34, 35, 38, 58, 63, 73–94; *Beyond the Pleasure Principle*, xix, 73–94
"Furies, The" (*Death Notebooks*), xx, 67, 268
"Fury of Cocks, The" (*Complete Poems*), 269, 282

George, Diana Hume (*Oedipus Anne: The Poetry of Anne Sexton*), 15, 18, 143
God. *See* Father-God
Goddess. *See* Mother-Goddess
Goddesses and Everywoman (Bolen), 118
"Gold Key, The" (*Transformations*), 58, 283
Great Mother: An Analysis of the Archetype, The (Neumann), 119, 122–23, 134, 135, 143

"Hansel and Gretel" (*Transformations*), 258, 260
Harding, M. Esther: *Woman's Mysteries*, 130–31, 133, 136, 143
Heart's Needle (Snodgrass), xviii, 198
Hemingway, Ernest: *A Moveable Feast*, 294, 295
"Her Kind" (*Complete Poems*), 41, 276, 278
Hillman, James: *Re-Visioning Psychology*, 155–56, 159
"Hoarder, The" (*Book of Folly*), 106, 139
Holmes, John, 4–7, 31, 37, 50, 58, 197, 200, 201, 288
"House, The" (*Complete Poems*), 48, 50–51, 52
"Housewife" (*All My Pretty Ones*), 108, 254, 281
Howard, Richard, 274, 275, 280, 281
"How We Danced" (*Book of Folly*), 64
"Howl" (Ginsberg), 198
Hughes, Ted, 237, 238, 242
"Hurry Up Please It's Time" (*Death Notebooks*), 67–68, 69, 108, 114–15

"I Remember" (*All My Pretty Ones*), 203, 279
Ice baby, 78–80, 108, 150. *See also* Death Baby
"In Celebration of My Uterus" (*Love Poems*), xvii, 57, 115, 199, 264
"In the Deep Museum" (*All My Pretty Ones*), 47, 48, 206, 216, 263, 293
Incest, xii, xv, 12–13, 16, 19–25; aunt-niece, 20, 23–24, 25; father-daughter, xii, 12–13, 19, 20–25; mother-

daughter and pre-Oedipal sources, 22–25

"Is It True?" (*Awful Rowing Toward God*), 69, 182, 270

"January 24th" (*Words for Dr. Y*), 78
"Jesus Asleep" (*Book of Folly*), 152
"Jesus Awake" (*Book of Folly*), 152
"Jesus Cooks" (*Book of Folly*), 152, 265
"Jesus Dies" (*Book of Folly*), 152–53, 265
"Jesus Papers, The" (*Book of Folly*), xiv, xix, 47, 60, 151–53, 205–6, 254, 262, 263–67, 269, 271
"Jesus Raises Up the Harlot" (*Book of Folly*), 152
"Jesus Suckles" (*Book of Folly*), 151, 264, 266
"Jesus Summons Forth" (*Book of Folly*), 152, 265
"Jesus Unborn" (*Book of Folly*), 153, 266
"Jesus Walking" (*Death Notebooks*), 47, 48
Jocasta, 39, 43, 46, 289, 290, 292, 299n10
Jonah, 293–96, 298, 299n11
Juhasz, Suzanne, 146, 161, 281
Jung, C. G., xiv, xv, 118–19, 140; Jungian "soul-making," 145–59

"Keeping the City" (*Complete Poems*), 235–36
Kierkegaard, Søren, 178, 181, 190
"Killing the Spring" (*Book of Folly*), 60, 149
"Kind Sir: These Woods" (*To Bedlam and Part Way Back*), 40
"Kiss, The" (*Complete Poems*), 8
Kumin, Maxine, 88, 92–93, 94, 212, 215, 224, 291

Lauter, Estella, 95n17, 206, 207–8
Lawrence, D. H., 10, 29, 32
"Letter Written on a Ferry While Crossing Long Island Sound" (*Complete Poems*), 48, 203, 278, 281, 285
"Letting Down of the Hair, The" (*Complete Poems*), 262, 287–88

"Little Girl, My String Bean, My Lovely Woman" (*Live or Die*), xvii, 110, 127, 132, 133
"Little Peasant, The" (*Transformations*), 205, 260
"Little Uncomplicated Hymn, A" (*Live or Die*), 17, 54, 110–11, 125–26
"Live" (*Live or Die*), 56, 114, 130, 136
Live or Die, 34–35, 52–54, 62, 124–25, 133, 187–89, 208, 281
Logos, 174–76, 179, 181, 186, 191n11, 259, 265
Love Poems, xviii, 56–57, 133, 137, 139, 179, 313
"Love Songs" (*Live or Die*), 53
"Loving the Killer" (*Love Poems*), 57
Lowell, Robert, xvii, xviii, 30–33, 36, 40, 178, 197–98, 224, 233, 244, 253, 254, 255, 274
"Lullaby" (*Complete Poems*), 41

Madness, 4, 8, 17, 34, 36, 155–56, 200, 209, 210; in *Mercy Street*, 19, 24, 25–26; Nana's, 62–63
Madonna: and death baby, 84, 86–87, 89
Madwoman in the Attic (Gilbert and Gubar), 229
"Making a Living" (*Death Notebooks*), 284, 293–94
Marvel, Andrew: "To His Coy Mistress," xii, 3–6
Mary, 56, 151, 152, 157–58, 200, 235, 263, 264–65, 266–67
Mary Magdalene, 152, 153, 265
"Max" (*Death Notebooks*), 87–88, 91, 92–93
"Menstruation at Forty" (*Live or Die*), 53, 137, 282
Mercy Street, xii, 16, 19–26, 54, 255; plot summary of, 19
Middlebrook, Diane Wood, 4, 18, 209
"Moss of His Skin, The" (*Complete Poems*), 279
"Mother and Daughter" (*Book of Folly*), 11, 12, 61, 112, 131, 132, 262
Mother/daughter relationships: xi, xiii, 11–12, 86–87, 100–101, 130–34, 140–41; Sexton and her daughters, 108–13, 117, 120, 121–34, 233–34;

Sexton and her mother, 43–46, 99–108, 121
Mother-Goddess, xiv, xv, 119, 122–23, 139, 154, 157–59, 165–69, 267, 272
Moveable Feast, A (Hemingway), 294, 295
Ms. Dog: Sexton as, 107, 148, 150, 166, 207, 268
"Music Swims Back to Me" (To Bedlam and Part Way Back), 40, 41, 200
"My Friend, My Friend" (Complete Poems), 223–26

Nana. See Dingley, Anna Ladd
Neruda, Pablo, 29, 53, 203
Neumann, Erich: Amor and Psyche, 128, 129–30, 143; The Great Mother: An Analysis of the Archetype, 119, 122–23, 134, 135, 143; The Origins and History of Consciousness, 119, 139, 142
No Evil Star: Selected Essays, Interviews and Prose (Colburn, ed.), 10, 18
"Noon Walk on the Asylum Lawn" (Complete Poems), 41

"O Ye Tongues" (Death Notebooks), xx, 9, 67, 109, 134–35, 153–54, 156, 268–69, 307
Oedipus, 5, 37–38, 129, 289–92, 298, 299n10
Oedipus Anne: The Poetry of Anne Sexton (George), ix, 15, 17, 18, 143
Oedipus complex, 21–23, 25, 64–66, 205, 206
"Old" (Complete Poems), 292
"Old Dwarf Heart" (Complete Poems), 48–49
"Operation, The" (All My Pretty Ones), 48, 50, 59, 104, 203, 204, 210, 277, 279, 280
Oral stage, 105–6
Origins and History of Consciousness, The (Neumann), 119, 139
Ostriker, Alicia, x, xii, xv, 18
"Other, The" (Book of Folly), 62, 63, 262
Ouroboros, 126
"Oysters" (Book of Folly), 12–13, 64

"Pain for a Daughter" (Complete Poems), 127, 128–29, 133
Persephone, See Demeter-Kore
Personae, Sexton's: 6–7, 10–11, 13–17, 99–100, 104, 113–16, 146–48; Ms. Dog, 148, 150, 166, 207, 268
Plath, Sylvia: Ariel, 236, 239; "Daddy," 32, 132, 223, 224, 225–26; and Sexton, xvi, xvii, xviii, 17, 29, 30, 56, 117, 120, 198, 223–26, 232–33, 236–46, 251–55, 272, 274
"Poet of Ignorance, The" (Awful Rowing Toward God), 69
Poetic control: in early poetry, xiii, 274–81; formal, 274–81; narrative, 283–99

Radcliffe Institute, The, 211–18
"Rapunzel" (Transformations), 260, 288
Rats, xiii, 286–87, 303–11, 314
"Rats Live on No Evil Star" (Death Notebooks), 294, 304
"Red Shoes, The" (Complete Poems), 149, 262
Reik, Theodore: The Compulsion to Confess, 31–32
Religious poetry: Sexton's, xiii–xiv, xx, 26, 47–48, 69, 183, 224; spiritual quest in, xv, xvi, 19, 24–26, 140–41, 145–59, 165–69, 261–67, 268–73, 303–11
Repetition compulsion, 74–77, 84–86, 88–91, 92
Re-Visioning Psychology (Hillman), 155–56, 159
"Riding the Elevator into the Sky" (Awful Rowing Toward God), 203, 292
"Ringing the Bells" (To Bedlam and Part Way Back), 40, 276, 291
"Risk, The" (45 Mercy Street), 112–13
Roethke, Theodore, 48, 53, 254
"Rowing" (Awful Rowing Toward God), 7, 165–66, 172, 283, 303, 306–7
"Rowing Endeth, The" (Awful Rowing Toward God), 166, 172, 185, 270–71
"Rumpelstiltskin" (Transformations), 205, 256, 258, 260

"Said the Poet to the Analyst" (To Bedlam and Part Way Back), 38–39, 41, 284, 296–98

Salvation. See Religious poetry: Sexton's

Schopenhauer, Arthur: quote used as epigraph, 5, 37–38, 289, 290, 292

Seduction: of audience, xv, 4–17; laughter as, 12–13; in "To His Coy Mistress," 3–6

"Seven Times" (Death Notebooks), 83–84, 88

Sex. See Eroticism

Sexton, Joyce Ladd, 110, 111, 200, 216, 217, 230

Sexton, Linda Gray, 109, 110, 111, 112, 154, 199, 216, 217, 218, 230

Sexton, Mary Gray, 101–8, 109, 217, 218, 230

Smart, Christopher, 8, 21, 29, 67, 258

Snodgrass, W. D., xvii, xviii, 30, 33, 178, 255, 306; Heart's Needle, 30, 43

"Snow White and the Seven Dwarfs" (Transformations), 57, 256, 257, 260

"Some Foreign Letters" (Complete Poems), 42, 48, 54–55, 210, 276

Speakers. See Personae, Sexton's

"Starry Night, The" (Complete Poems), 278, 314

Stealing the Language: The Emergence of Women's Poetry in America (Ostriker), x

Suicide, 17, 62, 73–94, 96n22, 114, 117, 120, 132, 139, 158–59, 171–90, 210; Alvarez on, 186; Camus on, 189–90; Emerson on, 188; Sexton on, 186; Sexton's, 30, 32, 43, 56, 100, 155, 172, 186–90, 209, 312–15

"Talking to Sheep" (45 Mercy Street), 42, 99–100, 233, 308

Thoreau, Henry David, 227, 252

"Those Times . . ." (Live or Die), 52, 53, 273n5

"Three Green Windows" (Live or Die), 53, 104

To Bedlam and Part Way Back, xvii–xviii, 4, 5, 31, 37, 40, 47, 55, 122, 137, 171, 202, 224, 274, 277–80, 296

"To Lose the Earth" (Live or Die), 53, 187

Transformations, xviii, xiv, xix, 50, 57–60, 80, 90, 146–47, 205, 207, 235, 253, 254, 255–61, 262, 263, 268, 271, 281, 293, 313

"Truth the Dead Know, The" (Complete Poems), 49, 171, 203, 278

"Unknown Girl in the Maternity Ward" (To Bedlam and Part Way Back), 30, 171

"Wall, The" (Awful Rowing Toward God), 9, 155, 181–82, 187

"Wanting to Die" (Live or Die), 88, 126

Whitman, Walt, 36, 48, 177, 227, 228

"With Mercy for the Greedy" (All My Pretty Ones), 47, 201, 206, 284–89

Woman's Mysteries (Harding), 130, 133, 136, 143

"Woman with Girdle" (All My Pretty Ones), 279

Words for Dr. Y., xx, 78, 145, 149, 155, 158, 245

"You, Dr. Martin" (To Bedlam and Part Way Back), 41, 61, 200, 275–76, 281

"Young" (Complete Poems), 203

"Your Face on the Dog's Neck" (Complete Poems), 126